Tomáš G. Masaryk

Tomáš G. Masaryk

a Scholar and a Statesman

The Philosophical Background of His Political Views

Zdeněk V. David

HHP

H P

Helena History Press LLC
A division of KKL Publications LLC, Reno, Nevada USA
www.helenahistorypress.com
Publishing scholarship about and from Central and East Europe

ISBN 978-1-943596-13-3

Distributed by IngramSpark and available through all major e-retail sites
Order: *info@helenahistorypress.com*

Book Jacket photograph by permission of Getty Images

Copy Editor: Jill Hannum, Krisztina Kós
Graphic Designer: Sebastian Stachowski

Table of Contents

Preface

A lthough subject to some revisionism since the end of the Cold War (when he was considered one of the "Champions of Liberty"[1]), the importance of the political thought of Tomáš G. Masaryk (1850–1937), the first president of Czechoslovakia, has been based on two considerations. One was his image as the principal shaper of the democratic culture in inter-war Czechoslovakia, which was unique in East-Central Europe. The other image was as a model of political prudence and sagacity, not only for East-Central Europe but one recognized universally (like that of Václav Havel at the turn of the twentieth century). In the period between World Wars I and II, two leading European intellectuals – Thomas Mann and George Bernard Shaw – were asked on separate occasions, whom they would suggest as the first president of the United States of Europe. Both responded unequivocally that the best candidate was Masaryk.[2] He was called "the wisest European of today" by Emil Ludwig,[3] and "the greatest man in Europe" by Herbert G. Wells (due to "Masaryk's tireless struggle for the welfare of mankind").[4] John MacCormac, writing in the *New York Times* on March 2, 1930, saw in Masaryk a personage of the same

---

1   In a series of stamps issued by the U.S. Post Office in 1951–1960.
2   Thomas Mann, "In Memory of Masaryk," *The Nation*, vol. 145, no. 15 (October 9, 1937), 374; W. Preston Warren, *Masaryk's Democracy: A Philosophy of Scientific and Moral Culture* (Chapel Hill: University of North Carolina Press, 1941), 1. Masaryk met Shaw, as well as H. G. Wells, B. Russell, and F. Swinnerton, during his official visit in London in October 1923; see in Masaryk, Tomáš G., *Cesta demokracie II, Spisy* 34 (Prague: Masarykův ústav AV ČR, 2007), 489.
3   Emil Ludwig, *Defender of Democracy: Masaryk of Czechoslovakia* (New York: R. M. McBride, 1936), x.
4   "Rozhovor prezidenta s novinářkou Betty Rossovou," June 21, 1933, in Tomáš G. Masaryk, *Cesta demokracie IV, Spisy* 36 (Prague: Masarykův ústav AV ČR, 1997), 485.

caliber as Washington, Lincoln, and Wilson.[5] In May 1935, Masaryk received the medal of the Woodrow Wilson Foundation in recognition of his tireless struggle against tyrannical oppressors and for human rights. The citation pointed out that Masaryk originally declared the independence of Czechoslovakia in October 1918 in Washington, D.C., in agreement with the ideals of President Woodrow Wilson. Above all, according to the award, he kept the republic which he had established faithful to the principles of constitutional and parliamentary democracy, the principle of law, humanity ("valued by all civilized nations"), and the principle of freedom of expression, press, and conscience. The citation was signed by Hamilton Fish Armstrong (1893–1973), president of the Foundation. Other recipients of the medal included Viscount Cecil of Chelwood (Lord Robert Cecil, 1864–1958), Colonel Charles Lindbergh, Senator Elihu Root, and the entire League of Nations.[6] After World War II, Oscar Jászi compared Masaryk to Woodrow Wilson, but – according to him – Masaryk surpassed Wilson in his knowledge of Europe and a sense of the realities of life.[7] Later, in 1971, the prominent American statesman Hubert H. Humphrey stated: "Like all great national leaders, Masaryk had an appeal that was not limited to his countrymen. ... A militant democrat, he shares our affection with other great national founders and preservers: Gandhi and Lincoln and Churchill."[8]

More recently, in October 2011, the former US secretary of state Madeleine Albright defined the relationship between Masaryk and Woodrow Wilson by saying in Prague: "In real life, their partnership may not have been as warm as many of us were taught, but the connection between democratic ideals on one side of the Atlantic and the creation of a new republic here in the heart of Europe [Czechoslovakia] was genuine." Al-

---

5   John MacCormac, "Masaryk, at Eighty, Toils on at His Task," *New York Times*, March 2, 1930, 3, 14. See also Jaroslav Opat, "Masarykovo evropanství jako pojem a jako politický program," *Masarykův sborník* 8 (1993, Prague: Ústav T. G. Masaryka, 1993), 44.

6   Tomáš G. Masaryk, *Cesta demokracie IV, Spisy* 36 (Prague: Masarykův ústav AV ČR, 1997), 444. Masaryk, in fact, stated that the Czechoslovak independence was born on the soil of the United States, the oldest democracy in the world, and its models were the great figures of American history, and the noble ideas of President Wilson. "Nástupní audience amerického vyslance," September 8, 1933, Masaryk, Tomáš G., *Cesta demokracie IV, Spisy* 36 (Prague: Masarykův ústav AV ČR, 1997), 484.

7   Oscar Jászi, "Significance of Thomas G. Masaryk for the Future," *Journal of Central European Affairs*, April 1950, 1–2.

8   Hubert H. Humphrey, "Foreword," in Tomáš G. Masaryk, *Humanistic Ideals*, transl. W. Preston Warren (Lewisburg, PA: Bucknell University Press, 1971), 7.

bright went on to characterize Masaryk: "He was not the first leader ... to make the case for a world that was democratic, humane and just. But few sought to achieve these goals with as much persistence and integrity over a long period of time."[9]

Like Wilson, Masaryk brought to his political activity the assets of a profound background in scholarship as well as religious flavor. A leitmotif of Masaryk's intellectual search – and which separated him from the austere empirical realism of the Austrian philosophical tradition of his home environment – was his desire to establish a religious dimension to the human experience. Unable to accept his native Catholicism, whether traditional or liberal, he turned to the two modernizing trends in German Lutheranism that had jettisoned traditional dogma and liturgy. Among them, he rejected the intellectualizing trend leading to German Idealism (from Kant to Hegel) that transformed theological dogmas into secularized metaphysical concepts. Instead, he gravitated to the other, non-intellectualized approach of the religion of inner feeling that he found in Friedrich A. Lange and Paul A. de Lagarde.[10] In turn, the appeal of this approach engendered in Masaryk – rather surprisingly – a measure of sympathy for Schopenhauer and Nietzsche, who had participated to a considerable extent in that branch of secularized Lutheran tradition. For Masaryk, endowing every act of perception with an ethical significance could incorporate a religious dimension into the empirical realism of the Austrian school, while preserving an epistemological integrity. Thus, he could avoid an epistemological dualism like that of Kant's Pure and Practical Reason. Moreover, the religion of inner feelings that developed within German Lutheranism was virtually identical with the non-dogmatic moral theology of the Unity of Brethren that – in Masaryk's view – epitomized the universal cosmopolitan contribution of the Bohemian Reformation to world culture.

---

9   At the dedication of the restored monument to Woodrow Wilson in Prague on October 5, 2011; Madeleine Albright, "The Legacy of Masaryk and Wilson Today, Part II," *Slovo* (Cedar Rapids, IA), 12, 2 (2011), 19–20.

10 For the historian Heinrich von Treitschke, this approach recovered the purely moral content of Christianity, freed from the intellectual shackles of dogma. Thereby the Germans conducted another Reformation leading to free and unprejudiced intellectual life. With justified national pride they could claim to be at once "pious and free," creating a literature which was Protestant, but not tainted with dogma. See James E Bradley and Dale K. Van Kley, eds., *Religion and Politics in Enlightenment Europe* (Notre Dame, IN.: University of Notre Dame Press, 2001), 9, citing Heinrich von Treitschke, *Deutsche Geschichte im neunzehnten Jahrhundert*, vol. 1, 6th ed. (Leipzig: S. Hirzel, 1897), 51, 90, 93.

An important aspect of Masaryk's life, thought, and work was his kinship with the American president Woodrow Wilson, as noted above. The kinship was, most importantly, reflected in their shared political philosophy of the crucial importance of democracy and in the vision of a peaceful world achieved through the League of Nations. The relationship was sealed by their personal contact in Washington, D.C., between April and October 1918, as well as by Masaryk's expressed admiration for Wilson.[11] Moreover, like Wilson, Masaryk combined academic and political activity. Reflecting on the connection, he asserted that he never accepted knowledge for its own sake, just as he did not believe in art for art's sake. He maintained that knowledge was concerned with life and served life. Science and scholarship were not fruits of intellect only but also of morality. Academic knowledge involved labor, patience, precision, sincerity, and truthfulness, and those were not qualities of reason but of morality.[12] In his Wilsonian vision Masaryk sought to build democracy not only in Czechoslovakia but also abroad. In addition to his whole-hearted support of the League of Nations, he insisted on the admission of political figures from other European countries, who were threatened with persecution as their countries became totalitarian or dictatorial, beginning with Communist Russia and ending with Nazi Germany and Austria.[13]

In general in his decisions and actions, Masaryk actively embraced liberalism, tolerance, individualism, open society, and universal human culture, as opposed to authoritarianism, rigid ideology, intolerance, collectivism, utopianism, and essentialist nationalism. Despite his failure to appreciate the roots of Austro-Bohemian realism and universalism in the Catholic Enlightenment of the eighteenth century (which in Bohemia shared its roots with the Utraquism of the sixteenth century[14]), he became an heir to this tradition thanks to his immersion in the Austrian school of philosophy, as it had developed in the latter part of the nineteenth century, particularly when guided by Franz Brentano. It is the realistic and

---

11   On Masaryk's personal relation to Wilson, see Alain Soubigou, *Thomas Masaryk* (Paris: Librairie Arthème Fayard, 2002), 254–58.

12   Statement at the inauguration of the Masaryk Chair of Central European History at the King's College of the University of London on October 24, 1923; see Tomáš G. Masaryk, *Cesta demokracie II, Spisy* 34 (Masarykův ústav AV ČR, 2007), 491.

13   Opat, "Masarykovo evropanství jako pojem a jako politický program," 43.

14   Zdeněk V. David, Realism, *Tolerance, and Liberalism in the Czech National Awakening: Legacies of the Bohemian Reformation* (Washington, D.C.: Wilson Center Press; Baltimore: Johns Hopkins University Press, 2010), 64–82.

anti-Hegelian orientation of this tradition that can be helpful in explaining the resistance to totalitarianism in twentieth-century Czech political culture that was manifest in inter-war Czechoslovakia (1918–1938) and distinctive in East-Central Europe. The attempts to diminish Masaryk's intellectual and political stature after the end of the Cold War could hardly affect the core of his achievement.[15]

Of course, there exists a voluminous literature on Masaryk in various languages and on various levels of erudition. My main interest is to probe the mind of the man as revealed through his writings on philosophy and religion, and to map out his position in relation to the principal Austrian, British, French, and German – to some extent also American and Russian – thinkers with whom he dealt in his philosophical and religious writings. I mean to focus on the ideas behind his political pronouncements and activities, rather than just on his political pronouncements and activities alone. The latter have been emphasized in the past and have received rather abundant coverage.[16] As Erazim Kohák has recently pointed out:

> Masaryk today as a philosopher is virtually unknown. In part this may be because so much of his philosophizing remained oriented to the special issue of the Czech national rebirth in the nineteenth century, but even in greater part it is because his philosophical work has been overshadowed by his spectacular career as a statesman during the final two decades of his life.[17]

In fact, Masaryk's achievements as a philosopher did not equal those of the major figures in the field, such as Locke, Kant, Hegel, Comte, or Berg-

---

15   Prominent examples of this revisionism are Andrea Orzoff, *Battle for the Castle: The Myth of Czechoslovakia in Europe, 1914–1948* (New York: Oxford University Press, 2009); see also review by Matěj Spurný, Austrian History Yearbook, 43 (2011), 245–46; and Mary Heimann, *Czechoslovakia: The State That Failed* (New Haven: Yale University Press, 2009); see also reviews by Igor Lukes, American Historical Review, 116 (2011), 893–94; and Jindřich Dejmek, *Český časopis historický*, 109 (2011), 344–58.

16   For instance, Nejedlý in his extensive biography of Masaryk maintains that he has dealt with his subject more as a political actor than as a philosophical thinker; see Zdeněk Nejedlý, *T. G. Masaryk*, 4 vols. (Prague: Melantrich, 1930–1937), 2d ed., vols. 1–2, *Sebrané spisy*, 31–32 (Prague: Orbis, 1949–1950), 1: 25. Eva Schmidt-Hartmann, *Thomas G. Masaryk's Realism: Origins of a Czech Political Concept*, Veröffentlichungen des Collegium Carolinum, 52 (Munich: Oldenbourg, 1984), 65–66, points to a lacuna in the knowledge of sources from which Masaryk developed his thought.

17   Erazim Kohák, ed., *Jan Patočka: Philosophy and Selected Writings* (Chicago: University of Chicago, 1989), 10. See also Zdeněk Novotný, *Korektiv Masarykovy filosofie* (Prague: Filosofia, 2011), 9.

son, and he himself originally did not aspire to be a scholar and a professor, but instead a diplomat and a politician.[18] Thus, there were critics who deplored Masaryk's inability to produce a perfectly coherent and consistent system that would account in an overarching manner for all the major aspects of philosophy, including metaphysics, epistemology, and axiology.[19]

Nevertheless, in the end, his philosophical as well as religious ideas supplied the essential infrastructures of his political views and activities. Many commentators have noted that Masaryk met Plato's desideratum that rulers should be philosophers and philosophers should be rulers.[20] Moreover, Masaryk was exceptional among philosophers, for he had significant influence in politics. In comparison, Plato had only a modest effect on the Tyrant of Syracuse, Seneca on Nero, Voltaire on Frederick the Great, or Diderot on Catherine the Great.[21] Karel Čapek summed up cogently in the mid-1930s the relationship between philosophy and politics in Masaryk's life: "Masaryk's road to politics leads even today through philosophy. Politics is for him a practical realization of philosophy; and philosophy is an authoritative (scientific) search for answers to questions posed by practical, that is political, life."[22] Jan Patočka has called attention to what Franz Brentano, Masaryk's philosophy professor at the University of Vienna (1874–1879), said about Masaryk to fellow student Edmund Husserl, namely that Masaryk was mostly interested in the practical effect of philosophical doctrines. He was not interested in the doctrines themselves, but in their political consequences. This led him specifically to the study of Marxism and its impact on Russian politics.[23] Patočka highly prized Masaryk's insight into the nature of World War I as a symptom of the intellectual crises of modern man.[24] Hence Masaryk's philosophy was not purely theoretical, but orient-

---

18   Tomáš G. Masaryk, *Světová revoluce za války a ve válce, 1914–1918*, Spisy 15 (Prague: Masarykův ústav AV ČR, 2005), 266–67.

19   For outstanding examples of such criticism, which some might consider pedantic, see Jan Patočka, "Pokus o českou národní filosofii a jeho nezdar (1946)," idem, *Sebrané spisy*, 12, (Prague: 2006), 346–47, 348–49, 358, 365; and Karel Vorovka, "Několik myšlenek o Masarykově filosofii a jeho Světové revoluci," *Ruch filosofický* 5 (1925), 280, 283.

20   E.g., Ludwig, *Defender of Democracy: Masaryk of Czechoslovakia*, 53–54.

21   Soubigou, *Thomas Masaryk*, 17.

22   Karel Čapek, *Čtení o T. G. Masarykovi* (Prague: Melantrich, 1969), 61, cited by Zdeněk Novotný, *Korektiv Masarykovy filosofie* (Prague: Filosofia, 2011), 46.

23   Jan Patočka, "České myšlení v meziválečném údobí (Záznam přednášky)," [1974] in his *Češi II, Sebrané spisy*, 13 (Prague: Oikoymenh, 2006), 358.

24   Jan Patočka, "České myšlení v meziválečném období (Koncept přednášky)," (1975, 13:479) in his *Češi II, Sebrané spisy*, 13 (Prague: Oikoymenh, 2006), 341–42.

ed to practical life; it was activist, not passively observing; and it was constructive, not skeptical or pessimistic.[25] In essence, Masaryk's philosophical realism can be defined in the broadest sense as anchored in two areas, Platonic idealism and English empiricism. His philosophy "provided the foundation of his political work and has had an immense impact in molding the intellectual and civic climate of Bohemia."[26]

This book opens by discussing two neglected influences that grounded Masaryk's basic philosophical orientation, the German Friedrich A. Lange (1825–1875) and the Englishman Henry George Lewes (1817–1878). The text turns to the formation of his epistemological outlook, which involved a rejection of the metaphysics of German Idealism, epitomized by Georg Hegel, and the embracing instead of the realistic empiricism of John Locke. The orientation toward empirical realism was bolstered by his exposure to the paragons of the Austrian philosophical tradition stemming from Bernard Bolzano and transmitted to Masaryk by his university teachers Franz Brentano and Robert Zimmermann. The secularized Lutheran idea of personal faith, manifested in his paradoxical interaction with the views of the xenophobe and anti-Semite Paul de Lagarde (1827–1891), provided him with a straightforward religious insight without intricate metaphysical ratiocination or resorting to a revealed knowledge or truth. In a parallel intellectual advance, he had to steer his philosophical barque through the reefs of the ontological monism of Arthur Schopenhauer and Friedrich Nietzsche, and around the shoals of the social collectivism of Plato, Johann G. Herder, and Auguste Comte. Ultimately, he overcame both the specter of metaphysical monism and the limitations of empirical realism by appeals to the epistemological function and the ontic value of the emotion of faith (in his paradoxical intellectual encounter with Lagarde) and the emotion of love (finally and fully crystalized in his latter-day romantic relationship with the modest author and journalist, Oldra Sedlmayerová [1884–1954]).[27]

Turning from the philosophical to the political part of the book, the trajectories of moral and religious progress, according to Masaryk, aimed

---

25 Nejedlý, T. G. Masaryk, 1: 376–77.
26 Josef Novák, "Masaryk's Criticism of Romantic Titanism," in *T. G. Masaryk und die Brentano Schule*, Josef Zumr and Thomas Binder, eds. (Prague and Graz: Filozofický ústav Československé akademie věd and Forschungstelle und Dokumentationszentrum für österreichische Philosophie, 1992), 144.
27 See Chapters 3 and 4.

at worldwide development from the intellectual, political, and social stage of theocracy to that of democracy. Exploring the national, ethnic, and linguistic differences within humankind, Masaryk strove to establish the universality of human culture, which transcended such differentiations. His tracing on the grand scale of history the gradual prevalence of democracy over theocracy (represented by royal absolutism and the aristocratic social system) culminated, in his view, in a decisive victory of democracy as a result of World War I. As a sign of this victory Masaryk saw a democratic element, though perverse, even in the modern totalitarianism of the interwar era. In the trend toward a cultural and political unification of humankind, symbolized by the creation of the League of Nations (1918–1934), Masaryk sought to fend off tendencies toward limiting the process to a parochial unification of Europe. In his vision of the future, a single culture and civilization, although derived from the context of Europe's intellectual, political, and cultural development, should and would prevail on a global scale, embracing all of humankind worldwide.

The concluding part of the book deals with the worldwide legacy – eventually through Václav Havel – of Masaryk's philosophy and politics. An examination of Masaryk's intellectual and political inheritance has first to deal with the eclipse of Masaryk's vision in the shadow of the totalitarian systems during the half-century after his death. This vision was not only denounced by the propaganda of the Communist bloc, but there were also doubts about its viability and future even among committed democrats and dissidents from the totalitarian regime, exemplified by the courageous and outstanding Czech philosopher, Jan Patočka (1907–1977). Except for the brief respite of the Prague Spring (1967–1969), Masaryk's intellectual and political legacy could exert its full influence only after the Communist regime in Czechoslovakia was swept away in the wake of the Velvet Revolution of November 1989. Then Václav Havel could embrace Masaryk's ideas as a political program, retaining its globalism and democratic framework; although Havel's vision allowed for a greater cultural diversity, limiting – though not eliminating – Masaryk's cultural Eurocentrism. This concession was consistent with the international developments during the second half of the twentieth century, particularly the occurrence of decolonization.

I

Philosophy

Chapter 1

Masaryk's Path Toward Empiricism

Perhaps the most crucial issue in Masaryk's philosophical teaching was his approach to the juxtaposition of Idealism, which saw the ultimate (ontic) reality as thought, and Empiricism, for which the ultimate reality consisted of sense perceptions. Applied to politics, Idealism's concept of reality as a cosmic thought fostered the image of social and national wholes, postulating an ultimate singularity (or monism) of nations and states, and therefore also standing for political collectivism (or authoritarianism), downgrading the individual. On the other hand, Empiricism's view of reality as an assemblage of autonomous perceptions, when applied to states and societies, promoted the vision of multiplicity and the autonomy of individual entities, or pluralism – therefore, also political individualism. In his philosophical preferences, Masaryk often expressed his negative view of German Idealism, as exemplified by Johann G. Fichte (1762–1814) and Georg W. Hegel (1770–1831), and this became one of the main leitmotifs of his teaching. In his vision of ultimate (ontic) reality, he definitely gravitated towards British-style Empiricism, as expressed, above all, in the works of John Locke (1632–1704) and Franz Brentano (1838–1917) (as discussed in Chapter 2). Thanks to his immersion in the Austrian school of philosophy, as it had developed in the latter part of the nineteenth century and particularly when guided by Franz Brentano, Masaryk became an heir to the tradition of Austro-Bohemian realism and universalism (despite his failure to appreciate its roots in the Catholic Enlightenment of the eighteenth century[1]).

---

1   In Bohemia this tradition shared its roots with the Utraquism of the sixteenth century. Zdeněk V. David, *Realism, Tolerance, and Liberalism in the Czech National Awakening: Legacies of the Bohemian Reformation* (Washington, D.C.: Wilson Center Press; Baltimore: Johns Hopkins University Press, 2010), 64–82.

This chapter addresses the roots of Masaryk's nuanced stance on the issues of ultimate reality (ontology), through the seminal influence of Friedrich A. Lange (1828–1875) and Henry Lewes and the evolution of his lifelong opposition to Hegel and German Idealism.

Masaryk's Philosophical Progenitors

Lange's seminal influence on Masaryk

Early in Masaryk's intellectual development, Lange helped him to reject metaphysical idealism, to accept empiricism in a qualified way, and, in addition, to seek a religious dimension in life and existence that was compatible with empiricism.[2] Thus, Lange not only helped to orient Masaryk in the problems of ontology but also pointed the way to an undogmatic yet profound religiosity. But despite its significance, Lange's impact on Masaryk's thought has not received the attention it deserves, indeed, scholars have overlooked it almost entirely. The crucial source documenting Masaryk's interest in Lange is a passage in his autobiographical statement of August 25, 1875, which Jaromír Doležal discovered after World War I in the archives of the former Austrian Ministry of Education in Vienna. Masaryk wrote about his preoccupation with Lange's survey of Western philosophy while still a secondary school (Gymnasium) student in Vienna in 1869: "My favorite task in those days was a Czech translation of Lange's Geschichte des Materialismus [History of Materialism], which I provided with notes embodying my opinions, such as they were."[3] Masaryk's own admission can, therefore, be regarded as the "smoking gun" in an investigation of Lange's influence on him.

---

2   Friedrich A. Lange, while rejecting later German Idealism, accepted in a qualified way Kant's epistemology, and with Otto Liebmann he was the founder of the Neo-Kantian tradition, which dominated German philosophy during the second half of the nineteenth century. He was a professor of philosophy in Bonn, Duisberg, Zurich, and Marburg; Donald M. Borchert, ed., *The Encyclopedia of Philosophy*, 2nd ed., 10 vols. (New York: Macmillan, 2006), 5: 186–87.

3   "Meine Lieblingsarbeit war damals eine bömische Übersetzung Lange's *Geschichte des Materialismus* die ich mit noten versah, in denen ich meine unmassgeblichen Ansichten aussprach..." See Jaromír Doležal, *Masarykova cesta životem*, 2 vols. (Brno: Polygrafie, 1920–1921), 2: 15; see also ibid., 1: 17. Lange's history was originally written in German and published in 1865, followed by a two-volume extended second edition published in 1873–75, followed by a three-volume English translation in 1877–81.

The above passage from Masaryk's autobiography was cited by Paul Selver in his biography of Masaryk (1940),[4] and Jaroslav Opat's biography of Masaryk contained a brief reference to it as well. Opat noted that in his final *Gymnasium* years in Vienna, "Lange's *History of Materialism* in Czech translation was among his most favorite reading." This statement, however, tends to convey the mistaken impression that there was a pre-existing Czech translation of Lange.[5] In actuality, according to the autobiography cited by Doležal, Masaryk was preparing the Czech translation for himself, which attested to a much deeper involvement with the text than even Opat suggests.[6]

Apparently, the first author to call attention to Lange's role in its own right was Zdeněk Nejedlý in his grand biography of Masaryk (1930–37). He pointed out the importance of Lange in the formation of Masaryk's philosophical outlook,[7] and also stressed the importance of Masaryk's translation of Lange's *History of Materialism* into Czech, noting that the manuscript thereof was not extant.[8] He further suggested that Masaryk first became acquainted with eighteenth-century British empiricism through his study of Lange's work.[9] Stanislav Polák recognized Masaryk's translation as a seminal event in the statesman's intellectual development, pointing out that in Lange, Masaryk found a delineation

---

4   Paul Selver, *Masaryk: A Biography* (London: M. Joseph, 1940), 23.

5   Jaroslav Opat, *Filozof a politik: T. G. Masaryk, 1882–1893* (Prague: Melantrich, 1990), 30. A simple statement of Masaryk's early and deep interest in Lange's *Geschichte des Materialismus* is also in Vladimír Peška, "La France dans la formation intellectuelle de Masaryk," in Vladimír Peška and Antoine Mareš, eds., *Thomas Garrigue Masaryk, européen et humaniste* (Paris: Etudes et documentation internationales: Institut d'études slaves, 1991), 222.

6   Doležal, *Masarykova cesta životem*, 1: 17. See also Jaromír Doležal, "Masaryk na studiích ve Vídni," *Masarykův almanach* (Vienna: Akademický spolek, 1925), 21. There are no mentions of Lange in the following monographs on Masaryk: Antonie van den Beld, *Humanity: The Political and Social Philosophy of Thomas G. Masaryk* (The Hague: Mouton, 1975); Roman Szporluk, *The Political Thought of Thomas Masaryk*, East European Monographs, 85 (New York: Columbia University Press, 1981); Eva Schmidt-Hartmann, *Thomas G. Masaryk's Realism: Origins of a Czech Political Concept*, Veröffentlichungen des Collegium Carolinum, 52 (Munich: Oldenbourg, 1984); *T. G. Masaryk, 1850–1937*, Stanley Winters and others, eds., 3 vols. (London: Macmillan, 1989–1990); Zwi Batscha, *Eine Philosophie der Demokratie: Thomas G. Masaryks Begründung einer neuzeitlichen Demokratie* (Frankfurt: Surkamp, 1994); H. Gordon Skilling, *T. G. Masaryk: Against the Current, 1882–1914* (University Park: Pennsylvania State University, 1994); Milan Machovec, *Tomáš G. Masaryk*, 3rd ed. (Prague: Česká expedice, 2000).

7   Zdeněk Nejedlý, *T. G. Masaryk*, 4 vols. (Prague: Melantrich, 1930–1937); 2nd ed., vols. 1–2, Sebrané spisy, 31–32 (Prague: Orbis, 1949–1950), 1: 320.

8   Nejedlý, *T. G. Masaryk*, 2: 281. Nejedlý again referred to Masaryk's youthful translation of Lange in his list of Masaryk's translations into Czech, also including texts from Plato and Descartes; ibid., 2: 305.

9   Nejedlý, *T. G. Masaryk*, 1: 370.

between the two approaches to knowledge that had preoccupied him in his youth: namely, the contrast between the realm of sense perception and that of intellectual speculation and imagination. Lange designated the former (simplistically and inaccurately) as Materialism and the latter as Idealism.[10]

Interestingly, in his own writings Masaryk did not refer to Lange conspicuously or frequently. There are simple references to Lange in *The Foundations of Concrete Logic* [Základové konkretné logiky],[11] in a review for the journal *Atheneum* in 1884,[12] and in his own first monograph, a study of suicide.[13] In *The Social Question*, Masaryk concerned himself with Lange in the latter's other capacity, as a writer on workers' movements.[14] In *The Spirit of Russia* Masaryk noted Russian populist Nikolai K. Mikhailovskii's fascination with Lange's writings, the reading of which Mikhailovskii considered essential for the education of Russian youth.[15] Later in his life, Masaryk included Lange among the seven German

---

10   Stanislav Polák, *T.G. Masaryk*, 6 vols. (Prague: Masarykův ústav AV ČR, 2000–2012), 1: 136.

11   Tomáš G. Masaryk, *Česká otázka. Naše nynější krize. Jan Hus*, Spisy 6 (Prague: Masarykův ústav, 2000); idem, *Pokus o konkrétní logiku; třídění a soustava věd*, Spisy 3 (Prague: Masarykův ústav AV ČR, 2001); Karel Čapek, *Hovory s T. G. Masarykem*, Spisy 20 (Prague: Československý spisovatel, 1990).

12   Review of Jan Kapras, *Zkušebná duševěda* (Prague: Otto, 1884), in Tomáš G. Masaryk, *Z počátků Athenea, 1883–1885*, Spisy 18 (Prague: Masarykův ústav AV ČR, 2004), 130.

13   Tomáš G. Masaryk, *Sebevražda hromadným jevem společenským moderní osvěty*, Spisy 1 (Prague: Masarykův ústav AV ČR, 2002), 62, refers to Lange, *Geschichte des Materialismus*, vol 2, p. 453 ff.: on the materialistic and hedonistic character of modern society.

14   Tomáš G. Masaryk, *Otázka sociální. Základy marxismu filosofické a sociologické*, 2 vols. Spisy 9–10 (Prague: Masarykův ústav AV ČR, 2000), 1: 28, lists in bibliography in category writings of "non-socialists" (*Nesocialisté*): Friedrich Albert Lange, *Die Arbeiterfrage in ihrer Bedeutung für Gegenwart und Zukunft beleuchtet* (Duisburg: W. Falk & Volmer, 1865); Lange, *Die Arbeiterfrage. Ihre Bedeutung für Gegenwart und Zukunft*, 5th ed. (Winterthur: Gescwister Ziegler, 1894) is unchanged reprint of ed. 3; Masaryk, *Otázka sociální*, 1: 195, refers to Friedrich Albert Lange, *Die Arbeiterfrage* [given as *Arbeitsfrage*] 1894–1895, 106, 140; concerning the question of development and progress once socialism/communism has been reached; cited together with J.S. Mill, *Principles of Political Economy* IV [1848], kapitola VI: On the Stationary State. There is no reference to Lange in either Tomáš G. Masaryk, *Moderní člověk a náboženství*, Spisy 8 (Prague: Masarykův ústav AV ČR, 2000); or in Tomáš G. Masaryk, *Juvenilie, Studie a stati, 1876–1881*, Spisy 16 (Prague: Masarykův ústav AV ČR, 1993).

15   In addition to those of Eugene Dühring, see Masaryk, *The Spirit of Russia*, 2: 139; Tomáš G. Masaryk, *Rusko a Evropa*, vol. 2, Spisy 12 (Prague: Masarykův ústav AV ČR, 1996), 133. Mikhailovskii was impressed by Lange's assertion in the *History of Materialism* that, while the materialist viewpoint was proper for the study of nature, the "ideal" dimension had to figure in the consideration of human problem. See James H. Billington, *Mikhailovsky and Russian Populism* (New York: Oxford University Press, 1958), 69. On the basis of Lange's Neo-Kantianism, he advanced the doctrine of a "two-sided truth," according to which the subjective and the objective perceptions were in full harmony. Ibid., 97,

Neo-Kantians whom he identified as the inspirers of revisionist Marxism in late nineteenth century Russia.[16]

Nejedlý recorded an interesting episode that bore on Masaryk's relation to Lange. According to Nejedlý, in 1874 the University of Vienna favored Lange over Franz Brentano, who was to become Masaryk's cherished teacher at that university, for appointment to a tenured position as a professor of philosophy. Brentano, who had been a Catholic priest, nevertheless secured the appointment on January 22, 1874, thanks to the secularist, Liberal, Council of Ministers in Vienna.[17] However, it seems unlikely that a rivalry between Lange and Masaryk's favorite mentor in Vienna would have caused Masaryk to hesitate to mention Lange's name. In a broader sense, Nejedlý does point out that Masaryk never felt the need to entertain a disciple's gratitude toward his mentors, especially where such gratitude would place him under an intellectual or personal obligation.[18] In any case, Masaryk's reticence helps to explain why Lange's effect on him has been underrepresented, if not entirely overlooked in scholarship.

Lange placed in opposition two philosophical principles that he claimed had dominated the thinking of humankind from the beginning to the present: materialism and idealism. The former relied on an empirical and rationalist approach and recognized the world of sensory phenomena. The latter rose above the world of the senses to seek allegedly higher truths.[19] Lange guided young Masaryk through the thought of Kant, Fichte, and Hegel, with the outcome that Masaryk eventually rejected philosophical Idealism and gravitated toward the Empiricism of Locke and Brentano, a perspective that influenced his politics and manifested itself in his rejection of collectivist authoritarianism and embrace of individualistic democratism. In other words, Lange's early influence significantly helped to establish Masaryk's basic philosophical matrix, underpinning his subsequent political theory and practice.

---

16 In addition to Wilhelm Schuppe, Alois Riehl, Hermann Cohen, Wilhelm Windelband, Heinrich Rickert, and Rudolf Stammler, see Masaryk, *The Spirit of Russia*, 2: 352.

17 Nejedlý, *T. G. Masaryk,* 1: 449.

18 Thus Masaryk likewise avoided mentioning Brentano's role in stimulating his interest in Hume's skepticism. Zdeněk Novotný, *Korektiv Masarykovy filosofie* (Prague: Filosofia, 2011), 56, citing Nejedlý, *T. G. Masaryk,* 4: 257.

19 Friedrich A. Lange, *Geschichte des Materialismus und Kritik seiner Bedeutung in der Gegenwart,* ed. Alfred Schmidt, 2 vols. (Frankfurt a. M.: Suhrkamp, 1974), 2: 987; the metaphysics of idealism "built castles in the air."

Negative view of Idealism

Lange was a critic of speculative metaphysics and a defender of the view that philosophy should incorporate the findings of the exact sciences.[20] Early in his first serious philosophical reading in Vienna, Masaryk imbibed a negative view of Hegel from Lange's survey of Western philosophy, *Geschichte des Materialismus und Kritik seiner Bedeutung in der Gegenwart*. Lange is considered a precursor, if not one of the founders, of neo-Kantianism. He allowed a space for the acceptance of Kant, whom he viewed as an advocate of transcendental knowledge, however, he condemned in no uncertain terms the use of Kant for the production of metaphysical constructs.

Hegel's metaphysics, according to Lange, ultimately rested on pantheism, which set out, a priori, as an axiom the unity of all human minds with the universal Spirit and all other spirits.[21] As the dominant way of thinking [*Denkweise*] not only for Hegel but also for Friedrich W. Schelling's (1775–1854) *Naturphilosophie*, pantheism represented a world view that, while not lacking a certain mystical depth, simultaneously contained the danger of fantastic mental aberrations.[22] Lange further maintained that Hegel's influence on the writing of history was at times particularly pernicious.[23]

Masaryk derived from his exposure to Lange his distaste for mainline German Idealism on the one hand, and on the other a way of allowing a certain space for ethics, esthetics and religion that went beyond strict empiricism.[24] However, he found Hegel's overt and implied pantheism to be particularly deplorable. Masaryk's view – originally imbibed from Lange – of the detrimental effect of Hegelian Idealism on both intellectual and social developments, particularly in Germany and Russia is discussed in detail below.

The limitations of empiricism and the issue of materialism

Aside from a negative view of Idealism, Masaryk shared not only Lange's preference for empiricism but also his concern for the epistemological lim-

---

20 *Concise Routledge Encyclopedia of Philosophy* (New York: Routledge, 2000), 450–51. An exact science, as defined by Merriam-Webster is "a science (such as physics, chemistry, or astronomy) whose laws are capable of accurate quantitative expression."
21 Ibid., 2: 546.
22 Ibid., 2: 514.
23 Ibid., 2: 579.
24 Borchert, *Encyclopedia of Philosophy*, 5: 186–87.

itations of empiricism. However, Masaryk differed with both Lange's diagnosis of the flaw in empiricism and with his prescription of Neo-Kantianism as a cure. Although clearly preferring Empiricism of the British and French type to Idealism, Lange nevertheless sensed that, ultimately, empiricism was unable to grasp the fullness of reality. In his opinion, empiricism actually denied any existence beyond sensory experience, and thus it led to the metaphysics of materialism.

According to Lange, the English philosophers since Francis Bacon (1561–1626) employed a method that was in particular harmony with a natural sciences approach. Hence, unlike the Continent, England had not experienced a significant conflict between philosophy and exact science. The world of phenomena was treated by the important English philosophers in the same manner as by the Continent's materialists, although only a few, such as Hobbes, would admit to being materialists. Locke in particular sought cover under the subjective approach of sensualism.[25] Nevertheless, Lange identified the British empirical thought of Bacon, Hobbes, and Locke as leading to the materialism of French Enlightenment thinkers. Subsequently, John Stuart Mill was added to the series of empiricists who paved the way for materialism in philosophy. Although Masaryk shared Lange's later concern with the lack of a spiritual dimension in English and French Empiricism, this deficiency did not diminish his own respect for British empiricists, in particular for Locke (see Chapter 2).

Space for a spiritual dimension

To balance the claims of what he called materialism and idealism, Lange sought a Neo-Kantian approach. Materialism led to knowledge of nature and its laws; idealism created art, religion, and metaphysics.[26] Hence, Lange felt that in seeking to apply philosophy to the understanding of nature, the French and British, with their "materialism," had made much greater advances in science than the Germans had with their metaphysics.[27] He also saw two sides of both philosophical systems: materialism led to egoism,

---

25   Ibid., 2: 593. Attributing irreligious views to Locke, however, was particularly inappropriate; in 1659–1662, he was an advocate of High Church Anglicanism, virtually an Anglo-Catholic; see Jacqueline Rose, "John Locke, 'matters indifferent,' and the Restoration of the Church of England," *Historical Journal*, 48 (2005), 601–21.

26   On Lange's Neo-Kantianism see Borchert, *Encyclopedia of Philosophy*, 5: 186–87, 344–45.

27   Lange's *Geschichte des Materialismus und Kritik seiner Bedeutung in der Gegenwart*, 2: 512–13.

Epicureanism, and passive resignation; idealism's chimerical products of fantasy hindered the development of the human spirit. On the positive side, idealism lifted man above purely personal interests, and aroused an instinct both to self-sacrifice and charity; materialism was a justifiable reaction to excessive idealism. The future called for achieving a balance between knowledge and poetry, empiricism and the transcendental, and a final establishment of political and intellectual freedom in which reason and the senses are given their rights while at the same time spiritual life could flourish.[28]

Masaryk's disagreements with Lange

Above all, Masaryk did not agree with Lange's conviction that empiricism necessarily led to the metaphysics of materialism (see Chapter 2). Likewise, he was not sympathetic to Lange's new way of enlisting Kantian concepts to rescue empiricism from its epistemological predicament. Along these lines, Masaryk was adamantly opposed to attempts by the so-called Neo-Kantians to enlist Austrian philosopher Johann F. Herbart (1776–1841) – an early opponent of German Idealism – as a supporter of Kant. In particular, Masaryk targeted Hermann Cohen (1842–1918), a professor of philosophy at the University of Marburg, for his *Kants Theorie der Erfahrung* in 1871. Masaryk felt that even the Neo-Kantians leaned too far in the direction of Kant. Thus, he was particularly harsh in censuring Josef Durdík, philosophy professor at the University of Prague (1882–1902), for his efforts to equate Herbart's ideas with those of Kant. Masaryk charged Durdík with transgressions such as "rashness, trickery, and absurdity" and pointed out that Herbart himself had excoriated Kant in his work on psychology.[29] For his part, Masaryk would seek a solution to the predicament of empiricism's epistemological poverty through the recognition of the ontic power of faith (see Chapter 3) and of love (see Chapter 4).

---

28 Lange's *Geschichte des Materialismus und Kritik seiner Bedeutung in der Gegenwart*, 2: 450; Borchert, *Encyclopedia of Philosophy*, 5: 186–87, 344–45. Lange's non-dogmatic religiosity was also a possible link between Masaryk and Nietzsche. Nietzsche read Friedrich Lange's *History of Materialism* about the same time as Masaryk; Friedrich Nietzsche, *The Anti-Christ, Ecce Homo, Twilight of the Idols, and Other Writings*, ed. Aaron Ridley and Judith Norman, trans. Judith Norman (Cambridge: Cambridge University Press, 2005), xxxv. He used ideas from Lange's *History* for inspiration throughout his creative life, see George J. Stack, *Lange and Nietzsche*, Monographien und Texte zur Nietzsche-Forschung, vol. 10 (Berlin and New York: W. De Gruyter, 1983), 1–9.

29 Masaryk, *Z počátků Athenea, 1883–1885*, 231. He refers to Hermann Cohen's *Kants Theorie der Erfahrung* (Berlin: F Dümmer, 1871).

Despite these differences, Lange was instrumental in establishing Masaryk's basic philosophical matrix, not only by his rejection of German Idealism and endorsement of empiricism but also by his insistence on augmenting the epistemological range of empiricism by supplying a spiritual dimension. And also despite their differences, Masaryk's primary respect for Lange as his primordial teacher of philosophy is clearly indicated by his attempt to translate the *Geschichte des Materialismus* into Czech.[30] This deep respect for Lange persisted into Masaryk's mature philosophical life.[31]

George Henry Lewes and the link to Lange

As a follow up to the discussion of the relationship between Masaryk and Lange, it is essential to point out that in his early pedagogical career at the University of Prague, Masaryk tended to link Lange's *Geschichte des Materialismus* with the work of George Henry Lewes (1817–1878). Masaryk was translating Lange's main work as early as 1869 and had become familiar with Lewes's ideas on philosophy of history by 1875, during his doctoral studies in Vienna.[32] Most likely, his principal university professor, Franz Brentano, called his attention to Lewes. Brentano became familiar with Lewes's *Biographical History of Philosophy from Its Origin in Greece down to the Present Day* (1871) during his stay in London in the spring of 1872 and found it remarkable, albeit somewhat superficial.[33] By 1882 Masaryk had begun recommending Lewes's book (probably the German edition of 1876[34]) to his students in Prague, as a fundamental text. And – significantly – he recommended Lewes in conjunction with Lange's treatise.[35] Masaryk's article "Spisy A. Comta"

30 Polák, *T.G. Masaryk*, 1: 192.
31 For example, in his intellectual history of Russia, Russland und Europa, published in 1913, he made a special note of appreciation for Vladimir S. Solov'ev's plan to translate the *Geschichte des Materialismus* into the Russian language. Masaryk, *Rusko a Evropa*, vol. 2, 212.
32 Masaryk asked for Lewes's history of philosophy as a Christmas present in 1875; see Jakub Všetečka, "Vzpomínky," *Masarykův sborník,* 4 (Prague: Čin, 1930), 336; Nejedlý, *T. G. Masaryk,* 1: 416.
33 Letter of April 22, 1972, see Franz C. Brentano, *Briefe an Carl Stumpf, 1867–1917,* ed. Gerhard Oberkofler with Peter Goller (Graz: Akademische Druck- u. Verlagsanstalt, 1989), 27.
34 He also recommended to his students another book by Lewes, in German translation, namely, *The Physiology of Common Life,* 2 vols. (Edinburgh and London: Blackwood, 1859); see Tomáš G. Masaryk, *Univerzitní přednášky I: Praktická filozofie,* Spisy 4 (Prague: Masarykův ústav AV ČR, 2012), 26. See also Nejedlý, *T. G. Masaryk,* 3: 201.
35 Zdeněk Franta, "Vzpomínky," *Masarykův sborník,* 4 (Prague: Čin, 1930), 412, 415. On the contrary,

[Writings of A. Comte] appeared in *Atheneum* in November 1883, during his the first year teaching in Prague. In it, he also made positive mention of Lewes among the English thinkers who were receptive to Auguste Comte's (1798–1857) positivist ideas.[36] The first of the five important viewpoints Masaryk shared with Lewis was that Masaryk strongly favored Locke's empiricism,[37] while also objecting to empiricism (in the form of Comte's positivism) for not allowing any scope for ontic reality.[38] Second, like Lewes, Masaryk considered Hume's skepticism to have been a fundamental issue at the start of modern philosophy, one that set its course in the direction of both Idealism and Positivism.[39] Third, Masaryk shared Lewes's special liking for Lessing and Goethe,[40] both of whom he tended to include (together with Herder) in a trinity of German thinkers who avoided the philosophical pitfall of radical subjectivism.[41] Fourth – on the other side of the ledger – Masaryk agreed with Lewes's aversion to German idealists from Kant through Fichte, Schelling,

---

Masaryk spoke disparagingly about Duehring because of his stress on social collectivism; see Nejedlý, *T. G. Masaryk*, 3: 162–63; Franta, "Vzpomínky," 411. Lewes's history of philosophy was originally published in 1845–1846; the fourth edition came out in 1871, and there were subsequent translations into German and Hungarian. See, "Lewis, George Henry," *Dictionary of National Biography* [DNB], 22 vols. (Oxford: Oxford University Press, 1921–1922), 11: 1046 (a revised edition was published by Longmans in London, 1871); Ashton, Rosemary, *G. H. Lewes: A Life* (New York: Oxford University Press, 1991), 337. The German edition that Masaryk may have used was published as: George H. Lewes, *Geschichte der Philosophie von Thales bis Comte*, 2 vols. Transl. of 4th English ed. from 1871 (Berlin: R. Oppenheim, 1876); vol. 1: *Geschichte der alten Philosophie*; vol. 2: *Geschichte der neueren Philosophie*.

36   Masaryk, *Z počátků Athenea, 1883–1885*, 22.

37   George Henry Lewes, *Biographical History of Philosophy from Its Origin in Greece down to the Present Day* (New York: Appleton, 1857), 527.

38   Lewes, *Geschichte der Philosophie von Thales bis Comte*, 2: 276–284. See, also, "Lewis, George Henry," DNB, 11: 1045.

39   Lewes, *Geschichte der Philosophie von Thales bis Comte*, 2: 344–51, 364–68 (on the relation to Kant).

40   Lewes's article on Lessing in "Lessingiana," *Edinburgh Review* (October 1845), 451–70, reveals the highest admiration for Lessing, partly as "the least German of all Germans;" see ibid., 453; "Lewis, George Henry," DNB, 11: 1044; his "Life of Goethe" appeared in 1855, and it became the standard English work on the subject, DNB, 11: 1045.

41   Regarding Masaryk making an exception for Lessing, Goethe, and Herder, see, for instance, Tomáš G. Masaryk, *Havlíček: Snahy a tužby politického probuzení*, Spisy 7 (Prague: Masarykův ústav AV ČR, 1996), 195; Masaryk, *Česká otázka. Naše nynější krize. Jan Hus*, 416–417; Tomáš G. Masaryk, *Světová revoluce za války a ve válce, 1914–1918*, Spisy 15 (Prague: Masarykův ústav AV ČR, 2005), 434; Tomáš G. Masaryk, "Řeč prezidenta Masaryka při inauguraci Institutu pro slovanská studia," *Národní listy*, October 18, 1923, in idem, *Cesta demokracie II*, Spisy 34 (Prague: Masarykův ústav AV ČR, 2007), 467; Emil Ludwig, *Defender of Democracy: Masaryk of Czechoslovakia* (New York: R. M. McBride, 1936), 204. Masaryk, however, considered Goethe to have been intellectually stagnated in the eighteenth century; he was improperly considered superior to the more advanced Lessing and Herder. Masaryk, *Moderní člověk a náboženství*, 154.

and Hegel for their pronounced epistemological and ontic "subjectivism."[42] Finally, Masaryk shared both Lewes's high opinion of Comte and also, more tellingly, a regret over Comte's neglect of psychology as a scientific discipline.[43] In his two early treatises on "concrete logic" (1885 and 1887),[44] Masaryk pointedly echoes Lewes's critique of Comte's failure to include psychology in his scale of classification of sciences, an indication of Lewes's influence on the formative years of Masaryk's philosophical career.

Overall, his early exposure to Lewes's history of philosophy undoubtedly helped to strengthen Masaryk's attitude toward German philosophy, particularly his lifelong aversion to German Idealism. The importance that he attributed to Lewes's views in the initial stages of his academic teaching is indicated by his having highlighted Lewes's text – together with Lange's – as an instrument for introducing young adepts to the field of philosophical studies. This can also be taken as a reflection of the crucial role Lewes's textbook played in reinforcing the role that Lange's history played in forming the fundamentals of Masaryk's philosophical outlook.

Against Hegel and German Idealism

Throughout his career as philosopher, statesman, and public figure, Masaryk focused his critical attention on Hegel's thought and influence as the crucial link with what was unhealthy in the German philosophical tradition. Building on perspective gleaned from both Lange and Lewes, Masaryk held that the vagaries of German Idealism culminated in Hegel's teaching, with Kant, Fichte, and Schelling as his precursors and contemporaries.[45] Masaryk saw Kant in particular as the initial source of the subsequent distortions in the intellectual life of Germany. Early in his career,

---

42 Lewes, *Biographical History of Philosophy from Its Origin in Greece down to the Present Day*, x; see also [George Henry Lewis], "Lessingiana," 453. On Kant's key position in the further development of German Idealism, see Lewes, *Geschichte der Philosophie von Thales bis Comte*, 2: 579.

43 "Lewis, George Henry," DNB, 11: 1044, 1045; Lewes, *Geschichte der Philosophie von Thales bis Comte*, 2: 774.

44 Masaryk, *Základové konkretné logiky: třídění a soustava věd*, 105. Masaryk, *Pokus o konkrétní logiku; třídění a soustava věd*, 139.

45 Roger Scruton, "Masaryk, Patočka and the Care of the Soul," in *On Masaryk: Texts in English and German*, Studien zur österreichischen Philosophie, ed. Josef Novák, vol. 13 (Amsterdam: Rodopi, 1988), 112.

Masaryk was repelled by Kant's effort to overcome his own subjectivism and individualism by means of fantasy and questionable resolutions. Later, however, he did gain a measure of respect for Kant's *Critique of Pure Reason* and for his endeavor in ethics,[46] noting that Kant did not directly anticipate the imperialist Pan-German ideal (having proclaimed his devotion to republican principles and political freedom)[47] and even at times conceding to Kant a place among the stalwarts of Germany's positive philosophical tradition, such as Herder, Lessing, Goethe, and Schiller.[48]

Nevertheless, on the whole, Masaryk remained aware of the weakness of Kant's Prussian pretentiousness, which he called Titanism (a term borrowed from Greek mythology), and he considered Kant's categorical imperative and his postulates of apriori category to be abdications before the postulates of Christian dogmatic theology and morality, and their imitations, referring presumably to the concept of soul, and to the Ten Commandments. According to Masaryk, Kant's followers exaggerated their mentor's faults, and these exaggerations were clearly visible both in the fantastic method by which the disciples sought to construct original philosophical systems and in the caricatures, at which German so-called idealism (really subjectivism) arrived – for example, Fichte's Ego, Schiller's Absolute, Hegel's Spirit, or Schopenhauer's Will. After Kant, German philosophy, with its subjectivism and fantasy, sank unavoidably into pessimism and egoism and sanctified the use of brutality as advocated by the devotees of Pangermanism.[49]

Eventually, it was specifically Hegel's teaching that served as a nexus between German Idealist philosophy and the subsequent reprehensible social and political ideologies that fostered amoral world views by replacing the individual conscience with submission to extrinsic historical forces. According to Masaryk, the first direction in which this led was to the dialectical and historical materialism of Marx and Friedrich Engels (1820–1895), as well as to the fateful susceptibility to Marxism of the Russian political culture, which was steeped in Hegel. The second direction

---

46 Tomáš G. Masaryk, *Světová revoluce za války a ve válce, 1914–1918*, Spisy 15 (Prague: Masarykův ústav AV ČR, 2005), 426.

47 Here Masaryk reacted to the attempts by the National Socialists in the 1930s to appropriate ideologically not only Kant but also Plato; see Emil Ludwig, *Defender of Democracy: Masaryk of Czechoslovakia* (New York: R. M. McBride, 1936), 204.

48 Masaryk, *Světová revoluce za války a ve válce, 1914–1918*, 434.

49 Ibid., 426. See also Chapter 8, "Masaryk's Perspective and Participation in World War I."

to which it led was to the pessimism of dominant German intellectuals such as Eduard Hartmann (1842–1906), Friedrich Nietzsche (1844–1900), and Richard Wagner (1818–1883). Masaryk felt that this second consequence of Hegelianism was conducive to violence as a psychological escape from nihilism and depression, thus fueling the national chauvinism of Pangermanism and triggering in Germany the drive toward the carnage of World War I.

Hegel and the German philosophical tradition: "unscientific" and "obscure"

In Masaryk's view, Hegel's philosophy, like that of Fichte and Schelling, relied on myths in its metaphysical concepts. He deemed it unscientific, because every discipline of knowledge as it progressed toward becoming a science had to discard the ballast of its mythical origins.[50] In this conviction, Masaryk mirrored the views of his teacher Brentano.[51] Hand in hand with the mythological character of Hegelianism, according to Masaryk, went a language so obscure that Hegel's concepts were not comprehensible to young students, often not even to adults.[52] It was in this context that Masaryk pointed out in *Sebevražda* [Suicide] that Americans had no use for Hegel – not because they were not interested in philosophy, but because their ideal needs (*ideální potřeby*) were satisfied by religion, and thus they did not need to resort to metaphysics.[53]

50   Tomáš G. Masaryk, *Základové konkretné logiky: třídění a soustava věd*, Spisy 2 (Prague: Masarykův ústav AV ČR, 2001), 168–67. See also Stanislav Polák, *T. G. Masaryk*, 6 vols. (Prague: Masarykův ústav AV ČR, 2000–2012), 1: 165; Zdeněk Nejedlý, *T. G. Masaryk*, 4 vols. (Prague: Melantrich, 1930–1937); 2d ed., vols. 1–2, Sebrané spisy, 31–32 (Prague: Orbis, 1949–1950), 4: 234.

51   Brentano argued for the sequential adoption of the scientific method by every discipline of knowledge in his Inaugural Lecture at the University of Vienna, April 1874; see Franz Brentano, *Über die Gründe der Ermutigung auf philosophischem Gebiete* (Vienna, 1874); also in Franz Brentano, *Über die Zukunft der Philosophie*, ed. Oskar Kraus (Leipzig, 1929), 83–100. According to Batscha, Masaryk's view of progress as a movement from mythology to science was reminiscent of Comte; Zwi Batscha, *Eine Philosophie der Demokratie: Thomas G. Masaryks Begründung einer neuzeitlichen Demokratie* (Frankfurt: Surkamp, 1994), 234.

52   Tomáš G. Masaryk, *Parlamentní projevy, 1891–1893*, Spisy, 21 (Prague: Masarykův ústav AV ČR, 2001), 101. Patočka noted that Masaryk, influenced by Brenato, viewed German Idealism as an extreme subjectivism and product of fantasy; see Jan Patočka, *Dvě studie o Masarykovi* (Toronto: Sixty-Eight Publishers, 1980), 61.

53   Tomáš G. Masaryk, *Sebevražda hromadným jevem společenským moderní osvěty*, Spisy 1 (Prague: Masarykův ústav AV ČR, 2002), 168.

Writing in the journal *Atheneum* in the mid-1880s, Masaryk agreed with the assessment of Hegel's philosophy by Alexius Meinong (1853–1920), a former fellow student at the University of Vienna: after Kant German philosophy had gone astray. This was widely recognized to be true in the case of Hegel, as well as Schelling and Fichte, and even Kant was being linked with this dubious company. Meinong concluded that German philosophy became stranded in a strange mixture of philology, theology, and unhealthy apriorism and would benefit from a healthy dose of English empiricism – a point with which Masaryk agreed.[54]

The subjective approach to knowledge and existence was – according to Masaryk – a curse of the German tradition that produced an epistemological and metaphysical asymmetry that had serious consequences, namely the interrelated extremes of solipsism and pantheism. In his early work *Pokus o konkrétní logiku* [An Attempt at Concrete Logic] (1887), Masaryk noted that Kant had reduced philosophy to logic, thus exaggerating his own view of the static condition of the world, and further that Hegel had committed the cardinal error of, in effect, turning logic into metaphysics.[55] Moreover, Hegel had tried to remedy Kant's static view with his own philosophy of development, which seemed to be a brilliant achievement, but unfortunately, just like Kant's criticism, it lacked psychological sobriety.[56] In *Modern Man and Religion* (1896–98), Masaryk pointed out that the Post-Kantian development of German philosophy revealed the great flaw of subjectivism, whereby Hegel, and Fichte as well, had pushed Kant's view into a logical dead end with their Absolute Idealism.[57]

---

54 Tomáš G. Masaryk, "Dr. Alexius Meinong, *Hume-Studien II*," vol. 1 1883–84," in Masaryk, *Z počátků Athenea, 1883–1885*, Spisy 18 (Prague: Masarykův ústav AV ČR, 2004), 93. In the same period, Masaryk endorsed the plea of Wilhelm Dilthey that the study of the humanities be freed from metaphysical viewpoints, of which Hegel's philosophy of history was a prime example; Tomáš G. Masaryk, "Wilh. Dilthey...*Einleitung in die Geisteswissenschaften*, vol. 2, 1883–84," Masaryk, *Z počátků Athenea, 1883–1885*, 114.

55 Tomáš G. Masaryk, *Pokus o konkrétní logiku; třídění a soustava věd*, Spisy 3 (Prague: Ústav T. G. Masaryka, 2001), 160.

56 Masaryk, *Pokus o konkrétní logiku*, 221.

57 Tomáš G. Masaryk, *Moderní člověk a náboženství*, Spisy 8 (Prague: Masarykův ústav AV ČR, 2000), 54. Jan M. Lochman noted that, for Masaryk, Hegel's dialectic undermined the existence of any permanent truths and values; Lochman, "Masaryk's Quarrel with Marxism," in *T. G. Masaryk, 1850–1937*, Stanley Winters and others, eds., 3 vols. (London: Macmillan, 1989–1990), 2: 121–22. See also Jan M. Lochman, "Masaryks Auseinandersetzung mit dem Marxismus," in *On Masaryk: Texts in English and German*, 231–32.

Masaryk reiterated his position in the 1920s. In his war memoirs, he recollected that after his appointment in Prague he had taught his students about the importance of one of the basic epistemological problems in philosophy: the relationship between Hume and Kant. Hume's scepticism derived from the egocentric predicament, an epistemological presumption that "a knower is unable to get outside his own mind because all that the knower can know is what is present to his own mind." Kant's alleged overcoming of Hume's egocentric predicament did not satisfy Masaryk, and he rejected Kant's subjectivism and "fantastic apriorism." Yet he devoted considerable time to studying Kant's teachings and those of his German followers and opponents, Gottlieb Schulze, Jakub Fries, Friedrich Beneke, and Wiegand Jacobi.[58] In his conversations with Karel Čapek, also in the 1920s, Masaryk further explained that Kant had set modern philosophy on the wrong path and had escaped radical subjectivism by postulating the unknowable thing-in-itself noumenon. Fichte had overcome Kant's dichotomy with "Absolute Idealism," that is, solipsism. Against this Fichtean extreme, Hegel posited a – presumably comforting – Objective Idealism, which made the individual mind a part of an overarching universal spirit.[59] After Masaryk's opinion of Kant eventually improved (due to his, Kant's, ethical earnestness [etická opravdovost] and the fact that he grasped the break [rozlom] in modern thought), he recommended that his students study both Hume and Kant for a necessary orientation in further independent thought.[60]

In another approach to what he saw as the extreme self-centeredness of the German Idealists, Masaryk postulated what he called the "Faust Complex" in German culture; namely that the Idealists made God out of the individual.[61] This extreme subjectivism was, Masaryk thought, the root cause of modern man's inclination toward suicide.[62] One way to escape the terrors of psychological isolation and pessimism that such a God-like status engendered was to embrace Hegel's pantheism. This pantheism – from

---

58 Masaryk, *Světová revoluce za války a ve válce, 1914–1918*, 423–24, 426.
59 Karel Čapek, *Hovory s T. G. Masarykem*, Spisy 20 (Prague: Československý spisovatel, 1990), 234.
60 Masaryk, *Světová revoluce za války a ve válce, 1914–1918*, 424.
61 Masaryk, *Moderní člověk a náboženství*, 163. See also Nejedlý, *T. G. Masaryk*, 3: 265. On the related concept of "Titanism," see, Milan Machovec, *Tomáš G. Masaryk*, 3rd ed. (Prague: Česká expedice, 2000), 150.
62 This was the theme of his first major philosophical work; see Masaryk, *Sebevražda hromadným jevem společenským moderní osvěty*.

the philosophical and sociological viewpoint – was an attempt to downgrade human particularity. In order to diminish the self, Hegel postulated what he called "the illusion of individual consciousness" and declared the individual mind to be a part of a the higher "dialectical" reason of the World Spirit.[63] Taking shelter under the umbrella of the World Spirit also had the unfortunate consequence of releasing the individual from his sense of personal moral responsibility.[64] According to Masaryk, Leo Tolstoy's (1828–1910) pantheism partly found its source in Hegel,[65] and within the Czech context, Hegel (and Schelling) had a decisive influence on Augustin Smetana's (1814–1851) adoption of pantheism.[66] For his part, Masaryk categorically rejected pantheism because he felt that it was a standpoint from which it was impossible to explain the world, as all of his own experiences contradicted pantheism.[67]

Hegel in Russia

Bewildering the Russian Slavophiles

Aside from its pervasive role in Germany, Masaryk was particularly concerned with the influence of Hegel's thought in Russia. In his opinion, the ideas of the Slavophiles in particular were largely based on German philosophy that derived from Hegel and Schelling.[68] Masaryk suspected that the Russians were attracted to Hegel in the 1830s and 1840s because his philosophy offered a grandiose view of the world and the security of the absolute, which was similar – as Alexander I. Herzen had recognized

---

63   Tomáš G. Masaryk, *Otázka sociální. Základy marxismu filosofické a sociologické*, 2 vols. Spisy 9–10 (Prague: Masarykův ústav AV ČR, 2000), 1: 144.

64   Concerning Masaryk's denial that extrinsic cosmic forces governed human life, see also František X. Šalda, "Těžká kniha," [*Rozhledy* 4 (1894–1895)] in Šalda, *Kritické projevy*, vol. 2 (Prague: Svoboda, 1950), 298–99.

65   Tomáš G. Masaryk, *Rusko a Evropa III*, Spisy 13 (Prague: Masarykův ústav AV ČR, 1996), 295.

66   Masaryk, *Moderní člověk a náboženství*, 94. See also Tomáš G. Masaryk, *Lectures at the University of Chicago, Summer 1902*, ed. Draga B. Shillinglaw (Lewisburg, PA: Bucknell University Press, 1978), 108. See also Polák, *T. G. Masaryk*, 3: 101–2.

67   Masaryk, *Moderní člověk a náboženství*, 109; see also on Hegel's pantheism in Tomáš G. Masaryk, "O hypnotismu (magnetismu zvířecím)," *Juvenalie: studie a stati, 1876–1881*, Spisy 16 (Prague: Ústav T. G. Masaryka, 1993), 136. On Masaryk's affirmation of individualism, see also Šalda, "Těžká kniha," 293–98.

68   Masaryk, *Lectures at the University of Chicago*, 137.

– to Byzantine theology, with its quasi-mystical characteristics.[69] Masaryk undertook a preliminary exploration of Hegel's role in Russia in an early series of articles that appeared in the journal *Atheneum* from 1889 to 1890. Titled "Slovanské studie" [Slavic Studies], they mainly analyzed the views of the founder of Slavophilism, Ivan V. Kireevskii (1806–1856).

Masaryk disagreed with Kireevskii's propositions concerning Hegel's place in the development of Western philosophy. First was Kireevskii's assertion that Western thought was purely abstract, and, having reached its limit in Hegel's teaching, it could advance no further.[70] Kireevskii's second assertion – dubious according to Masaryk – was that Western European thought inherently represented a one-dimensional intellectualism that had its roots in Aristotle, over whom even Hegel's achievement did not represent any qualitative advance. According to Kireevskii, the dialectic – long considered Hegel's unique accomplishment – was already known to the Eleatics, and if one read "Parmenides" it was like listening to Hegel.[71] Kireevskii further maintained that Hegel, like Aristotle, used philosophy as a weapon against religion in what was the main developmental line of Western thought, though Aristotle fought against the false religion of Greek polytheism, while Hegel was against the true religion of Christianity. Deprived of the inner religious dimension, Western thought thus turned one-sidedly objectivistic and formalistic, and in consequence, pessimism arose about the defectiveness of human experience.[72]

While Masaryk condoned Kireevskii's charge that Hegel's vision of history – as being driven by a higher rational necessity – resulted in denial of free will,[73] he argued against Kireevskii's assertion that Hegel and his German followers held philosophical dominance in current European intellectual life. First, there were several strands of Western philosophy, and they did not derive solely from Aristotle. Second, and more importantly, Hegelianism did not monopolize European thought. Discrediting

69 Tomáš G. Masaryk, "Slavjanofilství Ivana Vasiljeviče Kirejevského," publ. in *Atheneum,* vol. 6, 1889–1890, in Tomáš G. Masaryk, *Slovanské studie a texty z let 1889–1891,* Spisy 20 (Prague: Masarykův ústav AV ČR, 2007), 96.

70 Masaryk, "Slavjanofilství Ivana Vasiljeviče Kirejevského," 19; see also Dmytro Chyzhevskyi, *Hegel bei den Slaven* (Reichenberg: Stiepel, 1934), 154; Kireevskii had an opportunity to study personally under Hegel in Berlin, ibid., 151–53; see also Boris Jakowenko, *Geschichte des Hegelianismus in Russland,* Bd 1. (Prague: [Der russische Gedanke], 1938), 2–3.

71 Masaryk, "Slavjanofilství Ivana Vasiljeviče Kirejevského," 54.

72 Ibid., 36–37.

73 Ibid., 31.

Hegel and German Idealism, therefore, did not invalidate the West's philosophy in its entirety. According to Masaryk, Kireevskii was apparently unaware of the modern empirical trend, which was erecting European philosophy on a new, scientific foundation.[74]

Having rejected Kireevskii's diagnosis of the West's spiritual malaise, Masaryk naturally objected to the proposed cure as well. Initially enthusiastic about the teachings of Hegel (as well as Schelling) but then recognizing their deficiencies, Kireevskii, Masaryk wrote, decided to return to the Orthodoxy of the Russian people in order to find the religious dimension missing in Hegel. Convinced that, in the West, religion was replaced by philosophy that started from Aristotle and culminated in Hegel, Kireevskii was also certain that Western thinkers would have to proceed in the same direction, i.e., toward religion, if they wished to find a balanced worldview.[75] This would most likely be Eastern Orthodoxy, since Western religions were vitiated by the intellectualism endemic in the thought of the West. Moreover, reconciling Hegel and Orthodoxy would bring about the ideological reconciliation of the West and the East, a happy denouement that Kireevskii felt he had brought about in his own self when he turned from a Hegelian into an Orthodox believer.[76]

Masaryk sharply disagreed. He was convinced that the future did not belong to traditional religions, as Kireevskii assumed, but to the new empirical philosophy based on the scientific method, which would justify the existence of a theistic God without resorting to the revealed truths of traditional Christianity.[77] Masaryk, in fact, detected Hegel's devious influence in Kireevskii's prescription for curing the global intellectual crisis: the Russian Slavophile attributed to Russia, via Orthodoxy, the special role of a chosen nation; Hegel did the same for the Germans via his own philosophy.[78]

---

74 Masaryk evidently had in mind the development of the Austrian tradition in philosophy, then represented mainly by Franz Brentano; Masaryk, "Slavjanofilství Ivana Vasiljeviče Kirejevského," 53.

75 Ibid., 21.

76 Ibid., 31–32, 85.

77 Masaryk, "Slavjanofilství Ivana Vasiljeviče Kirejevského," 53. See also Zdeněk V. David, "Masaryk and Locke within the Context of the Austrian Philosophical Tradition," *Cestou dějin.* K poctě prof. Svatavy Rakové, ed. Eva Sematonová, 2 vols. (Prague: Historický ústav AV ČR, 2007), 2: 69–87.

78 Masaryk, "Slavjanofilství Ivana Vasiljeviče Kirejevského," 64. According to Masaryk, the praise of Slav/Russian characteristics as a parallel of Hegel's praise for Teutonic/German characteristics was true of other Slavophiles, such as Aleksei Khomiakov; see Tomáš G. Masaryk, *Rusko a Evropa I*, Spisy 11 (Prague: Masarykův ústav AV ČR, 1995), 212. See also Jaroslav Opat, *Filozof a politik: T. G. Masaryk, 1882–1893* (Prague: Melantrich, 1990), 202.

Inspiring the flaws in Marxist ideology

When Masaryk began his detailed analysis of Marx and Engels' teachings in *Otázka sociální* [The Social Question] (1898), he attributed serious flaws in Marxism's philosophy and social theory to the influence of Hegel – an influence he felt could not be overstated. Hegel affected Marx from the beginning of his academic career and persistently thereafter, providing the basis – the philosophical skeleton – for Marx's thinking.[79] Masaryk maintained that this dependence was not surprising, since both Marx and Engels accepted Hegel's idea that German thought represented the acme in human development[80] and held that Hegel's teaching was the final, highest stage of the era of Idealist thought. It would inevitably be followed by "a new philosophy" of the period of materialism, in which Hegel's Idealist metaphysics would be replaced by a materialistic world view, which, however, would retain much of Hegel's historical and cosmic principles. The founders of Marxism, of course, aspired to be the authors of this new ideology,[81] and Engels in particular avowed that Marxism grew out of German philosophy – above all, from Hegel.[82] (Later, Lenin was also convinced of the seminal role played by Hegel in the formation of Marx's and Engels' ideology.[83]) Accordingly, when arguing against the charge made by German anti-Semites, including in Adolf Hitler's *Mein Kampf*, that Marxism was essentially Jewish, Masaryk would point out that Marx actually drew his ideas from a German Lutheran, namely Hegel.[84]

Masaryk also credited Hegel with turning Marx's attention to the teaching of Ludwig Feuerbach (1804–1872).[85] According to Masaryk, Feuerbach was a kindred spirit of Marx and Engels, who also saw in Hegel the cul-

---

79   Masaryk, *Otázka sociální*, 1:53–54. Masaryk argued against those who would located Hegel's influence only in Marx's later life, especially after the revolutions of 1848. Masaryk sees them from the very beginning. Ibid., 1: 54, n. 3. See also Jaroslav Opat, *Průvodce životem a dílem T. G. Masaryka: Česká otázka včera a dnes* (Prague: Masarykův ústav AV ČR, 2003), 138.
80   Masaryk, *Otázka sociální*, 2: 103.
81   Ibid., 2: 124.
82   Ibid., 1: 38–39; 2: 163.
83   On Lenin's view see note 92, especially, V. I. Lenin, *Polnoe sobranie sochinenii*, 5th ed. 55 vols. (Moscow: Izdatel'stvo politicheskoi literatury, 1967–1970), vol. 29; on Hegel and dialectic see, especially 316– 22, including characterization of Hegel's view as ingenious [*kak genial'no zametil Gegel'*], 318.
84   As well as Feuerbach, and the English economist Ricardo. See "Masarykova recenze Hitlerovy knihy *Mein Kampf*," Tomáš G. Masaryk, *Cesta demokracie IV*, Spisy 36 (Prague: Masarykův ústav AV ČR, 1997), 352.
85   Masaryk, *Otázka sociální*, 1: 38–39.

mination of world philosophy. Feuerbach supplied materialism as the new metaphysical basis for the reconstruction of Hegel's teaching. According to Masaryk, Marx saw Feuerbach as having turned Hegel, who had stood on his head, upright to stand on his feet.[86] Nevertheless, in Masaryk's opinion, Feuerbach's influence on Marx was less important than Hegel's,[87] from whom Marx acquired several fundamental concepts: Hegel's dialectics were the inspiration for Marx's dialectical materialism; his emphasis on the history of philosophy and of society led to Marx's historical materialism; and Hegel's pantheism was transformed into the myth of the proletariat, which helped its adherents to evade personal moral responsibility.[88]

According to Masaryk, Hegel's idea of dialectic development had to be fundamentally altered in its adaptation as Marx's dialectical materialism. Hegel's idea of progress was based on logic, aimed at abstracting a view of development from a progress of thought. He saw in history and in nature, an epiphany of logic, and above all, a flow of contradictions and agreements of ideas, and he stressed contradiction as a law of progressive development.[89] Marx, on the other hand, transposed logical concepts into the realm of material reality and considered them to be the reflection of real events (such as the struggle of the masses), not just of different degrees of the Absolute Concept.[90] In this manner, Hegel's dialectic was flipped from its head onto its feet, and Marx transformed Hegel's idealistic dialectic into a materialistic one. Viewing world development as a process that overcame contradictions – in a dialectical movement – was a fundamental philosophical acquisition that Marx gained from Hegel. In fact, Masaryk maintained that the concept of a materialistic dialectic was the most characteristic aspect of Marx's dependence on Hegel.[91] At the same time, he pointed out that Marx never really attempted to explain how Hegel's dialectic, situated in the realm of logical processes, could be applied from

---

86   Masaryk, *Otázka sociální*, 1: 44–45. The fact that Hegel had depersonalized the Absolute Idea facilitated its conversion into the matter of dialectical materialism by Marx; Milíč Čapek, "Masaryk's Personalism," in *On Masaryk: Texts in English and German*, 171.
87   Masaryk, *Otázka sociální*, 1: 54.
88   Masaryk, *Otázka sociální*, 1: 35–36; 2: 164; Antonie van den Beld, *Humanity: The Political and Social Philosophy of Thomas G. Masaryk* (The Hague: Mouton, 1975), 22–23, 90.
89   Masaryk, *Otázka sociální*, 1: 60.
90   Ibid., 1: 194.
91   According to Masaryk, in Hegelianism ordinary reason saw contraries everywhere, the higher reason perceived an identity of contraries in a higher unity; Masaryk, *Otázka sociální*, 1: 58–59; Tomáš G. Masaryk, *Rusko a Evropa II*, Spisy 12 (Prague: Masarykův ústav AV ČR, 1996), 277.

the realm of logical processes of the cosmic mind (or the World Spirit) to the mindlessness of the material world.[92] By transposing them from the intellectual to the material sphere, Marx and Engels made Hegel's philosophical and historical principles even less plausible.

Masaryk stressed that Marx and Engels's dependence on Hegel was also reflected in the area of social sciences, which they treated historically (that is, as historical sciences), using concepts and methods of Hegel's philosophy of history. As a result, they closely connected the historical sciences with philosophy and also referred to their philosophical system as historical materialism.[93] Masaryk tells us that when he read *Das Kapital* in his youth in the early 1870s, he was already repelled by its philosophy of history, which seemed heavily influenced by Hegel.[94] Hegelian historicism furnished explanations for constant changes of social order; thus it also offered to Marx a purely objective reason for communism, as imposed by history itself.[95] Hegel passed on to Marx a tendency toward abstraction and a penchant for dialectical construction, and, as a result, the arbitrariness of Hegel's philosophical concepts of history was intensified in Marx's economic materialism.[96] Above all, according to Masaryk, Hegel justified the development of history as a violent process that destroyed

92 Masaryk criticized Marx for applying Hegel's dialectic, especially the negation of negation, to the interplay of material forces; it had no meaning there; Polák, *T. G. Masaryk*, 3: 181; also Alain Soubigou, *Thomas Masaryk* (Paris: Librairie Arthème Fayard, 2002), 126. It is interesting to point out that Lenin likewise considered Hegel's dialectic his most valuable contribution to the Marxist idelogy. Particularly, in his *Filosofskie tetradi* [Philosophical Notebooks], written in 1914–1916, Lenin replaced the contrast between materialism and idealism with one between dialectical and non-dialectical thinking; see, for instance, Ted Honderich, ed., *Oxford Companion to Philosophy* (New York: Oxford University Press, 1995), 480; Donald M. Borchert, ed., *The Encyclopedia of Philosophy*, 2nd ed., 10 vols. (New York: Macmillan, 2006), 5: 280; Lenin's *Filosofskie tetradi* are published in V. I. Lenin, *Polnoe sobranie sochinenii*, 5th ed. 55 vols. (Moscow: Izdatel'stvo politicheskoi literatury, 1967–1970), vol. 29; on Hegel and dialectic see, especially, 316–22, including characterization of Hegel's view as ingenious [*kak genial'no zametil Gegel'*], 318; otherwise extensive notes on *Science of Logic*, 77–218, and *History of Philosophy*, 219–90. Lenin relied on Georg W.F. Hegel, *Werke*, Vollständige Ausgabe, 22 vols. (Berlin: Duncker and Humblot, 1832–1845).

93 Masaryk, *Otázka sociální*, 1: 81. See also Paul Selver, *Masaryk: A Biography* (London: M. Joseph, 1940), 67–68.

94 Nejedlý, *T. G. Masaryk*, 1: 373.

95 Masaryk, *Otázka sociální*, 1: 90.

96 Masaryk, *Otázka sociální*, 1: 153. Lochman and Batscha have credited Masaryk with perceiving the seeds of Soviet Stalinist totalitarianism in Marx's Hegelian heritage, when Marx merged the developments in the natural world and in human society under the concept of historical materialism; Batscha, *Eine Philosophie der Demokratie: Thomas G. Masaryks Begründung einer neuzeitlichen Demokratie*, 162; Lochman, "Masaryk's Quarrel with Marxism," 2: 121–22. See also Lochman, "Masaryks Auseinandersetzung mit dem Marxismus," 231–32.

existing values, giving Marx and Engels a reason to praise the revolutionary tendency of Hegel's philosophy, and in their concept of the revolution, the Hegelian idea of the negation of negation specifically played a distinct role.[97] In addition, Marx and Engels attempted to bolster the operation of Hegel's metaphysical laws (existing in the mental world) by implanting them incongruously in the realm of economic and sociological data (borrowed from the Positivist philosophy of Auguste Comte).[98]

According to Masaryk, Hegel's pantheism, which attempted to overcome the "illusion of individual consciousness," was also mirrored in the ideology of Marxism,[99] which similarly declared individual consciousness to be an illusion, a false consciousness. However, Marx and Engels rejected subjectivism, and thus Hegel's pantheism was converted into a belief in the collectivism of the proletarians. In other words, in Marxism Hegel's Absolute Spirit became "the mass," the proletariat.[100] Masaryk pointed out that thus Marx appropriated Hegel's absolution of the individual of social responsibility (because he was just a plaything of the Absolute). Hegel imported the forces that really moved history from the outside – from philosophical ideology. For him, the motives of individual actors were not the ultimate causes of historical events. Marx likewise saw the driving forces of the dialectic as beyond the actions of individuals; humans were not accountable for the future.[101] Moreover, Marx accepted from Hegel's pantheism the teleological idea of progress, which, according to Masaryk, was quite unsuitable for his positivistic materialism. In Marx, faith in progress was nothing more than an inexplicable dogma.[102]

---

97 Masaryk, *Otázka sociální,* 1: 84, 166; Van den Beld, *Humanity: The Political and Social Philosophy of Thomas G. Masaryk,* 136.

98 Masaryk, *Otázka sociální,* 1: 193, 196. See also Lochman, "Masaryk's Quarrel with Marxism," 2: 124; or Lochman, "Masaryks Auseinandersetzung mit dem Marxismus," 234; Opat, *Průvodce životem a dílem T. G. Masaryka,* 148.

99 Masaryk, *Otázka sociální,* 1: 144.

100 Masaryk, *Otázka sociální,* 1: 63, 90, 182. In Masaryk's view, Hegel's pantheism applied by Marx to society as a social pantheism was psychologically and logically an absurdity because society was not a single organism – a uniform social consciousness did not exist. Masaryk, *Rusko a Evropa II,* Spisy 12: 316.

101 Masaryk,, *Otázka sociální,* 1: 158. See also Soubigou, *Thomas Masaryk,* 127; Batscha, *Eine Philosophie der Demokratie,* 107.

102 Masaryk, *Otázka sociální,* 1: 196. Masaryk noted that initially Marx had endorsed Hegel's high regard for the state, who identified, especially in the Prussian state, a crucial expression of the Absolute Spirit. By 1844, Marx, however, began to regard the state as an instrument of oppression and shifted his focus to the Masses and social classes; according to Masaryk, this shift was under the influence of French socialism. Masaryk, *Otázka sociální,* 2: 69, 72, 171.

Preparing the Russians for Marxism

After his wide-ranging examination of the ideology of Marxism, Masaryk returned once more to the assessment of Russia's intellectual tradition in his magisterial *Russland und Europa* [*Rusko a Evropa*] (1913), known in the Anglophone world under the title *The Spirit of Russia*.[103] While Masaryk had earlier emphasized that Hegel's teaching had caused confusion about the character of European philosophy in the minds of Russian Slavophiles during the 1830s and 1840s, this time he focused on the effects of Hegelianism through its acceptance by Russian Westernizers in the same period. One could not, he felt, attribute the great influence of German philosophy in Russia to Kant, with his static and ahistorical Weltanschauung. Rather, it stemmed from the historically and dynamically oriented Hegel – and after him, from Marx.[104] The Westernizers' enthusiasm for Hegel facilitated the reception of Marxism in Russia, which, in turn, built on the Russians' predisposition to Hegelianism. This predilection, as Masaryk had noted earlier, drew in part on the spiritual kinship between Hegel's Absolute Idealism and the apocalypticism of the Eastern Orthodox Church.

Masaryk emphasized that it was incorrect to assume that only the Slavophiles, and not the Westernizers, were ardent students of German Idealism.[105] It was mostly Russian Westernizers whose enthusiasm for Hegel paved the way for the vogue in Russia of philosophical materialism and subsequently, Marxism. The Westernizers appreciated the revolutionary potential of Hegel's philosophy, which Marx then developed further.[106] The ascendancy of German thought in Russia was in large part due to a hostile reaction to France in the post-Napoleonic period. Moreover, the Russian government encouraged students to study in Germany rather than France. Masaryk pointed out that prominent Westernizers such as Chernyshevskii, Belinskii, Herzen and Bakunin had received their principal philosophical education from Hegel.[107]

---

103 Tomáš G. Masaryk, *The Spirit of Russia: Studies in History, Literature, and Philosophy*, tr. by Eden and Cedar Paul, and W. R. and Z. Lee. 2nd ed,. 3 vols. London: Allen & Unwin, 1961–67.

104 Masaryk, *Rusko a Evropa I*, Spisy 11: 149. On Hegel's radicalizing influence in Russia, see also James H. Billington, *The Icon and the Axe* (New York: Knopf, 1966), 325–28.

105 Masaryk, *Rusko a Evropa I*, Spisy 11: 181, 249.

106 Tomáš G. Masaryk, *Válka a revoluce II: Články, memoranda, přednášky, rozhovory, 1917*, Spisy 31 (Prague: Masarykův ústav AV ČR, 2008), 64.

107 On Russian Hegelianism, see also Zdeněk V. David, *Realism, Tolerance, and Liberalism in the Czech National Awakening* (Washington, D.C.: Woodrow Wilson Center Press; Baltimore: Johns Hopkins University Press, 2010), 211.

According to Masaryk, the intellectual evolution toward Hegelianism had followed the same trajectory in Russia as it had in Germany. The Russians' eagerness to endorse Hegel was a reaction to the feeling of psychological isolation and pessimism brought on by the extremes of Romantic thought and the Idealism of Fichte and Schelling that had previously dominated Russia's intellectual scene. Looking for Hegel's influence among the early Westernizers, Masaryk found that Petr I. Chaadaev (1794–1856) utilized Hegel's dialectic to understand historical development and referred to the gradual revelation of "the universal reason" in history.[108] Early on, both Vissarion G. Belinskii (1811–1848) and Mikhail A. Bakunin (1814–1876) found in Hegel's teaching a liberating release from the oppressive self-centeredness of Romanticism. Likewise, Herzen was first introduced to philosophy by reading Hegel, and could not imagine further progress of philosophy beyond him.[109] Belinskii focused on Hegel's view that society and the state were superior to the individual, and found Hegel's dictum "What is real is rational" to be particularly reassuring. On the other hand, Bakunin was mainly impressed by Hegel's dialectic, which he applied to the modern world and concluded that two contrary forces within that world would negate each other, and something completely new would appear. In this scenario, Europe was perishing due to an endemic internal conflict, and Russia would rise to provide the epiphany of the future.[110] According to Masaryk, Nikolai G. Chernyshevskii (1828–1889), like Belinskii, Herzen, and Bakunin, was deeply affected by the idea and the laws of historical development, although Chernyshevskii modified Hegel's view of a linear development by positing a circular one, somewhat like Giambattista Vico's *ricorsi*.[111]

The Russian Westernizers were smoothly guided from Hegel to Marx because of the pre-established harmony existing between Hegelianism and

108 Masaryk, *Rusko a Evropa I*, Spisy 11: 177–178; on Chaadaev see also Jakowenko, *Geschichte des Hegelianismus in Russland,* 1: 13; with reference to Masaryk [(1934 ed.), 14–15].
109 Masaryk, *Rusko a Evropa I*, Spisy 11: 283, 292. On Belinskii, Bakunin, and Herzen see also Chyzhevskyi, *Hegel bei den Slaven,* 207–29, 263–68, 330–41; Jakowenko, *Geschichte des Hegelianismus in Russland,* 1: 31–80.
110 Masaryk, *Rusko a Evropa II*, Spisy 12: 13–14, 21. See also *The Encyclopedia of Philosophy,* 2nd ed., Borchert, 1: 538.
111 Masaryk, *Rusko a Evropa II*, Spisy 12: 55–56. According to Masaryk, also Turgenev and Petr L. Lavrov (1823–1900) were introduced to philosophy through the study of Hegel; Masaryk, *Rusko a Evropa III*, Spisy 13: 282; Masaryk, *Rusko a Evropa II*, Spisy 12: 118–19, but he notes that Nikolai K. Mikhailovskii (1842–1904) missed Hegel's influence and became an adherent of Comte; Masaryk, *Rusko a Evropa II*, Spisy 12: 135.

Marxism. After exposure to Hegel, there was – according to Masaryk – a natural progression among the Russian intelligentsia to the materialism of Feuerbach and Karl Vogt (1817–1895)[112] and subsequently to Marx or Ferdinand Lasalle (1825–1864), both of whom took Hegel and Feuerbach as their starting point.[113] As noted, Masaryk viewed the Russians' eagerness to endorse Hegel – as exemplified particularly by Belinskii and Bakunin – as a reaction to feelings of isolation and pessimism. An antidote to this psychological malaise was first sought in Hegel's Absolute Spirit, and was subsequently found in the absolute materialist objectivism of Marx, both of which openly downgraded individual consciousness by subordinating it to the external forces of the dialectic and thus provided an attractive escape route from the egocentric predicament.[114]

Masaryk illustrated the consequent erasure of personal responsibility by reference to the "Father of Russian Marxism," Georgii V. Plekhanov (1857–1918), who drew attention to the Hegelian origins of Marx's system. Plekhanov praised Hegel not only for showing how conflicts arose in society but also for revealing in a comforting way the amoral character of social struggles: in the dialectical conflict, the defenders of an established order clashed with their challengers, and both parties subjectively felt that they had right on their side. Many perished tragically in the struggle, but objectively there were no guilty parties, because both sides were only acting out the roles that the impersonal dialectical process had assigned to them.[115]

Hegel in Germany: radicalizing his homeland

Finally, Masaryk returned his attention from Russia to Hegel's homeland – Germany. Connecting Hegel with authoritarian Prussianism and aggressive Pangermanism would crescendo in Masaryk's writings during and after World War I, but not, however, due to the expediency of war propaganda. This nexus appeared in Masaryk's writings and statements much

---

112 Masaryk, *Rusko a Evropa II*, Spisy 12: 85.
113 Masaryk, *Rusko a Evropa I*, Spisy 11: 113. See also Roland J. Hoffmann, *T. G. Masaryk und die tschechische Frage* (Munich: Oldenbourg, 1988), 282.
114 Masaryk, *Rusko a Evropa I*, Spisy 11: 155. On Plekhanov as the first propagator of Hegelianism among Russian Marxists, see Chyzhevskyi, *Hegel bei den Slaven*, 371–73.
115 Masaryk, *Rusko a Evropa II*, Spisy 12: 355.

earlier, at least since the 1890s. As early as 1890, his "Bismarckův odboj" [Bismarck's revolt], published in the newspaper *Čas*, argued that Bismarck attempted to practice in reality what Hegel had preached about the omnipotence of the state.[116] On November 18, 1892, during his first tenure as member of its House of Deputies, Masaryk called the attention of the *Reichsrat* (the Austrian Parliament[117]) to Hegel's view that the only significant nation advancing the work of history was the German one. Masaryk warned that this vision was currently becoming the predominant way that the Germans thought of themselves.[118] The following day, he went on to elaborate that the visions of Hegel, as well as Fichte and Schelling, all generally considered to be unrealistic dreamers, had found concrete and real expression in the Iron Chancellor's policies.[119] In *Česká otázka* [The Czech Question] (1895), Masaryk again noted that Bismarck was unthinkable without Hegel, just as Napoleon was unthinkable without the French *philosophes* of the eighteenth century.[120] He added in *Otázka sociální* [The Social Question] (1898) that anyone who viewed German philosophy as a guide to practical action would discern an organic connection and inner kinship (*organickou spojitost a vnitřní příbuznost*) between speculation à la Hegel and Bismark's politics of blood and iron.[121]

In *Národnostní filosofie doby novější* [The Most Recent Philosophy of Nationality] (1905), Masaryk placed Hegel into the broader context of German nationalist ideology, portraying him as having further advanced German nationalist concepts beyond Fichte's arousal of national feelings in the struggle against Napoleon. (Napoleon, incidentally, feared the German philosophers more than the German armies.) Hegel developed

---

116 "Bismarckův odboj," *Čas*, 4 (1890), 194–197, in Masaryk, *Slovanské studie a texty z let 1889–1891*, 337

117 Since the Compromise (*Ausgleich*) of 1867, the Reichsrat (in Vienna) was a parallel legislative body to the Hungarian Parliament (in Budapest). It legislated for the non-Hungarian part of the Habsburg Monarchy, which was, in fact, legally defined as "Kingdoms and Lands Represented in the Reichsrat." Matters common to both parts of the Monarchy were dealt with by "Delegations" chosen from the two legislative bodies. See Robert A. Kann and Zdeněk V. David, *The Peoples of the Eastern Habsburg Lands* (Seattle: Washington University Press, 1984), 300–1, 350–51.

118 Masaryk, *Parlamentní projevy, 1891–1893*, 258.

119 Masaryk, *Parlamentní projevy, 1891–1893*, 265. Shortly afterwards, Masaryk called attention to an article in the *Norddeutsche allgemeine Zeitung* that reprimanded the Czechs for misunderstanding Hegel. Ibid., 272. See also Hoffmann, *T. G. Masaryk und die tschechische Frage*, 121.

120 Tomáš G. Masaryk, *Česká otázka. Naše nynější krize. Jan Hus*, Spisy 6 (Prague: Masarykův ústav AV ČR, 2000), 294.

121 Masaryk, *Otázka sociální*, 1: 52.

a full-fledged cult of *Germanismus*, which identified the German nation
– with special reference to Prussia – as chosen to complete the historical
development of humankind. Subsequently – after the deification of Prussian absolutism – "Prussian reason" (the Prussian intellectual outlook) and
"Prussian providence" (the belief in Prussia's historical mission) came to
dominate political thought all over Germany.[122] According to Masaryk,
Hegel's thought found its ideal successor in Eduard Hartmann (1842–
1906), in whom German nationalism reached a high point at the opening
of the twentieth century. Hartmann built a synthesis based on Kant's categorical imperative, Fichte's view of the missionary task of the Prussians
in particular and the Germans in general; and Hegel's eschatological view
of the state, especially the Prussian one. Hartmann's synthesis influenced
German opinion enormously.[123]

In his wartime statements,[124] published in the journals *La Nation
Tchèque* in Paris and *New Europe* in London, Masaryk continued to stress
Hegel's role in the genesis of Pangermanism. On February 22, 1916, he
delivered an important lecture at the Institute of Slavic Studies in Paris,
titled "The Slavs in the World" [Les Slaves dans le monde], in which he
contrasted the pacific character of the Slavs with German aggressiveness.
Slavs, he said, did not worship political power, unlike the Germans, who
were taught by Hegel.[125] In 1916, Masaryk serially published a lengthy article in *New Europe* titled "The Literature of Pan-Germanism," in which
he reviewed two books on the subject by the French scholar Charles Andler. Masaryk pointed out that Andler correctly traced the origins of Pan-
germanism to the eighteenth century but had neglected to deal with the
even more important nineteenth-century philosophers, such as Hegel.[126]
In another 1916 article in *New Europe*, "Pangermanism and the Eastern
Question," Masaryk considered the intellectual origins of political Pan-

---

122 Tomáš G. Masaryk, *Národnostní filosofie doby novější*, 2nd ed. (Prague: Melantrich, 1919), 23. See
also Polák, *T. G. Masaryk*, 4: 510.

123 Masaryk, *Národnostní filosofie doby novější*, 24–25. See also Batscha, *Eine Philosophie der Demokratie*, 31–32.

124 Discussed in greater detail in Chapter 8, "Masaryk's Perspective and Participation in World War I."

125 Tomáš G. Masaryk, *Válka a revoluce I: články, memoranda, přednášky, rozhovory, 1914–1916*, Spisy
30 (Prague: Masarykův ústav AV ČR, 2005), 202.

126 As well as Herder, Fichte, Schelling, Karl C. Krause, Schopenhauer, or most recently Hart-
mann and Nietzsche. Masaryk, *Válka a revoluce I*, 246–247. Masaryk reviewed Charles Andler's
Les origines du Pan-Germanisme (1800–1888) and *Le Pan-Germanisme continental sous Guillaume
II (1888–1914)*, 2nd ed. (Paris, 1915).

Germanism and traced its roots to the historical orientation of German philosophy from Herder to Paul de Lagarde, Hartmann, and Nietzsche, with Hegel serving as the connecting link.[127]

In his war memoirs, *Světová revoluce za války a ve válce* [*The World Revolution during and in the War*] (1925), Masaryk continued to look for the roots of radical nationalism in German history.[128] He argued that three primary characteristics of the German Empire – theocracy, militarism, and amorality – were what distinguished Prussianized Germany from the liberal and democratic countries of Western Europe and the United States, and these characteristics were most clearly exemplified in the ways Hegel was being taught.

First, the construction of the Prussian state as a theocracy owed much, in Masaryk's view, to the secularization of German Lutheran theology. This occurred in Hegel's teaching, as well as that of Fichte and Schelling, all three of whom were originally trained as theologians.[129] Hegel in particular had not been a theologian in vain. He formulated the principles of Prussian theocracy through his pantheism and his tendency toward fantasy, which led to the quasi-divinization of the state. Both Bismarck and Kaiser Wilhelm constantly referred to God, and, Masaryk added, it was, of course, a Prussian God.[130]

Second, Hegel was the philosopher of Prussian militarism, which had already been anticipated by Kant's categorical imperative.[131] As Masaryk stated repeatedly, after Kant, German philosophy necessarily was mired in pessimism and egoism (because of its self-centeredness and its visionary tendency). The Pangermanic appeal to force was sanctified by philosophy, beginning with Kant and then to Fichte and Hegel,[132] and Hegel's preaching

---

127 Masaryk, *Válka a revoluce I*, 235.
128 Masaryk, *Světová revoluce za války a ve válce, 1914–1918*, 413, 415. The passages dealing with the history of German thought were left out of the English translation of the war memoirs, which appeared as Thomas Masaryk, *The Making of a State: Memories and Observations, 1914–1918*, ed. Henry W. Steed (New York: George Allen and Unwin, 1927). See also Batscha, *Eine Philosophie der Demokratie*, 31, 65.
129 Masaryk, *Světová revoluce za války a ve válce*, 419. See also Ludwig, *Defender of Democracy: Masaryk of Czechoslovakia*, 79.
130 Masaryk, *Světová revoluce za války a ve válce*, 280, 381.
131 Ibid., 282. See also Nejedlý, *T. G. Masaryk*, 3: 175.
132 Masaryk, *Světová revoluce za války a ve válce*, 426. Patočka, however, considered simplistic and historically unproven Masaryk's claim that Hegel's absolute Idealism had served the authoritarianism of the Prussian state and had provided a justification for the theory and practice of the use of force; Patočka, *Dvě studie o Masarykovi*, 59.

of violence was a response to the solipsism of Fichte and Schelling.[133] In the final analysis, modern militarism of the Prussian type represented an escape from suicidal inclinations because it directed violence outward instead of against oneself.[134] Indeed, Masaryk, asserted that Hegel had declared not only the infallibility of the state but also the redemptive value of belligerence and war.[135]

Third, Hegel, with his "Absolute Idealism," had made it possible for the Prussian state to disregard common humanity and universal values.[136] Hegel furnished the absolutist state with a Machiavellian *modus operandi*, in which right and law were derived from power. On the level of the individual, the dependence on the Absolute Spirit erased any real distinction between good and evil. The vision of an inexorable progress of historical dialectics deprived the individual of a sense of personal moral involvement,[137] and thus, Hegel's teaching provided the basis for the state's unscrupulous theoretical and practical reliance on force.[138]

The Question of Hegel's Influence on Masaryk

The authors I discuss below have suggested that despite his harsh criticism of German Idealism in general and of Hegel in particular, Masaryk was actually indebted to Hegel for fundamental ideas of his own philosophy and political thought. The first of these alleged borrowed influences was Hegel's specific type of historicism, according to which overarching ideas of social progress became actualized in the unfolding of history (such as the victory of democracy over theocracy in World War I).[139] The second was the definition of the state as the highest embodiment and expression of human moral values. Explaining my use of "alleged" calls for a closer look at these two aspects of Masaryk's relationship with Hegel.

---

133 Masaryk, *Světová revoluce za války a ve válce*, 282. See also Nejedlý, *T. G. Masaryk*, 3: 175.

134 Masaryk, *Světová revoluce za války a ve válce*, 287.

135 Ibid., 282.

136 Ibid., 280. See also Opat, *Průvodce životem a dílem T. G. Masaryka*, 406; René Wellek, "Masaryk's Philosophy," in *On Masaryk: Texts in English and German*, 25.

137 Masaryk, *Světová revoluce za války a ve válce*, 282.

138 Ibid., 426

139 See Chapter 9, "Democracy and Totalitarian Regimes," and Chapter 11, "Legacy," on the transition from "theocracy" to "democracy" as a result of World War I.

Hegel's Historicism

Hegel saw the realization of the World Spirit in history, and on the issue of Hegel's historicism, Zwi Batscha has argued that Masaryk was
indebted to Hegel for the view of history as the medium through which
his own philosophy would be realized in the actual world. Batscha offered the example that Masaryk had seen the idea of the Bohemian Reformation (as exemplified by the Unity of Brethren) so realized.[140] In his
Základové konkretné logiky [The Foundations of Concrete Logic] Masaryk did indeed point out (in the section on sociology) that Hegel's famous philosophy of history was a powerful stimulus for a philosophical
study of the historical past.[141] Likewise, there was a tendency in Europe
to turn to the study of sociology under Hegel's impetus.[142] Thus Hegel,
together with Auguste Comte, became a paragon of pervasive historicism in the first half of the nineteenth century, although even his historicism had roots in the eighteenth century, in Herder, Vico, and Lessing.[143] In a parliamentary speech on June 9, 1891, Masaryk declared that
he did not oppose the application of logical patterns to the interpretation of historical processes, even if this approach made him vulnerable
to charges of adopting Hegelianism.[144]

However, in the final analysis Masaryk was not pleased with Hegel's
philosophy of history,[145] which he noted was influential not only on the
triangular relationship among Hegel, Marx, and the Russian intelligentsia, of which he was highly critical, but also among other Slavs as well,
particularly the Slovaks and the Poles.[146] He focused his criticism on
Hegel's influence on the prominent Slovak National Awakener, Jan Kollár
(1793–1852), who, like Hegel, mistakenly asserted that at a given historical
time a specific nation had a particular, exclusive historical task to perform.
Said nation was also destined to provide the leadership for the entirety of

---

140 Batscha, *Eine Philosophie der Demokratie*, 234.
141 Masaryk, *Základové konkretné logiky,* 106. See also Nejedlý, *T. G. Masaryk*, 4: 199.
142 Masaryk, *Základové konkretné logiky,* 107; also idem, *Pokus o konkrétní logiku*, 143.
143 Masaryk, *Moderní člověk a náboženství*, 72.
144 Masaryk, *Parlamentní projevy, 1891–1893,* 72. See also Hoffmann, *T. G. Masaryk und die tsche-
     chische Frage*, 139.
145 On his critical view of Hegel's philosophy of history, see Machovec, *Tomáš G. Masaryk*, 57, 101–3.
146 Concerning Hegel's influence on Polish philosophy, see Masaryk, *Rusko a Evropa I*, Spisy 11: 226;
     on the Slovak Awakener Ľudovít Štúr, see Masaryk, *Česká otázka. Naše nynější krize. Jan Hus,* 66.

humankind. According to Masaryk, the same objections could be applied to Kollár as to Hegel. It was obvious that in addition to the German/Teutonic nation, various nations that spoke Romance languages were simultaneously playing important historical roles in modern Europe. By combining the Germans and the Romance-language speakers into an imaginary national entity, Kollár (and hence Hegel) obscured rather than illumined the course of history.[147] Moreover, Hegel's philosophy of history was also fascinating to Kollár due to – what Masaryk considered – its pernicious teaching about the reconciliation of contradictions. On the positive side, Kollár, unlike Hegel, assigned no ontic role to the state.[148]

Toward the end of his famous polemic about the meaning of Czech history, Masaryk criticized his main opponent, the historian Josef Pekař, for being more attracted – for the purposes of historical periodization – by Hegel's dialectics than reality would warrant.[149] Earlier, in another general critique of historicism, Masaryk maintained in the parliamentary discussion of June 9, 1891, that studying the history of a discipline could not be substituted for the study of the discipline itself.[150] Masaryk opposed Hegel's historicism within the study of philosophy as well. Thus, he argued against the view propounded by of his former teacher in Leipzig, Konrad Hermann (1818–1897), that the study of philosophy could not be separated from that of history. In Masaryk's opinion, history of philosophy was only an auxiliary subject, not a substantial part of philosophy (just as history of mathematics was not a substantial part of mathematics as such); no discipline could be reduced to its history.[151] Masaryk also considered illusory Hegel's theory of three stages of dialectical historical development. In his view, it was only in retrospect that reason attempted to discern some system in a series of past events; but reason was often fallible.[152]

147 Masaryk, *Česká otázka. Naše nynější krize. Jan Hus*, 329, 341, 343.
148 Ibid., 417–18. Since Hegel was uncritically ascribing various outstanding qualities to the Germans, it was no wonder, according to Masaryk, that Kollár was emulating him by similarly glorifying the Slavs, ibid., 62.
149 Masaryk, *Cesta demokracie IV*, 275, referring to Josef Pekař, "O periodizaci českých dějin," *Česká mysl*, 28 (1932). On the polemic concerning the role of the Bohemian Reformation in Czech history, see Chapter 5.
150 The discussion concerned the curriculum of Law Schools; Masaryk, *Parlamentní projevy, 1891–1893*, 72.
151 Nejedlý, *T. G. Masaryk*, 3: 164. On Hermann see *Enciclopedia universal ilustrada europeo-americana*, 70 vols. (Madrid: Espasa-Calpe, 1907–1930), 27: 1195.
152 Opat, *Filozof a politik: T. G. Masaryk, 1882–1893*, 92.

In Masaryk's ultimate assessment, Hegel's philosophy of history was a brilliant construct, but unfortunately it lacked (just like Kant's criticism) intellectual sobriety.[153]

In his *Hovory* [Conversations] with Karel Čapek, however, Masaryk seemed, surprisingly, to approach the basic proposition of Hegel's metaphysics – that the Absolute Spirit realized itself through human history. Masaryk advanced the views that (1) humankind was fulfilling a divine plan on earth; (2) every human individual was to perform a role in the realization of this plan (the full-fledged development of Humanity); and hence (3) a certain degree of determinism was involved in history and in human life. Yet there was a fundamental distinction between Hegel's pantheism and what, for Masaryk, was an ontological pluralism. For Masaryk, first, individual human beings possessed an ontic identity; and second, God was theistic, that is, ontologically distinct from man and the rest of creation.[154] In addition, as Jan Zouhar has pointed out, Masaryk's idea of progress from the mythical stage to the scientific one is basically derived from Comte's sociology.[155] This view is also supported by Jan Patočka, who maintains that Masaryk embraced Comte's tenet that the main guiding forces of historical and social development are "ideas" or certain convictions. Masaryk's sociology and philosophy of history were always mostly analyses of the potential and real effects of ideas and convictions on society.[156]

Veneration of the State

On the second issue, the significance of the state, historian Roman Szporluk noted that in the 1920s Masaryk did, in fact, approach the Hegelian idea of the state as a moral embodiment. He quoted a speech that Ma-

---

153 Masaryk, *Pokus o konkrétní logiku*, 221.

154 Čapek, *Hovory s T. G. Masarykem*, 249, 252. For Hegel, as for Herder and Schelling before him: "Thus God is not an entity beyond the world, but the idea realized in history. Providence is not an 'external end', a supernatural plan imposed by God on nature, but an 'internal end', the ultimate purpose of history itself." See Frederick C. Beiser, "Hegel's Historicism," in idem (ed.), *Cambridge Companion to Hegel* (New York, 1993), 271.

155 Jan Zouhar, "Dějiny a dějinnost v Masarykově filozofii," in Jozef Leikert and others, *Politik s dušou filozofa; Miesto T. G. Masaryka v česko-slovenských dejinách* (Bratislava: Spoločnosť Pro Historia and Historický ústav SAV, 2007), 216.

156 Comte treats the contemporary crisis as a consequence of the transition to the stage of positivism, Masaryk agrees with him, seeing the crisis as a result of a conflict of the traditional religious and the new irreligious outlooks. Jan Patočka, "Masarykovo a Husserlovo pojetí duševní krise lidstva (1936)," idem, *Sebrané Spisy* 12 (Prague: Oikoymenh, 2006), 23.

saryk delivered in October 1928 on the tenth anniversary of the foundation of Czechoslovakia in which he said, "the state has a spiritual, a moral
meaning." Szporluk also noted that on another occasion Masaryk stated, "the state approaches the ethical maximum – the ideal – through the
ethical minimum – the law."[157] Szporluk further cited Karl Popper's assertion that Masaryk was misled by Hegel (and Fichte) in constructing
Czechoslovakia as a national state.[158] Masaryk had in fact already casually
observed in his *Česká otázka* that Hegel's introduction of the concept of
the state may have benefited the stateless nations, such as the Poles and
the Czechs, by reminding them of the need for a political organization or
the function of the state.[159] He sharpened his critique of the Czechs' sus-
picion of the state in his Conversations with Karel Čapek, pointing out
that they had adopted a disrespectful attitude toward the institution of
the state because, having lost their statehood in 1620, they were forced
to live under a monarchy they considered foreign and even hostile. After
the collapse of the Habsburg Empire and the creation of an independent
Czechoslovakia in 1918, it had, according to Masaryk, become incumbent
on the Czechs to adopt a positive view of the state as a part of their de-
Austrianization [*odrakouštění*].[160]

There was, however, an overwhelming and fundamental difference between Masaryk's and Hegel's political concepts. In defining the difference,
Masaryk himself proclaimed that, for him, the state was not a divine and
omniscient institution, as Hegel had imagined, but instead, was a human
institution with various human weaknesses and strengths.[161] Moreover, as
we have seen, Masaryk made several harsh statements about Hegel's political ideas, particularly concerning their detrimental role in the politics of Imperial Germany. He castigated Hegel for viewing the state (with

157 Roman Szporluk, *The Political Thought of Thomas Masaryk*, East European Monographs 85 (New
York: Columbia University Press, 1981), 116. The second quote is from Tomáš G. Masaryk, *The
Making of a State: Memories and Observations, 1914–1918*, ed. Henry W. Steed (New York: George
Allen and Unwin, 1927), 409.
158 Even though the state was exceptionally democratic; cited from Karl R. Popper, *Open Society and
Its Enemies*, 2 vols., 3rd ed. (London: Routledge and Kegan Paul, 1957), 2: 50–51, 318, by Szporluk, *The Political Thought of Thomas Masaryk*, 155, 216 n. 35.
159 Masaryk, *Česká otázka. Naše nynější krize. Jan Hus*, 74. See also Tomáš G. Masaryk, *Karel
Havlíček: Snahy a tužby politického probuzení*, Spisy 7 (Prague: Masarykův ústav AV ČR, 1996),
326–27.
160 The new state and statehood were democratic, not resting just on the bureaucracy and the military but on the entire citizenry; Čapek, *Hovory s T. G. Masarykem*, 339–40.
161 Masaryk, *Světová revoluce za války a ve válce*, 381. See also Šalda, "Těžká kniha," 287.

Hobbes) as a "*mortalis deus*," as "an absolute authority and majesty," as a re-flection of the divine idea or "an absolutely perfect ethical organism," and above all, for locating the Absolute Spirit in the Prussian state.[162] Hegel not only declared the infallibility of the state but also exalted the redemptive value of the militarism it imposed and the wars it conducted.[163] Particularly during World War I, Masaryk contrasted the pacifism of the Slavs with the militarism of the Germans, whom Hegel had taught to deify the state.[164]

In the final analysis, Masaryk held a dim view of Hegel's political and legal theories in their entirety. In his review of Josef Trakal's *Hlavní směry novější právní a státní filosofie* [Principal Trends in Recent Philosophy of Law and Politics] (Prague, 1885), he expressed his doubt that Hegel's thought deserved to be presented as a special stage in the development of political science and law.[165]

Masaryk and the Germans

As we have seen, Masaryk was not interested in the teachings of Hegel and his precursors and successors from the narrow perspective of philosophy as such. Rather, he was deeply concerned with the effects of Hegel's ideas on the political and social development of Central and Eastern Europe, effects with amoral and pessimistic consequences resulting in violence. It is also important to make two points: first Masaryk did not object to Hegel and other philosophers in the (technically speaking) German (as opposed to Austrian) tradition on ethnic grounds – that is, that they were Germans. Rather, it was because they taught metaphysical monism, stressing the hegemony of universals over individual, extant beings, and thus trivializing the status and the rights of particular individuals. Hegel's philosophy in particular discounted individual consciousness and conscience as "unreal," in favor of the collective consciousness and conscience of the World Spirit as "real." And second, Masaryk's dislike of Hegel and the philosophical tradition which he epitomized was free of any national

---

162 Masaryk, *Otázka sociální*, 2: 69.
163 Masaryk, *Světová revoluce za války a ve válce*, 280, 282.
164 Masaryk, *Válka a revoluce I*, 202.
165 Masaryk, *Z počátků Athenea, 1883–1885*, 243, 226.

prejudice.[166] Masaryk's disregard for the ethnic or linguistic criterion in intellectual life was ultimately evident from his avid participation in the Austrian philosophical school, which consisted largely of German speakers.[167] He considered it perfectly normal that philosophical ideas crossed state and ethnic frontiers, and that, for example, ideas originating in Germany could take root in Russia.[168]

---

166 He also had some doubts about Hegel's intellectual honesty and judgment. He noted that Hegel obtained university tenure on the basis of a dissertation in which he sought to prove – on the basis of Plato's *Timaues* – that no planet could exist between Jupiter and Mars, a year after asteroid Ceres was discovered. See Masaryk, *Slovanské studie a texty z let 1889–1891*, 404.

167 See also his positive attitude toward Herbart's ontic individualism, which opposed Hegel's metaphysical monism, in Masaryk, *Moderní člověk a náboženství*, 100; also Batscha, *Eine Philosophie der Demokratie*, 69.

168 Masaryk, *Česká otázka. N, 1aše nynější krize. Jan Hus*, 20, 103.

Chapter 2

Masaryk's Preference for John Locke and British Empiricism

M asaryk's preference for empiricism was life-long, and it exerted strong influence on him in his principal role in the second half of his life span as a political actor. As noted in the Preface, in the broadest sense, Masaryk's philosophical realism "had an immense impact in molding the intellectual and civic climate of Bohemia,"[1] and it can be defined as having had two anchors: Platonic idealism and English empiricism.

Within the Austrian school of philosophy, he shared with his precursors and his contemporaries a strong aversion to German idealist philosophy, in particular to Hegel (as discussed in Chapter 1),[2] and a strong attraction to empirical philosophers, especially British ones. John Locke occupied a prominent place as a founder of the English empirical tradition in philosophy[3] and as a fountainhead of liberalism in political theory in the United States and elsewhere.[4] This chapter concentrates on Ma-

---

1   Josef Novák, "Masaryk's Criticism of Romantic Titanism," in *T. G. Masaryk und die Brentano Schule*, ed. Josef Zumr and Thomas Binder (Prague and Graz: Filozofický ústav Československé akademie věd and Forschungstelle und Dokumentationzentrum für österreichische Philosophie, 1992), 144.

2   This particular facet of the Austrian philosophical tradition became deeply embedded in Bohemia's intellectual life. As Masaryk had his Brentano, his eminent predecessor, Karel Havlíček, had had his Bolzano to immunize him against the allures of the Hegelian Weltanschauung.

3   ... which, in the words of the *DNB,* "substituted a scientific psychology for a transcendental metaphysic." See *Dictionary of National Biography*, 22 vols. (Oxford: Oxford University Press, 1921–1922), 12: 36.

4   "In America, [Locke's] influence on Jonathan Edwards, Hamilton, and Jefferson was decisive." James G. Clapp, "John Locke," in *The Encyclopedia of Philosophy*, ed. Donald M. Borchert, 2nd ed., 10 vols. (New York: New York: Macmillan, 2006), 5: 392. Just prior to the American Revo-

saryk's interest – within the context of the Austrian philosophical school – in this outstanding philosopher, and examines his treatment of Locke's epistemology, psychology, political theory, and religious views.

When seeking the roots of Masaryk's preference for empiricism, it is important to recall that his primary introduction to the field of philosophy came with his immersion in Friedrich A. Lange's survey of Western philosophy while still at Gymnasium (see Chapter 1) and that later his philosophical outlook was shaped to a considerable extent at the University of Vienna by the teaching and scholarship of Franz Brentano from 1872 to 1876.[5] Independently of Brentano, he also developed an attachment to English empiricism,[6] which was strengthened after he began delving into Hume's philosophy in 1877 in connection with what he considered to be Kant's unsuccessful attempts to overcome Hume's skepticism.[7] His October 16, 1882, inaugural lecture at the University of Prague was devoted to "The Calculus of Probability and Hume's Skepticism" (*Počet pravděpodobnosti a Humova skepse*),[8] and his interest deepened when he and his wife, Charlotte, began translating selections from Hume from English into German in 1883.[9]

Moreover, Masaryk had an opportunity to gain a positive impression of another strand of empiricism in the philosophy of Johann F. Herbart (1776–1841), which was entrenched in Bohemia and Austria, largely thanks to the teaching of Leopold Rembold at the University of Vienna and Franz Exner at the University of Prague. Masaryk had had a chance to become familiar with Herbart's teaching in his early studies of Friedrich A.

---

lution in 1773, Locke's *Second Treatise of Government* was reprinted in Boston and often cited in debates. Subsequently, Locke's account of the origin and limits of government continued to be influential in the United States; see *Oxford Dictionary of National Biography*, 61 vols. (Oxford: Oxford University Press, 2004), 34: 228.

5   On the Czech participation in the Austrian philosophical tradition, see also Barry Smith, "Von T. G. Masaryk bis Jan Patočka: Eine philosophische Skizze," in *T. G. Masaryk und die Brentano-Schule*, ed. Josef Zumr and Thomas Binder, 95. For a more detailed discussion of Masaryk's participation in the school of Brenatono, see Zdeněk V. David, "Masaryk and the Austrian Philosophical Tradition: Bolzano and Brentano," *Kosmas: Czechoslovak and Central European Journal*, vol. 27, no. 1 (Fall 2013), 1–16.

6   Tomáš G. Masaryk, *Světová revoluce za války a ve válce, 1914–1918*, Spisy 15 (Prague: Masarykův ústav AV ČR, 2005), 422.

7   Masaryk, *Světová revoluce za války a ve válce, 1914–1918*, 427.

8   Zdeněk Novotný, *Korektiv Masarykovy filosofie* (Prague: Filosofia, 2011), 14.

9   Vladimír Peška, "La France dans la formation intellectuelle de Masaryk," in *Thomas Garrigue Masaryk, européen et humaniste*, ed. Vladimír Peška and Antoine Mareš (Paris: Etudes et documentation internationales: Institut d'études slaves, 1991), 226–27.

Lange's philosophical works,[10] and he was also exposed to Herbart's philosophy at the University of Vienna by Robert Zimmermann. Zimmermann represented a connecting link between the empirical realism of Bernard Bolzano (1741–1848) – considered the godfather of that philosophical tradition – and the Austrian empirical philosophy of Brentano. Having started as a favorite student of Bolzano, Zimmermann later taught philosophy, first at the University of Prague (1852–1861) and then at the University of Vienna (1861–1898), much of that time, as Brentano's colleague.[11]

British Empiricism and the Austrian Philosophical Tradition

In his later memoirs, Masaryk stated that English thinkers were his principal early teachers, next to Plato.[12] In particular, discussing his early political activity, Masaryk declared that Locke, Hume, and other empiricists had moderated his attachment to Plato.[13] Within the Austrian tradition, concern with British empirical philosophy, particularly with Locke and his precursors and successors (such as Hume, James Mill, and John Stuart Mill), reached all the way back to Bolzano.[14] Despite Locke's importance, however, the reception of his ideas in Central Europe has not yet been adequately explored.[15]

To begin with, Bolzano, in opposing Kant, paid attention to Locke's empiricism[16] and – to a lesser extent – to the kindred Scottish philosophy

---

10 Lange listed Herbart, together with Leibniz and Kant, among the most intelligent [*scharfsinnigsten*] thinkers; see Friedrich Albert Lange, *Geschichte des Materialismus und Kritik seiner Bedeutung in der Gegenwart*, ed. Alfred Schmidt, 2 vols. (Frankfurt a. M.: Suhrkamp, 1974), 1: 172.

11 Petr Urban, "Bolzano a raný Husserl," in *Osamělý myslitel, Bernard Bolzano*, ed. Kateřina Trlifajová (Prague: Filosofia, 2006), 174; Rudolf Haller, "Bolzano and Austrian Philosophy," in: *Bolzano's Wissenschaftslehre, 1837–1987*, International Workshop, Firenze, 16–19, September 1987 (Florence: Olschki, 1992), 197–201; Robert Zimmermann, *Robert Zimmermanns Philosophische Propädeutik und die Vorlagen aus der Wissenschaftslehre Bernard Bolzanos*, intro. and ed. Eduard Winter (Vienna: Verlag der Österreichischen Akademie der Wissenschaften, 1975).

12 Masaryk, *Světová revoluce za války a ve válce, 1914–1918*, 427.

13 Karel Čapek, *Hovory s T. G. Masarykem*, Spisy 20 (Prague: Československý spisovatel, 1990), 152–53, 237.

14 See, for instance, Alexius Meiong, *Philosophenbriefe: Aus der Wissenschaftlichen Korrespondenz*, Rudolf Kindinger, ed. (Graz: Akademische Druck- und Verlagsanstalt, 1965), 141.

15 John W. Yolton, "John Locke," in *The Encyclopedia of Philosophy*, ed. Donald M. Borchert, 2nd ed., 5: 395.

16 He read John Locke's *An Essay Concerning Human Understanding* in a German translation as *Versuch über den menschlichen Verstand*, transl. Wilhelm G. Tennemann, 2 vols. (Jena: 1795–1797); see Bernard Bolzano, *Philosophische Tagebücher*, in Gesamtausgabe, ed. Eduard Winter, Jan Berg,

of common sense as expressed in the works of Dugald Stewart, Thomas Reid, and James Beattie.[17] He was primarily interested in Locke's views on psychology. In the section in his principal work, *Wissenschaftslehre* (Theory of Science) (1837), in which he sought to define his concept of "the proposition in itself" (*der Satz an sich*), Bolzano cited (in English) Locke's basic definition of knowledge.[18] He also explored Locke's criterion of truth (*Wahrheit*),[19] and disagreed with Locke's distinction between "mental" and "verbal" truths.[20] Also, unlike Locke, he maintained that there could be "clear ideas" not just of perceptible objects but also of those that were imperceptible, such as moral and physical qualities (courage, weight).[21] Yet he praised Locke for grasping correctly the distinction between concept sentences (*Begriffssätzen*) and perception sentences (*Anschauungssätzen*), the former expressing full certainty, the latter only probability.[22] Locke, according to Bolzano had outdone Kant, for in his "trifling propositions," Locke had more appropriately defined the meaning of "analytical sentences" than Kant done in his *Analytische Sätze* (Analytical sentences).[23] He agreed with Locke in rejecting the concepts of "innate ideas," but felt that Locke did not carefully specify "how experience brought forth cer-

---

Friedrich Kambartel, Jaromír Loužil, and Bob van Rootselaar, 40 Bände in 57 (Stuttgart-Bad Cannstatt: 1969-in progress), Reihe II, Nachlass, B. Wissenschaftliche Tagebücher; Band 17, *1817–1827*, 116, 142.

17 Bolzano, *Philosophische Tagebücher*, Gesamtausgabe, Reihe II, Nachlass, B. Wissenschaftliche Tagebücher; Band 17, *1817–1827*, 89–91.

18 "Knowledge then seems to me to be nothing but the perception of the connexion and agreement, or disagreement and repugnancy of any of our ideas." John Locke, *An Essay Concerning Human Understanding* London 1690, Book 4, chapter 1, par. 2, cited by Bolzano, *Wissenschaftslehre*, Gesamtausgabe, Reihe I, Schriften, Band 11, Teil 1, 121.

19 "Er erklärte die Metaphysische Wahrheit als die reale Existenz der Dinge, sofern sie mit unseren Vorstellungen übereinstimmt." Citing from J. Locke, *An Essay Concerning Human Understanding*, Book 4, chapter 5, par. 11, see Bolzano, *Wissenschaftslehre*, Gesamtausgabe, Reihe I, Schriften, Band 11, Teil 1, 166.

20 J. Locke, *An Essay Concerning Human Understanding*, Book 4, chapter 5, par. 2, cited by Bolzano, *Wissenschaftslehre*, Gesamtausgabe, Reihe I, Schriften, Band 11, Teil 1, 145.

21 Bolzano, *Wissenschaftslehre*, Gesamtausgabe, Reihe I, Schriften, Band 13, Teil 1, 49, referring to Locke's statement: "As a clear idea is that, where of the mind has such a full and evident perception, as it does receive from an outward object, operating duly on a well disposed organ." Cited from J. Locke, *An Essay Concerning Human Understanding*, London 1700, Book 2, chapter 29, paragraph 4.

22 Bolzano, *Wissenschaftslehre*, Gesamtausgabe, Reihe I, Schriften, Band 12, Teil 1, 96, referring to J. Locke, *An Essay Concerning Human Understanding* (London: 1775) Book 4, chapter 3, paragraph 31; chapter 4, paragraph 6, 16.

23 Bolzano, *Wissenschaftslehre*, Gesamtausgabe, Reihe I, Schriften, Band 12, Teil 1, 144, referring to J. Locke, *An Essay Concerning Human Understanding*, Book 4, chapter 8, paragraph 4.

tain ideas."[24] Bolzano was likewise interested in Locke's theory concerning the grounds of the possibility of error.[25]

Brentano and Locke

Masaryk studied under Franz Brentano during his stay at the University of Vienna from 1874 to 1876 and 1879 to 1882. This was after Brentano, formerly a Catholic priest, had broken from the Roman Church over the dogma stipulating papal infallibility (at the First Vatican Council in 1870).[26] While Comte's positivism left Brentano cold, he had developed an early interest in English empirical philosophy and corresponded with John S. Mill until the latter's death in 1873.[27] He also studied Hume's works and, later, those of William Hamilton (1730–1788), the leading exponent of the Scottish philosophy of "common sense."[28] A study tour took him to England from April to June 1872, where he sought language fluency and a better acquaintance with the local philosophy.[29] After resigning his academic position in Würzburg, and before settling in Vienna, Brentano sought a position at the University of Leipzig in 1873, but was disillusioned by its lack of English philosophical literature.[30] In the introduction to his basic work, *Psychology from an Empirical Standpoint* (1874) Brentano stressed that he had relied as much on English philosophical literature as on German.[31]

Locke played an eminent and specific role in Brentano's interpretation of the course of European philosophy. In Brentano's fourfold scheme of philosophical development, Locke (together with Leibniz) represented the third high point of philosophy, followed by a phase of decay, then skepti-

---

24 Bolzano, *Wissenschaftslehre*, Gesamtausgabe, Reihe I, Schriften, Band 13, Teil 1, 114, referring to J. Locke, *An Essay Concerning Human Understanding* (London, 1700), Book 1, chapter 3.

25 "...dass wohl die meisten unserer Irrthümer blosse *Gedächtnissfehler* wären..." See B. Bolzano, *Wissenschaftslehre*, Gesamtausgabe, Reihe I, Schriften, Band 13, Teil 2, 48, referring to J. Locke, *An Essay Concerning Human Understanding*, Book 4, chapter 2, paragraph 7; chapter 20, paragraph 1.

26 Čapek, *Hovory s T. G. Masarykem*, 71–72.

27 Oskar Kraus, *Franz Brentano: Zur Kenntnis seines Lebens und seiner Lehre*. With contributions from Carl Stumpf and Edmund Husserl (Munich: Beck, 1919), 7–8.

28 Franz Brentano, *Psychologie vom empirischen Standpunkt*, 2nd ed., 3 vols., ed. Oskar Kraus (Leipzig: Felix Meiner, 1924–1928), 1: 23–24 (on Hume); 1: 25–26 (Hamilton); originally published in 1874.

29 Kraus, *Franz Brentano: Zur Kenntnis seines Lebens und seiner Lehre*, 125.

30 Ibid., 130. In his old age, he translated into German the English hymn "Nearer, my God to Thee" [*Näher zu Dir mein Gott*], which was played on the Titanic during its sinking in 1913; ibid., 142.

31 Brentano, *Psychologie vom empirischen Standpunkt*, ed. Oskar Kraus, 1: 2.

cism, then mysticism (the pantheistic mysticism of Schelling and the absolute idealism of Hegel). The previous peaks had been attained by Aristotle in ancient times and by Thomas Aquinas in the Middle Ages. The
ancient decline involved Stoics with Epicureans, then Skeptics, and finally the Neo-Platonists; the medieval cycle proceeded from the dogmatic
hair-splitters, to the skeptical nominalists, and finally to the mystics of
the type of Ramon Sibiud, Nicolas of Cues, and the disciples of Ramon
Lull.[32] According to Carl Stumpf, Brentano had arrived at this interpretation (of three stages with quadruple steps) early in life, probably by 1860,
when he wondered why pretentious systems that were once universally admired now seemed to be universally rejected. It occurred to him that this
was happening in his own time to the philosophies of Fichte, Schelling,
and Hegel.[33] He returned to this theme in 1893 when he predicted a new
blossoming of philosophy that would be comparable to the age of Locke
(as well as Leibniz and Descartes) and would establish philosophy on the
basis of scientific knowledge.[34]

Despite the high place that he assigned to Locke in the development of
European philosophy, Brentano referred to him infrequently in his magisterial *Psychology from an Empirical Standpoint*.[35] He preferred to cite more
recent representatives of empirical philosophy, especially William Hamilton, Johann F. Herbart, and John S. Mill.[36] He did defend Locke (together with other earlier philosophers) against Henry Maudsley's (1835–1918)
charge that his ideas on psychology failed because he did not provide insight from the physiology of brain activity. Brentano agreed with John S.
Mill that the study of brain functions was not yet sufficiently advanced
to shed light on psychological phenomena.[37] Brentano further criticized

---

32 Etienne Gilson, "Franz Brentano's Interpretation of Medieval Philosophy," in *The Philosophy of Brentano*, ed. Linda L. McAlister (Atlantic Highlands, NJ: Humanities Press, 1977), 56–57; Lucie Gilson, "Franz Brentano on Science an Philosophy," in *The Philosophy of Brentano*, 69; Franz C. Brentano, *Die vier Phasen der Philosophie und ihr augenblicklicher Stand. Nebst Abhandlungen über Plotinus, Thomas von Aquin, Kant, Schopenhauer und Auguste Comte*, ed. Oskar Kraus, new intro. Franziska Mayer-Hillebrand, 2nd ed. (Hamburg: Meiner, 1968), 18.

33 Kraus, *Franz Brentano: Zur Kenntnis seines Lebens und seiner Lehre*, 90; Gilson, "Franz Brentano's Interpretation of Medieval Philosophy," 57–58

34 Kraus, *Franz Brentano: Zur Kenntnis seines Lebens und seiner Lehre*, 20.

35 Franz Brentano, *Psychology from an Empirical Standpoint*, ed. Oskar Kraus; English edition ed. Linda L. McAlister, transl. Antos C. Rancurello, D.B. Terrell, and Linda L. McAlister, new intro. by Peter Simons (London and New York : Routledge, 1995).

36 He also refers to Wilhelm T. Krug, see Brentano, *Psychologie vom empirischen Standpunkt*, Oskar Kraus, ed., 2: 12–13, 28; to Thomas Reid, ibid., 2: 10, 265–266; as well as to Bolzano, ibid., 2: 265.

37 Ibid., 1: 77.

Maudsley for misrepresenting Locke's approach by claiming that he focused on his own individual mental phenomena and ignored others. In actuality, Locke – according to Brentano – took into account noteworthy phenomena observed in other men, as well as in animals.[38] In the case of animals, Locke agreed with Aristotle that they lacked the capacity for general abstract concepts.[39] Along similar lines, Brentano called attention to Locke's interest in studying "life simpler than our own," such as that of little children and of "primitive" peoples. In that approach, Locke was ahead of his time.[40] Locke was, however, remiss in not undertaking a proper analysis of mental phenomena; he simply noted their general aspects rather than seek to separate out the simpler phenomena that made up the more complex one. It was – Brentano claimed – as if a chemist noted "the color and taste of cinnabar" and considered them constituent elements, instead of conducting a proper chemical analysis.[41] According to Brentano, Locke (as well as John S. Mill) also wrongly denied the existence of "unconscious consciousness," even though the concept of "unconscious mental activity" had been accepted by many recent philosophers and psychologists.[42]

Brentano noted Locke's rejection of objective existence of secondary qualities (such as taste or color), contrasting them with primary qualities (such as shape or movement). To Brentano, the Lockean secondary qualities were just contributed by the mind, although he admitted that the transmental existence of "physical qualities" was possible.[43] On the issue of free will, Brentano argued that Locke failed to distinguish between absolute or "causeless" free will and the ability to avoid an unrighteous decision.[44] In his later writings, Brentano commented on Locke's concepts of inner perception [*innere Wahrnehmung*] and of time,[45] and in his book on ethics, *The Origin of Our Knowledge of Right and Wrong*, he further agreed with Locke

---

38 Brentano refers to Henry Maudsley, *Physiology and Pathology of the Mind* (New York: Appleton, 1876), and defends also John Stuart Mill and Aristotle, see Brentano, *Psychologie vom empirischen Standpunkt*, Oskar Kraus, ed., 1: 78.

39 Brentano, *Psychologie vom empirischen Standpunkt*, ed. Oskar Kraus, 2: 30–31.

40 Ibid., 1: 56.

41 Ibid., 1: 64.

42 Among others, he refers to Herbart and Beneke, and he cites James Mill that: "...that there are sensations of which we are not conscious, because of habitual inattention." See Ibid., 1: 143–44.

43 Ibid., 1: lxxiii, 13; see also Barry Smith, *Austrian Philosophy: The Legacy of Bretano* (Chicago: Open Court, 1994), 43.

44 Brentano, *Psychologie vom empirischen Standpunkt*, ed. Oskar Kraus, 2: 111.

45 Brentano, "Neue Abhandlasse," in *Psychologie vom empirischen Standpunkt*, ed. Oskar Kraus, 2: 199, 264.

that there were no innate moral ideas that might constitute a natural law of reason – which antiquity had known as the law of nations (*ius gentium*).[46]

Masaryk's colleagues Anton Marty and Carl Stumpf both showed interest in Locke among the representatives of philosophical empiricism. Like Masaryk, they were students of Brentano and, also in the 1880s, were professors of philosophy in Prague. According to the 1915 recollections of Hugo Bergmann, Marty had dealt with Locke in his philosophy seminar, as well as with Aristotle, Descartes, Hume and Leibniz,[47] but he was especially fond of Locke.[48] As an empiricist, Stumpf preferred Locke and George Berkeley to the traditional German idealists.[49] Among Masaryk's other student peers, Alexius Meinong (1853–1921) discussed Locke in his correspondence with Johannes Fries (concerning judgment) and Max Heinze (concerning the psychological theory of value).[50] The more famous Edmund Husserl (1859–1938) dealt with Locke in his *Second Logical Investigation*, scrutinizing Locke's doctrine of "abstract" or "universal" ideas that replaced the doctrine of real (Platonic-style) universals. Husserl was mainly concerned that Locke wrongly arrived at a "psychological hypostatization of the universal," making the universal a real datum in consciousness.[51] He considered Locke to be the true teacher of Hume in employing the empirical-psychological method in epistemology.[52] It was, in fact, Masaryk who first turned Husserl's attention to Locke and English empiricism during their student years in Leipzig (1876–1877). [53]

---

46 Franz C. Brentano, *The Origin of Our knowledge of Right and Wrong*, ed. Oskar Kraus; English edition Roderick M. Chisholm, transl. Roderick M. Chisholm and Elizabeth H. Schneewind (London: Routledge & K. Paul; New York: Humanities Press, 1969), 5. Originally published as Franz C. Brentano, *Vom Ursprung sittlicher Erkenntnis* (Leipzig: Duncker and Humblot, 1889).
47 Meinong, *Philosophenbriefe: Aus der Wissenschaftlichen Korrespondenz*, 205.
48 William M. Johnston, *The Austrian Mind: An Intellectual and Social History, 1848–1938* (Berkeley: University of California Press, 1972), 77–78.
49 *The Encyclopedia of Philosophy*, 2nd ed., ed. Donald M. Borchert, 9: 280.
50 Meinong, *Philosophenbriefe: Aus der Wissenschaftlichen Korrespondenz*, 124, 141.
51 Edmund Husserl, *Logical Investigations*, transl. John N. Findlay (London: Routledge, 2001), 251, 254. A case in point was the non-existence of the idea of a universal triangle; it had no mental existence because such would also be real existence; ibid., 255. See also 270, 277, 283–84; Barry Smith, *Austrian Philosophy: The Legacy of Bretano*, 17 n12.
52 Husserl, *Logical Investigations*, 292. He further cautioned that the opposition to Locke's "general ideas" had led to the opposite extreme of modern nominalism. The latter, exemplified by John Stuart Mill, rejects not only realism, but also "conceptualism" in the realm of ideas. It is based on the psychologically regulated association of the same signs, instead of on the generality, which belongs to the intentional conceit of the logical experiences themselves. Ibid., 262–64.
53 Vasil Škrach, "Edmund Husserl," *Česká mysl.* 25 (1929), 189. On their contacts in Leipzig see also Chapter 4.

Masaryk and Locke

Masaryk's concern with British philosophy began before his contact with Brentano and can be traced to the beginning of his secondary school *(Gymnasium)* studies in Vienna in 1869 and his general fascination with Anglophone culture. He took up the study of English specifically to be able to read English literature (above all Shakespeare and Byron) in the original.[54] (As a student in Vienna in 1871, Masaryk is said to have considered Shakespeare's plays superior to Goethe's "Faust."[55]) Zdeněk Nejedlý, in his monumental, although unfinished, biography of Masaryk, suggests that he probably first learned about Locke's philosophy from Friedrich Albert Lange's *Geschichte des Materialismus und Kritik seiner Bedeutung in der Gegenwart.*[56] (As noted in Chapter 1, Masaryk wrote about his preoccupation with Lange while still a Gymnasium student in 1869.[57]) Nejedlý likewise suggests that Masaryk was particularly attracted to Locke for his status as a philosopher who was also involved in politics.[58] In speaking of this connection between theory and practice, the Encyclopedia of Philosophy notes that "Locke's zeal for truth as he saw it ... may account for the fact that his works prepared the ground for action as well as thought."[59] Masaryk himself considered English Empiricists as his principal philosophical teachers[60] and has stated that Locke (as well as Hume and other empiricists) provided him with a salutary counterbalance to Plato's speculative idealism.[61] Indeed, ear-

54 Stanislav Polák, *T.G. Masaryk*, 6 vols. (Prague: Masarykův ústav AV ČR, 127 :1 ,(2012–2000. See also Jaromír Doležal, *Masarykova cesta životem*, 2 vols. (Brno: Polygrafie, 1920–1921), 2: 15; Emil Ludwig, *Defender of Democracy: Masaryk of Czechoslovakia* (New York: R. M. McBride, 1936). His early fondness for English led him to send on December 20, 1870, verses of a British poet to Anna Chotěnovská, a young lady he then courted: "When I shall meet Thee / After long years - / How shall I greet Thee? / With silence and tears?" see Polák, *T.G. Masaryk*, 1: 131.

55 Polák, *T.G. Masaryk*, 1: 141. [There is no such reference in Thomas G. Masaryk, "Můj poměr ke Goethovi," *Goethův sborník*. Památce 100. výročí básníkovy smrti vydali čeští germanisté (Prague: Státní nakladatelství, 1932), 9–11.

56 Zdeněk Nejedlý, *T. G. Masaryk*, 4 vols. (Prague: Melantrich, 1930–1937); 2nd ed., vols. 1–2, Sebrané spisy, 31–32 (Prague: Orbis, 1949–1950), 1: 317. The reference is to: Lange, *Geschichte des Materialismus und Kritik seiner Bedeutung in der Gegenwart.*

57 "... meine Lieblingsarbeit war damals eine bömische Übersetzung Lange's Geschichte des Materialismus die ich mit Noten versah, in denen ich meine unmassgeblichen Ansichten aussprach...;" see Doležal, *Masarykova cesta životem*, 2: 15; see also ibid., 1: 17.

58 Nejedlý, *T. G. Masaryk*, 1: 25.

59 James G. Clapp, "John Locke," in *The Encyclopedia of Philosophy*, 2nd ed., ed. Donald M. Borchert, 5: 392.

60 Masaryk, *Světová revoluce za války a ve válce, 1914–1918*, 427.

61 Čapek, *Hovory s T. G. Masarykem*, 153.

ly in his career as professor of philosophy at the University of Prague, during the academic year 1886–1887, Masaryk devoted his winter- and summer-semester seminars to the exclusive study of Locke.[62]

Empiricism/Epistemology

According to Masaryk, Locke, like Francis Bacon before him and Hume after, contributed to the development of empirical thought, to which Englishmen remained faithful to the turn of the nineteenth century.[63] Locke had a special advantage in this field because his training as a physician accustomed him to external observation.[64] Masaryk thought that English empiricism always had a beneficial effect on German philosophy: thus, Leibniz, in particular, learned from Locke, and whatever was valuable in Kant was owed to Hume. Subsequently, psychologist Friedrich E. Beneke (1798–1854) relied primarily on Locke in his opposition to the speculative idealism of Kant, Fichte, and Schelling.[65] Masaryk also praised the creative use of Locke's epistemology by his own younger colleague, Alexius Meinong. In his theory of relations, Meinong strengthened Locke's empiricism substantively and methodologically by judicious use of "a sober rationalism."[66] Masaryk used Locke's empiricism as a criterion for judging defections to idealism. Thus, he saw Leibniz escaping Locke for Plato and his pre-established harmony, and he preferred Hume for his reliance on Locke over Kant, who relied on Leibniz – hence, ultimately on Plato.[67] Masaryk endorsed Locke's opposition to standard rationalism by rejecting the concept of innate ideas, ideas that, because they do not de-

---

62 Tomáš G. Masaryk, *Univerzitní přednášky I: Praktická filozofie*, Spisy 4 (Prague: Masarykův ústav AV ČR, 2012), 448.
63 Tomáš G. Masaryk, *Sebevražda hromadným jevem společenským moderní osvěty*, Spisy 1 (Prague: Masarykův ústav AV ČR, 2002), 163.
64 Tomáš G. Masaryk, *Pokus o konkrétní logiku*, Spisy 3 (Prague: Masarykův ústav AV ČR, 111 ,(2001).
65 Masaryk, *Pokus o konkrétní logiku*, 113; see also Beneke's correspondence, concerning British philosophy with William Whewell (1794–1866) and with Sir John F. W. Herschel (1792–1871) in Friedrich Eduard Beneke, *Ungedruckte Briefe*, ed. Renato Pettoello and Nikola Barelmann (Aalen, Germany: Scientia, 1994), 84–85. To Whewell he complained in 1842 about the sway of idealist philosophy in Germany, as well as expressed his hope that he might find more understanding in England; see Beneke, *Ungedruckte Briefe*, 228, 238.
66 Masaryk, "Dr. Alexius Meinong, Hume-Studien II," in *Z počátků Athenea, 1883–1885*, 93–94.
67 Tomáš G. Masaryk, *Moderní člověk a náboženství*, Spisy, 8 (Prague: Masarykův ústav AV ČR, 53–52 ,(2000.

rive from our sense experience, have no explanation for their origin. Their source appeared to be like a revelation, as if they were inserted into human minds by God.[68]

Psychology

To Masaryk, Locke was the unequivocal founder of modern psychology. Thanks to him, the study of psychology was able to advance so much that it left behind scholastic psychology, which had offered empty verbal constructs instead of substantive learning.[69] From Locke the "empirical" trend continued in England through Hume, Hartley, James Mill and John S. Mill. In Germany, however, Locke's stand on the importance of empiricism over rationalism in the origin of ideas met a challenge from Leibniz and Kant, although the former started from Locke and the latter from Hume. Eventually – according to Masaryk – an ascendancy was gained in Germany by Kant's artificial psychologism of apriori notions that were embedded in human minds to organize sense perceptions. This ascendancy came to play the unfortunate role of opening the door to various "psychological myths." However, Kant's influence in psychology was overcome in Germany when Beneke, relying primarily on Locke's teaching, returned his focus to English psychology and stood in opposition to Kant. Beneke's approach was, therefore, more successful than Herbart's, which attempted to make psychology more precise through the application of mathematics.[70] In addition, Masaryk credited Beneke with the idea that psychology should serve as the basis of philosophy,[71] a notion which both Masaryk and Brentano strongly upheld.[72] Masaryk further point-

---

68 Čapek, *Hovory s T. G. Masarykem*, 232.

69 Tomáš G. Masaryk, "Tři knihy o filosofii," in Tomáš G. Masaryk, "Dr. Alexius Meinong, Hume-Studien II," *Z počátků Athenea, 1883–1885*, 189.

70 Masaryk, *Pokus o konkrétní logiku*, 113. On Beneke's inspiration from British thought, and his high regard for Locke, see also *The Encyclopedia of Philosophy*, 2nd ed., ed. Donald M. Borchert, 1: 544; and Frederick Copleston, *History of Philosophy*, 8 vols. (London: Burns and Oates, 1947–1966), 7: 255.

71 See, e.g., *Encyclpedia Britannica* (2002), Micropaedia, 2: 98.

72 Rudolf Haller, "Brentanos Spuren im Werk Masaryks," in *T. G. Masaryk und die Brentano-Schule,* ed. Zumr and Binder, 14. Brentano does not mention Beneke, except for a minor reference in his own major work Brentano, *Psychologie vom empirischen Standpunkt,* ed. Oskar Kraus, 1: 168. Brentano's reference is to Friedrich Eduard Beneke, *Lehrbuch der Psychologie als Naturwissenschaft,* 2nd ed. (Berlin: E. S. Mittler, 1845), par. 57.

ed out that also for Locke psychology represented the philosophical basis of logic.[73] Finally, he viewed Meinong's work as a worthy continuation of Locke's teaching in both psychology and logic.[74]

Political Theory

Masaryk considered Locke to be a principal founder of modern political philosophy, continuing the work of Bacon and Hobbes.[75] In this context, Masaryk opposed Josef Trakal's assertion that Locke located the mainspring of human behavior in instinct; rather, he located it in reason.[76] Above all, for Masaryk, Locke was the first interpreter and systematizer of liberalism. During the eighteenth century, liberalism's intellectual essence came to include deism, freethinking, and the rest of the philosophy of the Enlightenment.[77] In the *Spirit of Russia*, Masaryk emphasized Locke's influence on liberal thought in the tsarist empire. For instance, Catherine the Great admired Locke second only to Montesquieu. Mikhail Speranskii drew not only on jurist Sir William Blackstone (1723–1780) and the English constitutionalists but also on the philosophy of Locke for his own proposed constitutional reforms for Russia at the opening of the nineteenth century.[78] However, as far as Masaryk was concerned, Locke's close association with liberalism was not unambiguously favorable to his, Locke's, image. These qualms grew out of Masaryk's own ambiguous view of liberalism, especially as it had developed in the nineteenth century.[79] It trod this slippery slope when Voltaire and the encyclopedists became the representatives of liberalism in the philosophic field and attempted to organize, with the aid of pamphleteering and journalism, so-called "sound

73 Masaryk, *Pokus o konkrétní logiku*, 160.
74 Masaryk, "Dr. Alexius Meinong, Hume-Studien II," 93–94.
75 Masaryk, *Pokus o konkrétní logiku*, 136.
76 Tomáš G. Masaryk, "Dr. Josef Trakal, *Hlavní směry novější právní a státní filosofie.* (V Praze 1885)," in *Z počátků Athenea, 1883–1885*, 226–27; Masaryk, "Hovorna," *Z počátků Athenea, 1883–1885*, 245.
77 Tomáš G. Masaryk, *Rusko a Evropa II*, Spisy 12 (Prague: Masarykův ústav AV ČR, 1996), [1913], 323; see also Masaryk, Thomas, *The Spirit of Russia: Studies in History, Literature, and Philosophy*, trans. Eden and Cedar Paul, and W. R. and Z. Lee. 2d ed,. 3 vols. (London: Allen & Unwin, 1961–67), 2: 413.
78 Masaryk, *Rusko a Evropa I*, Spisy 11, 58, 69; see also Masaryk, *The Spirit of Russia*, 1: 69, 85.
79 On Masaryk's questioning of liberalism, see Chapter 5 in this book and David, "Thomas G. Masaryk's Ambivalent View of the Enlightenment and Political Liberalism," 83–93.

human reason" as a public authority.[80] The character of what passed for liberalism further deteriorated after the Napoleonic Wars, when Locke's penchant for toleration was (mis)applied towards support for ideas and trends against which liberalism had previously fought, especially in support of the notion that historical law was superior to natural law. This perversion even included the endorsement of reactionary royal legitimism to counter the revolutionary ferment.[81]

On the positive side, Masaryk stressed that as the first philosopher of liberalism, Locke was also the first advocate of the separation of church and state. This endeavor was in line with liberalism's objective to secure freedom, in this case freedom from the spiritual oppression imposed by what Masaryk called theocracy – the union of church and state.[82] Yet, he was also deeply impressed by the fact that even Locke, despite his religious tolerance, would consider atheism a threat to social order and thus a crime.[83] Masaryk was apparently either puzzled or troubled by this fact, and returned to it on several occasions in his writings and statements.[84]

In the area of the social sciences, according to Masaryk, Locke, like Hobbes, made a major contribution to the development of abstract sociology, helping to formulate the laws of both social statics and social dynamics;[85] and, like Adam Smith and David Ricardo, Locke also stressed the importance of "labor," from both philosophical and social viewpoints.[86] As a committed socialist, Nejedlý, in his previously-mentioned biography of Masaryk, expressed disagreement with Masaryk's endorsement of Locke's views concerning the rights of private property.[87] More relevantly, Zwi Batscha has called attention to the fact that Masaryk did not deal

---

80 Masaryk, *Rusko a Evropa II*, 323; see also Masaryk, *The Spirit of Russia*, 2: 413.
81 Masaryk, *Rusko a Evropa II*, 326; see also Masaryk, *The Spirit of Russia*, 2: 416.
82 Masaryk, *Rusko a Evropa II*, 379; see also Masaryk, *The Spirit of Russia*, 2: 492.
83 Masaryk, *Rusko a Evropa II*, 383, 409, see also Masaryk, *The Spirit of Russia*, 2: 418, also 2: 534.
84 Masaryk, *Světová revoluce za války a ve válce, 1914–1918*, 406 [see also Tomáš G. Masaryk, *Světová revoluce za války a ve válce, 1914–1918* (Prague: Čin, 1933), 608]; and Ludwig, *Defender of Democracy: Masaryk of Czechoslovakia*, 82. However, James P. Scanlan, "Masaryk as an Interpreter of Russian Philosophy," *T. G. Masaryk, 1850–1937*, ed. Stanley Winters et al., 3 vols. (London: Macmillan, 1989–1990), 2: 91, has shown that Masaryk was mistaken when he was under the impression that Locke considered atheism a capital offense.
85 Tomáš G. Masaryk, *Otázka sociální. Základy marxismu filosofické a sociologické*, 2 vols. Spisy 9–10 (Prague: Masarykův ústav AV ČR, 151 :1 ,(2000 n. 82 .2. For Masaryk's concept of «abstract sociology," see Masaryk, *Pokus o konkrétní logiku*, 123–25.
86 Masaryk, *Otázka sociální. Základy marxismu filosofické a sociologické*, 1: 270.
87 Nejedlý, *T. G. Masaryk*, 3: 297, 300.

with Locke's notable idea of the right of resistance to unjust political authorities, a particularly ironic omission in light of Masaryk's subsequent
leadership in the struggle against Austria-Hungary for an independent
Czechoslovakia.[88]

Metaphysics/Materialism

Masaryk defended Locke against Karl Marx's claim that together with Bacon and Hobbes, Locke was a founder of "materialism," which then came to
Europe from Britain. Masaryk saw this interpretation as Marx's attempt to
portray the rise of materialism as a product of an inevitable trend of modern European philosophy. In what Masaryk considered a fanciful scenario, Marx further claimed that this materialism migrated to France, where
Claude Adrian Helvétius (1715–1771) applied it to social life. Marx crowned
this fictitious history by maintaining that, while French materialism was
mostly mechanistic, it was the original English version, especially Locke's,
that was applied to intellectual life and culture and, therefore, led to socialism. In Masaryk's opinion, Marx showed a gross lack of discrimina-
tion and historical understanding in viewing altogether Bacon, Hobbes,
Locke, Helvétius, Condillac and Feuerbach as generic "materialists." This
lack of refinement reflected Marx's own confused idea of the concept of
"materialism," his own version of which actually stemmed from Feuerbach.[89]

Masaryk did admit, however, that Locke's empiricism and his opposition to the trans-phenomenal world of innate ideas might later have been
misinterpreted in a materialist and antireligious direction. Thus, during
the eighteenth century, the influence of Locke, Hume, and other deists
inadvertently helped to lead representatives of the French Enlightenment,
such as Etienne Bonnot de Condillac, Pierre Jean Georges Cabanis, Antoine Destutt de Tracy, and Julien Offray de La Mettrie, toward sensualism and materialism in their struggle against the church and state of the
ancien régime.[90] Earlier, Hume had misused Locke to deny non-empirical reality; he turned Locke's empiricism into "ultra-empiricism" direct-

---

88   Zwi Batscha, *Eine Philosophie der Demokratie* (Frankfurt a/M: Suhrkamp, 1994), 207.
89   Masaryk, *Otázka sociální. Základy marxismu filosofické a sociologické*, 1: 62–63.
90   Masaryk, *Pokus o konkrétní logiku*, 114.

ed against theology and religion.[91] Masaryk's view concerning Locke's alleged "materialism" coincided with that of his early teacher Friedrich A. Lange. According to Lange, even though the realm of phenomena was construed by the English empiricist without any reference to an underlying ideal (or, in Kant's term, noumenal) reality, and thus resembled the viewpoint of current German materialists, Locke did not attribute a material reality to phenomena, instead he considered them to be products of subjective perceptions – albeit of a sensory type.[92]

Deism/Theism

In classifying Locke from the religious point of view, Masaryk shifted from an early characterization of him as deist, to a later one as theist. In *Pokus o konkrétní logiku* (An Attempt at Concrete Logic), he places Locke, together with Hume, among the eighteenth-century British deists.[93] Masaryk presents Locke as a theist when writing about Hume's reaction to Locke's religious views in *Moderní člověk a náboženství* (The Modern Man and Religion). Although Hume thought that Locke's empiricism had demolished any previous religious orthodoxy, according to Masaryk, Hume considered Locke "the first true Christian," who had freed the human mind from the burden of superstition that was the source of false piety. Inasmuch as Christianity before Locke was based on superstition, Locke – not Christ – was the first true Christian.[94] Masaryk concluded that Hume could even tolerate theism, as long as it was philosophical, à la Locke.[95] Identifying Locke as a theist brought Masaryk into agreement with his own teacher, Brentano.[96]

In classifying Locke as either a deist or a theist, Masaryk actually still neglected a major area of Locke's religiosity that modern research has since

---

91 Masaryk, *Moderní člověk a náboženství*, 39.
92 Lange, *Geschichte des Materialismus und Kritik seiner Bedeutung in der Gegenwart*, 2: 593.
93 Masaryk, *Pokus o konkrétní logiku*, 114.
94 Masaryk, *Moderní člověk a náboženství*, 45.
95 Ibid., 113.
96 Brentano, "Epicurus and the War," in Brentano, *The Origin of Our Knowledge of Right and Wrong*, ed. Oskar Kraus, English edition, ed. Roderick M. Chisholm, 123. Despite Masaryk's clear commitment to theism, it is surprising that Arne Novák could maintain that Masaryk professed "a religion without God," see his "Světová revoluce," *Lumír* 53 (1926) in Novák, *Nosiči pochodní; kniha české tradice* (Prague, Literární odbor Umělecké besedy a Kruh českých spisovatelů, 1928), 213.

emphasized.[97] Locke's late writings on religion indicated beliefs in the divinity of Christ, the Virgin Birth, the Resurrection, as well as sin and redemption. These mysteries, according to Locke, could not be discovered by unaided reason, but instead were disclosed by revelation. Normally, reason had to be followed as far as it could lead, but in the case of religious mysteries, it could not lead far enough by itself. True revelation, however, could not violate the canons of reason but had to be consonant with them.[98] These findings defy the assertions that Locke was either a deist or an anti-trinitarian (Socinian) theist.[99] While it was true that classical British empiricism "limited knowledge wholly and solely to experience,"[100] and some of its practitioners, like John S. Mill, were indeed hostile to any form of religion, this was not the case with Locke. Although his religious outlook was not, strictly speaking, ecclesiastical, it was, in fact, much more orthodox than Masaryk's rational theism. The latter did not accept the divinity of Christ or the doctrine of Christ's Resurrection. Likewise, he did not accept Locke's epistemological disconnect between natural and revealed knowledge. He insisted that religious truth, particularity the existence of a theistic God and the immortality of the soul, could be proved by natural reason. He therefore did not accept the concept of revelation.[101] Masaryk may not have been aware of this facet of Locke's latter-day religiosity, inasmuch as he assumed that Locke had sought only "a natural religion" [*náboženství přirozené*];[102] or, if he had an inkling of it, he considered it irrelevant, as something that lay outside the legitimate precincts of philosophy.

---

97 These views can be derived particularly from John Locke, *A Paraphrase and Notes on the Epistles of St. Paul to the Galatians, 1 and 2 Corinthians, Romans, Ephesians*, ed. Arthur W. Wainwright, 2 vols. (Oxford: Clarendon Press, 1987). See, for instance, Jeremy Waldron, *God, Locke and Equality: Christian Foundations in Locke's Political Thought* (Cambridge: Cambridge University Press, 2002); Paul E. Sigmund, "Jeremy Waldron and the Religious Turn in Locke Scholarship," and Jeremy Waldron, "Response to Critics," in "Symposium on God, Locke, and Equality," in *Review of Politics*, 67 (2005), 407–12, 498–99.

98 Arthur Wainwright, "Introduction," to John Locke, *A Paraphrase and Notes on the Epistles of St. Paul to the Galatians, 1 and 2 Corinthians, Romans, Ephesians*, Arthur W. Wainwright, ed., 2 vols. (Oxford: Clarendon Press, 1987), 28–57.

99 Wainwright, "Introduction," to John Locke, *A Paraphrase and Notes*, 58. See also "Locke," *Oxford Dictionary of National Biography*, 24: 226; compared with "Locke," *The Encyclopedia of Philosophy*, ed. Paul Edwards, 8 vols. (New York: Macmillan, 1967), 4: 502.

100 Tom Rockmore, *Hegel, Idealism, and Analytic Philosophy* (New Haven, NJ: Yale University Press, 2005), 21.

101 Otakar A. Funda, "Náboženství: téma pro české myšlení," in *Cesta a odkaz T.G. Masaryka : fakta, úvahy, souvislosti*, ed. Jarmila Lakosilová (Prague: 2002), 134; Ludwig, *Defender of Democracy: Masaryk of Czechoslovakia*, 74–75.

102 Masaryk, *Moderní člověk a náboženství*, 35.

Proximity to the Austrian Philosophical Tradition

Masaryk insisted that some of the ultimate questions – treated in orthodox Christianity as eschatological – could be explored philosophically (by natural human reason) as questions of ontology. In this he differed from both Locke's and orthodox Christianity's acceptance of the limits of natural knowledge. He rejected both the concept of "tabula rasa" and that of a revealed truth.[103] In his effort to overcome the barrenness of Locke's empiricism, Masaryk tended to turn to Hume concerning the need to supplement the images of sensory perception with the feelings of emotion.[104] He pointed out that Plato, too, opposed the theory of "tabula rasa" – the mind was not as passive as "radical empiricism" claimed; internal human experience contradicted such a notion.[105]

More importantly, in his search for feeling beyond sense perception, Masaryk came close to straying across the boundary into the German philosophical tradition. It was the methodology of the secularized theology of German Lutheranism (in the form of Herderian Romanticism and/ or idealism) that sought to explicate the ultimate eschatological questions through natural knowledge. The philosophical elaboration of secularized eschatology culminated in German idealism. Masaryk, indeed, showed an – evidently fluctuating – interest in the metaphysical entity of Herder's Humanity or, for that matter, Comte's kindred concept of collective humanity as the *Grand Être*.[106]

By and large, however, Masaryk would remain within the empirical bounds shared with the Austrian philosophical tradition. His way of overcoming the austerity of Locke's empiricism was to maintain that every cognitive perception was combined with a moral perception. Thus, the construction of a moral universe leading to the conviction of immortal-

---

103 Masaryk, *Pokus o konkrétní logiku,* 22.
104 Masaryk, *Moderní člověk a náboženství,* 117. Later, Masaryk noted that, according to Hume, human beings were from nature provided with an immediate, selfless feeling of sympathy for their neighbor, despite their also natural egotism; Masaryk, *Světová revoluce za války a ve válce, 1914–1918,* 371 [Thomas Masaryk, *Světová revoluce za války a ve válce, 1914–1918* (Prague: Čin, 1933), 552]. See also Novotný, *Korektiv Masarykovy filosofie,* 145–46, 151.
105 Masaryk, *Pokus o konkrétní logiku,* 22.
106 Zdeněk V. David, "Realism and Religion in Masaryk's Political Thought," *Per saecula ad tempora nostra,* sborník prací k šedesátým narozeninám prof. Jaroslava Pánka, ed. Jiří Mikulec and Miloslav Polívka, 2 vols. (Prague: Historický ústav AV ČR, 2007), 2: 657–63. For a further discussion of Masaryk's philosophical relationship to Herder and Comte, see Chapter 5 in this book.

ity and of a personal anthropomorphic deity did not need to indulge in speculative metaphysics. Instead, it remained on the level of mental phenomena without touching on the Kantian noumenal realm. As we have already seen, Masaryk considered Kantian noumena to be the very root of the misguided metaphysical speculation by the German idealists from Fichte onward. In this, he once more stood close to his mentor Brentano.[107] Their view that acts of cognition were properly imbued with an ethical purpose established for both Masaryk and Brentano a bridge to a religious purposefulness that had dispensed with revelation.[108] However, Masaryk eventually would find Brentano too reticent in leavening empirical perceptions with the emotion of faith.

In this, Masaryk also differed from his earliest teacher, Lange, who did insist on the need to go beyond purely cognitive perceptions to deal with the realm of religion, as well as art. Unlike Masaryk, Lange did not consider religion and esthetics to be the product of empirical epistemology, but instead viewed them as results of poetical creativity.[109] Finally, Masaryk's position may appear to resemble, in a way, Kant's approach to immortality and to God through "Practical Reason." However, Masaryk rejected both Kant's metaphysical rationalism[110] and his ontological distinction between theoretical and moral knowledge, or between "Pure" and "Practical" Reason.[111] For Masaryk, in this sense, Brentano prevailed over Kant (including the Neo-Kantians, like Lange) and Comte. However, as it will become evident in the subsequent discussion, Masaryk would advance beyond Brentano's empiricism, and would discover trans-phenomenal reality in the ontic experience of faith (Chapter 3), and ultimately in the ontic experience of love (Chapter 4).

---

107 In the words of Ján Pavlík – Masaryk owed to Brentano a peculiar synthesis of strong empiricism with an ethical transcendence that became a hidden paradigm of Masaryk's total Weltanschauung; see Ján Pavlík, in "Brentano und Masaryks Auffassung seiner Ethik," in *T. G. Masaryk und die Brentano-Schule*, ed. Zumr and Binder, 90.

108 For Brentano, the revival of religious consciousness was an important objective of philosophy, perhaps its highest calling; see Carl Stumpf, "Erinnerungen an Franz Brentano," in Kraus, *Franz Brentano: Zur Kenntnis seines Lebens und seiner Lehre*, 116; also cited by Josef Novák "Masaryk and the Brentano School," in *On Masaryk: Texts in English and German*, Studien zur österreichischen Philosophie, ed. Josef Novák, Bd. 13 (Amsterdam: Rodopi, 1988), 36–37.

109 Religious thinking was a field governed by poetizing. It answered an essential human need and was not illegitimate, yet, it did not yield scientific knowledge, nor was it a substitute for the latter; see Arnulf Zweig, "Friedrich Albert Lange," in *The Encyclopedia of Philosophy*, 2nd ed., ed. Donald M. Borchert, 5: 186–87.

110 On his rejection of "innate ideas," see Čapek, *Hovory s T. G. Masarykem*, 232; Masaryk, *Moderní člověk a náboženství*, 48–50.

111 Masaryk, *Moderní člověk a náboženství*, 55.

Chapter 3

Lutheran Theological Revisionism: The Ontic Value of Faith

Along the lines indicated in the preceding chapter, Masaryk gradually supplemented the empiricism of the Austrian School of Bolzano/Brentano by recourse to the ontic value of faith that would not contradict the ontic character of empirical experience. For him, the ontic force of faith was primarily derived from a feeling of order and purposefulness in the perceived world pointing toward the existence of God.[1] Masaryk saw this faith exemplified in the religion of inner feeling of Paul A. de Lagarde, which was foreshadowed in his youthful study of the writings of Friedrich A. Lange. This solution had a double advantage. First, it did not violate (for Masaryk) the empirical approach; the perceptions of moral impulses were just as much a matter of experience as the perception of physical objects. Second, the religion of inner feelings, which developed within German Lutheranism, was virtually identical with the non-dogmatic moral theology of the Unity of Brethren, which to him was to become the epitome of the Czech contribution to the spiritual advancement of humanity (see Chapter 5).

Masaryk and Lagarde

It is, therefore, illuminating to explore his neglected relationship, both personal and intellectual, with the German philosopher and theologian,

---

1   See Oskar Kraus, "Die Grundzüge der Welt- und Lebensanschauung T. G. Masaryks," *Slavische Rundschau,* vol. 2, no. 3 (1930), 163.

Paul Anton de Lagarde (1827–1891). Lagarde taught at the University of Göttingen from 1869 to 1889, and Masaryk corresponded with him in the 1880s both from Vienna and Prague and remained concerned with his teaching even after Lagarde's death in 1891, until the end of his own life. Masaryk's relationship with Lagarde was complex. What continued to inspire his enthusiasm was Lagarde's view of religion and of its necessary and inherent relationship to politics. What repelled him were Lagarde's ideas about practical politics.

This relationship was not only complex, but also highly paradoxical in view of Masaryk's own reputation for humanitarianism and tolerance – which may explain why scholars have shied away from the topic. Lagarde tended to appeal to radical nationalists in Germany, eventually including the National Socialists, as a result of his avid promotion of the German mission of colonization in the East, and his sharp critique of Jewish influences in Christianity, which he blamed mainly on the Epistle's of St. Paul. Alfred Rosenberg, the chief ideologist of the German National Socialist movement, considered himself Lagarde's disciple.[2] Other prominent Nazi theorists sought to interpret politics and religion in the spirit of Lagarde, and his influence has been traced to Nietzsche's image of St. Paul in the *Antichrist*.[3]

As noted earlier, the key to understanding Lagarde's attractiveness for Masaryk is Masaryk's search for a religious dimension to round out his own weltanschauung. This theological dimension had to harmonize with the empirical realism of his philosophy, which he derived from the

---

2   Concerning Rosenberg's enthusiasm for Lagarde, see Ernst Piper, "Der Orient als Dystopie: Paul de Lagarde und der Mythus der deutschen Nation," in *Der Orient im Okzident: Sichtweisen und Einflussungen*, ed. Irene Diekmann et al. (Potsdam: Verlag für Berlin-Brandenburg , 2003), 174, 176. The linkage of Masaryk with Rosenberg through Lagarde is reminiscent of a recent attempt by Robert B. Pysent to link – through the works of Friedrich L. Jahn – Božena Němcová with Adolf Hitler's *Mein Kampf*; see his "Božena Němcová jahnující: pokus o Babičku," in *Božena Němcová: život, dílo, doba*, ed. Milan Horký and Roman Horký, Sborník příspěvků z konference 7. - 8. září 2005. Česká Skalice: Muzeum Boženy Němcové, 2006, 186–95. See also Jan Randák's review of the Conference in *Český časopis historický* 103 (2005), 980–981. Jahn (1778–1852) in the famous book, *Deutsches Volkstum* (Frankfurt: C. Naumanns,1810), aside from his ideas on education and physical fitness, embraced extreme nationalism, racism, and antisemitism. Due to his popularity after World War I, he was considered a precursor of National Socialism; *Neue deutsche Biographie*, 10: 302.

3   Andreas-Urs Sommer, "Zwischen Agitation, Religionsstiftung und 'Höher Politik': Friedrich Nietzsche und Paul de Lagarde," in *Nietzscheforschung*, Jahrbuch Band 4 (1998), ed. Volker Gerhardt, 169–94. See also Karl D. Bracher, *Die deutsche Diktatur: Entstehung, Struktur, Folgen des Nationalsozialismus*, 6th ed. rev. (Frankfurt/M: Ullstein, 1979), 32–33, 97.

Austrian tradition, represented particularly by Bolzano and Brentano.[4] In his search for the compatible religious complement, he gravitated to German theology, deriving from the Lutheran tradition of theological revisionism. Masaryk rejected the intellectualizing trend leading to German Idealism, and he was drawn, instead, to the other, non-intellectualized approach of the religion of inner feeling and moral practice that stemmed from the Pietist tradition, and stressed the belief in a theistic God and in the immortality of human souls, but without the traditional Christian dogma.[5] Masaryk found this orientation in Lagarde, as well as – to some extent – in Gustav T. Fechner, and it was foreshadowed for him by his first philosophical mentor, Friedrich A. Lange.[6] This intuitive approach to religion, a pure faith (replacing dogmatic theology) led to a sacralization of everyday life.

Rosenberg on Lagarde

To delineate the paradoxical character of Masaryk's interest in Lagarde, it is germane to briefly point out the latter's role in the ideology of German Nazism. Above all, Alfred Rosenberg embraced Lagarde as the spiritual ancestor of National Socialism already in the 1920s while serving as a commentator for the party newspaper, *Völkischer Beobachter*. In September 1927, he wrote: "Among the men, who one day will be named as the prophets of the new world outlook and co-constructors of the folkish state, one will shine especially forth: Paul de la Garde [sic!]."[7] In particular, Rosenberg endorsed Lagarde's 1887 criticism of the spiritual poverty under the Second German Empire, when the German nation thirsted for a new *Weltanschauung* and rejected contemporary religion. As for religion, Rosenberg agreed with Lagarde that it was St. Paul who imposed

---

4   See Chapter 2 in this book.
5   See, for instance, Josef Táborský, *Reformní katolík Josef Dobrovský*, Pontes pragenses, 48 (Brno: L. Marek, 2007), 20.
6   Zdeněk V. David, "Thomas G. Masaryk's Ambivalent View of the Enlightenment and Political Liberalism," *Kosmas: Czechoslovak and Central European Journal*, 19 no. 2 (Spring 2006), 83–85.
7   "Unter den Männern, die einst als Propheten der neuen *Weltanschauung* und Mitbauer des völkischen Staates gennant sein werden, strahlt einer besonders hervor: Paul de la Garde." See Rosenberg, Alfred, "Paul de Lagarde," *Völkischer Beobachter*, September 10, 1927, reprinted in Rosenberg, *Blut und Ehre: Ein Kampf für deutsche Wiedergeburt: Reden und Aufsätze von 1919–1933*, ed. Thilo Trotha, 24th ed. (Munich: Zentralverlag der NSDAP, Franz Eher nachf., 1941), 228.

the Old Testament onto the Church to a virtual exclusion of the Gospels. He approved Lagarde's view that religion was a personal relationship with God; it was unconditionally in the present, having no essential relationship with past events as recorded in Christian mythology.[8] Moreover, religion should favor the national interest, and Rosenberg quoted Lagarde's statement: "[A] German's religion is his fatherland."[9]

Rosenberg continued to highlight Lagarde's pioneering role in his famous *Der Mythus des 20. Jahrhunderts,* originally published in 1930 and, after Hitler's *Mein Kampf,*[10] the most influential text of German National Socialism. Rosenberg included Lagarde among the eight great heroes who exemplified the nobility of German life that was due to the Nordic race; the others included Siegfried, Hercules, Leonardo da Vinci, Copernicus, Meister Eckhart, Frederick the Great, and Bismarck. The virtue of the Nordic race was made evident by Siegfried and Hercules in military matters, by Frederick the Great and Bismarck in political affairs, by Copernicus and Leonardo da Vinci in science, and by Meister Eckhart and Lagarde in religion.[11] Rosenberg paired Eckhart and Lagarde because Lagarde dared to restate Eckhart's claim that the concept of divine grace rendered the ideas of sin and penitence irrelevant. As Eckhart was denounced for his stand by the Roman priesthood in the Middle Ages, so was Lagarde by the Protestant clergy in his own time.[12]

In addition to Rosenberg, other prominent Nazi ideologists sought to reinterpret politics and religion in the spirit of Lagarde. The official Party journal, *Nationalsozialistische Monatshefte,* declared in November 1932 that Lagarde's views, in a somewhat altered form, were "still today alive in Na-

8   Ibid., 229.
9   Alfred Rosenberg, "Stille in Sturm," *Völkischer Beobachter,* December 25, 1929, reprinted Rosenberg, *Blut und Ehre: Ein Kampf für deutsche Wiedergeburt: Reden und Aufsätze von 1919–1933,* ed. Thilo Trotha, 24th ed. (Munich: Zentralverlag der NSDAP, Franz Eher nachf., 1941), 53.
10 Adolf Hitler in *Mein Kampf* (Boston: Houghton and Mifflin, 1971) does not refer to Lagarde, nor for that matter to Hegel or Nietzsche; there are numerous references to Marx and Georg Schönerer, and one to Richard Wagner.
11 Alfred Rosenberg, *Der Mythus des 20. Jahrhunderts. Eine Wertung der seelisch-geistigen Gestaltenkämpfe unserer Zeit,* 5th ed. (Munich: Hoheneichen-Verlag, 1934), 138.
12 Ibid., 237. It is of interest that the Diedrichs publishing house of Jena, which – as shown below – had relations with both Lagarde and Masaryk, had advertised Eckhart's works in its 1908 catalog as works by one who had created the German religion of the most profound inwardness, and also one to accomplish that "without the Jews, without a mediator, without dualism." Stefan Breuer, "Kulturpessimist, Antimodernist, Konservativer Revolutionär?" in Justus H. Ulbricht, and Meike G. Werner, eds., *Romantik, Revolution und Reform: der Eugen Diedrichs Verlag im Epochenkontext, 1900–1949* (Göttingen: Wallstein, 1999), 58.

tional Socialism, even more alive than before."[13] The authoritative bibliography of works for the ideological background of National Socialism, Erich Unger's *Das Schrifttum zum Aufbau des neuen Reiches* (1934), listed nine entries for Lagarde, compared to none for Hegel or Nietzsche, and only one each for Treitschke and Heidegger.[14]

The attractive Lagarde

Masaryk expressed his high opinion of Lagarde's writings just after completing his first book, *Suicide as a Mass Social Phenomenon of Modern Culture* [*Sebevražda hromadným jevem společenským moderní osvěty*], in 1880–1881. In his private notes he wrote about the great joy that he derived from reading Lagarde's *Deutsche Schriften* [German Writings], and regretted that he had not known them before writing his own book.[15] He sent Lagarde a copy of his new book with an extremely cordial note, dated in Vienna on March 14, 1881: "Please accept my monograph on 'Suicide' as a feeble contribution to the noble endeavors to which you have dedicated your head and heart."[16]

In his next book, *Základové konkretné logiky* [*Foundations of Concrete Logic*], published in 1885, Masaryk cited Lagarde's *Deutsche Schriften*, (1878 and 1881), in a list of literature dealing with the relationship between philosophy, on one side, and theology and religion on the other.[17] In his sub-

---

13   Georg Schweinshaupt, "Nationalsozialismus und Lagarde," *Nationalsozialistische Monatshefte* 3 (November 1932), 502–3.

14   Erich Unger, ed., *Das Schrifttum zum Aufbau des neuen Reiches, 1919 - 1. 1. 1934* (Berlin: Junker und Dünnhaupt, 1934). The entries are to Heinrich Treitschke, *Deutsche Geschichte in 19. Jahrhundert*, intro. Alfred Rosenberg (Berlin: Safari, 1933), and to Martin Heidegger, *Die Selbstbehauptung der deutschen Universität*, Rektoratsrede, May 27, 1933 (Breslau: Korn, 1933).

15   "Lagardes deutsche Schriften machen mir eine grosse Freude: Schade dass ich sie früher bevor ich mein Buch geschrieben habe, nicht gekannt habe. Er ist Einer der sehr Wenigen: man scheint ihn todschweigen zu wollen und deshalb wohl kamen mir seine Schriften so spät zu Gesichte." [prior to April 17, 1881]; Prague, Masarykův ústav - Archiv Akademie věd České republiky (MSÚ - A AV ČR), "Aforismy: (1880–1881)," cited by Stanislav Polák, *T.G. Masaryk*, 5 vols. (Prague: Masarykův ústav AV ČR, 2000–2009), 1: 343n73. For his book on suicide, see Tomáš G. Masaryk, *Sebevražda hromadným jevem společenským moderní osvěty*, in Spisy vol. 1 (Prague: Masarykův ústav AV ČR, 2002).

16   "Wien 14. III. 81. Sehr geehrter Herr Professor! Nehmen Sie, ich bitte, meine Monographie über den 'Selbstmord' als schwachen Beitrag zu den edlen Strebungen auf, denen Sie Herz und Kopf geweiht. In aufrichtiger Hochachtung, Th. G. Masaryk." A copy is in Prague, Masarykův ústav - Archiv Akademie věd České republiky (MSÚ - A AV ČR), March 14, 1881, in Korespondence I, 7, 19.

17   Tomáš G. Masaryk, *Základové konkretné logiky: třídění a soustava věd*, in Spisy vol. 2 (Prague: Masarykův ústav AV ČR, 2001), 164.

sequent work, *Pokus o konkrétní logiku* [*Essay on Concrete Logic*], which was originally published in German as *Versuch einer concreten Logik* (1887), the same reference to Lagarde's *Deutsche Schriften* was presented in the same bibliographical list, which, however, this time was intended to reflect the developing antagonism between theology and philosophy since the time of the Renaissance and the Reformation.[18] Masaryk sent a copy of his *Concrete Logic* to Lagarde with an accompanying note, dated in Prague on October 30, 1886, in which he again stressed his "deep-felt need" in some way to express his gratitude for Lagarde's *Deutsche Schriften*.[19]

In any case, Lagarde thanked him in a letter dated November 6, 1886, in which he wrote: "I have become thoroughly familiar with the structure of the book and I have read many parts. One needs to wish for students who can, on the basis of such a guide, gain the first overview of science in its entirety. I wish you to find many people capable of grasping this wholeness; with us, such individuals are scarce."[20] A year later, in a letter of September 19, 1887, Masaryk recommended to Leo Tolstoy to study Lagarde's *Deutsche Schriften*.[21]

The religion of inner feeling

Unable to accept Catholicism, whether traditional or liberal, Masaryk turned to the two modernizing trends in German Lutheranism –with which he had personal experience during his study at the University of Leipzig (1876–1877) – that had jettisoned traditional dogma and liturgy.[22]

---

18   Tomáš G. Masaryk, *Pokus o konkrétní logiku; třídění a soustava věd*, in Spisy vol. 3 (Prague: Ústav T. G. Masaryka, 2001), 205. The German version appeared as *Versuch einer concreten Logik. Classification und Organisation der Wissenschaften* (Vienna: C. Konegen, 1887).

19   "Hochgeehrter Herr Professor, wenn ich mir erlaube Ihnen meine Arbeit über concrete Logik vorzulegen, so thue ich es, Herr Professor, aus innerem Bedürfnis, Ihnen irgendwie für Ihre *Deutsche Schriften* meine Dankbarkeit aussprechen..." A copy of Masaryk's letter is in Prague, Masarykův ústav - Archiv Akademie věd České republiky (MSÚ - A AV ČR), October 30, 1886 in Korespondence I, 7, 101.

20   Jaroslav Opat, *Filozof a politik T. G. Masaryk, 1882–1893* (Prague: Melantrich, 1990), 104.

21   Ibid., 199; Josef Jirásek, "Z korespondence T. G. Masaryka L. N. Tolstému," *Bratislava, Časopis učené společnosti Šafaříkovy*, 6 (1932): 611; Masaryk's letter to Tolstoy was also published in a German translation – and with Lagarde misnamed as "Raul de Lagarde" – in I. Silberstein, "L. N. Tolstoi und T. G. Masaryk: Neues aus den Archiven der Sowjetunion," *Slavische Rundschau* 7 (Berlin, 1935): 148–49.

22   Zdeněk V. David, "Realism and Religion in Masaryk's Political Thought," in *Per saecula ad tempora nostra, contribution to a Festschrift for Jaroslav Pánek*, ed. Jiří Mikulec, Miloslav Polívka, and Pavel Kůrka, 2 vols. (Prague: Historický ústav AV ČR, 2007), 2: 657–59.

He felt, however, that one of these trends – German Idealism (from Kant to Hegel and Hartmann) – had merely transformed theological dogmas into secularized metaphysical concepts and processes. Instead, he gravitated to the other, non-intellectualized approach of the religion of inner feeling, drawing on the Pietist attitude that – while rejecting the traditional Christian dogmas and liturgy – nevertheless affirmed the existence of a theistic God and the immortality of the human soul. He found the latter approach in Paul A. de Lagarde, as he had earlier in Gustav T. Fechner and in Friedrich A. Lange.[23]

Masaryk pointed out what he considered the strength of Lagarde's theological standpoint: "As a professor of the University of Göttingen and a Protestant theologian he wished not only to strengthen German national feeling, but also to purify it on the basis of a renewed evangelical Protestantism."[24] He referred to Lagarde as "an important theologian and reformer,"[25] and considered him one of the strong religious spirits of the time.[26] Moreover, Masaryk pointed out that Lagarde rejected not only Catholicism, but also traditional Protestantism with its emphasis on the need of justification, claiming that neither the Old, nor the New Testament mentions "Messianism."[27]

Lagarde's opposition to traditional Christianity in general, and to Luther's theology in particular became dramatically evident in his disputes with Albrecht Ritschl, a colleague at the University of Göttingen who tried to restore the original teaching of Luther in *Die christliche Lehre von der Rechtfertigung und Versöhnung* (1870–1874). Lagarde categorically objected when Ritschl sought to rehabilitate the Lutheran dogmatic theology within the context of celebrating the 400th anniversary of Luther's birth in 1883.[28] He predicted that the religion of the future would dispense

23 Zdeněk V. David, "Thomas G. Masaryk's Ambivalent View of the Enlightenment and Political Liberalism," *Kosmas: Czechoslovak and Central European Journal*, 19, no. 2 (Spring 2006): 83–85.
24 Tomáš G. Masaryk, *Parlamentní projevy, 1891–1893*, in Spisy, vol. 21 (Prague: Masarykův ústav AV ČR, 2001), 258.
25 Ibid., 265.
26 Tomáš G. Masaryk, "Ze zápisníku čtenářova," *Naše doba* 10 (1902–1903): 708, cited in Roland J. Hoffmann, *T. G. Masaryk und die tschechische Frage*, Veröffentlichungen des Collegium Carolinum, 58 (Munich: Oldenbourg, 1988), 266.
27 Tomáš G. Masaryk, *Národnostní filosofie doby novější*, 2nd ed. (Prague: Melantrich, 1919), 25–26.
28 Robert W. Lougee, *Paul de Lagarde, 1827–1891: A Study of Radical Conservatism in Germany* (Cambridge, Mass.: Harvard University Press, 1962), 92–93; Paul de Lagarde, *Ausgewählte Schriften*, vol. 2 of *Schriften für das deutsche Volk*, ed. Paul Fischer, 2nd ed. (Munich: J. F. Lehmanns Verlag, 1934), 282, 288; Jean Favrat, *Pensée de Paul de Lagarde, 1827–1891: contribution à l'étude des*

with Lutheran theology altogether.[29] In his treatise, *Über die gegenwärtige Lage des deutschen Reiches* (1875), Lagarde described the true religion that expressed itself in ethical striving. This striving arose from a feeling of gratitude to God and to his messengers for the impetus to infuse the physical world with an uplifting moral purpose. Prior to the contact with God's Apostles this drive had existed only in an embryonic form. Acting within this ethical dynamic, one gives of himself with an overflowing heart, while an identification with the everlasting moral purpose frees him from the horror of death.[30]

Detesting Hegel and German Idealism

Masaryk shared common ground with Lagarde in their dim view, if not contempt, for the attempts to modernize Lutheran theology by the German Idealists, which involved Kant and his successors culminating in Hegel and Hartmann. According to Lagarde, Hegel's significance for religion was nil; he had reduced theology to a subordinate part of philosophy.[31] He disagreed with Hegel's concept of God as "the apotheosis of idea," which he considered hopelessly inadequate. Such an abstraction failed to meet Lagarde's Pietistic sense of an inner, emotional participation in God.[32] Together with other critics, Masaryk and Lagarde thought Hegel foolish in assuming that world history culminated politically in the Prussian state of 1830, and intellectually in his own philosophical system.[33]

Masaryk, therefore, saw Lagarde in an entirely different class from that of the German Idealists. In his opinion, the development of German Idealism from Kant and Fichte, which peaked out in Hegel, had eventually led to a full-fledged denial of Christian religion in Eduard von Hartmann.[34]

---

rapports de la religion et de la politique dans le nationalisme et le conservatisme allemands au XIXème siècle. Thesis: Université de Paris IV. (Lille: Atelier Reproduction des thèses, Université de Lille III; Paris: H. Champion, 1979), 90–91. The work appeared as Albrecht Ritschl, *Die christliche Lehre von der Rechtfertigung und Versöhnung,* 3 vols. (Bonn: A. Marcus, 1870–1874).

29 Favrat, *Pensée de Paul de Lagarde,* 229, 231.

30 Paul de Lagarde, *Deutsche Schriften,* Gesammtausgabe letzter Hand, 5th ed. (Göttingen: Dieterich'sche Universitäts-Buchhandlung, 1920), 144.

31 Lagarde, *Ausgewählte Schriften,* 69.

32 Lougee, *Paul de Lagarde,* 132.

33 Lagarde, "Über die gegenwärtige Lage," *Deutsche Schriften,* 173 ; idem "Über die Klage," *Deutsche Schriften,* 405–6, See also Lougee, *Paul de Lagarde,* 121.

34 Masaryk, *Národnostní filosofie doby novější,* 24–5; originally published in 1904 (page numbers based on the 1919 second edition).

Kant, Fichte, Hegel, and Hartmann had substituted abstract concepts (Absolute, Will, Unconscious) for God.[35] Lagarde, in contrast, wished not only to strengthen German national feeling, but – as a Protestant theologian – he also sought to purify German nationalism on the basis of a renewed evangelical Protestantism, retaining belief in a personal God and in an inherently religious purpose of human life.[36]

Lagarde also denounced what he considered Hegel's baneful influence on government, education, and religion in Prussia. He decried the divinization of the state by Hegel. The state was not "the divine" on the earth, but a changing institution according to particular needs, and it was designed to fulfill certain mundane functions; it was not an end in itself. Lagarde characterized Hegel's standpoint in the following way: "Hegel and [those who] followed him saw in the state (I must not alter the bombastic phrases) the reality of the moral idea, the divine will at present, unfolding itself to a true form and organization of the world, the spirit realizing itself in consciousness through the world..."[37] For Lagarde, on the contrary, the state had a subservient and impermanent character: religion, the arts, and sciences stood above it.[38]

The denunciation of St. Paul

As for the most conspicuous aspect of their agreement in theology, Masaryk shared with Lagarde a negative view of St. Paul's Epistles. Masaryk pointed out that Lagarde saw in the doctrines of St. Paul the roots of the dogmatism and ritualism of traditional Protestantism that he had decried.[39] Lagarde, therefore, transferred his negative view of St. Paul to Luther as well.[40] Luther's Reformation, by placing at its center an essentially Pauline theology – the doctrine of justification by faith alone – represented a further step in the process of Judaization. It made the notion of sacrifice (by Christ) crucial to human history.[41]

---

35 Masaryk, *Základové konkretné logiky*, 168; idem, *Pokus o konkrétní logiku*, 221.
36 Masaryk, *Parlamentní projevy, 1891–1893*, 258.
37 Lagarde, *Deutsche Schriften*, 355. See also Favrat, *Pensée de Paul de Lagarde*, 288.
38 Lagarde, *Deutsche Schriften*, 353.
39 Tomáš G. Masaryk, *Válka a revoluce: články, memoranda, přednášky, rozhovory, 1914–1916*, in Spisy, vol. 30 (Prague: Masarykův ústav AV ČR, 2005), 247.
40 Lougee, *Paul de Lagarde*, 41.
41 Favrat, *Pensée de Paul de Lagarde*, 216.

Stressing the distinction between St. Paul's Epistles and the Jesus of
the Gospels, Masaryk maintained that Christ's teaching was free of any
formalism or ritualism. It embodied a noble theism, connected with a belief in immortality and a moral teaching of love. The life of Jesus offered
a perfect application of his own teaching – not a dry and abstract one,
but a living teaching.[42] In contrast to the cheery Christ, St. Paul posited
a gloomy opposition between morality and nature.[43] Masaryk illustrated
this dichotomy between the humane Jesus and the ascetic Paul by their
respective attitudes toward divorce, which Jesus was willing to permit,
while Paul was adamantly opposed. Masaryk concluded that it was Paul
who set the tone for the subsequent institutional Christianity.[44] Masaryk
objected to Paul's teaching not only on the grounds of theology and ecclesiology, but also of political theory. St. Paul bluntly advocated a dominion
of priests and kings over the people. In the Epistle to the Romans he expounded unambiguously the doctrine of the divine rights of kings, declaring that all the powers that be were ordained by God. "Wherefore ye must
needs be subject, not only for wrath, but also for conscience sake" (13:5).
He declared again: "Whosoever therefore resisteth the power, resisteth the
ordinance of God: and they that resist shall receive to themselves dam-
nation" (13:2). Paul wrote as a Jew, accustomed to the form of Jewish theocracy, but at the same time he advocated elements from Rome's imperial rule. No wonder then, according to Masaryk, that – in view of Pauline
emphasis on submissiveness – Nietzsche and other modern thinkers regarded Christianity as a religion of slaves.[45] During World War I, Masaryk
claimed that the state power in the Habsburg monarchy had rested on St.
Paul's commandment of obedience to established authorities, and that the
Church propagated his principle of state authority based on divine grace.[46]

---

42 Masaryk, *Sebevražda hromadným jevem*, 132–33.
43 Tomáš G. Masaryk, *Moderní člověk a náboženství*, in Spisy, vol. 8 (Prague: Masarykův ústav AV
    ČR, 2000) [originally published 1896–1898], 89.
44 Alain Soubigou, *Thomas Masaryk* (Paris: Fayard, 2002), 156, 159; Tomáš Masaryk, "Žena u Ježíše
    a u Pavla," in *Masarykův sborník*, 2 (1926–1927), 233–41. On Masaryk's approval of divorce, see
    Masaryk, *Otázka sociální. Základy marxismu filosofické a sociologické*, 2 vols. in Spisy vol. 9–10
    (Prague: Masarykův ústav AV ČR, 2000), 2: 64.
45 Thomas G. Masaryk, *The Spirit of Russia: Studies in History, Literature, and Philosophy*, trans. by
    Eden and Cedar Paul, and W. R. and Z. Lee. 2d ed,. 3 vols.(London: Allen & Unwin, 1961–67),
    2: 498–99. Masaryk notes St. Paul's dictum that political power comes from God also in ibid.,
    1: 355.
46 Tomáš G. Masaryk, *Světová revoluce za války a ve válce, 1914–1918* in Spisy vol. 15 (Prague:
    Masarykův ústav, 2005), 374.

Like Masaryk's, Lagarde's criticism of St. Paul was based on an alleged contrast between the Old Testament and the teaching of Jesus. His critical view of St. Paul was part of his negative attitude toward what he considered a "vulgar legalism" of the Old Testament. Paul propounded the messianic interpretation of Jesus, and to this he added the doctrine of the justification by faith, both of which he had foisted on Luther.[47] Having no association with Jesus and little with any of the Apostles, Paul proceeded to construct Christian theology from Judaic elements. He brought into Christian religion the old Jewish beliefs: the concept of sin, sacrifice of the mass for the purposes of atonement, a legalist insistence on literal interpretation, and an unfeeling dogmatism. St. Paul focused the new religion on Christ's sacrifice instead of his message. Above all, the point of view was shifted from the freshness of experience and the immediacy of the divine to a historical occurrence. Contemplation of a past event became merely a sentimentality and obscured the power of immanent life.[48] Lagarde wrote in his treatise, *Über das Verhältnis des deutschen Staates zu Theologie, Kirche und Religion* (1873): "Paul has brought the Old Testament into the Church; under his influence the Gospel was – as far as possible – suppressed: Paul has blessed us with a Pharisaic exegesis, which proves everything from everything, it brings along (in its pocket) a beforehand defined content of what should be found in the text, and it takes pride in following only the Word; Paul has brought the Jewish theory of sacrifice, and everything that depends on it, into our house."[49]

As far as the New Testament was concerned, Lagarde argued that justification by faith alone, highlighting Christ's redemptive sacrifice, was advanced only by Paul; it was absent in the Gospels, in the Epistles of Peter and John, and it was rejected by the Epistle of James. It could not have been a belief current in primitive Christianity.[50] More specifically, Lagarde contrasted St. Paul's teaching that introduced Jewish elements into Christianity (particularly the notions of messianism and of "a new covenant") with the Gospel of St. John, which was supposedly allergic to the

---

47 Lougee, *Paul de Lagarde*, 41; Wolfgang Wiefel, "Zur Würdigung William Wredes," *Zeitschrift für Religions- und Geistesgeschichte*, 23 (1971): 69–72.
48 Lougee, *Paul de Lagarde*, 153–4, citing Lagarde, "Über das Verhältnis des deutschen Staates zu Theologie, Kirche und Religion," in Lagarde, *Deutsche Schriften*, 63–64.
49 Lagarde, *Deutsche Schriften*, 62.
50 Ibid., 48–49. See also Favrat, *Pensée de Paul de Lagarde*, 220.

presence of any Jewish elements in Christianity.[51] Lagarde declared categorically: "Whatever Paul said about Jesus and the Gospel had no claim to truthfulness."[52]

The religious foundation of politics

Masaryk highly appreciated Lagarde's insistence on the infusion of the non-dogmatic religion into politics, with religion manifest in the form of an ethical guidance.[53] According to Lagarde, political life had to rest on the foundation of a new religiosity, independent of traditional church organizations. A direct sense of Providential presence was to imbue political and social life with a moral purpose and a search for truth. Likewise, the definition of a nation's interest or the national idea should fit into this religious parameter.[54]

Masaryk repeatedly praised Lagarde's combination of politics and religion. He declared in the Austrian *Reichsrat* – the Imperial Parliament – on November 18, 1892: "As a professor of the University of Göttingen and a Protestant theologian [Lagarde] wished not only to strengthen German national feeling, but also to purify it on the basis of a renewed evangelical Protestantism."[55] In his lectures, *Moderní člověk a náboženství* [*The Modern Man and Religion*] (1896–1898) Masaryk claimed that Lagarde demonstrated the need for a religious inspiration in national politics, even in such a great nation as that of the Germans.[56] In an article of 1903, he placed Lagarde among the strong religious spirits that could provide a role model.[57] In his treatise, *Národnostní filosofie doby novější* [*The Philosophy of Nationality in Recent Times*] (1904), Masaryk credited Lagarde once more with

---

51   Lagarde, *Deutsche Schriften*, 58–59. See also Favrat, *Pensée de Paul de Lagarde*, 194. Ultimately, however, not only the other Apostles, but also John had not understood Jesus; Lagarde, *Deutsche Schriften*, 60; and Jesus was "clearly unlucky" in the choice of the Evangelists; ibid., 59.
52   Lagarde, *Deutsche Schriften*, 61.
53   Tomáš G. Masaryk, *Cesta demokracie: projevy, články, rozhovory IV, 1929–1937*, in Spisy vol. 36 (Prague: Masarykův ústav AV ČR, 1997), 101, 109. See also Jaroslav Opat, *Průvodce životem a dílem T. G. Masaryka: česká otázka včera a dnes* (Prague: Masarykův ústav AV ČR, 2003), 134–35, 444.
54   Lougee, *Paul de Lagarde*, 212; "Lagarde," *Allgemeine Deutsche Biographie*. 2nd ed. 56 vols. (Berlin: Duncker und Humblot, 1968), 51: 536.
55   Masaryk, *Parlamentní projevy, 1891–1893*, 258.
56   Masaryk, *Moderní člověk a náboženství*, 37.
57   Masaryk, "Ze zápisníku čtenářova," 708; also in Tomáš G. Masaryk, *Česká otázka. Naše nynější krize. Jan Hus*, in Spisy vol. 6 (Prague: Masarykův ústav, 2000), 431.

seeking to ground the national idea in a religious idea and with a conviction that neither an individual nor a nation could exist without a religion.[58] Finally, Masaryk included Lagarde on the honor roll of those who also grounded German nationalism in philosophy.[59]

With his insistence on the religious basis for politics, Masaryk shared Lagarde's conviction about the defects of the typical nineteenth-century liberalism. Since according to Lagarde the "national idea" had to be defined in religious terms, Lagarde deprecated political liberalism as lacking the necessary spiritual and moral depth. He further equated the liberals and the Jews in their alleged contempt for genuine culture and their penchant to live by doctrinal abstractions. The liberals' mentality interfered with the need of the Germans to live according to distinctly national ideals in order to realize their *Deutschtum* [German-ness].[60] In his view, humanitarian sentimentalism that often served as a distinguishing mark of the liberals did not derive from a truly religious inspiration. It had nothing to do with the Gospels or with Christianity.[61]

While not blaming the Jews, as Lagarde did, Masaryk often voiced in his philosophical and political writings a jaundiced view of the French-style liberalism. Although a liberal himself, Masaryk rejected the antireligious liberalism springing from the French Enlightenment, which focused solely on secular experience and, therefore, was inherently disposed to ignore the religious and ethical meaning of life and culture.[62] Consequently, according to Masaryk, the cultural and social policy of such liberalism was deficient in philosophical depth, and its adherents could not avail themselves of a religious, or even an ethical, guidance for their political conduct.[63] Specifically in Bohemia, the Voltairean version of the Enlightenment turned into the Young Czechs' liberalism, which became indifferent to the questions of religion, philosophy, and morality.[64]

Masaryk could also be impressed by Lagarde's apparent – albeit rather ambiguous – respect for what he himself proposed as the proper reli-

---

58　Masaryk, *Národnostní filosofie doby novější*, 25–26.

59　Polák, *T.G. Masaryk*, 4: 510 n60.

60　Lagarde, *Deutsche Schriften*, 339–43. See also Lougee, *Paul de Lagarde*, 212.

61　Lagarde, *Deutsche Schriften*, 144. See also Favrat, *Pensée de Paul de Lagarde*, 257.

62　Masaryk, *Česká otázka*, 315; on the anti-religious tenor of German nineteenth-century liberalism see also Masaryk, *Otázka sociální*, 2: 121.

63　Masaryk, *Česká otázka*, 316–17.

64　Ibid., 178. See also Felix Vodička, *Cesty a cíle obrozenské literatury* (Prague: Československý spisovatel, 1958), 142–44.

gious mainsprings for Czech national politics: the teaching of the Unity of Brethren and the philosophy of Johann G. Herder. In contrast to the secularism of the Voltairean Enlightenment, Masaryk recognized in the ideas of the Unity of Brethren another strand in the Enlightenment which was beneficent and rested solidly on a religious foundation. The Brethren represented, in his view, an eighteenth-century extension of the sound and authentic spirit of the Bohemian Reformation which moreover was not parochial, but cosmopolitan.[65] Masaryk traced the religious and philosophical effervescence from the Bohemian Reformation to this positive Enlightenment mainly to Jan Komenský [John Comenius] (1592–1670), the exiled bishop of the Unity.[66] The intellectual transmission continued through the German Protestant philosophers Gottfried W. Leibniz and Johann G. Herder, who were both deeply influenced by Komenský's writings. To Masaryk, Komenský's impact on Herder was particularly strong and Herder, in turn, affected Josef Dobrovský and Jan Kollár, the leading figures in the early phases of the National Awakening in Bohemia.[67]

Lagarde sympathized with the Unity of Brethren for its cultivation of a personal Pietist-like relationship with God, and of an internalized morality, as opposed to the dogmatism and ritualism of the Utraquist Church (the mainstream in the Bohemian Reformation). He attributed to their exile community in Berlin an influence on Friedrich Schleiermacher, whose concept of religion – in contrast to that of Hegel – he greatly admired.[68] As for Herder, Lagarde shared Herder's belief in a close bond between religion and nationality.[69] Lagarde agreed with Herder that the nation, like man, had a soul as befitted a spiritual being.[70]

The Diederichs connection

A circumstantial link to Lagarde was also Masaryk's personal and professional involvement with the book publisher in Jena, Eugene Diederichs (1867–1930). The latter focused his book production, as well as the contents of the house journal, *Die Tat*, on the role of philosophical and religious

---

65   Masaryk, *Česká otázka*, 15, 347; Masaryk, *V boji o náboženství*, 38.
66   Masaryk, *V boji o náboženství*, 30.
67   Masaryk, *Světová revoluce za války a ve válce*, 391, 396, 399.
68   Lagarde, *Ausgewählte Schriften*, 70.
69   Klamroth, *Staat und Nation bei Paul de Lagarde*, 57; Favrat, *Pensée de Paul de Lagarde*, 300.
70   Lougee, *Paul de Lagarde*, 130, referring to Lagarde, "Über die Klage," *Deutsche Schriften*, 407.

ideas in politics. In that regard, he paid close attention to the teaching of Lagarde. At the same time, Diederichs published in 1912 the German original of Masaryk's major work on Russian philosophy and religion, *Russland und Europa* (later published in English as *The Spirit of Russia*).[71] Diederichs' interest in Lagarde's work extended deep into the twentieth century. In 1911, Diederichs had adopted a quote from Lagarde, "When the winds would want to blow" [*Wenn die Winde wehen wollten*], as a motto of his publishing house.[72] The issue of *Die Tat* of April 1913 was dedicated to Lagarde, his thought and influence.[73]

The celebration of Lagarde by Diederichs continued after World War I. In the mid-1920s, his publishing house arranged for an idealized bust of Lagarde by Felix Pfeifer to be placed in the *Deutsche Bücherei* in Leipzig.[74] In a speech on March 21, 1929, Diederichs referred to Lagarde as his most valued mentor.[75] It has been widely assumed that in the 1920s the publishing house and the group around its journal, the *Tatkreis*, helped ideologically pave the way for National Socialism's rise in Germany.[76] In any case, Masaryk remained on friendly terms with Diederichs even after World War I, as their exchange of postcards indicates.[77]

The repugnant Lagarde

The rights of small nations

Despite their areas of agreement, Masaryk, of course, could not overlook the glaringly repugnant features of Lagarde's Weltanschauung, particularly his intolerant German chauvinism and rabid anti-Semitism. He in

71 Hans Lemberg, "Masaryk and the Russian Question against the Background of German and Czech Attitudes to Russia," in *T. G. Masaryk, 1850–1937*, Stanley Winters et al., eds., 3 vols. (London: Macmillan, 1989–1990), 1: 288. Diedrichs established his publishing house in Florence in 1896, transferring it to Leipzig in 1897, and finally to Jena in 1904. See Justus H. Ulbricht and Meike G. Werner, eds., *Romantik, Revolution und Reform: der Eugen Diedrichs Verlag im Epochenkontext, 1900–1949* (Göttingen: Wallstein, 1999), 12.
72 Imgard Heidler, *Der Verleger Eugen Diederichs und seine Welt, 1896–1930* (Wiesbaden: Harrassowitz, 1998), 378.
73 Ibid.
74 Ibid., 381.
75 Ulbricht and Werner, eds., *Romantik, Revolution und Reform*, 7.
76 *Meyers Enzyklopädische Lexikon* (1978), 23: 244.
77 Heidler, *Der Verleger Eugen Diederichs und seine Welt*, 387.

fact reacted quite forcefully. Lagarde voiced an undisguised contempt for the non-German nationalities of East Central Europe, which eventually covered the Czechs as well. He thought that the nations of the Austrian monarchy, except the South Slavs, should be absorbed into the German nation: "The peoples of the Empire with the exception of the Germans and the South Slavs are politically worthless. At best they are the material for a new Germanic edifice."[78] In the Habsburg monarchy it was a waste to learn Magyar, Ruthenian, Polish, Czech, Slovene, Serbian, and Romanian, because such efforts sapped the individual's energy for doing something more substantial.[79] Furthermore, Lagarde asserted that Germanization would be of great material and moral benefit to the nationalities themselves, writing: "To rebuild village after village on German lines...would be to show the Magyars, Czechs, Ruthenians, Moravians [*Hannaken*] and Slovaks who the better men are, and who, therefore, ought to rule."[80]

As for Germany proper – Lagarde pointed out – there were large numbers of Poles, as well as Casubians. While they made good soldiers, their presence "in our [German] midst" absolutely could not be tolerated: "The Germanization of the strips of land, inhabited by them, is from every point of view a necessity."[81] The Croats (as well as the Serbs) were the only nationalities of the Habsburg Empire who might have a chance to form an independent state, provided that Turkey was pushed out of Europe and the South Slav state could spread from the Mediterranean to the Black Sea, thus securing a sufficient territorial base for its existence.[82] As for the Czechs, he had lost his early enthusiasm for the Bohemian Reformation, and became highly skeptical about the emergence of Czech statehood. Later he wrote derisively about the possibility of a restored "Wenzelland" [Land of St. Wenceslaus].[83] Further, Lagarde concluded that, while all the Slavs hated Germans, the Czechs hated them the most, citing as evidence of this hatred the forged manuscript of Dvůr Králové, by which, according to him, the Czechs sought to "ennoble" their nationality.[84]

---

78   Lagarde, *Deutsche Schriften*, 121; see also Lougee, *Paul de Lagarde*, 188.
79   Lagarde, *Deutsche Schriften*, 121.
80   Ibid., 122.
81   Ibid., 118.
82   Ibid., 27, 121.
83   Ibid., 28, 121; see also Lougee, *Paul de Lagarde*, 188.
84   Lagarde, *Deutsche Schriften*, 428; see also Favrat, *Pensée de Paul de Lagarde*, 376.

Masaryk, of course, could not remain indifferent to Lagarde's opinions concerning the smaller nations of East Central Europe, and especially the Czechs. He called attention to this issue already in his university lectures, "Practical Philosophy on the Basis of Sociology," in 1885.[85] A year later, thanking Lagarde for a copy of the *Deutsche Schriften* in his letter of October 30, he added: "At a later time I shall deal with them [i.e., the *Deutsche Schriften*] more specifically, that is, correct some of your political judgments, for example, of the Czechs, because I do not believe that you wrote with detachment on this point. Of course this in no way impairs my sincere esteem for you."[86] Lagarde replied in a letter, dated November 6, 1886, in which he also reacted to Masaryk's reservations about the political judgments in the *Deutsche Schriften*. After praising Masaryk's *Základové konkretné logiky* [*Foundations of Concrete Logic*], which Masaryk had just sent him, he continued: "The Czechs have the same right to exist like any other nation, however, not against us, but alongside us; and as long as Germany is not certain that the Czechs do not serve Russian masters, and that the Poles are not subservient to the Jesuits, we shall be enemies of the Czechs and the Poles... In any case with Masaryk [i.e. you], it is certainly possible to come to an agreement in all these problems."[87]

After Lagarde's death, Masaryk referred to his correspondence with him in a debate on the nationality issues in the *Reichsrat* on November 22, 1892.[88] He called Lagarde an "important, independent and original thinker," whom he had avidly studied, and later tried to induce to modify his views vis-a-vis the Czechs and other nations of the Austrian Empire. Masaryk then quoted Lagarde's letter of November 1886 to show that a reasonable discussion was possible with a German opponent concerning the Austrian and hence also the Czech problem.[89] Nevertheless, in 1890, Masaryk caustically referred to Lagarde's "remarkable" [*znamenitý*] political writings as assuming an extermination of "us Czechs and the Austrian

85 Tomáš G. Masaryk, *Praktická filosofie na základě sociologie: Litografovaná příručka k přednáškám* (Prague, [1885]), 412. [Copy in the National Library of the Czech Republic, call no. NUK: 54 D 7938]
86 A copy of Masaryk's letter is in Prague, Masarykův ústav - Archiv Akademie věd České republiky (MSÚ - A AV ČR), October 30, 1886, in Korespondence I, 7, 101.
87 The letter of Lagarde, dated November 6, 1886 is cited by Hoffmann, *T. G. Masaryk und die tschechische Frage*, 55n61from: Niedersächsische Staats- und Universitätsbibliothek, Göttingen, manuscript division, Abschrift an Profesor Masaryk, Prag.
88 Of which he was a member 1890–1893, and again 1907–1914.
89 Masaryk, *Parlamentní projevy, 1891–1893*, 257, 269–70. See also Emil Ludwig, *Defender of Democracy: Masaryk of Czechoslovakia* (New York: R. M. McBride, 1936), 197.

Slavs."[90] As an extenuating circumstance, Masaryk, however, later (in 1898) pointed out that skepticism about the viability of small Central European nations was a malady which endemically afflicted German intellectuals over a wide spectrum of ideologies. Thus, according to Masaryk, Lagarde followed Marx in his attitude toward denationalization of the Slavs, and was himself followed by Theodor Mommsen.[91]

Pan-Germanism

Since the 1890s, and especially after the outbreak of the World War in 1914, Masaryk became increasingly critical of what he eventually called Lagarde's Pan-Germanism. At the same time, however, he continued to stress his high regard for Lagarde as a theologian. He summed up his view in the study, *Národnostní filosofie doby* (1904), when he wrote: "In the teaching of Lagarde, there is a strange mixture of Teutonic brutality and noble religious ideas."[92] His sense of contrast between benign theology and rabid nationalism was not new in this period, although it seemed to intensify as time went on. Masaryk's divided opinion about Lagarde's teaching originated in the first encounter with the *Deutsche Schriften*. In his personal private notes, he had written as early as ca. 1880: "Lagarde's *Schriften* contain much that is atrocious [*viel Ungeheuerliches*] about the nationalities and kindred subjects... how can one be so wrong despite a great moral power."[93]

Masaryk began to associate Lagarde with what he considered a sinister general plan of Germanization in Central Europe already during the major debate on the nationality issue in the *Reichsrat* on November 18, 19 and 22, 1892. On November 18, he cited from the early parts of Lagarde's *Deutsche Schriften*, particularly from the drastic "Über die gegenwärtige Lage des deutschen Reiches" (1875). In his speech, Masaryk pointed out that Lagarde referred to Bohemia pejoratively as "Wenzelsland." He stressed that

---

90 Masaryk, "Člověk a příroda," in his *Slovanské studie a texty z let 1889–1891*, in Spisy vol. 20 (Prague: Masarykův ústav AV ČR, 2007), 264.

91 Masaryk, *Otázka sociální*, 2: 112 n8.

92 Masaryk, *Národnostní filosofie doby novější*, 26. Other commentators have similarly separated Lagarde's ideas on theology and education from his "antisemitism, imperialism, and aggressive nationalism." See Heidler, *Der Verleger Eugen Diederichs*, 379.

93 "Lagardes Schriften enthalten viel Ungeheuerliches: über Nationalitäten und Ähnl. Hat er keine gesunden Ideen: wie man bei grosser moralischer Kraft ungerecht sein kann." Prague, Masarykův ústav - Archiv Akademie věd České republiky (MSÚ -- A AV ČR), Aforismy: (1880–1881), f. 10, cited by Polák, *T.G. Masaryk*, 1: 343 n73.

Lagarde was willing to make an exception for the South Slavs, and thus help to secure Trieste as a gateway of German expansion through the Adriatic and into Africa.[94] On November 19, Masaryk identified Lagarde as part of a powerful German nationalist current, which included Franz Löher, Karl Walcker, Eduard Hartmann and "last but not least" (he said in English), the Iron Chancellor, Bismarck.[95]

In his *Otázka sociální* (1898), Masaryk outlined the genealogy of radical German nationalism. Referring to Fichte with his idea of a nationalist education, then to Hegel "with an apotheosis of the Teutonic-Germanic culture and the Teutonic-Germanic spirit," Masaryk significantly added: "I have to name here especially Lagarde...."[96] In his *Národnostní filosofie doby novější* (1904), Masaryk depicted Lagarde's teaching as the culmination of the German apotheosis. Lagarde was not a mere shallow agitator, like the Austrian advocate of Pan-Germanism, Georg Schönerer, but he provided a solid ideological infrastructure for German nationalism, as evident from his *Deutsche Schriften*. He wished to create a Great Germany and a Great Austria, with the latter serving as a territorial reserve for Germany. The Czechs, Poles, and Magyars were to Lagarde just raw material for augmenting the German nation.[97] *In The Spirit of Russia* (1913), returning to the genealogy of radical nationalism that started with Herder and Fichte, Masaryk continued: "but in this connection we must also think of Hegel, of Schopenhauer and his pupil Hartmann, of Lagarde, Richard Wagner, and [Joseph A. de] Gobineau."[98]

Objections to Pan-Germanism, and hence also to the political ideas of Lagarde's legacy, escalated in Masaryk's statements during World War I. In the confidential memorandum "Independent Bohemia," which Masaryk prepared for the British Foreign Office in late April 1915, he portrayed Lagarde as the father of modern Pan-Germanism. He had formulated a program for colonization of Austria by Germany and had also broached the German claims for acquisition of the port of Trieste.[99] Masaryk continued to depict Lagarde, as one of the key progenitor of aggressive German expansionism in his inaugural lecture at the University of London on Oc-

94 Masaryk, *Parlamentní projevy, 1891–1893*, 257–58. See also Polák, *T.G. Masaryk*, 2: 283.
95 Masaryk, *Parlamentní projevy, 1891–1893*, 265.
96 Masaryk, *Otázka sociální*, 2: 103.
97 Masaryk, *Národnostní filosofie doby novější*, 25–26.
98 Masaryk, *The Spirit of Russia*, 1: 281.
99 Masaryk, *Válka a revoluce: články, memoranda, přednášky, rozhovory, 1914–1916*, 62–63.

tober 19, 1915[100] and in the "Declaration of the Czech Committee Abroad," issued in Paris on November 14, 1915.[101] The same is true of the "Memorandum on the Military Situation," which Masaryk prepared for his British supporters in January 1916.[102]

Masaryk's harsh attitude toward Lagarde's political objectives, continued even after World War I. In his statement after he returned to Prague on December 23, 1918, he stressed that the war's outcome foiled "the barbaric exhortations of the Mommsens, Hartmanns and Lagardes."[103] In his war memoirs, *Světová revoluce za války a ve válce* [*The World Revolution During and In the War*] (1925) seeking the roots of radical nationalism in German history, Masaryk maintained that Lagarde and his adherents continued in the footsteps of Hegel, who had preached the infallibility of the state, and glorified the idea of war and militarism. Masaryk added that Lagarde's view of German superiority was also evident in Marx, who judged the Slav nations inferior the same way as Lagarde or Treitschke.[104]

Masaryk lived long enough to pronounce a judgment on Lagarde's relationship to German National Socialism after Adolf Hitler's assumption of power. Asked for his opinions about racism in the fall of 1933 Masaryk, still president of Czechoslovakia, pointed out that for a long time before World War I, he had been interested in the Pan-German ideas, a movement which then was merely theoretical; during the war he had written articles about it in *New Europe*. Now this set of ideas was called National Socialism or racism, and became practical politics, but the views of Lagarde, Schönerer, and others, still provided its intellectual foundation. The pure races that the Nazi propagandists posited as a criterion of nationality did not exist in Europe.[105]

---

100 Ibid., 123.
101 Ibid., 138.
102 Ibid., 169–71.
103 "Poselství prezidenta republiky," *Pražské noviny*, December 23, 1918, in Tomáš G. Masaryk, *Cesta demokracie: projevy, články, rozhovory I, 1918–1920*, in Spisy vol. 33 (Prague: Masarykův ústav AV ČR, 2003), 25.
104 Masaryk, *Světová revoluce za války a ve válce*, 280, 282. The passages dealing with the history of German thought were omitted from the English translation of the war memoirs, which appeared as Masaryk, *The Making of a State: Memories and Observations, 1914–1918*, ed. Henry W. Steed (New York: George Allen and Unwin, 1927). See also Zwi Batscha, *Eine Philosophie der Demokratie: Thomas G. Masaryks Begründung einer neuzeitlichen Demokratie* (Frankfurt: Surkamp, 1994), 31, 65.
105 "Masaryk o demokracii a diktatuře," *Právo lidu*, October 1, 1933; *Národní politika*, September 30, 1933, in Masaryk, *Cesta demokracie: projevy, články, rozhovory IV, 1929–1937*, 374–75.

Anti-Semitism

Lagarde's anti-Semitism highlights the paradoxical character of Masaryk's linkage with him. He believed not only that Jews could never assimilate to the host nation, but also that they constituted an outright detrimental element that, at the very least, should be severely restricted, if not barred, from positions in high finance, the government, and the universities. As we shall see, he would even admit the possibility of ritual murders by the Jews. He was among those who early (in 1885) proposed a resettlement of European Jews on Madagascar.[106] Likewise, he decried the emancipation of the Jews in Germany and connected political liberalism (for which he felt a deep distaste) with Jewish influences.

Lagarde's anti-Semitism related to his Kulturkritik; he regarded the Jews as a part of the cause and manifestation of the cultural decay of current Germany. His attack focused on Jewish culture within the German context and charged that it was not faithful to the ancient Hebrew heritage. Since the Jews had become bearers of liberalism (in his definition of the term), they represented a corrupting element standing in the way of Germany's national rebirth.[107] His feelings about the Jews mounted and crescendoed in the 1880s, with the opening salvo coming in his treatise *Stellung der Religionsgesellschaften im Staate* (1881). In every European state, the Jews remained strangers and bearers of corruption and decay; it was therefore impossible to fuse Jewish and German culture. Lagarde observed that the Jews were kept apart from the rest of society by several factors. First, there was their observance of laws that had already been outmoded in the time of Jesus. Second, they regarded with horror the Middle Ages, which gave birth to German civilization. Third, like the Jesuits and the Free Masons, they reached out to their confreres abroad and thus disdained the national boundaries.[108] Moreover, in the treatise *Die graue Internationale* (1881), Lagarde equated the liberals and the Jews in their common contempt for genuine culture and their willingness to live by doctrinal abstractions.[109]

---

106 Magnus Brechtken, 'Madagaskar für die Juden': Antisemitische Idee und politische Praxis, 1885–1945 (Munich: Oldenbourg, 1997), 17–18, 32, 285.
107 Lougee, Paul de Lagarde, 210–11.
108 Lagarde, Deutsche Schriften, 276–80, especially 278.
109 Ibid., 344–49.

In the late 1880s, Lagarde accused the Jews of hindering Germany's union with Austria and her expansion to the East because they feared that the country would become economically independent and thus no longer forced to rely on Jewish finance. Emancipation of the Jews in 1830 was an enormous mistake because it deprived the Jews of an incentive to give up their Jewishness. With a glaring inconsistency, Lagarde maintained that prior to the Emancipation large numbers of them had "turned German in religion, in customs, and in national feeling."[110] In Lagarde's correspondence, cited from the archives by Lougee, it appears that he opposed – in writing to the relevant government ministers – the appointment of Jews to professorships at the University of Göttingen in 1888. More shockingly, he lent credence to the alleged Jewish practice of ritual murders. In an 1889 letter to the Minister of Justice, he wrote about the 1882 murder of a Christian girl in Tiszaeszlár, Hungary, accusing the Austro-Hungarian authorities of not prosecuting the case vigorously because they were intimidated by Jewish financiers like the Rothschilds. As for ritual murder as such, while admitting that there was no basis in Jewish law for that crime, he argued that superstitious Jews sometimes used blood in their rituals despite the lack of a Talmudic prescription.[111] In the end, Lagarde recognized neither the right of the Jews to a separate existence, nor the right to integrate into the German national community.[112]

Masaryk's attitude toward the Jews was diametrically opposed to Legarde's. It resembled Lagarde's only to the extent that he considered the Jews a distinct nation and their integration into another national milieu problematic. Hence, he was sympathetic to Zionism.[113] Unlike Lagarde, however, Masaryk did not maintain that the presence of the Jews had a detrimental effect on the society in which they lived. In particular, he did not blame them for nineteenth-century liberalism. By 1898, he advocated Zionism not necessarily as a collective emigration to Palestine, but as a way to the desired moral restoration. He thought that Jews lacked the self-criticism such as was found in the Old Testament prophets, and he saw an excessive self-satisfaction as the

---

110 Lagarde, *Ausgewählte Schriften*, 225–49, cited by Lougee, *Paul de Lagarde*, 213.
111 Lougee, *Paul de Lagarde*, 213–14. On the Hungarian case, see Peter G. J. Pulzer, *The Rise of Political Anti-Semitism in Germany and Austria* (New York: Wiley, 1964), 140–41.
112 Lougee, *Paul de Lagarde*, 215.
113 Felix Weltsch, "Masaryk und der Zionismus," in *Masaryk und das Judentum*, ed. Ernst Rychnovský (Prague: Marsvelagsgesellschaft, 1931), 68; Michael A. Riff, "The Ambiguity of Masaryk's Attitudes on the 'Jewish Question'," in Winters, et al, eds., *T. G. Masaryk, 1850–1937*, 2: 79.

main fault in the current Jewish character. However, he attributed the same moral malady to anti-Semitic Christendom.[114] Cultural assimilation was legitimate and natural, and the Jews could, indeed, become culturally Czech. He concluded: "By the way, it is by no means a misfortune when the Jews live for a time among a people as a distinct element."[115] The clearest criterion of the difference in Masaryk's attitude toward the Jews,[116] compared to Lagarde's, was, however, the issue of ritual murder Masaryk demonstrated his utter abhorrence of the superstitious belief in the practice of ritual murder by his energetic intervention into the case at Polná in Moravia in 1899–1900, in which Leopold Hilsner was accused of murdering a young Christian woman, Anežka Hrůzová.[117] Even, while President of Czechoslovakia in August 28, 1933, he would denounce Nazi Germany for depriving the Jews of their civil rights and possibility of earning a living.[118]

Cosmopolitanism

Masaryk held a very different view from Lagarde's as to the aim of history. His vision of mankind's destiny was its uplifting into a condition of common humanity, while Lagarde considered the state of common humanity to be a primitive condition (indeed, allegorically a sinful state) to be overcome and remedied by an increasing differentiation. Unlike Herder, whom Masaryk cherished, Lagarde did not regard the differentiation as a harmonious process, but a predatory one.[119] Lagarde further believed that a nation's religion derived from its national characteristics; Masaryk

---

114 Masaryk, *Otázka sociální*, 2: 119. See also George J. Kovtun, *Tajuplná vražda: případ Leopolda Hilsnera* (Prague: Sefer, 1994), 241–42; also Weltsch, "Masaryk und der Zionismus," 70–71.
115 Weltsch, "Masaryk und der Zionismus," 72–74. Incidentally, Diederichs maintained that even Lagarde would ultimately tolerate the presence of Jews, citing him as stating: "once the Germandom becomes strong and creative, the Jewish question will no longer exist." See Heidler, *Der Verleger Eugen Diederichs*, 868.
116 Masaryk was aware of Lagarde's antisemitism, but he did not comment on it; see, for instance, Masaryk, *Národnostní filosofie doby novější*, 26: "Lagarde is also an uncompromising [důsledný] Anti-Semite."
117 Kovtun, *Tajuplná vražda*, 268–74; Steven Beller, "The Hilsner Affairs: Nationalism, Anti-Semitism and the Individual in the Habsburg Monarchy at the Turn of the Century," in Stanley Winters, and others eds., *T. G. Masaryk, 1850–1937*, 3 vols. (London: Macmillan, 1989–1990), 2: 54. In addition, Masaryk provided a survey of literature refuting any theological grounds for ritual murder in early 1900; see Tomáš G. Masaryk, "O pověře rituelní," *Naše doba*, 7 (1899–1900), especially, 579–89.
118 Tomáš G.Masaryk, "Keine interne Frage Deutschlands," *Prager Abendzeitung*, August 25, 1933, in Tomáš G.Masaryk, *Cesta demokracie IV*, Spisy 36 (Prague: Masarykův ústav AV ČR, 1997), 368.
119 Lougee, *Paul de Lagarde*, 18.

held that religion transcended ethnic boundaries. Lagarde disliked the Enlightenment because of its cosmopolitan culture; Masaryk had reservations towards the Enlightenment, especially in its French variant, because of its irreligious secularism.

Lagarde commented concerning the dissolution of mankind into pugnacious nations: "It is necessary to break with [the idea of] humanity because our actual mission does not consist in what we have in common with all human beings, but in what is ours alone. Humanity is our guilt; individuality our obligation." Humanity to Lagarde thus designated the state of nature and of sin, "the old man" of the Gospels. The individual rises from this humanity through intermediate stages, such as nationality and ethnic differentiation.[120] In his struggle against cosmopolitanism and universalism, Lagarde even blamed Jesus for ignoring the existence of national communities and addressing himself directly to humankind (*Menschheit*). Jesus did not know a nation in the proper sense of the word.[121]

For Masaryk, on the contrary, individual and societal activities in the world derived their religious meaning from the advancement of the Providential plan, which aimed at a realization of the ideal of universal Humanity. Within this framework, he felt optimistic that – despite occasional setbacks – there was a progress toward an ever fuller perfection of morals and intellectual life.[122] Particularly in the early years of the twentieth century, the meaning of religious life in the most quintessential sense became embodied, for him, in the implementation of the idea of Humanity.[123]

In Lagarde's view, on the contrary, religion was based on nationality. Religious life was specific to a given community, and was tied to the moral norms of that community. He stated: "Every conscience receives its distinctiveness from its relationship to the ethical views of its society."[124] In other words, the religious consciousness of a nation was

---

120 "Mit der Humanität müssen wir brechen: denn nicht das allen Menschen Gemeinsame ist unsere eigenste Pflicht, sondern das nur uns Eigene ist es. Die Humanität ist unsere Schuld, die Individualität unsere Aufgabe." Lagarde, *Deutsche Schriften*, 398; Favrat, *Pensée de Paul de Lagarde*, 269.
121 Lagarde, *Deutsche Schriften*, 258; Favrat, *Pensée de Paul de Lagarde*, 270–71.
122 Ludwig, *Defender of Democracy*, 255–56. For Masaryk's understanding of this process see, for instance, Masaryk, *Moderní člověk a náboženství*, 71.
123 Otakar A. Funda, "Náboženství: téma pro české myšlení," in Jiří Brabec et al., *Cesta a odkaz T.G. Masaryka: fakta, úvahy, souvislosti*, ed. Jarmila Lakosilová (Prague: Nakl. Lidové noviny, 2002), 137.
124 "Jedes Gewissen nun erhält seine Bestimmtheit durch sein Verhältnis zu der sittlichen Anschauung einer Gemeinschaft." Lagarde, *Deutsche Schriften*, 43; Favrat, *Pensée de Paul de Lagarde*, 267.

relative to the morals of a community and to the spirit of the time [*Zeit-geist*]. Consequently, there was a necessary plurality of religions among nations, and each nation held an essential position in the development of a religion.[125] In postulating the relationship between religion and nationality Lagarde approached Herder's position. Herder, however, had recognized an equal right of existence for all races and nations, while Lagarde regarded certain nations as worthless and as a "burden in the history of humanity."[126]

In his campaign against cosmopolitanism, Lagarde also took a dim view of the Enlightenment for its cultural universalism. In his dislike of Enlightenment internationalism, he went as far as to deny to the German literary classicism of the eighteenth century the quality of being "German." Because of its "cosmopolitan tendency," this cultural trend reflected not German, but Greek and Roman ideals. According to Lagarde, even Hegel was guilty of introducing cosmopolitanism into the German/Prussian educational system by furnishing it with a "cosmopolitan, un-German, indeed, anti-German content."[127]

Masaryk's qualms about the Enlightenment stemmed from his assessment of its intellectual temper, especially in France, as irreligious.[128] According to Masaryk, the inspiration of the Czech National Awakening, should have derived properly from the ideas of the Bohemian Reformation, particularly from the cosmopolitan Unity of Brethren which operated in a global ambiance.[129] Unlike Lagarde's strictures, Masaryk's jaundiced remarks about the Enlightenment were not inspired by its cosmopolitanism or teaching of universal culture, both of which he embraced.

Empirical Realism with a Religious Dimension of Faith

Behind Masaryk's straying from the austere empirical realism of the Austrian philosophical tradition, and the key to his admiration for Lagarde, was his desire to establish a religious dimension to the human experience.

---

125 Lagarde, *Deutsche Schriften*, 43; Favrat, *Pensée de Paul de Lagarde*, 267–68.
126 Lagarde, *Deutsche Schriften*, 28, 111, 121; Favrat, *Pensée de Paul de Lagarde*, 375–76.
127 Lagarde, *Deutsche Schriften*, 260; Favrat, *Pensée de Paul de Lagarde*, 515.
128 Masaryk, *Česká otázka*, 15, 347; idem, *V boji o náboženství*, 38.
129 Masaryk, *Česká otázka*, 15, 88, 99, 110.

Unable to accept Catholicism, whether traditional or liberal, he turned to the two modernizing trends in German Lutheranism that had jettisoned traditional dogma and liturgy. As stated earlier, he rejected the intellectualizing trend leading to German Idealism (from Kant to Hegel) that transformed theological dogmas into secularized metaphysical concepts and processes. Instead, he gravitated to the other modernizing trend, namely, the non-intellectualized approach of the religion of inner feeling, drawing on the Pietist attitude that he found in Friedrich A. Lange and Paul A. de Lagarde, and to some extent also in Gustav T. Fechner.[130] The appeal of this approach, in turn, engendered in Masaryk – rather unexpectedly (in view of his generally low opinion of German Idealism) – a measure of sympathy for Schopenhauer and Nietzsche, who had shared considerably in that branch of secularized modernizing tradition in German Lutheranism.[131] Endowing every act of perception with an ethical significance, Masaryk could incorporate this religious dimension into the empirical realism of the Austrian school and preserve an epistemological integrity. Thus, he felt that he could avoid the epistemological dualism like that of Kant's Pure and Practical Reason. Masaryk's admiration for Lagarde as a religious thinker was, of course, combined with an utmost contempt for Lagarde as a political theorist, who expressed "the noblest religious ideas" in a peculiar mixture with "Teutonic brutality." [132]

Later in life, in his *Hovory* with Karel Čapek, Masaryk discussed his view on the ontic basis of his epistemology. He then defined his modification of empiricism as critical realism. Critical realism rejected materialism, pantheism or dualism; its metaphysics was not monistic, but rather pluralistic. Pluralism accepted the material world, even though it might

---

130 Heinrich von Treitschke, like Lagarde and Fechner, advocated a Lutheranism free of the traditional religious dogmas. For him the crucial connecting link was the Pietist movement, represented by Jakob Spener and Hermann Franke, which recovered the purely moral content of Christianity. Hence the Germans conducted another Reformation leading to free and unprejudiced intellectual life. With justified national pride they could claim to be at once Apious and free," creating a literature which was Protestant, but not tainted with dogma. See James E Bradley and Dale K. Van Kley, eds., *Religion and Politics in Enlightenment Europe* (Notre Dame, Ind.: University of Notre Dame Press, 2001), 9, citing Heinrich von Treitschke, *Deutsche Geschichte im neunzehnten Jahrhundert*, vol. 1, 6th ed. (Leipzig: S. Hirzel, 1897), 51, 90, 93. Masaryk, however, did not appreciate Treitschke's observations on religion, and regarded him primarily as an extreme German nationalist and an inspirer of Pangermanic ambitions.

131 See Zdeněk V. David, "Masaryk on Schopenhauer and Nietzsche within the Austrian Philosophical Tradition," *Kosmas: Czechoslovak and Central European Journal,* vol. 23, no. 1, Fall 2009, 19–36.

132 Masaryk, *Národnostní filosofie doby novější*, 26.

not be exactly such, as it appeared to a human observer; it also accepted the inner world of personal consciousness and the consciousness of others; and finally, it accepted the world of souls, and accepted God.[133] This religious ingredient in Masaryk's critical empiricism rested on faith, that is, in a conviction that a judgment was correct.[134] Thus Masaryk anchored his empiricism in reality and made space for a religious dimension of faith (especially for God and immortality), as well as reaffirmed his belief in ontic pluralism.

---

133 Čapek, *Hovory s T. G. Masarykem*, 241–42.

134 "…in that sense faith is a substantial function of reason…" Čapek, *Hovory s T. G. Masarykem*, 284. See also Jan Šímsa, "Česká otázka otázkou náboženskou?" in *Náboženská dimenze Masarykova myšlení*, Semináře Masarykova Muzea, ed. Chovančíková, Irena (Hodonín: Masarykovo Muzeum, 1995), 5; Jan Patočka, "Masarykovo a Husserlovo pojetí duševní krise lidstva, 1936)," idem, *Češi I*, Sebrané spisy, 12 (Prague: 2006), 33.

Chapter 4

Against Philosophical Monism and Social Collectivism: the Ontic Value of Love

During his career as a philosopher lecturing at the universities of Vienna and Prague, Masaryk became gradually fascinated by the teaching of Plato, Comte, and Herder. While other philosophers – English and Austrian empiricists, as well as German idealists – served largely as foils against whom to define his own opinions,[1] it is fair to say that he cherished Plato, Comte, and Herder more than any other thinkers for their own sake. Initially, moreover, the metaphysical concepts of these philosophers might have provided tempting channels to the divine purpose of the universe. While the austerity of Brentano's empirical realism was to a large extent ameliorated by an appeal to the emotion of faith – derived primarily from Lagarde – nevertheless there remained potential space for the allurements of metaphysical concepts.

The basic issue in Masaryk's encounter with his three cherished thinkers, addressed in this chapter, however, was the clash between his ontic pluralism, anchored in the Austrian philosophical tradition, and the metaphysical monism of the three favorites. He had to deal with Plato's adherence to the ontic reality of Ideas, with Comte's view that all human-

---

[1] See, for instance, Zdeněk V. David, "Masaryk and Locke within the Context of the Austrian Philosophical tradition," *Cestou dějin. K poctě prof. Svatavy Rakové*, ed. Eva Sematonová, 2 vols. (Prague: Historický ústav AV ČR, 2007), 2: 69–87; idem, "Masaryk and Hegel within the Context of the Austrian Philosophical Tradition," *Fiftieth Anniversary of the SVU*, Selected Papers from the Twenty-Fourth World Congress of the Czechoslovak Society for Arts and Sciences, ed. Dalibor Mikuláš, Karel Raška, Zdeněk David, and Jill Pokorney, 2 vols. (Žilina, Slovakia: University of Žilina, [2010]), 1: 15–38.

kind constituted a single ontic entity as a *Grand Être*, and with Herder's similar view that humanity was a single evolving organism. Unlike the marked stability of most of Masaryk's philosophical views, his treatment of Plato, Comte, and Herder underwent considerable fluctuations during his lifetime. His early interest in Plato in the 1880s receded in the middle period of his life (1890s–1900s), only to reach an unprecedented intensity in his old age (1914–1934). In the case of Comte, his early enthusiasm continued into the middle period, but began to decline before World War I and through its aftermath. In the case of Herder, Masaryk's early relative indifference was replaced by an intense attachment in the middle period, and – following a measure of ambiguity during World War I – the highly positive attitude was fully restored after 1918. Therefore, the understanding of Masaryk's intellectual relationship with his three favorite philosophers calls for a chronological approach.[2]

Specifically, Masaryk's relationship with his three favorite philosophers, had a number of pitfalls. In particular, his critics have been concerned about Plato's preference for philosophers as rulers of the state, about the reconciliation of Comte's and Herder's providential purpose in human and natural history with the freedom of individual human beings, and about the inclination toward social collectivism of all the three philosophers. Thus the philosophies of Plato, Comte, and Herder offered serious challenges to some of Masaryk's core values. Some of these challenges will be further touched upon in the following chapter, in connection with Masaryk's philosophy of Czech history. Treating these gauntlets helps to place Masaryk's relationship to those philosophers into a proper perspective. Ultimately, Masaryk overcame the daunting metaphysical constructs by transcending them with the overarching ontological concept of love.

Political Elitism

It has been asserted by his critics that Masaryk's attachment to Plato distorted his ideas of democracy. Thus, Eva Schmidt-Hartmann has written that Masaryk, in his youthful essay on Plato, showed a certain doubt

---

2   For a detailed discussion of this chronology, see Zdeněk. V. David, "Appeal and Challenge: Masaryk's problem with Plato, Comte, and Herder," *Comenius: Journal of Euro-American Civilization*, (2014), n. 2, 9–35.

about democracy as a form of government, suggesting instead the advantages (à la Plato) of philosophers as rulers.[3] Similarly, Roman Szporluk has maintained that the Platonic ideal always affected Masaryk's concept of democracy.[4] An examination of his early essays, however, shows that Masaryk treated Plato's concept of democracy with considerable detachment, as early as in his youthful piece, "Plato as a Patriot." Although opposed to democratic equality, Plato was impressed by the aristocracy of intellect, not the aristocracy of birth.[5] Masaryk defended Plato's ideal state from the suggestions that it was essentially a theocratic entity. He explained that the rulers would be philosophers, not priests, and that their teaching would not be just theoretical, but a moral guide to practical life. In fact, Masaryk understood that these rulers would be really sociologists, which impressed him deeply.[6] Although Plato did not consider democracy to be the best form of government, he did not think it was the worst form either – that was tyranny.[7]

In his more advanced years, Masaryk still dealt with the charge that Plato was an enemy of democracy by explaining that Plato misconstrued democracy as an anarchistic, laissez-faire state of utter selfishness, in which nobody had any consideration for one another.[8] Finally, Masaryk had a chance to express most fully and openly his relationship with Plato's understanding of politics in his own conversations with Čapek. He explained that the relationship between philosophy and politics was very close: ethics was the essential ingredient in politics, and ethics was always a part of philosophy. In a way, politics was the practical applica-

---

3   Eva Schmidt-Hartmann, *Thomas G. Masaryk's Realism: Origins of a Czech Political Concept*, Veröffentlichungen des Collegium Carolinum, 52 (Munich: Oldenbourg, 1984), 79.
4   Roman Szporluk, *The Political Thought of Thomas Masaryk*, East European Monographs, 85 (New York: Columbia University Press, 1981), 45; see also H. Gordon Skilling, *T. G. Masaryk: Against the Current, 1882–1914* (University Park: Pennsylvania State University, 1994), 36.
5   "Plato jako vlastenec," in Tomáš G. Masaryk, *Juvenalie: studie a stati, 1876–1881*, Spisy 16 (Prague: Ústav T. G. Masaryka, 1993), 34–35.
6   Ibid., 41.
7   "Plato jako vlastenec," in Masaryk, *Juvenalie: studie a stati, 1876–1881*, 43. Batscha categorically denies that Masaryk derived his ideal of democracy from Plato, because Plato considered democracy the worst form of government, except for tyranny. He does admit that Masaryk was influenced by Plato's stress on the tie between ethics and politics, and the importance of education. Zwi Batscha, *Eine Philosophie der Demokratie: Thomas G. Masaryks Begründung einer neuzeitlichen Demokratie* (Frankfurt: Surkamp, 1994), 73, 126.
8   Masaryk quipped that even donkeys did not wish to be controlled in a democracy, according to Plato; Tomáš G. Masaryk, "Syndikalismus a demokracie, 1913," in *Politika vědou a uměním, 1911–1914*, Spisy 28 (Prague: Masarykův ústav AV ČR, 2011), 319. 332. Also: Tomáš G. Masaryk, *Rusko a Evropa II*, Spisy 12 (Prague: Masarykův ústav AV ČR, 1996). 394.

tion of philosophy. In that sense, Plato maintained that society should be ruled by philosophers. According to Masaryk, modern statesmen should consequently be educated and wise, and not only conventionally wise, because modern politics was to a great extent based on vision: they had to immerse themselves in the thought of their times and delve into history as well, in order to glean the direction of social development and to perceive the ideal to which this development pointed. In short, the statesman should rely on something poetic; it was, however, an imagination, not a fantasy or utopia.[9]

Historical Determinism

An apparent discrepancy between Masaryk's assumption of man's individual moral responsibility and of the simultaneous existence of a providential plan of historical development was emphatically noted by Jan Patočka in an essay published in 1946.[10] Masaryk, however, was conscious of the conflict between social determinism and individual liberty.[11] As early as in his *Pokus o konkrétní logiku* (1887), he denied that Comte intended to establish historical stages that were metaphysically binding. Comte's idea of social dynamics was merely a heuristic device to help the study of history by showing how the present had developed from the past, and how the future was developing from the present. This study had to be guided by some theory of development, hence his stages of progress. As it was true of every scientific theory, these stages were not iron-clad, but were subject to adjustment in response to subsequent observation. Masaryk pointed out that this seemingly circular trend was true of all empirical sciences.[12] Learning from

9   Karel Čapek, *Hovory s T. G. Masarykem*, Spisy 20 (Prague: Československý spisovatel, 1990), 309. See also Emil Ludwig, *Defender of Democracy: Masaryk of Czechoslovakia* (New York: R. M. McBride, 1936), 160.

10   Jan Patočka, "Pokus o českou národní filosofii a jeho nezdar (1946)," Sebrané spisy 12 (Prague: Oikoymenh, 2006), 350; see also Karel Hrubý, "Masaryk's Political Outlook," in *T.G. Masaryk In Perspective: Comments and Criticism*, ed. Milič Čapek and Karel Hrubý ([Ann Arbor, Mich.]: SVU, c1981), 133. Patočka's argument is discussed further in Chapter 11.

11   As in the case of Bakunin, see Masaryk, *Rusko a Evropa II*, 23. According to Kraus, he also felt that it was possible to choose among different chains of determining causes; See Oskar Kraus, "Die Grundzüge der Welt- und Lebensanschauung T. G. Masaryks," *Slavische Rundschau*, vol. 2, no. 3 (1930), 165.

12   Tomáš G. Masaryk, *Pokus o konkrétní logiku; třídění a soustava věd*, Spisy 3 (Prague: Ústav T. G. Masaryka, 2001), 118.

history, according to Masaryk in "Teorie a praxis," was to search history for useful truths and laws, which could be suitably applied. Comte himself had said that the living were increasingly guided by the dead. These trends should be taken into account by a statesman. Discernment of them, however, should not lead to fatalism, such as that which prevailed among the nations of the Near East.[13] Furthermore, Masaryk praised Comte's abstract sociological laws of human progress for their cosmopolitan and universal character. Thus, Comte identified the progress from fetishism through polytheism to monotheism as an ideal eternal law that he claimed to apply generally, without naming specific nations, persons, or events.[14]

Later, Masaryk went even further to undermine the cogency of the critique that he had ignored the gap between historical laws and individual freedom. By 1913, he questioned Comte's view of the historical stages as simply governed by historical laws of progression from the theological stage to the metaphysical one, and then from the metaphysical stage to the positivist one. According to Masaryk, this position failed to specify the obligation of each individual to actively cooperate in the spread and elaboration of a positive (anti-theological and anti-metaphysical) outlook on the world and on life.[15] In his war memoirs, Masaryk stated categorically: "Just because Providence takes care of us and of our world, does not mean that a fatalism of inactivity should follow, but rather an optimism of synergy – a strict command of work, the work for an ideal." [16]

The problem raised by Comte's positivist philosophy of history was also relevant to Herder's vision of the cosmic realization of the Ideal of

13 Tomáš G. Masaryk, "Teorie a praxis," in *Juvenalie: studie a stati, 1876–1881,* 19–20. See also Zdeněk Nejedlý, *T. G. Masaryk,* vols. 3–4 (Prague: Melantrich, 1930–1937); 2d ed., vols. 1–2, Sebrané spisy 31–32 (Prague: Orbis, 1949–1950), 2: 332.

14 Masaryk, *Pokus o konkrétní logiku; třídění a soustava věd,* 124.

15 Masaryk, *Rusko a Evropa II,* 121. Also Masaryk believed that with the progress of history man changes not only physically put also intellectually and further develops powers, hitherto underdeveloped, ibid. *II,* 424. Zdeněk Nejedlý has pointed out another crucial difference. Comte presented a detailed set of stages and substages in transitions from the theocratic to the metaphysical and finally to the positive stage. Masaryk's scheme was simple and thus freer of rigid determinism. He recognized just two poles, myth and science, in a more fluid transition from theocracy to democracy. Nejedlý, *T. G. Masaryk,* 3: 311.

16 Masaryk, Tomáš G., *Světová revoluce za války a ve válce, 1914–1918,* Spisy 15 (Prague: Masarykův ústav AV ČR, 2005), 265, cited by Karel Vorovka, "Několik myšlenek o Masarykově filosofii a jeho *Světové revoluci,*" *Ruch filosofický* 5 (1925), 277. According to Hrubý, Masaryk sought to reconcile the cooperation of human freedom and the providential action of God on the basis of *synergism.* He drew a sharp distinction between determinism and fatalism. Karel Hrubý, "Concluding Remarks," in *T.G. Masaryk in Perspective: Comments and Criticism,* 277.

Humanity. Herder's ideal could likewise be viewed as creating an incompatibility between Masaryk's insistence on the moral responsibility of the individual and the predetermined course of historical development. Herder's assumption of the divine involvement in leading mankind and nature to a happy denouement, according to Alexander Gillies, moreover created the presumption of pantheism. A pantheist process would obviously clash with Masaryk's assertion of man's free will and Herder's pantheist stand could actually lead directly into German idealism, culminating in Hegel, which Masaryk resolutely opposed. [17]

F. M. Barnard attempted to reconcile the seeming disharmony between Herder's Ideal of Humamity and Masaryk's belief in Providential purpose and the idea of human freedom. He wrote:

> Humanity, Herder concedes, is part of Nature and subject to her laws; at the same time it inhabits the realm of culture....in which it is subject as well as object, agent as well as instrument and in which realm choice rather than necessity prevails. It is by virtue of being an inhabitant of both realms that human beings can be said to have a "will of their own," that they are not only subject to law, but also 'a law to themselves.'[18]

Josette Baer has similarly argued that Masaryk, with Herder, saw in humanity a metahistorical goal of moral development of mankind, which expressed itself not collectively, but on the individual level. Thus humanity is the meaning and the aim of the existence of individuals (without the behavior of individuals being determined).[19] According to Masaryk, however, what Herder actually envisaged in the realization of the ideal Humanity was something more prosaic, the establishment of a natural religion that was in fact deism. This was the reason why Herder had reprimanded the Holy Roman Emperor, Joseph II, for the persecution of the

---

17 Alexander Gillies, "Herder and Masaryk: Some Points of Contact," *The Modern Language Review* 9 (1945), 120–23.

18 F. M. Barnard, "Humanism and Titanism. Masaryk and Herder," in T. G. *Masaryk, 1850–1937*, Stanley Winters et al, eds, 3 vols. (London: Macmillan, 1989–1990), 1: 29; he refers to Herder's own definition of the concept of Humanity in Johann G. Herder, *Sämmtliche Werke*, ed. Bernhard Suphan (Berlin: Weidmann, 1877–1913), 15: 133, 17: 143; 18: 339. See also Batscha, *Eine Philosophie der Demokratie*, 123.

19 Josette Baer, *Politik als praktizierte Sittlichkeit. Zum Demokratiebegriff bei Thomas G. Masaryk und Vaclav Havel* (Sinzheim: Pro Universitate Verlag, 1998), 323.

deists in the Empire. Hence, the attainment of Humanity did not mean a metaphysical fusion of mankind into a single body or entity, but the adoption of a natural religion – which stood above the religion of the traditional churches – by all of mankind.[20]

Otakar Funda has pointed out that Masaryk did not seek to be a philosopher of history like Herder (or, for that matter, Hegel or Marx); he was not interested in delimiting certain epochs, or defining the driving forces in history, or determining the pattern of the historical development. He tried to discern the meaning and the direction of certain ethical ideas and endeavors – above all, the movement from theocracy to democracy. [21]

Social Collectivism

Masaryk, like other advocates of modern democracy, viewed the safeguarding of individual freedom not merely as a concern for humanity's future, but primarily as a current requirement in the functioning of contemporary states. Plato, Comte, and Herder have been seen, on the contrary, as placing the interests and the stature of society above those of its individual members, and subordinating the interests of the individuals to those of the collective whole. In the case of Plato, Roman Szporluk has called attention to Karl R. Popper's suggestion that Masaryk (as well as Woodrow Wilson) fell victim to the metaphysical theories of Plato and built their concepts of nationalist movements on them.[22] Masaryk, however, actually denounced Plato's social collectivism, which he saw applied in the teaching of Marx and Engels. Marx and Engels viewed the masses as a single organism, whereby they transferred the characteristics of a single person to a social whole. Already Plato had committed this organicist error, which then passed on to Spencer and Marx.[23] As noted earlier, Masaryk was also convinced that Plato influenced Marxist ideas about communism. He resolutely rejected Plato's communism, although he was

20 Tomáš G. Masaryk, *Česká otázka. Naše nynější krize. Jan Hus,* Spisy 6 (Prague: Masarykův ústav, 2000), 416–17.

21 Otakar A. Funda, *Thomas Garigue Masaryk: Sein phiosophisches, religiöses und politisches Denken* (Bern: P. Lang, 1978), 193–94.

22 Quoting from Karl R. Popper, *The Open Society and Its Enemies* (Princeton, NJ.: Princeton University Press), 246. Roman Szporluk, "Masaryk's Republic: Nationalism with a Human Face," in *T.G. Masaryk in Perspective: Comments and Criticism,* 228.

23 Tomáš G. Masaryk, *Otázka sociální. Základy marxismu filosofické a sociologické,* vol. 1, Spisy 9 (Prague: Masarykův ústav AV ČR, 2000) [1898], 173–74, 194.

convinced that the collectivist theory derived from the very core of Plato's philosophy, particularly his teaching about Ideas.[24] Masaryk traced Plato's strong tendency toward the organicist concept of society to a contemporary underdevelopment of the study of psychology, which otherwise would have bolstered the countervailing status of individualism. Plato had not yet distinguished psychology from other humanities; the Socratic dialogs still mixed psychological, political, esthetic, and logical theories. Only Aristotle emancipated psychology, regarding it as an independent science.[25] Zdeněk Nejedlý notes that Masaryk was fortified against Plato's collectivism by the power of his own individualism.[26] This individualism prevented him from employing an analogy between society and organism that would result in an entirely collectivist view of society.[27]

According to Nejedlý, Masaryk's resistance to collectivism by the power of his individualism, while evident in the case of Plato, was manifest even more strongly with respect to Comte's collectivist view of society.[28] According to Masaryk, the individual, although living within society, did not dissolve in the societal whole, and it was not true that he was nothing when by himself. Likewise, it was wrong to view society as an organism, in which the individual lost independence, as if a part of a larger entity, analogous to the human body.[29] As Masaryk pointed out in his *Rusko a Evropa,* even Leo Tolstoy opposed Comte's view that mankind was a single organism.[30]

Masaryk rejected Comte's concept of the *Grand Être* that was not simply mankind as perceived by positive sociology, but an actual being that was to be what God was to a Christian or a theist. The worship of the *Grand Être* was, to Masaryk, a restoration of fetishism that Comte had condemned in its original form. [31] Masaryk opposed not only the metaphysical concept of the *Grand Être,* but also the political arrangement of the *Grand Être* as a social ideal of positivism, which he viewed as derived

---

24 Tomáš G. Masaryk, *Otázka sociální. Základy marxismu filosofické a sociologické,* vol. 2, Spisy 10 (Prague: Masarykův ústav AV ČR, 2000), 24–25.

25 Masaryk, *Pokus o konkrétní logiku; třídění a soustava věd,* 112. See also Tomáš G. Masaryk, "Teorie dějin dle zásad T. H. Buckla," in idem, *Přednášky a studie z let 1882–1884,* Spisy 17 (Prague: Masarykův ústav AV ČR, 1998), 125.

26 Nejedlý, *T. G. Masaryk,* 1: 393–94.

27 Ibid., 3: 257.

28 Ibid., 1: 380.

29 Ibid., 2: 494–95.

30 Masaryk, *Rusko a Evropa III,* 314.

31 Tomáš G. Masaryk, *Moderní člověk a náboženství,* Spisy 8 (Prague: Masarykův ústav AV ČR, 2000), 73–74.

from the model of an old-fashioned absolutist regime.[32] According to Masaryk, Comte wished to ultimately replace theocracy by an authoritarian "sociocracy," which would combine the allegedly best parts of the previous political systems in a universal, historically contextualized, synthesis.[33] Finally, Masaryk pointed out that Comte's positive politics involved a great paradox. Initially, priding himself on the strict objectivism of a scientific outlook, Comte ended up in pure subjectivism. Positive logic was to be replaced by the logic of the heart and by fantasy; Romanticism, in the worst sense of the word, permeated Comte's positive politics.[34]

Masaryk attributed Comte's adherence to the concepts of social collectivism to two main factors: his receptivity to the reactionary Catholic political theory, and – already noted in Plato – his disregard of psychology as a distinct scientific discipline. In a way, Comte, in his political thought, exemplified the widespread appeal of the ecclesial Catholic statehood evident in the nineteenth century. Masaryk showed Comte's thorough grasp of the papal political power, manifest in the administration of the former Papal States.[35] Masaryk further concluded that the political arrangements, which Comte presented as a social ideal of positivism, were derived from the absolutistic papalist vision of de Maistre.[36] Thus Comte, inspired by de Maistre, proclaimed a religion of humanity and, in a mystical enthusiasm, proclaimed himself its high priest.[37] According to Masaryk, Comte as a born Catholic could not resist, and introduced the positivist form of religion as fetishism.[38] Comte's religion of Humanity preserved Catholic institutions and rituals, but gave them another meaning; it was a Catholicism without Christianity.[39]

In addition to the residual Catholicism, according to Masaryk, Comte's downgrading of psychology to a part of biology was the other major fac-

---

32 Masaryk, *Pokus o konkrétní logiku; třídění a soustava věd*, 222; Masaryk, *Moderní člověk a náboženství*, 73.
33 Masaryk, *Moderní člověk a náboženství*, 74.
34 Ibid., 76.
35 It compared favorably with the knowledge of an expert, Heinrich von Eicken; see Tomáš G. Masaryk, "Heinrich von Eicken, *Geschichte und System der mittelalterlichen Weltanschauung.* Stuttgart, 1887," in idem, *Slovanské studie a texty z let 1889–1891*, Spisy 20 (Prague: Masarykův ústav AV ČR, 2007), 305.
36 Masaryk, *Moderní člověk a náboženství*, 73–74; Masaryk, *Pokus o konkrétní logiku; třídění a soustava věd*, 222.
37 Masaryk, "Katolický sjezd ve Vídni." in Masaryk, *Slovanské studie a texty z let 1889–1891*, 561.
38 Tomáš G. Masaryk, *Rusko a Evropa III*, Spisy 13 (Prague: Masarykův ústav, 1996), 54. See also František Fajfr, *Masaryk a Comte* (Kdyně: Okresní sbor osvětový, 1925), 90.
39 Prayers were directed toward women. Masaryk, *Rusko a Evropa III*, 206.

tor, which led to a downgrading of an individual consciousness in favor of a collective mentality.[40] A proper recognition of the independence and importance of psychology would have undermined Comte's anti-individualist stand. Comte rejected the supremacy of psychology because of his belief that true reality was the collective humankind, and because, for him, the individual was just an abstraction. Comte felt that human reason developed within society, and thus in the knowledge of social development rested the unifying principle of all human cognitions. As a further negative consequence, neglecting psychology, Comte did not recognize that every historical and social phenomenon was, at the same time, a psychical one. This, in turn, prevented him from accepting psychology as the unifying science. Psychology alone could provide a common thread – the point of departure for the unification of knowledge, which Comte had sought through his classification of sciences.[41] Masaryk also criticized Comte, for his exclusion of introspective psychology from the list of sciences. As a result of Comte's sternly objectivistic epistemology, other aspects of the cognitive process were neglected. Above all, this excluded the grasp of the moral significance in perceptions, which would, in turn, point to the providential theistic purpose in the world. [42]

Turning to the last of the three philosophers, critics have suggested that Masaryk, as an admirer of Herder, had to deal with not one, but two collectivist social entities: humanity, and the nation. Moreover, he had to face the ambiguity of the German philosopher's idea of the relationship between the two entities. Jan M. Lochman framed the conflict as if between a tribal conception of the nation and a cosmopolitan vision of humanity.[43] On a more specific level, Michael A. Riff has maintained that the Herderian view of nationality as something inherent, even derived from divinity, prevented Masaryk from arguing for Jewish membership in the Czech nation. [44]

---

40 Masaryk's stress on the importance of psychology for the philosophical discourse was, in part, a legacy of Brentano's influence. Masaryk, *Rusko a Evropa II*, 120.
41 Masaryk, *Pokus o konkrétní logiku; třídění a soustava věd*, 201.
42 Milič Čapek, "The Presence of Masaryk's Thought," in *T.G. Masaryk in Perspective: Comments and Criticism*, 26–27.
43 Jan Milič Lochman, "Emanuel Rádl: In Masaryk's Footsteps," *T.G. Masaryk in Perspective: Comments and Criticism*, 88–89; citing: Emanuel Rádl, *Válka Čechů s Němci* (Prague: Čin, 1928), 96, 132.
44 Michael A. Riff, "The Ambiguity of Masaryk's Attitude on the 'Jewish Question'," in *T. G. Masaryk, 1850–1937*, Stanley Winters et al, eds, 3 vols. (London: Macmillan, 1989–1990), 2: 83, 85. This issue is discussed in Chapter 3.

Masaryk was aware of the collectivist aspects verging on panthe-ism in Herder's philosophical outlook. He wrote in his *Moderní člověk a náboženství* that – while David Hume understood humanity purely indi-vidualistically – Herder (like Comte, Spencer, and Rousseau) conceived of humanity collectively. For them, historical and contemporary human-ity constituted a single organic whole. Thus, also for Herder, the ideal of humanity was identical with mankind, and mankind, to him, was God.[45] Masaryk pointed out that Kollár also adopted from Herder the concept of humanity as a single entity.[46]

It has been mentioned that Masaryk endorsed Herder's view that the nation as a natural group was a superior entity to the state, which was an artificial concept. Nature organized humankind into nations. Ma-saryk, however, felt that Herder overemphasized the importance of the nation so much so that he almost lost the sight of the singleness of Hu-manity. His attachment to the nation idea reached a high level of ex-clusivity, even to the point of justifying injustice to other nations.[47] In addition, Masaryk argued that Kollár distorted Herder's idea of the na-tion even further.

Kollár specified that one nation or national group assumed a leading position in the development of mankind at a time. The primacy of the leading nation violated Herder's view of humanity as an organic whole, whereby the historical task was being performed by the various nations concurrently, not consecutively. Kollár adopted from Hegel the idea of certain nations holding an exclusive status; while Herder was a federal-ist, Kollár was a centralist, even an absolutist.[48] In addition, unlike Herd-er, Kollár engaged in an extremely harsh critique of the existing state of European civilization that contrasted with the bright future of humani-ty, and reflected especially in the current degeneration of nations speak-ing Germanic and Romance languages. The source of this devastating cri-tique of civilization, according to Masaryk, was best sought not in Herder but in Rousseau. Kollár, however, did not agree with Rousseau's remedy

---

45 Tomáš G. Masaryk, *Moderní člověk a náboženství*, 114. See also Batscha, *Eine Philosophie der Demokratie*, 114.
46 Masaryk, *Česká otázka. Naše nynější krize. Jan Hus,* 394.
47 Ibid., 23–24.
48 Masaryk, *Česká otázka. Naše nynější krize. Jan Hus,* 394. The dichotomy between the federalists and the centralists might have been inspired by the late nineteenth-century conflict on the nationality issue in the Habsburg monarchy.

of returning to the state of nature. The Slavs would, on the contrary, engage in advancing a purified civilization.[49]

Finally, Masaryk's major objection to Kollár's philosophy of history was the identification of humanity with Slavdom in the future advancement of mankind. This was a serious deviation from Herder's teaching, which did not exclude any national group from participation in the providential realization of humanity. Masaryk pointed out that, according to Herder, even the most belligerent Germans would be able, in the future, to adopt the peaceful humanitarian denouement.[50] Hence, there was a sharp dichotomy in Kollár's teaching between the Herderian humanitarianism and his own exclusivist nationalism, expressed especially in his famous epos *Slávy dcera*.[51] It was the former, the message of harmony with humanitarianism that Kollár transmitted to the Czech awakeners, from Dobrovský on, and even to Bernard Bolzano.[52]

Most importantly, Masaryk decisively rejected the collectivist conception of the nation as a person, or as an organism, the view of Herder and the subsequent Romanticists.[53] As early as 1877, in his review of Théophile Funck-Brentano's book, *La civilisation et ses lois. Morale sociale* (Paris: E. Plon et Cie, 1876), Masaryk defined his belief in the ontic reality of the individual human being. An individual did not dissolve in society and was not reduced to nothing in isolation. Utilizing an analogy from the natural sciences, he pointed out that the linking of individuals in society was physical, not chemical. It constituted a physical mixture, not a chemical compound. Masaryk admonished that one must not lose sight of a concrete individual, and see only the sheer abstraction, which is society. What acted and suffered in life was a specific, concrete human being, not an abstract concept, like society.[54]

Masaryk saw in the nation only an aggregate of individuals, because individuals alone were bearers of consciousness. Society did not have a con-

49 Although Kollár may have read some Rousseau in his early years, most of the knowledge of Rousseau was probably transmitted to him by Herder. Herder was much under Rousseau's influence and concerned with him in his own writings; Masaryk, *Česká otázka. Naše nynější krize. Jan Hus,* 417–18.
50 An additional problem was how could Kollár, under these circumstances, accept the idea of Humanity from a German; Masaryk, Tomáš G., *Česká otázka. Naše nynější krize. Jan Hus,* 402.
51 Masaryk, *Česká otázka. Naše nynější krize. Jan Hus,* 41.
52 Ibid., 40.
53 Tomáš G. Masaryk, *Rusko a Evropa I*, Spisy 11 (Prague: Masarykův ústav AV ČR, 1996). 209.
54 Masaryk, "Zákony osvěty a budoucnost Slovanstva," in *Juvenalie: studie a stati, 1876–1881,* 70–71; see also Jaroslav Opat, *Filozof a politik: T. G. Masaryk, 1882–1893* (Prague: Melantrich, 1990), 34.

sciousness of its own. The so-called collective or "national consciousness" simply meant that individuals agreed among themselves, giving rise to a "shared spiritual climate."[55] Nationality was a concept central to the outlook of both Herder and Masaryk. For Masaryk, however, the nation was a pluralistic bridge to a pluralistic humanity, for Herder an ontically monistic part of an ontically monistic humanity.[56]

Thus throughout his lifetime, Masaryk would deal creatively with the views of Plato, Comte, and Herder, while at the same time coping with the challenge of their metaphysical monism to his ontic pluralism. Starting with Plato, Masaryk derived from him his realism in epistemology, recognizing the reality of perceptions. Hence he was critical of Comte's positivism which held that phenomena – the perceptions – were not real, appealing to Kant's dichotomy between the illusory phenomena and the real, but unknowable noumena beyond them. In ontology, however, Masaryk did not accept the reality of Plato's Ideas, regarding them as abstract notions. In that respect he remained a nominalist, also vis-à-vis Comte's *Grand Être* and Herder's *Humanität*. Thus his realism was not radical like Plato's, or later, John Wyclif's and Jan Hus's, but a moderate one, applying only to perceptions, but not to concepts.

Empirical Love over Speculative Metaphysics

No matter how much Masaryk admired Plato's moralism and argument for the immortality of the soul, Comte's endorsement of scientific empirical knowledge and rejection of any revealed lore, and Herder's elevation of the nation over the state and the providential road the human perfection, his own staunch conviction of ontic human individualism prevented him from endorsing their collectivist visions. Plato's organicism and communism, Comte's positive society, and Herder's nation and humanity as organisms, all fell predictably short.

---

55 Hrubý, "Masaryk's Political Outlook," in *T.G. Masaryk in Perspective: Comments and Criticism*, 128, citing Masaryk, *Social Question*, 249–50; Hrubý adds: "In Masaryk's rejection of a 'preordained nation' I see a politician of a predominantly nominalist outlook."
56 Alexander Gillies, "Herder and Masaryk: Some Points of Contact," *The Modern Language Review* 9 (1945), 125. See also Jaroslav Opat, "Glosy ke dvěma kritikám T. G. Masaryka," *Slovanský přehled*, 76, 3 (1990), 244.

Ultimately Masaryk saw the metaphysical concepts of Plato's Ideas, Comte's Grand Être, and Herder's Humanity, transcended and overridden by the epistemology and the ontic status of the empirical emotion of love, as the principle of social cohesion and of the divine cosmic purpose. This standpoint, which seems to have fully crystalized only late in Masaryk's life, harmonized with the empirical approach to epistemology that he had derived from his background in the Austrian philosophical tradition. It also supplemented and harmonized with his earlier realization, largely thanks to Lagarde, that the experience of faith supplied an epistemological dimension enhancing the ontic status of sensory perceptions involved in empirical realism. By the transcendent elevation of the epistemological and ontic experience of love, metaphysical concepts were relegated to a subordinate level in the scale of ontology.

Love

This elevation of the emotion of love into a key instrument of the divine purpose for human society undoubtedly germinated in Masaryk's mind for a long time. Paradoxically – in view of his rejection of a substantial part of Plato's metaphysics, namely, the reality of Ideas – it is safe to assume that his concept of ontic love was substantially affected by Plato. This time the source was not the intellectualized aspects of the ancient philosopher's teaching, but the emotive aspects, derived from Plato's dialogs dealing with the ontology of love, in particular *Lysis, Symposium,* and *Phaedrus.*[57] It was especially in *Phaedrus* that Plato recognized love as a powerful, emotional motive force in the human soul. He regarded passionate earthly love as a stimulus to propel the soul to participate in the supreme super-cosmic reality.[58] Sexual love was the seed of ideal love.[59] What was undoubtedly most important to Masaryk was Plato's concept of love as a path to immortality and to God. Thus in the "Symposium" Pla-

---

57   "Plato," *The Encyclopedia of Philosophy*, 2nd ed., Donald M. Borchert, 10 vols. (New York: Macmillan, 2006), 7: 589.

58   Plato, "Phaedrus," in *The Dialogs of Plato*, Great Books of the Western World 7 (Chicago: Encyclopedia Britannica, 1952), 124, 125; see also "Platonism," *The New Encyclopedia Britannica*, 15th ed. (Chicago: Encyclopaedia Britannica, 2002), 25: 897; Stanislav Polák, *T.G. Masaryk*, 6 vols. (Prague: Masarykův ústav AV ČR, 2000–2012), 6: 155, 277.

59   Plato, "Phaedrus," in *The Dialogs of Plato*, Great Books of the Western World 7: 127, 129; "Love," in *The Encyclopedia of Philosophy*, ed. Paul Edwards, 8 vols. (New York: Macmillan, 1967), 5: 90.

to has Socrates assert that love was the quest for the possession of eternity: "Wherefore love is of immortality."[60] Likewise in the "Symposium," the philosophical importance of love (*eros*) for Plato was its function as the source of energy driving human beings to pursue the supreme good, or to serve as a link between "mortal" man and the divine.[61]

In addition, Masaryk had earlier intimated that his concept of "humanity," the realization of which was the goal of history under divine guidance, was in fact identical with "the love for one's neighbor" in the Gospels.[62] In his history of Russian thought, *Russia and Europe*, he cited with approval even Bakunin's assertion that "the champions of democracy fulfil the supreme commandment of Christ and attest to the sole substance of Christianity – love."[63] According to Josette Baer, similarly the Herderian striving for the realization of the ideal of Humanity, for Masaryk, assumed the form of love of an individual for another. This development expressed itself in the work of everyone.[64]

Aside from the occasional and rather cryptic references, Masaryk stated his master concept of ontic love explicitly and forcefully only late in life. This view was clearly formulated by him in the following statement that was inserted into his conversations with Karel Čapek:

Love, sympathy is the greatest moral force – out of it there springs all the mutual participation [*účast*], help and cooperation; moral life that is the co-active share in the divine order of the world – love, sympathy, synergy, that is the law of life in the relationship between two people, in the family, in the nation, in the state, in humanity. I do not know of any other.[65]

---

60 Plato, "Symposium," in *The Dialogs of Plato*, Great Books of the Western World, 7 (Chicago: Encyclopedia Britannica, 1952), 165; see also Frederick Copleston, *History of Philosophy*, 8 vols. (London: Burns and Oates, 1947–1966), 1: 199–200; "Love," *The Encyclopedia of Religion*, ed. Mircea Eliade, 16 vols. (New York: Macmillan, 1987), 9: 36–38.

61 Plato, "Symposium," in *The Dialogs of Plato*, Great Books of the Western World, 7: 163; see also "Plato," *The Encyclopedia of Philosophy*, 2nd ed., Donald M. Borchert, 7: 589.

62 Masaryk, *Světová revoluce za války a ve válce*, 374; Tomáš G. Masaryk, "Humanita, pacifismus a voják," *Naše vojsko*, October 15, 1928, Masaryk, Tomáš G., *Cesta demokracie III*, Spisy 35 (Prague: Masarykův ústav AV ČR, 1994), 312; Miloš Havelka, "Demokracie, humanita, odpovědnost," Jarmila Lakosilová, ed., *Cesta a odkaz T.G. Masaryka : fakta, úvahy, souvislosti..*, by Jiří Brabec et al. (Prague: Nakl. Lidové noviny, 2002), 13. See also Batscha, *Eine Philosophie der Demokratie*, 113–27; Schmidt-Hartmann, *Thomas G. Masaryk's Realism*, 183.

63 Masaryk, *Rusko a Evropa II*, 16.

64 Baer, *Politik als praktizierte Sittlichkeit. Zum Demokratiebegriff bei Thomas G. Masaryk und Vaclav Havel*, 323.

65 Čapek, *Hovory s T. G. Masarykem*, 98.

Sedlmayerová

The force of this latter-day statement was almost certainly inspired and crystalized under the impact of the powerful emotions which were elicited by Masaryk's concurrent and intense relationship with Oldra – or Ola as Masaryk referred to her in private – Sedlmayerová nee Michálková (1884–1954), which extended from 1928 to 1933. Thus, Sedlmayerová was then in her late forties, and Masaryk in his late seventies and early eighties. There exists direct evidence that Masaryk's friendship with Sedlmayerová had a seminal influence on the formulation of his cosmic concept of ontic love. The standpoint on love, presented in Masaryk's statement to Čapek – as quoted above – is found explicitly articulated in his contemporary correspondence with Sedlmayerová. In a letter of August 28, 1928, he wrote to Oldra: "A wonder – that immortal soul, that eternal soul is not satisfied with aloneness, it yearns for a connection in the same way as the body does; people shake hands, embrace, kiss each other – why?"[66]

Sedlmayerová, first a postal worker, then a journalist of relatively modest accomplishments, was born in Kouřim near Kolín in central Bohemia, but was raised in Mikulovice near Znojmo in southern Moravia, that is in an area which was also the setting of Masaryk's youth.[67] She completed her secondary schooling in 1903 and started working as a postal clerk in Žďár near Havlíčkův Brod. She was fascinated by Masaryk, by his appearance, and by his political activities already during her school attendance.[68] According to the recollections of Pavlína Mocová, Sedlmayerová was first formally introduced to Masaryk and his wife Charlotte by Karla Zátková, a descendant of Karel Havlíček Borovský, in 1906 during festivities in Havlíček's birthplace of Borová.[69] In 1911, she started working for Masaryk's Realist Party, and became chairperson of the Party's local organization in Havlíčkův Brod. [70] In the capacity of – albeit a minor – functionary of Masaryk's political Party, she had opportunities to travel

---

66 Jiří Kovtun, *Republika v nebezpečném světě. Era prezidenta Masaryka, 1918–1935* (Prague: Torst, 2005), 586.
67 As a peculiarity, since early youth she spoke of herself as an illegitimate daughter of the prominent actor of the National Theater, Karel Želenský; Michaela Košťálová, *Rodokmen a soukromí T. G. Masaryka* (Prague: Petrklíč, 2013), 87.
68 Košťálová, *Rodokmen a soukromí T. G. Masaryka*, 88–89.
69 Jana Bártová and Jan Bílek, "Oldra Sedlmayerová ve vzpomínkách Pavly Mocové," *Tvar*, 12 (1999), June 10, 14. See also Košťálová, *Rodokmen a soukromí T. G. Masaryka*, 90.
70 Košťálová, *Rodokmen a soukromí T. G. Masaryka*, 91.

to Prague and attend meetings of the Party's central committee, at which Masaryk usually presided. [71] The only surviving piece of correspondence from this period between Sedlmayerová and the future President, from July 10, 1914, ironically contains Masaryk's rejection of her article, submitted to the journal *Naše doba* [Our Times], which he then edited.[72] After the war in 1919 she sought a nomination as the Party's candidate for Czechoslovak Parliament, and after the Party's dissolution in 1925 she joined with other former Realists to form the National Party of Labor [*Národní strana práce*]. [73] Her journalistic activity in the 1920s, however, led her to know Masaryk's secretary Vasil K. Škrach, who in turn mediated her personal contact with the President in early 1928.[74]

Their first private meeting in the Presidential chateau of Lány on July 16, 1928 led to a passionate embrace on a couch.[75] Masaryk found in Sedlmayerová a woman completely devoted to him, whom he considered in the late 1920s and early 1930s a close friend in whom he could confide. They discussed politics and literature, with Sedlemayerová editing Masaryk's articles printed in newspapers under a pseudonym.[76] In fact, she became more than a confidante or a friend to Masaryk.[77] In the fall of 1928, they began to share ideas about love when Masaryk suggested that a strong bond [*štranek*] had developed between them and wrote further: "...this bond permits us, nay forces us to also discuss exactly the intimate aspects of life. After all, we both have our experiences, why should we shy away from talking about them? I think that I could say something new exactly about love, i.e., about what people have hitherto avoided saying."[78] Soon after, Masaryk expressed his conviction that Ola truly loved him and

71   Tomáš G. Masaryk, *Dopisy Oldře*, ed. Dagmar Hájková (Prague: IN ŽIVOT, 2006), 14; see also 10, 13, 35.
72   Masaryk, *Dopisy Oldře*, 9.
73   In seeking the nomination for parliamentary deputy she compared her life story to that of the famous novelist. Božena Němcová; Polák, *T.G. Masaryk*, 6:48, 242; Kovtun, *Republika v nebezpečném světě*, 587.
74   Anna Gašparíková-Horáková, *U Masarykovcov. Spomienky osobnej archivárky T. G. Masaryka* (Bratislava: Academic Electronic Press, 1995), 131–32.
75   Polák, *T.G. Masaryk*, 6: 158–60, 279.
76   Dagmar Hájková, "T.G. Masaryk," in Tomáš G. Masaryk, *Dopisy Oldře*, 109–10. Kovtun characterized the relationship as "a love relationship of fluctuating intensity, as literary collaboration with dubious results, and as a confidential friendship in which both of them related their life experiences and desires to the most intimate details." Kovtun, *Republika v nebezpečném světě*, 587.
77   Bártová and Bílek, "Oldra Sedlmayerová ve vzpomínkách Pavly Mocové," 14.
78   Masaryk, *Dopisy Oldře*, 12–13.

asked God to reward her for her love. In this letter, he suggested the idea of "living together" [*spolužití*] and overcoming the obstacles standing in the way.[79] Subsequently, in October 1928, Masaryk was able to arrange to spend ten days together with Ola in the spa of Topolčianky in Slovakia.[80] At Christmas time in 1928, Masaryk referred to their faithful friendship as the great event of the year, and speculated that this occurrence was neither accidental nor fortuitous.[81] In Prague, their meetings in the presidential seat of the Castle were usually informal, not officially recorded as audiences. Whenever possible they also met in the hotel *Esplanade* or in Malá Strana in the house of Klára Červenková, an old friend of the Masaryk family. At the height of his intense feeling, in April 1929, Masaryk, in fact, thought about renting a house for Ola where he might see her daily. [82] In this period, Masaryk's erotic conversations with Ola were regularly overheard by the telephone operators at the Central Post Office of Prague in Jindřišská Street.[83]

Perhaps, as a way to explain their frequent contacts, the focus of Sedlmayerová's literary activity was ostensibly a biography of Masaryk's close associate in World War I, Milan R. Štefánik.[84] Masaryk's family, especially his daughters Alice and Olga, looked askance at Masaryk's relationship with Sedlmayerová, who was estranged but not divorced from her husband Jan Sedlmayer, a railroad official.[85] Probably, to distract Masaryk's attention from Sedlmayerová, Alice Masaryková arranged in April 1929 for a young Slovak historian, Anna Gašparíková, to work with him as a research assistant until 1936. [86] Gašparíková joined Masaryk's daughters and his granddaughter Anna in their dislike of Sedlmayerová. Sedl-

79 Ibid., 20–21.
80 Masaryk's letter to Sedlmayerová of September 29, 1928, in Masaryk, *Dopisy Oldře*, 23. See also Vítězslav Houška, *Lidé kolem T.G.M.* (Prague: Paris/Hlas, 2006), 207.
81 Masaryk, *Dopisy Oldře*, 35.
82 The plan was not realized, apparently because of the opposition of his family entourage; Literární archiv Památníku národního písemnictví v Praze (LA-PNP), fond Oldra Sedlmayerová, Deník, cited by Kovtun, *Republika v nebezpečném světě*, 592, 850. See also Masaryk, *Dopisy Oldře*, 37, 56, 59, 66, 75, 81.
83 Ivo Tretera, *Vzpomínky na Bohuslava Hrabala a na život vůbec* (Prague: Paseka, 2011), 14–15.
84 Gašparíková-Horáková, *U Masarykovcov. Spomienky osobnej archivárky T. G. Masaryka*, 85, 106.
85 Polák, *T.G. Masaryk*, 6: 166, 281. She was married in 1905, ibid., 281. See also Gašparíková-Horáková, , *U Masarykovcov*, 131–32. As Sedlmayerová explained about her unhappy childhood in a letter to Masaryk of March 4, 1929; she was born as an illegitimate child; her mother then married a man who had five children of his own, in addition to being an alcoholic, see Polák, *T.G. Masaryk*, 6: 281.
86 Ibid., 5, 11.

mayerová encountered the four ladies at a festival in Slavkov, Moravia, on July 5, 1931 and she recorded in her diary: "Dr. Gašparíková called Dr. Alice's attention to me and noted with a malicious smile: 'That is a Iago[87] in skirts.' [...] I am not afraid of those fairies (*sudičky*)."[88] Masaryk's secretary, Dr. Antonín Schenk was helpful to Masaryk in maintaining contact with Sedlmayerová, despite the hostility of family members, especially Alice. When Masaryk's health began to fail, Schenk read Sedlmayerová's letters to him.[89]

The main objective of Masaryk's literary collaboration with Oldra turned out to be writing a novel in which their emotions toward each other would be expressed.[90] Masaryk felt that only in this form he might be able to set forth his ideas about the power of love and its role in human life. Thus, with the President's support Sedlmayerová undertook to write a lengthy novel "Marie" which depicted the transition of a young woman from an unhappy marriage to the great ideals of Masaryk's realism. Masaryk was making his appearance not only as a philosopher, but also as Maria's fictional partner Jan Volynsky.[91] As the work progressed, as late as August 1931, he wrote enthusiastically about the passages of the novel which Sedlmayerova sent him: "How should I thank you for this proof of love, faith?...I felt it so vividly – o, Ola my sweet, oh, so sweet."[92] Again in September of the same year, he wrote while vacationing in Slovakia: "I feel parched without you, it is terrible... but only to be with you and then there will be calm and peace...if there is not in it a yearning for the lost paradise? I do not understand myself, I only know that day and night I think of you and yearn."[93]

---

87   A sinister character in Shakespeare's "Othello," who drove the protagonist to kill his own virtuous wife, Desdemona.

88   Literární archiv Památníku národního písemnictví v Praze (LA PNP), fond Sedlmayerová. Inv. no. 702, cited by Polák, *T.G. Masaryk*, 6: 288; see also 191–92.

89   Košťálová, *Rodokmen a soukromí T. G. Masaryka*, 145, 147, citing from Marie Holmová, "Ženy prezidenta Masaryka," *Mladá fronta dnes*, January 2006, in ww.cs-magazin.com.

90   The plan to compose a novel, written by Sedlmayerová under his guidance, was the last echo of his desire, dating to his student years to write a novelistic version of his autobiography; see Košťálová, *Rodokmen a soukromí T. G. Masaryka* , 167.

91   Košťálová, *Rodokmen a soukromí T. G. Masaryka* , 80.

92   "Jak Ti mám děkovat za ten důkaz lásky, víry?... tak živě jsem to cítil – Olo moje sladká, ach, jak sladká." Cited by Kovtun, *Republika v nebezpečném světě*. 589. At this time, Masaryk was addressing Sedlmayorová in the intimate second person singular; see Masaryk, *Dopisy Oldře*, 16–25.

93   "Já jsem vyprahlý po Tobě, je to hrozné...ale jen být s Tebou a bude pak klid a pokoj... jestli to není...touha po ztraceném ráji? Já si nerozumím, jen vím,že dnem a nocí vzpomínám a toužím." Masaryk, *Dopisy Oldře*, 83.

At this time Masaryk's feelings for Oldra again reached a high level of intensity and he started addressing her as his "sweet girl" (*sladká holka*) and using the intimate second person singular.[94] According to Jiří Kovtun, who had a chance to examine the manuscript of Sedlemayerová's unfinished draft of the novel, the love scenes between the protagonists in the novel, Jan (Masaryk) and Marie (Sedlmayerová), echo Masaryk's letters. As an example, he cites the following statement of the fictional Marie: "Your loneliness will disappear, my dear, with me, in my embrace,"[95] which responded to Masaryk's statement, complaining about his lonesomeness in his letter of August 28, 1928, cited above. Masaryk also contributed intimate passages, depicting what the characters emotionally experienced: "With her mouth in an insane yearning she submitted to him… And they belonged to each other, a man and a woman…" [96]

In their exchanges on the subject of love in the jointly written novel, Masaryk, however, also had a tendency to correct what he considered Ola's excessive stress on the physical aspects of the relationship by supplementing references to the intellectual or spiritual aspects. Thus he crossed out the following sentence in Ola's draft: "If our bodies do not become creators and enablers of life through a physical fruit…" and added a note "love is not just physical." In another sentence: "And my own body – I love it because of you," he crossed out the second part and replaced it with "and also my soul I commit to you."[97] This reflected Masaryk's previously expressed view – in his essay on Leo Tolstoy – "a marriage can and should be a joining of not only bodies, but also of souls."[98]

Nevertheless, sometime at the turn of 1932, Masaryk appeared to experience a gradual disillusionment in his relationship with Sedlemayerová, and his interest in her literary activity – in particular, the novel – which

---

94 Masaryk, *Dopisy Oldře*, 83.
95 Kovtun, *Republika v nebezpečném světě*, 590.
96 "S ústy mu v šíleném toužení podala sebe… A byli svoji muž a žena…" See Košťálová, *Rodokmen a soukromí T. G. Masaryka*, 80.
97 Polák, *T.G. Masaryk*, 6: 166, citing from Literární archiv Památníku národního písemnictví v Praze (LA-PNP), fond Oldra Sedlmayerová, inv. č. 461, 462.
98 Masaryk, *Rusko a Evropa III*, 305. In a way, Masaryk's love relationship with Sedlmayerová is reminiscent of Franklin D. Roosevelt's relationship with Lucy Mercer Rutherford, initiated in 1918 and resumed in 1943. It is characterized by one of the American president's major biographers, thus: "…FDR had allowed himself to be vulnerable to Lucy in 1918; they had talked of love and need; he had allowed himself to express strong passions…" and "whether or not they made love, the ardor of their caring was intense." Hugh G. Gallagher, *FDR's Splendid Deception* (New York: Dodd, Mead & Company, 1985), 144.

was to be based on their loving relationship, weakened and gradually evaporated. During 1933, when their communication, now mainly by correspondence, diminished and finally ceased completely, Masaryk shifted his attention to collaboration with Emil Ludwig and particularly Karel Čapek as vehicles to sum up his philosophical ideas for posterity.[99] This was despite the fact that originally he had been reluctant to talk with Čapek on the subject, because he assumed that Čapek entertained a different concept of love than he himself did.[100]

Masaryk's letters to Sedlmayerová, as well as the drafts of Sedlmayerová's novel, inspired by their erotic relationship, remained unpublished until the first decade of the twenty-first century.[101] As for other earlier amorous experiences, Masaryk mentioned only two to Čapek: one while a student in the German gymnasium in Brno in the late 1860s, and the other as a student in the gymnasium in Vienna in 1869–1872.[102] He notably avoided references to any intimacies in the relationship with his wife, Charlotte, who had died in 1923. He did, however, confide to Sedlmayerová that he had deeply loved and revered his wife, but that her psychological problems worried him. After these complications, he was delighted to find very late in life a loving woman even if she lacked Charlotte's depth and intellectuality.[103]

On the onset of Masaryk's disability in the late spring of 1934, Sedlmayerová lost contact with him altogether. She complained bitterly in a surviving letter of November 1936 to Jaroslav Stranský, a member of Czechoslovak Parliament, that Masaryk's entourage, primarily his family members, who had hindered her in seeing Masaryk when he was well, prevented her from seeing him completely after he became ill in 1934. She considered their attitude toward her not only indecent, but outright inhu-

---

99 Masaryk, *Dopisy Oldře*, 90, 93; see also Kovtun, *Republika v nebezpečném světě*, 591. This was despite the fact that originally he was reluctant to talk with Čapek on the subject, because he assumed that Čapek had a different concept of love than he himself. Masaryk, *Dopisy Oldře*, 10.

100 Masaryk, *Dopisy Oldře*, 10, 13–14.

101 These materials appeared in part in Masaryk, *Dopisy Oldře*; and earlier in *Masarykův sborník*, 10 (2000), 318–22, and 11–12 (2004), 424–31; and were discussed in Kovtun, *Republika v nebezpečném světě*, particularly, 586–96.; Stanislav Polák, *T.G. Masaryk: Za ideálem a pravdou*, 6 vols. (Prague: Masarykův ústav AV ČR, 2000–2012), Previously these documents had been deposied inaccessible in Literární archiv Památníku národního písemnictví v Praze (LA-PNP),fond Oldra Sedlmayerová, inv. č. 461, 462; and in Archiv Ústavu T. G. Masaryka, Prague, see Dagmar Hájková, "T. G. Masaryk," in Masaryk, *Dopisy Oldře*, 112–13.

102 Čapek, *Hovory s T. G. Masarykem*, 52–53, 57–58.

103 Polák, *T.G. Masaryk*, 6: 166, 279.

man.[104] She died alone in the Bohemian spa of Poděbrady on June 6, 1954.[105] In her advanced years her loneliness was relieved by correspondence with, and visits from, several devoted female literary friends.[106]

Two Routes to Ultimate Reality: Faith and Love

Masaryk's philosophical journey involved the search for an ontic reality beyond the empirically perceived phenomena. This endeavor led him, in the first place, to the channel of faith , inspired largely by Paul de Lagarde's concept of non-dogmatic religion, devoid of the theological narrative of traditional Christianity, and springing from secularized German Lutheranism. Such a religious orientation was also kindred to his American wife Charlotte's native Unitarianism (see Chapter 3). Masaryk supplemented this avenue by a second channel, derived from Plato, not from the rationalist metaphysics of transcendent Ideas, but from the emotive concept of immanent love. Eventually the epistemological aspect of love crescendoed, and was fully crystallized, in Masaryk's encounter with Oldra Sedlmayerová, as discussed in this chapter.

Hence, Masaryk essentially taught that the ascent to ultimate reality took either the route of faith, as derived from de Lagarde, or the route of love, as posited by Plato. In this way, Masaryk was in a position to safeguard the ontic character of individual beings, as well as the moral character and the divine rule of the universe. At the same time, his standpoint enabled him to escape the siren song of German metaphysics and to remain faithful to the realism of the Austrian philosophical tradition. Thus, as discussed in the following section of this study (Chapters 5–10), Masaryk's philosophical teaching, when applied to the realms of politics and social relations, supported the conditions of individual freedom and militated against the ideological underpinnings of collectivism.

---

104 Cited by Kovtun, *Republika v nebezpečném světě*, 594–95, from Hoover Institution Archives (HI), letter of Sedlmayerová, February 9, 1936.
105 Bártová and Bílek, "Oldra Sedlmayerová ve vzpomínkách Pavly Mocové," *Tvar*, 12 (1999), June 10, 14–15, cited by Kovtun, *Republika v nebezpečném světě*, 595.
106 Bártová and Bílek, "Oldra Sedlmayerová ve vzpomínkách Pavly Mocové," 14–15.

II
Politics

Chapter 5

Bohemian Reformation, Enlightenment/Liberalism, Ideal of Humanity

As noted earlier, Masaryk's basic conception of political life involved his vision of a morally oriented society, indicating the existence of a theistic divinity. His study of philosophy led him to conclude – despite his sympathy for Locke – that a stark empiricism could not sustain the proper moral dimension of politics and social life. On the contrary, empirical epistemology inspired the amoral character of the French or Voltairean Enlightenment and of its nineteenth-century offspring, the contemporary irreligious political liberalism. Masaryk's insistence – deriving from his "rational theism" – on the necessary role of religion not only in private life, but also in public affairs, may appear on its surface rather paradoxical.

Although reared as a Catholic and later a formal member of the Reformed (Calvinist) Church, Masaryk's religious views did not conform to the beliefs of traditional Christianity.[1] As discussed (in Chapter 3), in the context of his intellectual relations with the theologian and philosopher Paul de Lagarde, he did not accept the dogmas of the incarnation and the resurrection, or the concept of original sin and the consequent need for redemption. Jesus, for him, was a man and a prophet, whose teaching contained the gist of both theology and ethics; namely, the love of God and the love for one's neighbor, pointing to his eventual adoption of ontic love as the binding force within society and mankind (in Chapter 4). Unable

---

[1]   Tomáš G. Masaryk, *V boji o náboženství*, 3rd ed. (Prague: Čin, 1947), 24, 38–39, 40–41.

to accept the dogma of the Trinity, he held a theological position close to the Unitarianism practiced by his American wife, Charlotte, although he never became a Unitarian himself. He was, however, considerably embarrassed when, at his admission into the Reformed Church, he was asked to recite the Nicene Creed, which expressed beliefs that he did not hold.[2]

On the positive side, Masaryk strongly avowed the need to accept a theistic (personal or anthropomorphic) God who guaranteed the order and the meaning of the universe.[3] Masaryk stated that he would have found it impossible to live and engage in political and other public activity without the belief in Providence or the sense that he was participating in the fulfillment of a divine plan. According to him, the concept of God also provided an assurance that moral behavior in private and public had a deep meaning in God's plan to realize the ideal of Humanity. Within this framework, Masaryk felt optimistic that – despite occasional setbacks – there was a process toward the ever-fuller perfection of morals and intellectual life.[4] There was nothing mystical, according to Masaryk, in the perception and recognition of one's relationship to God and to the world process; these were just experiences, like the perceptions of nature and of specific mental states.[5]

According to Otakar Funda, that was the gist of the "rational theism," which Masaryk derived primarily from the teaching of Franz Brentano at the University of Vienna. Following this theological viewpoint, it was more reasonable to assume that the world and the life it supported were given a purpose by God rather than having no meaning at all. Within this context, Masaryk took the role of religion with a grave – one might say deadly – seriousness. Without the belief in a providential design, modern man would run the risk of losing the sense of a purposeful life and become a candidate for suicide.[6] As a particular illustration, Masaryk traced the advance of the divinely-inspired drama – "the national pursuit of Hu-

2   Otakar A. Funda, "Náboženství: téma pro české myšlení," in Jiří Brabec et al., *Cesta a odkaz T.G. Masaryka: fakta, úvahy, souvislosti,* ed. Jarmila Lakosilová (Prague: Nakl. Lidové noviny, 2002), 134.

3   See, for instance, Masaryk's statements in Emil Ludwig, *Defender of Democracy: Masaryk of Czechoslovakia* (New York: R. M. McBride, 1936), 74–75.

4   Ludwig, *Defender of Democracy: Masaryk of Czechoslovakia,* 255–256. For Masaryk's understanding of this process see, for instance, Tomáš G. Masaryk, *Moderní člověk a náboženství,* Spisy 8 (Prague: Masarykův ústav AV ČR, 2000), 71.

5   Masaryk, *V boji o náboženství,* 24.

6   Masaryk, *Moderní člověk a náboženství,* 31.

manity" – through the history of Bohemia from the Reformation through the National Awakening to the modern politics.[7]

The Bohemian Reformation

According to Masaryk, the proper religious underpinning of Czech political life derived historically from the ideas of the Bohemian Reformation. As we saw (in Chapter 3), however, the situation was complicated by what he considered the presence of two dissonant (virtually contradictory) currents that emanated from that Reformation. One, which was contrary to the spirit of the Czech National Awakening, stemmed from the Utraquist Church that was religiously sterile or worse; the other, which was in harmony with the spirit of the Awakening, stemmed from the Unity of Brethren that, in fact, aimed at the realization of the ideal of Humanity.[8] Masaryk's identification of the Czech idea with the ideal of Humanity – a sign of his cosmopolitanism or globalist view – has been subjected to criticism, as theologically misleading, and politically unpatriotic, because of its unwarranted exaggeration of the Czech penchant for Europeanism, world democracy, and universal humanism.[9]

Utraquism and its link to Voltairean liberalism

Paradoxically, Masaryk saw the negative influence of the Utraquist Church's legacy to the Czech National Awakening manifest in the amoral Voltairean Enlightenment. In the long run, the irreligious Enlightenment and the amoral Liberalism that the former had engendered, according to Masaryk, by their interference, vitiated the proper course of

---

7   The pursuit of Humanity involved on the intellectual level spread of education and increase of knowledge, and on the moral level expansion of freedom, tolerance, and democracy. See, for instance, Miloš Havelka, "Masaryk ve sporu o smysl českých dějin," Jarmila Lakosilová, ed., *Cesta a odkaz T.G. Masaryka: fakta, úvahy, souvislosti*, by Jiří Brabec et al. (Prague: Nakl. Lidové noviny, 2002), 124.

8   Tomáš G. Masaryk, Česká otázka. Naše nynější krize. Jan Hus, Spisy 6 (Prague: Masarykův ústav AV ČR, 2000), 88.

9   For instance, Arne Novák, "Světová revoluce," *Lumír* 53 (1926) in Novák, *Nosiči pochodní; kniha české tradice* (Prague, Literární odbor Umělecké besedy a Kruh českých spisovatelů, 1928), 221–222, 224.

the National Awakening. The main proponent of this negative Enlightenment, which was out of harmony with the intellectual ambiance of the
Awakening in Bohemia, was Josef Jungmann, the prominent figure in the
second generation of the Awakeners.[10] Jungmann imbibed the irreligious
current from Voltaire, who had also introduced him to the French Encyclopedists.[11] Aside from Jungmann, Masaryk discerned this "Liberalist in-
differentism" [liberalistický indiferentismus] to religion in other Awakeners,
such as Antonín Puchmajer and Václav Hanka.[12]

For Masaryk, the Voltairean Enlightenment was, likewise, contradictory to the core of the Bohemian Reformation, which was represented by
the uncompromising moralism of the militant Taborites and, above all,
of the Unity of Brethren. He saw congruence between the moral mias-
ma of the irreligious Liberalism and the moderate strand within the Bohemian Reformation, the mainline Utraquism of the sixteenth-century.
The latter's defect was epitomized by the theological via media or "a fear
of firm religious commitment" of Archbishop Jan Rokycana, vacillating
later, according to Masaryk, between Rome and the Protestant Reformation. For Masaryk, Jungmann was the Rokycana of the nineteenth century, and thus, Masaryk arrived in a back-handed way at the concept of
a liberal symbiosis between the National Awakening and Utraquism.[13] Of
course, for him this was merely a sideshow (and a rather undesirable one)
to the main glorious drama of the symbiosis between the Awakening and
the moralism of the Unity of Brethren, as discussed later in this chapter.

Masaryk apparently derived his ideas about Utraquism from secondary
literature. As a result, he repeated the widespread (albeit erroneous) claim
that the Utraquist theologian, Bohuslav Bílejovský (1537) sought the origin
of the Bohemian Christianity in Eastern Orthodoxy.[14] In addition, nine-

---

10 Masaryk, Česká otázka. Naše nynější krize. Jan Hus, 15, 88.
11 Ibid., 110.
12 Masaryk, Česká otázka. Naše nynější krize. Jan Hus, 19, 330, 347. Concerning Masaryk's distinc-
    tion in the 1890s between the humanism of the Unity of Brethren and that of the French Revo-
    lution, see Karel Vorovka, "Několik myšlenek o Masarykově filosofii a jeho Světové revoluci," Ruch
    filosofický 5 (1925), 268–69.
13 Masaryk, Česká otázka. Naše nynější krize. Jan Hus, 347–348. On the via media of Utraquism,
    see Zdeněk V. David, Finding the Middle Way: The Utraquists' Liberal Challenge to Rome and Lu-
    ther (Washington, D.C.: Woodrow Wilson Center Press; Baltimore: Johns Hopkins University
    Press, 2003).
14 Masaryk, Česká otázka. Naše nynější krize. Jan Hus, 141. See also Kamil Krofta, "Slovo o knězi Bo-
    huslavu Bílejovském," in Krofta, Listy z náboženských dějin českých (Prague: Historický klub, 1936),
    300; David, Finding the Middle Way: The Utraquists' Liberal Challenge to Rome and Luther, 100–101.

teenth-century historians, particularly Václav Tomek and Josef Kalousek, mistakenly assumed that sixteenth-century Utraquism had become virtually synonymous with a morally lax Lutheranism.[15] This view passed on to Masaryk through the prestigious work of the French historian of Bohemia, Ernst Denis, and affected his interpretation of the long-term political influence of Utraquism.[16]

Considering the claim of the alleged contamination of Utraquism by Luther's teaching, it is relevant to note that Masaryk also had his own reservations against Lutheranism, of which he gained firsthand knowledge during his university studies in Leipzig in 1876–1878. In his view, Luther's main weakness was his heavy reliance on the message of St. Paul, rather than the message of Jesus. Paul had been affected by mysticism and ecstasy, and his example led Luther into a state of agitation and excitement. Agitated people, according to Masaryk, even if prophets or reformers, engendered a religion of turbulence. The true religion of Jesus, on the contrary, was calm, unexcited, and sunny.[17]

In addition to its convergence with "middle of the road" Utraquism, Voltairean Liberalism – according to Masaryk – continued the demoralizing and debilitating work of the Jesuit Counter-Reformation by undermining principled morality. The Counter-Reformation (1620–1773), for Masaryk had engendered among the Czechs insincerity, half-heartedness, and a lack of character (due to its religious coercion).[18] If there was any Catholic input into this secular Liberalism, it stemmed not from the benign Jansenist Enlightenment, but from the echoes of the Counter Reformation. He attributed to Jungmann a casuistic attitude learned from the Jesuits.[19] For Masaryk, Jungmann also exhibited – based on his secret diary – the main detrimental effect of the Counter Reformation on

15 Otakar Josek, Život a dílo Josefa Kalouska (Prague: Historický spolek, 1922), 292, cited by Krofta, Nesmrtelný národ: Od Bílé Hory k Palackému (Prague: Laichter, 1940) 350–351; Jaroslav Čechura and Jana Čechurová, eds., Korespondence Josefa Pekaře a Kamila Krofty (Prague: Karolinum, 1999), 87; František Šamalík, Úvahy o dějinách české politiky: Od reformace k osvícenství, 2nd ed. (Prague: Victoria Publishing, 1996), 79.

16 Masaryk, Česká otázka. Naše nynější krize. Jan Hus, 150. See also, for instance, Ernst Denis, Fin de l'indépendance bohême, 2nd ed. (Paris: Librairie Leroux, 1930), 2:83, 91–94, 295–302. See also Doubravka Olšáková, "Český překlad Denisova díla v kontextu sporu o smysl českých dějin," Dějiny a současnost, no. 5 (2001), 28–32; Doubravka Olšáková, "Husitství, Ernst Denis a spor o smysl českých dějin," Husitský Tábor, 14 (2004), 83–110.

17 Masaryk, V boji o náboženství, 23–24.

18 Masaryk, Česká otázka. Naše nynější krize. Jan Hus, 317.

19 Ibid., 88–89.

the Czech mind: teaching individuals to conceal their strongest innermost convictions.[20] He pointed out that Jungmann in that respect cited the Jesuit rule: "Vult mundus decipi, ergo decepiamur."[21]

Returning to Utraquism's connection with modern political life, Masaryk maintained that its middle-of-the-road approach to public life was resurrected and perpetuated (in a symbiosis with the Voltairean Enlightenment) not only in the influential outlook of Jungmann and his cohorts during the Bohemian National Awakening, but also in subsequent Czech politics. Jungmann's mantle as the Rokycana of the early nineteenth century was passed on to later generations. These liberal Rokycanas of the late nineteenth century, who claimed to represent the Czech national idea, were mere imposters – despite their large number. They found their ultimate embodiment (and abomination) in the Young Czechs, the major political party in Bohemia in the late nineteenth century.[22] Jungmann's Voltairean version of the Enlightenment turned into the Young Czechs' Liberalism, which became indifferent to the questions of religion, philosophy and morality.[23] To Masaryk, Jungmann's legacy shaped the Young Czechs' ideological program, while exemplifying much that was wrong with the Enlightenment in Bohemia: "for its emphasis on reason, it easily neglected the soul and its moral and religious life, and that meant that its efforts were not sufficiently deep, satisfied by-and-large with a superficial luster."[24]

Even when certain members of the Young Czech Party tried to fill the religious vacuum, these Liberals –bedeviled by their narrow nationalism – took the wrong turn. The propagation of the heritage of Saints Cyril and Methodius, seeking support in Byzantine Christianity, led them down a blind alley, eliciting no significant response from the Czech public. A flagrant example of this inappropriateness was the demonstrative conversion to Eastern Orthodoxy by Karel Sladkovský, one of the leaders of the Young

---

20 Ibid., 330.
21 Masaryk, Česká otázka. Naše nynější krize. Jan Hus, 89. For Masaryk's reference to Jungmann, see Josef J. Jungmann, *Zápisky*, ed. Radek Lunga (Prague: Budka, 1998), 49–50. See also Masaryk, *V boji o náboženství*, 40.
22 Masaryk, Česká otázka. Naše nynější krize. Jan Hus, 347–348. On Masaryk's continued aversion to the "golden middle road;" see also Tomáš G. Masaryk, *Světová revoluce za války a ve válce, 1914–1918*, Spisy 15 (Prague: Masarykův ústav AV ČR, 2005), 269.
23 Masaryk, Česká otázka. Naše nynější krize. Jan Hus, 178. See also Felix Vodička, *Cesty a cíle obrozenské literatury* (Prague: Československý spisovatel, 1958), 142–44.
24 Masaryk, Česká otázka. Naše nynější krize. Jan Hus, 330.

Czechs.[25] Masaryk strongly rejected the idea of Russian Slavophiles that the Bohemian Reformation had its roots in Eastern Orthodoxy, dating to the mission of Sts. Cyril and Methodius.[26] As far as there were outside influences on the Bohemian Reformation, they came from the West, especially England.[27] Masaryk had attempted to reform the Young Czech Party from within during his brief membership in 1891–1893, when he served as a deputy for the party in the Austrian parliament, the Reichsrat, in Vienna.[28] He went on to establish his own Realist Party in 1900.

In sum, the Voltairean Enlightenment led to the diffusion of irreligious Liberalism, which contradicted the proper program of the Czech National Revival that had its roots in the Bohemian Reformation, as exemplified by the Unity of Brethren. Masaryk drew a correlation between – on one hand – the religious via media of mainline Utraquism and – on the other hand – the secularist Liberalism which (some four hundred years later) attempted to vitiate the philosophical orientation of the National Awakening. Considering Rokycana's Utraquists amoral in their lukewarm "middle-of-the-road" position, Masaryk saw their intellectual openness (or latitudinarianism), combined with liberal ecclesiology, not as positive distinctions, but as signs of uncertainty, weakness, and degradation.[29]

The source of Masaryk's view of Utraquist amorality

In a way, Masaryk's depiction of Rokycana's Utraquism reflected the prevalent views of the nineteenth century historiography, many of which have carried on into the twenty-first century. While the radical sect of the Bo-

---

25 Ibid., 137, 348.

26 Masaryk, Tomáš G., *Rusko a Evropa I*, Spisy 11 (Prague: Masarykův ústav AV ČR, 1996). 229.

27 Masaryk, Tomáš G., *Slovanské studie a texty z let 1889–1891*, Spisy 20 (Prague: Masarykův ústav AV ČR, 2007), 50. Subsequently, Masaryk returned to the denunciation of the Cyrilo-Methodian Idea in an article in *Naše doba* in 1894, as a misuse to bolster the claim for a Czech statehood, independent from Austria and/or Germany; see Masaryk, Česká otázka. Naše nynější krize. Jan Hus, 423.

28 Masaryk's understanding of the Czech intellectual tradition, however, did not simply reflect his disagreement with the Young Czechs in the 1890s, which he would then read back into history. Rather his assessment of that tradition bore a clear imprint of his earlier philosophical values, which he had – as noted in the beginning of this article – also shared with Lange. See Havelka, "Masaryk ve sporu o smysl českých dějin," in Lakosilová, ed., *Cesta a odkaz T.G. Masaryka*, 123, 126.

29 On the sources of Masaryk's view of the amoral character of Utraquism, see Josek, Život a dílo Josefa Kalouska, 292, cited by Kamil Krofta, *Nesmrtelný národ: Od Bílé Hory k Palackému* (Prague: Laichter, 1940), 350–51; Čechura and Čechurová, eds., *Korespondence Josefa Pekaře a Kamila Krofty)*, 87; see also David, *Finding the Middle Way: The Utraquists' Liberal Challenge to Rome and Luther*, 12.

hemian Reformation, the Unity of Brethren, was acclaimed for its virtues, the mainstream Utraquist Church was widely regarded as afflicted by a low moral threshold of its clergy and laity.[30] Another charge was that of duplicity and toadyism of its Administrators and Consistories toward the agents of the Habsburg monarchs and the Roman Church in the issues of priestly ordinations and of other relations with the Church of Rome.[31] Ironically, as a result (and as we see in Masaryk's interpretation), the Utraquist Church, albeit the most substantial legatee of the Bohemian Reformation, did not receive – in contrast to the Unity of Brethren – positive credit in Czech historiography for its normative role in shaping the Czechs' political culture.

The image of Utraquists as lacking in moral stamina resulted largely from the types of sources used in historical literature. The Utraquists have traditionally been depicted on the basis of the Consistory's administrative and court records, revealing primarily the seamy side in the behavior of their clergy and laity. Their historical self-descriptions, like the crucial work of Bohuslav Bílejovský, have been almost routinely dismissed.[32] In contrast, the Bohemian Brethren have been assessed on the basis of their historical self-descriptions. Reliance on the Brethren's accounts of

---

30 Kamil Kofta, "Nový názor na český vývoj náboženský v době předbělohorské," in his *Listy z náboženských dějin českých* (Prague: Historický klub, 1936), 380–381. Kamil Krofta provides a comprehensive overview of these charges in his *Nesmrtelný národ: Od Bílé Hory k Palackému* (Prague: Laichter, 1940), 344–429. A recent writer has still characterized the period as one of "social and moral laxity and abulia;" see Zdeněk Rotrekl, *Barokní fenomén v součastnosti* (Prague: Trost, 1995), 129. See also František Kameníček, "Pod obojí (utrakvisté)," *Zemské sněmy a sjezdy moravské, 1526–1628*, 3 vols. (Brno: Zemský výbor Markrabství moravského, 1900–1905), 3: 418–19; Ferdinand Hrejsa, Česká konfesse: Její vznik, podstata a dějiny (Prague: Česká akademie pro vědy, slovesnost a umění, 1912), 58; Václav Novotný, "Náboženské dějiny české ve století 16.," in *Česká politika*, ed. Zdeněk V. Tobolka, 5 vols. (Prague: Jan Laichter, 1906), 1: 634, 637;

31 On the Consistory's abject and evasive dealings with archbishops Antoním Brus and Martin Medek, and with papal nuncios see, for instance, Kamil Krofta, "Boj o konsistoř podobojí v l. 1562–1575 a jeho historický základ," Český časopis historický, 17 (1911), 386, 391, 401–3; Josef Matoušek, "Kurie a boj o konsistoř pod obojí za administrátora Rezka," Český časopis historický, 37 (1931), 23, 27–8, 31, 252, 274, 281; Karel Stloukal, "Počátky nunciatury v Praze: Bonhomi v Čechách, 1581–84," Český časopis historický 34 (1928), 15–16, 256; Zikmund Winter, Život církevní v Čechách: Kulturně-historický obraz z XV. a XVI. století. 2 vols. (Prague: Česká akademie pro vědy, slovesnost a umění, 1895), 1: 182–83, 330–34. On the topic of diplomatic deception see David, *Finding the Middle Way: The Utraquists' Liberal Challenge to Rome and Luther*, 156–58.

32 The typical sources for the treatment of the Utraquists have been Klement Borový, *Jednání a dopisy konsistoře katolické a utrakvistické* (Prague: I. L. Kober, 1868) or Julius Pažout's *Jednání a dopisy konsistoře pod obojí způsobou přijímajících, 1562–1570* (Prague: Historický spolek, 1906), see especially page v. The lurid cases of clerical transgressions were dredged up with great diligence and colorfully presented with a definite *Schadenfreude*, for instance, by Zikmund Winter in Život církevní v Čechách; and by Antonín Podlaha in "Úpadek strany podobojí na sklonku XVI. století," *Sborník historického kroužku*, 5 (1904), 29–36, 65–69, 161–64, 219–27.

events has tended to skew the record not only in favor of the Brethren, but also strongly against the Utraquists; the Brethren, despite their many virtues, were notoriously uncharitable toward their opponents.[33] One is tempted to apply to them the critical characterization of the Puritans as those "who delighted in nothing so much as the contemplation of their own virtue and the condemnation of the supposed vices of others."[34] For instance, even the sympathetic Kamil Krofta, one of the leading historians of the Bohemian Reformation, demurs at the Brethren's verbal assaults on Utraquist clergy.[35]

Aside from the Brethren, the adherents of the Roman Curia had a singular reason to depict Utraquist priests in an uncomplimentary way. The Utraquist Church received a steady supply of priests by transfers from the Roman obedience and, in the eyes of Rome, such converts were *ipso facto*, tainted morally or intellectually. The blanket and unsubstantiated charges from the Roman side, which ordinarily might be dismissed as self-serving, gained credibility when they were reproduced – for reasons of their own – by Protestant and secular historians.[36] Finally, some of the disparaging characterizations of the Utraquists have, in all likelihood, stemmed from the reports of papal nuncios, like Cesare Speciano and Giovanni Dolfin who, from the vantage point of Italian cultural refinement, marveled at the crude manners and behavior of the transalpine central Europeans.[37]

---

33 In addition, the Brethren carried much of their documentation into the safety of exile, while material favorable to the Utraquists tended to perish during the Counter Reformation in Bohemia and Moravia. The typical sources for the treatment of the Brethren have been *Akty Jednoty bratrské*, ed. Jaroslav Bidlo (Brno: Matice moravská, 1915–23), vols. 1–2; Anton Gindely, *Quellen zur Geschichte der böhmischen Brüder* (Vienna: Hof und Staatsdruckerei, 1859); or "Diarium... Bratří českých," *Sněmy české*, 4: 392–464. On the Brethrens' expressions of vengefulness, see Winter, *Život církevní*, 1: 495–96.

34 Peter Lake, *Anglicans and Puritans? Presbyterianism and English Conformist thought from Whitgift to Hooker* (London: Unwin Hyman, 1988), 5. On Puritan invectives against the Church of England clergy, see Penry Williams, *The Later Tudors: England, 1547–1603* (Oxford: Clarendon Press, 1995), 481. Richard Hooker, *The Folger Library Edition of the Works*. 6 vols. ed. W. Speed Hill (Cambridge, MA.: Harvard University Press, 1977–1993), 1: 18; 6: 14; see also John S. Marshall, *Hooker and the Anglican tradition: an historical and theological study of Hooker's Ecclesiastical Polity* (Sewanee, Tenn.: The University Press at the University of the South, 1963), 32–33.

35 Thus, he is dismayed at their unsubstantiated characterization of the Utraquist Administrator Martin Mělnický, as "a dishonorable man, a liar, a drunkard, an obvious whoremonger..." ["... člověk nevážný, lhář, ožralec, kurevník zjevný...,"] see Krofta's "Boj o konsistoř," 302, n. 2.

36 Kameníček, *Zemské sněmy a sjezdy moravské*, 3: 419.

37 Matoušek, "Kurie a boj o konsistoř," 31, 267; *Nuntiaturberichte aus Deutschland*. Dritte Abteilung, 1572–1585, 8. Band: *Nuntiatur Giovanni Delfins, 1575–1576*, ed. Daniela Neri (Tübingen: Max Niemayer, 1997), 74; also Anna Skýbová, "Cesta po Čechách v roce 1561," *Český lid* 63 (1975), 99; Hrejsa, *Česká konfesse*, 58.

As for the willingness of historians to accept at face value slanderous assertions against the Utraquists, Krofta supplies an intriguing insight in this area. As noted earlier, Krofta has traced this image of Utraquism to nineteenth-century historians, particularly Václav Tomek and Josef Kalousek, who mistakenly assumed that sixteenth-century Utraquism became synonymous with Lutheranism, and that Luther's solafideism fostered immorality.[38] Passed on to Masaryk through the prestigious work of the French historian of Bohemia, Ernst Denis, this view affected his interpretation of the long-term political influence of Utraquism. In fact, these views were expressed in Masaryk's Česká otázka (The Czech Question), also cited earlier.[39] Thus, for Masaryk, the Bohemian Reformation ended in a moral morass and chaos in the sixteenth century under the modern label of Neo-Utraquism.[40] On a practical level, it has been shown that Utraquist theology and homiletics, in fact, run counter to the charges of Utraquism's inherent immorality. The exhortation to good deeds in fulfillment of the "Law of God" was one of the leitmotifs of Utraquist education. If Luther indeed had taught his followers not to worry – because of Christ's redemptive sacrifice – about observing religious laws and commandments, the Utraquists contrarily held the observance of the Law of God among their highest priorities. Responsible Utraquist ecclesiastics looked askance at Lutheranism's denial of the soteriological value of works.[41] Consequently, the charge of immorality or Epicurean-like licentiousness on the basis of solafideism was not applicable to Utraquism at all. Far from indifference to moral values, examples of fervent exhortation to virtue and good works can be found in surviving homiliaries from each of the three centuries of Utraquist preaching.[42] Contrary to the Breth-

---

38   Josek, Život a dílo Josefa Kalouska, 292, cited by Krofta, Nesmrtelný národ: Od Bílé Hory k Palackému, 350–51; Čechura and Čechurová, eds., Korespondence Josefa Pekaře a Kamila Krofty, 87; Šamalík, Úvahy o dějinách české politiky: Od reformace k osvícenství, 79.

39   Masaryk, Česká otázka, Naše nynější krize. Jan Hus, 150–55.

40   See the evidence presented in Zdeněk V. David, "Celistvost české církve pod obojí a otázka novoutrakvismu" Český časopis historický, vol. 101, no. 4, 2003, 882–910; and idem, "The Integrity of the Bohemian Reformation: The Problem of Neo-Utraquism," in The Transformation of Czech and Slovak Societies on the Threshold of the New Millennium and Their Role in the Global World, Selected Papers from the 21st World Congress [SVU], University of West Bohemia, Plzeň, Czech Republic, June 23–30, 2002, ed. Jan P. Skalny and Miloslav Rechcígl, Jr. (Plzeň: Aleš Čeněk, [2004]), 167–98.

41   On the Utraquist views of the good works, see the attitudes of Pavel Bydžovský and Vavřinec Leander Rvačovský of Rvačov in David, Finding the Middle Way, 118–19, 223–24.

42   For instance, Václav Koranda, Jr., in 1489 to Valentin Polon in 1589 and Jan Cykáda in 1607; see Krofta, Nesmrtelný národ, 381–82; Jan Cykáda, Hody křesťanské (Prague: Impressí Šumanská,

ren's assertion, Utraquist priests held a particularly exalted view of their calling and duties.[43]

Thus, from the present-day viewpoint, the Utraquists' intellectual openness or latitudinarianism, combined with liberal ecclesiology, is likely to be perceived as a positive distinction rather than a detrimental aspect.

The Unity of Brethren: the positive aspect of the Bohemian Reformation

In contrast to the critical remarks about the Voltairean Enlightenment, a movement that Masaryk claimed spawned irreligious Liberalism, he recognized another strand in the Enlightenment which was sound and rested solidly on a religious foundation. This strand of the eighteenth-century Enlightenment in Germany, England, and France was, in fact, an extension of the sound and authentic spirit of the Bohemian Reformation stemming from the Unity of Brethren, which separated from the Utraquist church in 1457.[44] Once more relying heavily on the French historian Ernst Denis, Masaryk claimed that the religious and philosophical input of the Bohemian Reformation in this positive Enlightenment was derived, above all, from Jan Komenský (John Comenius), the exiled bishop of the Unity,[45] and continued through the German Protestant philosophers Gottfried W.

1607), f. B1r-v; Valentin Polon, *Pomni na mne: Knižka obahující v sobě kratičká spasidedlná Naučení a sebrání...* (Staré Město Pražské: Buryan Valda, 1589), see his exhortations to priests, f. A6-2a-b, parents and youth, f. K5-3a - L5-1a, and to laity in general, f. B2a-b.

43 Polon summed up his view of the glory and duty of priesthood stipulating the following for the clergy: "...they should conscientiously tend to their office, remain steady in their calling, lead the people in goodness and morality, follow Christ in his footsteps and [follow] the holy Fathers in their salvific teachings, point the way to good order and Christian piety, provide examples of virtue, avoid scandal, shine like lights and radiate virtue among the faithful (Matthew 5), and resist the sins and temptations of the world..." Polon, *Pomni na mne*, f. A7r; see also A8r-v. Regarding the priests' duty to set a good example by deeds, not only by words, see Vavřinec Leander Rvačovský of Rvačov, *Masopust* (Prague: Jiří Melantrich, 1580), f. D2v.

44 Masaryk, *Česká otázka. Naše nynější krize. Jan Hus*, 15, 347; Masaryk, *V boji o náboženství*, 38. It can be argued that British Enlightenment, which chronologically preceded and influenced the French variant, remained, especially in religious matters, more moderate than its Gallic counterpart; see also J. C. D. Clark, *Revolution and Rebellion: State and Society in England in the Seventeenth and Eighteenth Centuries* (New York: Cambridge University Press, 1986), 104–11, especially 110, on the religious element in the political thought of British Enlightenment, cited by Dale K. Van Kley, "Christianity as Casualty and Chrysalis of Modernity: The Problem de Dechristianization in the French Revolution," *American Historical Review*, 108 (2003), 1087.

45 Masaryk, *V boji o náboženství*, 30.

Leibniz and Johann G. Herder, who were both deeply influenced by Komenský's writings. To Masaryk, Komenský's impact on Herder was particularly strong and Herder, in turn, affected Josef Dobrovský and Jan Kollár,
the leading figures in the early phases of the National Awakening in Bohemia.[46] Thus, Dobrovský and Kollár became the counterparts to Jungmann with the former representing the positive aspects of the Bohemian
Awakening, and the latter the negative ones.

To the extent that this positive Enlightenment was mediated to Bohemia through German philosophy, especially by Herder, the service represented – according to Masaryk – just a payment on an earlier debt, as
the Bohemian Reformation had previously fertilized German soil for the
growth of new ideas. This enrichment was thanks to the Czech religious
refugees and exiles after the Battle of the White Mountain (1620). They
represented the most upstanding members of the oppressed nation and
helped to ennoble the German spirit. The German input, in turn, assist-
ed in overcoming what Masaryk considered to be the Bohemian intellectual coma, precipitated by the Counter Reformation.[47]

Likewise, Masaryk recognized a positive Liberalism in Karel Havlíček
Borovský and František Palacký, the two seminal figures in the beginning of formal Czech politics in 1848.[48] Both called themselves "liberals,"
with Havlíček explicitly describing the political current to which he belonged as the "national liberal party."[49] However, according to Masaryk,
both Havlíček and Palacký found later liberalism distasteful and rejected
its irreligious or even anti-religious character that was apparent in much of
mid-century Germany, and which was indifferent to the ultimate purpose
of human life.[50] For Havlíček and Palacký, Liberalism had a moral content, which derived from a religious basis, and Masaryk quoted Havlíček's
statement that Christianity was the foundation and essence of true Liberalism. Both Havlíček and Palacký had proclaimed their devotion to re-

---

46 Masaryk, *Světová revoluce za války a ve válce, 1914–1918*, 391, 396, 399. See also in the English
    trans., Masaryk, *The Making of a State: Memories and Observations, 1914–1918*, ed. Henry W.
    Steed (New York: George Allen and Unwin, 1927), 424, 433. This view has been disputed by Kon-
    rad Bittner, *Herders Geschichtsphilosophie und die Slawen*. (Reichenberg: Gebr. Stiepel, 1929), 106.
47 Masaryk, Česká otázka. Naše nynější krize. Jan Hus, 15.
48 They provided a corrective to the irreligious Liberalism stemming from Jungmann and Voltaire;
    Masaryk, Česká otázka. Naše nynější krize. Jan Hus, 89, 178; see also 330.
49 Tomáš G. Masaryk, *Karel Havlíček: Snahy a tužby politického probuzení*, Spisy 7 (Prague:
    Masarykův ústav AV ČR, 1996), 141.
50 Masaryk, *Karel Havlíček: Snahy a tužby politického probuzení*, 183.

ligion; for Palacký, religion represented the Reformation principles of the Unity of Brethren; for Havlíček, those of Jan Hus.[51]

In this regard, Masaryk highlighted Palacký's reservations toward the famous compendium of liberal statecraft by Karl Rotteck and Karl Welcker. Although this reference work was considered paradigmatic in Central Europe at the time, the Czech statesman viewed it as excessively secularistic.[52] For Masaryk, Havlíček was far from indifferent to religion. His lifelong endeavors to mitigate clericalism and the hierarchical church administration served as proof of that.[53] On that score, Masaryk argued that Havlíček's attention to church affairs was not merely political, but reflected genuine religious convictions[54] and a wish to reform the church according to the principles of Hus.[55] Somewhat unexpectedly – and despite his skepticism about liberal Catholicism – Masaryk also saw evidence of Havlíček's religiosity in his respect and affection for Bernard Bolzano.[56]

In view of their religious orientations, Havlíček and Palacký, according to Masaryk, sought to apply Kollár's plan for the fulfillment of Humanity in politics. This plan stemmed from Herder, and Masaryk traced its origins ultimately to the Unity of Brethren.[57] Palacký had already emphasized the significance of the Unity of Brethren, which had excelled over any other attempts at religious reformation. The Brethren rejected both the existing church and state, and thus they perspicaciously perceived the substance of medieval theocracy as an intimate connection between the state and the church. The anarchism of their progenitor, Petr Chelčický, was soon moderated by his successors. Jiří of Poděbrady, although an opponent of the Brethren, agreed with a fundamental ideal of the Unity, that of an eternal peace. Komenský, the last bishop of the Unity, advocated schooling

51   Masaryk, *Karel Havlíček: Snahy a tužby politického probuzení*, 196; Tomáš G. Masaryk, *Národnostní filosofie doby novější*, 2nd ed. (Prague: Melantrich, 1919), 38.

52   Karl W. Rotteck and Karl T. Welcker, *Das Staats-Lexikon. Encyklopädie der sämmtlichen Staatswissenschaften für alle Stände*, 12 vols. (Altona: J. F. Hammerich, 1845–1848); see Masaryk, *Karel Havlíček: Snahy a tužby politického probuzení*, 102.

53   Masaryk, *Karel Havlíček: Snahy a tužby politického probuzení*, 187.

54   Ibid., 199–200.

55   Ibid., 193.

56   Masaryk, *Česká otázka. Naše nynější krize. Jan Hus*, 78–79, 329.

57   Masaryk, *Karel Havlíček: Snahy a tužby politického probuzení*, 181–82.

and education aimed at a development of Humanity; through education he expected to realize a program which was national and at the same time entirely cosmopolitan.[58] As Jan Patočka has pointed out, Masaryk could also appreciate the fact that Palacký saw a manifest example of humanitarianism in the Bohemian Reformation, a synthesis of democratic equality, freedom of thought, and deep moralism, which Masaryk cherished as a continuing leitmotif of Czech history.[59]

To those who would object that the ideas of Palacký and Havlíček lack the religious tenor of the Brethren's original teaching, Masaryk pointed out that a similar genesis of modern political ideas from antecedent religious ones may be observed elsewhere throughout history. He cites the example of Kant, who was indisputably rooted in the Protestant tradition, but who did not adopt Luther's catechism; and who, on the contrary, rejected all theology. Nevertheless, his individualism, subjectivism, and moralism were indubitably rooted in Lutheran Protestantism. In other words, he transformed the crucial ideas of Lutheranism into a secular philosophical system, which might even be contrary to Protestant orthodoxy. [60]

Thus, for Masaryk, the sound political liberalism of both Havlíček and Palacký was in harmony with the genuine elements of Bohemia's religious past. Masaryk recognized in them an adherence to a strand of the Enlightenment that, unlike the Voltairean one, was positive and rested solidly on a religious base. That version of the eighteenth-century Enlightenment was not restricted to Bohemia but represented a Europe-wide intellectual legacy of the radicals of the Bohemian Reformation, the Unity of Brethren.[61] Masaryk felt that Havlíček's and Palacký's views and attitude should, in turn, inform Czech politics in the future. From what was said, it is evident that Masaryk's understanding of the Czech intellectual tradition did not simply reflect his current conflicts with the Young Czech Party in the 1890s, which he would then read back or project into history. Instead, his negative assessment of nationalist liberalism bore the distinctive and clear imprint of his earlier philosophical values.

---

58 Masaryk, *Světová revoluce za války a ve válce,* 391.
59 Jan Patočka, "Filosofie českých dějin," *Sociologický časopis* 5 (1969), no. 5, 461.
60 Masaryk, *Světová revoluce za války a ve válce,* 391.
61 Masaryk, Česká otázka. Naše nynější krize. Jan Hus, 15.

Disregard of Catholic Enlightenment

In view of Masaryk's focus on the Bohemian Reformation and his conviction that Catholicism was inherently incompatible with modern science and
thought, he found it difficult, if not impossible, to appreciate the phenomena of the Catholic Enlightenment and the ensuing liberal Catholicism, to
which it gave birth.[62] Masaryk, in fact, adopted an ambivalent view on the
role of the Josephist Enlightenment in the National Awakening as a whole.[63]
In the case of the Catholic Enlightenment, he did not attempt to fit its outstanding representative, Dobrovský, into this clear religious pattern and rather imposed on him the unlikely role of propagator of the ideals of the Unity of Brethren.[64] As far as can be judged, Dobrovský respected the linguistic
skills of the Brethren, but otherwise viewed them as extremist sectarians.[65]
Beyond that, Masaryk did not recognize the line of thinkers including Karl
H. Seibt, Bolzano, Michael J. Fesl, František Příhonský, and Franz Exner,
who, in the spirit of Catholic Enlightenment, molded the intellectual life of
Bohemia from the late eighteenth into the mid-nineteenth century, as I have
argued in a previous book.[66] He recognized, albeit rather marginally, only
the most remarkable figure among them – Bolzano. Masaryk noted him as
a protégé of Dobrovský (with whom he shared a humanistic ideology), and
as Havlíček's teacher.[67] Masaryk's rather lukewarm appreciation of Bolzano
may be in part explained by the latter's adherence in his political theory to
utilitarianism, which Masaryk deplored, considering it ethically shallow.[68]

---

62 Masaryk, *Moderní člověk a náboženství*, 133.
63 Masaryk here appeared to follow the widespread identification of the Austro-Bohemian Enlightenment with French variant which indeed exhibited, especially in its later phases, strong
anti-religious tendencies. Recent research has considered the French type more of an exception
than the rule; see Jonathan Sheehan, "Enlightenment, Religion, and the Enigma of Secularization: A Review Essay," *American Historical Review*, 108 (2003), 1068, citing J. G. A. Pocock, *Bar-
barism and Religion: The Enlightenments of Edward Gibbon, 1737–1764* (Cambridge Cambridge
University Press, 1999); Jonathan Clark, *English Society, 1660–1832*, 2nd ed (Cambridge, Cambridge University Press, 2000), 28; David Sorkin, *Moses, Mendelsohn and the Religious Enlightenment* (Berkeley, CA.: University of California Press, 1996).
64 Masaryk, *Česká otázka. Naše nynější krize. Jan Hus*, 148.
65 Josef Dobrovský, *Dějiny české řeči a literatury v redakcích z roku 1791, 1792 a 1818*, ed.. Benjamin
Jedlička (Prague: Melantrich, 1936), 421.
66 Zdeněk V. David, *Realism, Tolerance, Liberalism in the Czech National Awakening: Legacies of
the Bohemian Reformation* (Washington, D.C.: Wilson Center Press; and Baltimore: The Johns
Hopkins University Press, 2010), 134–54, 215–28.
67 Masaryk, *Česká otázka. Naše nynější krize. Jan Hus*, 15, 39–40,
68 See his references to Jeremy Bentham in Masaryk, *Moderní člověk a náboženství*, 88; Masaryk,
Karel Havlíček: Snahy a tužby politického probuzení, 200.

As for liberal Catholicism, the fact that Masaryk did not appreciate the liberal feature of Utraquism and its ecclesiology makes it evident that he would not anticipate anything positive stemming from a renewal of the Roman Church. This was, indeed, expected by some of his immediate predecessors among the leading intellectual figures on Bohemia's political stage in 1848. They included František Náhlovský, Václav Tomek, and Havlíček, the last of whom Masaryk admired, as previously noted.[69] For Masaryk, the main weakness of liberal Catholicism was that it focused on the reform of church administration, not on the reform of dogmatic theology.[70] Needless to say, after 1848 (and during Masaryk's lifetime) the Roman Church did not give any signs of moving in a liberal direction of any kind.

The declaration of papal infallibility by the First Vatican Council in 1870 finally confirmed Masaryk's worst suspicions. Prior to his joining the Reformed Church ten years later, his immediate reaction in response to the Vatican Council's decision was to consider himself an Old Catholic (a member of the church which went into schism over the issue of infallibility), and to declare himself as such to the professor of religion at his gymnasium in Vienna. Yet worship in the Old Catholic Church was not immediately available. Instead, he began attending Eastern rite churches, both Uniate and Orthodox. In the official school registry he had his religious affiliation changed from Roman Catholic to Greek Uniate.[71] Later, he dated to the 1870s the watershed when the Catholic clergy did (or was forced to) embrace the spirit of the Counter Reformation once more.[72]

In the end, however, Masaryk's lack of appreciation for the Christian via media, evident already in his lack of sympathy for Utraquism, also made him skeptical of the value of Old Catholicism. He saw it as something half-hearted and devious. Its orientation appeared to him to be little more than futile efforts for the minor refurbishment of the Roman

---

69 Masaryk, Česká otázka. Naše nynější krize. Jan Hus, 89. However, he submitted Havlíček's religious views to a detailed analysis in Masaryk, *Karel Havlíček: Snahy a tužby politického probuzení*, 187–203.

70 Masaryk, *Karel Havlíček: Snahy a tužby politického probuzení*, 191.

71 Later, for an unknown reason and in an unknown way the religious classification was changed back to Catholic; see Jaromír Doležal, *Masarykova cesta životem*, 2 vols. (Brno: Polygrafie, 1920–1921), 1: 18; Stanislav Polák, *T.G. Masaryk*, 6 vols. (Prague: Masarykův ústav AV ČR, 2000–2012), 1: 132. This was, of course, prior to his formally joining the Reformed Church in 1880.

72 Masaryk, Česká otázka. Naše nynější krize. Jan Hus, 351.

Church.[73] Consequently, he remained likewise cool toward the attempts for rapprochement among the Old Catholics, the Anglicans, and the Russian Orthodox, which were manifest in the Bonn Conferences of 1875 that were assembled on the initiative of the German theologian Johann Döllinger.[74] Masaryk, however, eventually defended Döllinger against the views of Vladimir Solov'ev, who deplored Old Catholicism's disruptive Protestant-like attack on the Roman ecclesiastical centralism.[75]

H. Gordon Skilling has considered Masaryk's reserve toward liberal Catholicism rather paradoxical, pointing out his attachment to certain liturgical aspects of Catholicism so that "inwardly he remained Catholic for the rest of his life." Skilling cites Masaryk's claim of 1902: "I feel myself above all to be Catholic."[76] In fact, Masaryk did pay considerable attention to the writings of Catholic thinkers since the beginning of his academic career in Prague,[77] and later he gave a left-handed approval to Catholic modernist literature for challenging the spiritual vacuum of secular Liberalism.[78] However, considering Masaryk's categorical rejection of revealed religion and liturgical service, these statements cannot be taken too seriously.

It is now possible to summarize Masaryk's master narrative of Czech national development. He identified as the salient feature of this history the crucial relationship between the Bohemian Reformation, on the one hand, and on the other, the Czech National Awakening and the consequent political culture of the nineteenth century. Masaryk did not see the relationship as a single process; instead, he discerned a double-track bond. The negative one – at which he looked askance – proceeded from the sixteenth-century Utraquism via the Voltairean Enlightenment (and even the Jesuits) to

---

73 "...liberální a polovičaté starokatolictví...", see Masaryk, Česká otázka. Naše nynější krize. Jan Hus, 140.
74 Masaryk, Česká otázka. Naše nynější krize. Jan Hus, 139–40.
75 Tomáš G. Masaryk, *Rusko a Evropa II, Spisy* 12 (Prague: Masarykův ústav AV ČR, 1996), 213.
76 H. Gordon Skilling, *T. G. Masaryk: Against the Current, 1882–1914* (University Park: Pennsylvania State University, 1994), 94–95. Funda, "Náboženství: téma pro české myšlení," 138, cites a similar statement.
77 Josef Zumr, "Katolická kritika Masarykových *Základů konkretné logiky* a jiných prací téže doby," *Filosofický časopis*, 48 (2000), 293–99. Likewise, an appeal was apparently made to Masaryk by Christian von Ehrenfels to establish a so-called "real Catholicism." See M. Pauza, "Der Aufruf von Christian von Ehrenfels an T. G. Masaryk zur Gründung des sogennanten 'Realen Katholizismus'," in Josef Zumr and Th. Binder, eds., *T. G. Masaryk und die Brentano-Schule* (Prague and Graz: Filosofický ústav Československé akademie věd, 1992), 160ff.
78 Masaryk, Česká otázka. Naše nynější krize. Jan Hus, 90.

Josef Jungmann and the nineteenth-century Party of Young Czechs. The positive track – that he cherished – proceeded from the Unity of Brethren of the sixteenth century through Jan Komenský and the Herderian Enlightenment to the nineteenth-century teaching of František Palacký and Karel Havlíček. Thus the two tracks had sharply distinguished, even contrary, values. In any case, it was the positive track that performed, according to Masaryk, the magnificent role in the intellectual and moral development of Czech history, and radiated its benefits to the outside world.[79]

The Conundrum of Herder's "Humanity"

Next it is important to explore the ontological implications of Masaryk's philosophy of Czech national history. The reliance on the religious developmental axis from the Unity of Brethren through Komenský to Herder brought Masaryk on a collision course with cultural monism (a belief in the singularity of a universal human culture) and with ontic pluralism (a belief in the ontic distinctiveness of individual beings),[80] both of which were embedded in the Bohemian intellectual outlook by the Josephist Enlightenment of Seibt and Dobrovský. This philosophical outlook continued to characterize the liberal Catholicism of Bolzano, Fesl, Příhonský, and Exner into the first half of the nineteenth century.[81]

According to Masaryk, the crucial role in the triad – Brethren/Komenský/Herder – belonged to Herder, who actually provided the intellectual direction to the Bohemian Awakening primarily through Kollár. The latter adopted the German philosopher's ideal of Humanity as the guiding principle and goal of the Czech National Awakening. According to Masaryk, the Herderian idea was shared by key personalities in the Awakening such as Palacký, Havlíček, Augustin Smetana, and lesser figures, such as Karel S. Amerling.[82] The fact that he relied on Smetana, one of the few

---

79   Masaryk, *Světová revoluce za války a ve válce, 1914–1918*, 346; Masaryk, *Cesta demokracie I*, 197.

80   Concerning this problem see also Jan Zouhar, "Filozofie, metafyzika a pozitivní vědění," in Jarmila Lakosilová, ed., *Cesta a odkaz T.G. Masaryka: fakta, úvahy, souvislosti*, by Jiří Brabec et al. (Prague: Lidové noviny, 2002), 105.

81   Zdeněk V. David, *Realism, Tolerance, Liberalism in the Czech National Awakening: Legacies of the Bohemian Reformation* (Washington, D.C.: Wilson Center Press; and Baltimore: The Johns Hopkins University Press, 2010), 215–27.

82   Masaryk, *Česká otázka. Naše nynější krize. Jan Hus*, 93.

Hegelians among the Czech Awakeners, as an emblematic figure particularly runs against the idea of cultural monism. In his American lectures on the Czech intellectual tradition, delivered in Chicago in 1902, Masaryk additionally featured Smetana along with Dobrovský, Kollár, Palacký, and Havlíček, but, he – unsurprisingly – omitted Jungmann completely.[83]

The first consequence of Masaryk's search for the roots of the Awakening in Herderian nationalism was a seeming endorsement of cultural pluralism, contrary to the universalist view on culture of the Josephist Enlightenment and its aftermath. For Herder, the primary reality was the individual nations that pursued their peculiar distinctive ethnic destinies. Masaryk was, in fact, aware that Herder elevated the nation above the individual. He summed up Herder's view by saying "In the course of history, Humanity expresses itself through individual nations; individual nations lead humankind, each for a certain time." [84] Masaryk went so far as to suggest that the ideal of Humanity expressed the core of Czech national thought in the same way that Polish Messianism expressed Polish national thought, and Slavophilism expressed Russian national thought.[85] This view appears to be almost a direct contradiction of Bohemian cultural universalism, growing out of the developmental line of Seibt to Dobrovský to Bolzano. Moreover, Masaryk asserted elsewhere that, in every nation, a distinctive ethnic coloring became manifest in the various areas of public and intellectual life, such as the state, economic and social conditions, morality and law, art, religion and church, and even in science and philosophy.[86]

The second questionable consequence of Masaryk's derivation of the line of religious development from the legacy of Herder risked embracing of metaphysical monism as opposed to the ontic pluralism of the Austro-Bohemian Catholic Enlightenment. It proposed to merge God, the world, and mankind into the collective being of Herder's "Humanity." The latter did not stand for the sum of individual human beings, but rather for

---

83 Tomáš G. Masaryk, *The Lectures of Professor T. G. Masaryk at the University of Chicago, Summer 1902*, ed. Draga B. Shillinglaw (Lewisburg, PA: Bucknell University Press, 1978), 99–110.
84 See Masaryk, *Česká otázka. Naše nynější krize. Jan Hus*, 84. For attempts to portray Masaryk as a pupil of Herder see Frederick M. Barnard, *Herder's Social and Political Thought: From Enlightenment to Nationalism* (Oxford: Clarendon Press, 1965), 174–77; Alexander Gillies, *Herder* (Oxford: Blackwell, 1945), 131–32.
85 Masaryk, *Moderní člověk a náboženství*, 92–93.
86 Masaryk, *Národnostní filosofie doby novější*, 8–16.

a real mystical entity.[87] It undoubtedly held appeal for Masaryk, as it endowed social and political life with a religious dimension, yet remained outside of the parameters of Christian orthodoxy. The main reason for the appeal of the religious or quasi-religious aspects of Herder's philosophy of history, for Masaryk, seems to have been that Herder provided the last link in the chain of continuity in the paradigm from the Unity of Brethren to the Awakening, which he esteemed so highly. According to Masaryk's over-optimistic view, Herder, as a disciple of the Unity's famous bishop, Komenský, was actually transmitting the humanistic ideas from the Bohemian Reformation back into the Czech intellectual milieu, primarily through Kollár.[88]

This chain of causation worked well in the link between Kollár and Herder, but was highly questionable in the relationships between Herder and Komenský, and especially between Kollár and the Bohemian National Awakening. Even if Komenský's influence on Herder were significant, which is doubtful,[89] Herder's involvement with Komenský would have produced a dissonance with the Enlightenment nub of the Awakening. Komenský stood for the tradition of secularized eschatology or mystical collectivism which anticipated the core metaphysics not only of Herder's philosophy of history, but also of the subsequent Absolute Idealism of Hegel. Komenský's theologized historiography, identifying human progress with the process of divinization,[90] implied the obverse of Realism and

---

87   "Christ was much less his God than Humanity his goddess" [Christus war viel weniger sein Gott als die Humantät seine Göttin]," see Josef Kaizl, České myšlenky, 2nd ed. (Prague: Edvard Beaufort, 1896), 26; see also Samson B. Knoll, "Herder's Concept of Huminität," in *Johann Gottfried Herder, Innovator Through the Ages*, ed. Wulf Koepke and Samson B. Knoll (Bonn: Bouvier, 1982), 9. Humanity was thus a part of Herder's "doctrine of vitalist pantheism," which subsequently became important for Schelling and Hegel. "Thus God is not an entity beyond the world, but the idea realized in history. Providence is not an 'external end', a supernatural plan imposed by God on nature, but an 'internal end', the ultimate purpose of history itself." See Frederick C. Beiser, "Hegel's Historicism," in idem, ed., *Cambridge Companion to Hegel* (New York: Cambridge University Press, 1993), 271.

88   According to Masaryk, "Comenius...still speaks to us through Leibnitz and Herder whose influence on Dobrovský and Kollár Professor [Ernst] Denis has finely demonstrated...;" see Tomáš G. Masaryk, *The Making of a State: Memories and Observations, 1914–1918* (London: Allen and Unwin, 1927), 424. Denis seems rather vague about the connection to Komenský, see Ernest Denis, *La Bohême depuis la Montagne-Blanche*, Part 2: *La renaissance tchèque vers le fédéralisme*, (Paris: Ernest Leroux, 1903), 10–11.

89   Actually, Herder became familiar with Comenius's writings only in the 1790s. See Alexander Gillies, *Herder* (Oxford: Blackwell, 1945), 131–32.

90   Comenius envisioned the attainment of a millennial kingdom through a general improvement of education leading to a fuller understanding of both humanity and divinity. The Neo-Platonic idea of lifting up the humans to the level of the divine universal harmony was expounded par-

ontic individualism, which the Awakeners drew from the intellectual ambiance of the Enlightenment and recaptured from the Utraquist tradition of the Bohemian Reformation. The Europe of the Enlightenment tended to look askance at Komenský's secularized eschatology, and the leading figures of the Czech National Awakening, including Mikuláš Adaukt Voigt, František Faustin Procházka, František M. Pelcl, and Karel Ignác Thám, shared this negative view.[91]

Furthermore, it may be noted that Kollár's intellectual commitments likewise clashed with the prevailing ethos of the Bohemian Awakeners. His genuine attachment to Herder's philosophy and – more broadly – to Romanticism, was atypical of Bohemian intellectual life.[92] On the one hand, it was dissonant with the sober philosophical Realism of Dobrovský, Jungmann, František L. Čelakovský, Palacký, and Havlíček.[93] On the other hand, Kollár's Herderianism linked him with the mental universe of other Slovak Lutheran intellectuals, such as Ľudevít Štúr, Michal M.

ticularly in his *De rerum humanarum emendatione consultatio catholica*. See Jozef Pšenák and Zuzana Bugáňová, eds., *De rerum humanarum emendatione consultatio catholica a odkaz Jana Amosa Komenského pre tretie tisícročie* (Bratislava: Univerzita Komenského, 2001); Jaroslava Pešková, Josef Cach, and Michal Svatoš, eds., *Pocta Univerzity Karlovy J. A. Komenskému* (Prague: Karolinum, 1991), especially, 117–26, 185–92; Jan Patočka, *Komeniologické studie II*, Spisy 10, ed. Věra Schifferová (Prague: Oikoymenh, 1998), 149–211. A partial edition of Comenius's opus was known to Herder, but the entire work was published from a manuscript, rediscovered by Dmitrii Chyzhevskyi in Halle in 1934, only in the mid-twentieth century, as Johann Amos Comenius, *De rerum humanarum emendatione consultatio catholica*, 2 vols. (Prague: Academia, 1966); see also Patočka, *Komeniologické studie II*, 128–33.

91 Karel Rýdl, "Jan Amos Komenský ve vývoji evropského pedagogického a filozofického myšlení v 18. Století," in *Pocta Univerzity Karlovy J. A. Komenskému*, ed. Pešková, Cach, and Svatoš, 190–91. Masaryk was aware of Descartes' criticism that Komenský mixed philosophy with theology, but, according to Masaryk, Komenský thus resembled the most modern theologians, who strove for a "philosophical theology;" see Thomas G. Masaryk, "Předmluva," to *Johanes Amos Comenius* (Prague: Orbis, 1928), 3–7, cited in Tomáš G Masaryk, *Cesta demokracie III*, Spisy 35 (Prague: Masarykův ústav AV ČR, 1994), 321.

92 Concerning the influence of Herder on Kollár, see Walter Schamschula, *Geschichte der tschechischen Literatur* 2 vols. (Cologne: Böhlau, 1990–1996), 2: 65, 82; Vladimír Macura, *Znamení zrodu: české národní obrození jako kulturní typ*. Rev. ed. (Prague: H & H, 1995), 18; Jan Jakubec, ed., *Literatura česká devatenáctého století*, with Josef Hanuš, Jan Máchal, and Jaroslav Vlček. 2nd ed. 2 vols. (Prague: Jan Laichter, 1911–1917), 2: 366.

93 Antonín Měšťan, *Geschichte der tschechischen Literatur im 19. und 20. Jahrhundert* (Colgne: Böhlau, 1984), 100. On Czech critique of Kollár see Hana Šmahelová, "Kollárova vize slovanské vzájemnosti," *Česká literatura*, 50 (2002), 135–36, 139–40; František Pastrnek, "Starožitnických spisech Kollárových," in *Jan Kollár, 1793–1852. Sborník statí o životě, působení a literární činnosti pěvce 'Slávy dcery,'* ed. Fratišek Pastrnka (Vienna: Český akademický spolek, 1893), 231; Pavel Vašák, *Literární pouť Karla Hynka Máchy: Ohlas Máchova díla v letech 1836–1858* (Prague: Odeon, 1981), 36–37. On the contrast between Kollár's Romanticism and the realism of Havlíček and Palacký, see, for instance, Kaizl, *České myšlenky*, 40–41.

Hodža, and Josef M. Hurban,[94] although he disapproved of their more extreme passion for metaphysical Idealism, and especially for Hegel's philosophy.[95]

Incidentally, a problem – analogous to that stemming from the ontic monism in Herder's Humanity – also derived from Masaryk's off-and-on endorsement of Comte's philosophy, which included a collectivist concept of Humanity as a single Being.[96] Masaryk parted ways with his own teacher, Brentano, with regard to Comte. While Brentano only appreciated Comte's advocacy of a strictly scientific approach to reality, Masaryk was also fascinated by the other – quasi-religious – aspect of Comte's teaching, namely a messianic effort to redeem mankind.[97] In the early years of the twentieth century, the meaning of religious life for Masaryk became virtually synonymous with the implementation of the idea of Humanity.[98]

Moreover, Masaryk's linking of the Bohemian Reformation with modern Czech political culture led some to portray him as a Platonist who believed in the substantiality of essences or Ideas (like the Czech Idea), which were objectively real and eternal and which would seek a metaphysically-based reincarnation in different historical periods.[99] Indeed, in certain respects Masaryk expressed his preference for Plato over Aristotle. Once more he felt that Aristotle's Empiricism did not allow sufficient space to accommodate religious feelings, but Plato's Idealism permitted a certain scope for intuitive knowledge, leading to religious inspiration.[100] In ad-

---

94   Sam. Št. Osuský, *Filozofia Štúrovcov*, 3 vols. (Myjava: Daniel Pažický, 1926–1932), 1: 132–35; Elena Várossová, "Hegelovské inšpirácie u Štúra a Hurbana," in Várossová, *Filozofia vo svete: svet filozofie u nás* (Bratislava: Veda, 2005), 168; Albert Pražák, České obrození (Prague: E. Beaufort, 1948), 321.

95   Jan Kollár, *Rozpravy o slovanské vzájemnosti*, ed. Miloš Weingart (Prague: Slovanský ústav, 1929), xlvi, 106. See also Kollár's letter of February 1846 in Ľudovít Štúr, *Listy*, ed. Jozef Ambruš and Vladimír Matula, 4 vols. (Bratislava: Vydavateľstvo Slovenskej akadémie vied, 1954–1999), 4: 100. He also cited a derisive comment about Hurban's "deep, high, and broad Hegelian philosophizing." See ibid., 4: 115.

96   For the French positivist, Humanity constituted a single entity, for which moreover he proposed rituals of quasi-religious worship. See, for instance, Auguste Comte, *Auguste Comte and Positivism: The Essential Writings*, ed. Gertrud Lenzer (New York: Harper Torchbooks, 1975), 461–76; James Collins, *A History of Modern European Philosophy* (Milwaukee: Bruce, 1954), 728–35.

97   Polák, *T.G. Masaryk*, 1: 178.

98   Funda, "Náboženství: téma pro české myšlení," 137.

99   Miloš Havelka, ed., *Spor o smysl českých dějin, 1895–1938* (Prague: Torst, 1995), 15–16; Miloš Havelka, "Demokracie, humanita, odpovědnost," Jarmila Lakosilová, ed., *Cesta a odkaz T.G. Masaryka: fakta, úvahy, souvislosti*, by Jiří Brabec et al. (Prague: Nakl. Lidové noviny, 2002), 16–17.

100 Polák, *T.G. Masaryk*, 1: 178–79. This contrasted again with the view of his teacher Brentano. The latter considered Aristotle the outstanding figure in ancient philosophy who by his scientific approach surpassed Plato's inclination to mythologizing; see Polák, *T.G. Masaryk*, 1: 197.

dition, Masaryk was not immune to the appeal of Romanticism and the search for transcendental ideas about the meaning of life. He found this search exemplified in the writings of the poet Karel H. Mácha, who represented a striking exception to the Realism of the literary Biedermeier style prevalent in Bohemia's belles lettres under the continued impact of the Josephist Enlightenment in the 1830s and 1840s.[101]

The ideal of humanity as a Non-Herderian concept

In the final analysis, in any case, Masaryk's adherence to individualism, epistemological realism, and a universal culture was incompatible with Herder's teaching of metaphysically based cultural pluralism, and ontic monism. On the first issue, it appears upon closer inspection that Masaryk, in a tour de force, identified the specificity of the Czech national idea, in contrast to the other (Polish, or Russian) national ideas, as exactly that of an a-national cultural monism; in other words, the ideal of Humanity which (unlike Herder's) fostered a single culture for all of mankind.[102] The universalism of Masaryk's idea of Czech culture is placed in a sharper relief when juxtaposed – as it was in his monumental debate with Josef Pekař on the meaning of Bohemia's history – with Pekař's idea of the particularist and ethnic self-assertion of the Czech nation.[103]

More generally, Masaryk denied that on the ultimate ontic level the Providential Plan for mankind's development assigned distinctive roles to ethnic communities. There were no inherently superior or inferior nations

---

101 Karel Čapek, *Hovory s T. G. Masarykem*, Spisy 20 (Prague: Československý spisovatel, 1990), 70, 93, 152, 415; Masaryk, *Národnostní filosofie doby novější*, 39–40. On Biedermeier in Czech literature, see Virgil Nemoianu, *The Taming of Romanticism: European Literature and the Age of Biedermeier* (Cambridge, MA, 1984), 130, 142; Jan Lehár, Alexandr Stich, Jaroslava Janáčková, and Jiří Holý, *Česká literatura od počátků k dnešku* (Prague: Lidové noviny, 1998), 208–9, 237, 246. On the campaign against Mácha by the Realistic generation of Czech intellectuals of the 1830s and 1840s, such as Tyl and Havlíček, see Zdeněk V. David, "Karel H. Mácha's Philosophical Challenge to the Catholic Enlightenment in Bohemia," *Sborník Národního muzea v Praze*; Řada C, Literární historie / Acta Musei nationalis Pragae, Series C, *Historia litterarum* 56 (2011), no. 1–2, 3–14; and Zdeněk V. David with Christina N. Wall, "The Josephist Enlightenment Tradition in Bohemia and the Poetry of Karel H. Mácha," *Bohemia: A Journal of History and Civilization in East Central Europe* 57 (2017), no. 2, 322–345.

102 Masaryk, *Moderní člověk a náboženství*, 92–93.

103 See Havelka, "Masaryk ve sporu o smysl českých dějin," in Lakosilová, ed., *Cesta a odkaz T.G. Masaryka*, 128.

or races, and all proceeded along the same developmental trajectory, although at different rates.[104] Claims for special destiny were either perverse or ignorant. The perverse were exemplified by German Idealism from Hegel to Karl R. Hartmann to Paul de Lagarde,[105] the ignorant one by Russian Slavophilism from Ivan Kireevskii and Aleksei Khomiakov to Ivan Aksakov and Nikolai I. Danilevskii.[106]

On the issue of ontic monism, as discussed in Chapter 4, it was auspicious that Masaryk did not embrace the metaphysical status of "Humanity" which, for Herder, tended to deny the ontic reality of individuals.[107] Had he propounded an explicit and genuine attachment to such a metaphysical entity, he might have produced a jarring inconsistency on metaphysical grounds with the individualism of his political and social principles. Actually, Masaryk's idea of "Humanity" as the organizing principle of life was derived from individualist political and social principles, rather than from Herder, as has often been argued. His acknowledgment of Herder's role in this field was, in fact, rather grudging, and entirely without enthusiasm.[108] At times, Masaryk treated the pursuit of "Humanity" simply as an ethical approach in which "one does not do unto others what he would not want them to do unto him."[109] A case can be made

---

104 Masaryk, *Národnostní filosofie doby novější*, 17–18.

105 Masaryk, *Národnostní filosofie doby novější*, 23–26. Despite his extreme nationalism, Masaryk could not help, but be impressed by the "radical frankness and subjective candour" [die radikale Ehrlichkeit und subjektive Aufrichtigkeit] of Lagarde's thought; Hans-Christof Kraus, "Lagarde," *Deutsche biographische Enzyklopädie*, 12 vols. (Munich: K. G. Saur, 1995–2000), 6: 198.

106 Russian economic and political system was comparable to that of other European countries at a comparable stage of development. Even the Slavophile arguments for distinctiveness were derived from Western thought; Masaryk, *Národnostní filosofie doby novější*, 33–34.

107 See his discussion of Herder's "Humanity" in Masaryk, Česká otázka. Naše nynější krize. Jan Hus, 416–17.

108 Karel Mácha, *Glaube und Vernunft: Die Böhmische Philosophie in geschichtlicher Übersicht, vol. 2: 1800–1900* (Munich: Sauer, 1987), 151; Frederick M. Barnard, "Humanism and Titanism: Masaryk and Herder," in *T. G. Masaryk, 1850–1937*, 3 vols, ed. Stanley Winters et al. (London: Macmillan, 1989–1990), 1: 23–43.

109 Masaryk, *Karel Havlíček: Snahy a tužby politického probuzení*, 181; Masaryk, *Světová revoluce za války a ve válce*, 374–75. For Masaryk, the pursuit of Humanity involved on the intellectual level spread of education and increase of knowledge, and on the moral level expansion of freedom, tolerance, and democracy. See, for instance, Havelka, "Masaryk ve sporu o smysl českých dějin," in Lakosilová, ed., *Cesta a odkaz T.G. Masaryka*, 124. For Herder, as noted earlier, Humanity was a part of his "doctrine of vitalist pantheism," which subsequently became important for Schelling and Hegel. "Thus God is not an entity beyond the world, but the idea realized in history. Providence is not an 'external end', a supernatural plan imposed by God on nature, but an 'internal end', the ultimate purpose of history itself." See Frederick C. Beiser, "*Hegel's Historicism*," in Idem, ed., *Cambridge Companion to Hegel*, New York 1993, 271.

that Masaryk's "Humanity" could be understood simply in terms of the New Testament injunction of love for one's neighbor.[110] As also discussed in Chapter 4, Masaryk identified love as "the greatest moral force," and as "the law of life" in the relationship not only between two people and in the family, but also in the nation and in humanity.[111] After World War I, Masaryk sought to define his non-Herderian Idea of Humanity more precisely (see Chapter 7).

Likewise, in his teaching of sociology (his other primary academic field, along with philosophy), Masaryk embraced an anti-collectivist position that has been described as "radical individualism," and which asserted that societal phenomena could be properly investigated only through the psychology of individuals.[112] Finally, the impression that Masaryk perceived the intellectual transfer from the Bohemian Reformation to the Czech National Awakening as a migration of Platonic eternal Ideas would be erroneous. In fact, he proposed a genuine historical causation in the process of transmission from the Brethren via Komenský and Herder. In addition, he portrayed the Brethren as originators of the idea of Humanity in the West thanks to their dispersal and activities in foreign lands.[113] Hence, according to Masaryk, concrete empirically verifiable historical processes, not metaphysical incarnations and re-incarnations, were involved in the cultural and ideological transfers from the sixteenth to the nineteenth century by the Brethren back to Bohemia and to mankind at large.

Concerning the philosophical underpinnings of his political theory and practice, it can be concluded that Masaryk's adherence to Realism and

---

110 See, for instance, the interpretation in Havelka, "Demokracie, humanita, odpovědnost," in Lakosilová, ed., *Cesta a odkaz T.G. Masaryka*, 13. For further discussion of Masaryk's concept of Humanity, see Zwi Batscha, *Eine Philosophie der Demokratie: Thomas G. Masaryks Begründung einer neuzeitlichen Demokratie* (Frankfurt: Surkamp, 1994), 113–27; Eva Schmidt-Hartmann, *Thomas G. Masaryk's Realism: Origins of a Czech Political Concept*, Veröffentlichungen des Collegium Carolinum, 52 (Munich: Oldenbourg, 1984), 143, 183.

111 See also Čapek, *Hovory s T. G. Masarykem*, 98.

112 Miloslav Petrusek, "Pojetí sociologie," in Jarmila Lakosilová, ed., *Cesta a odkaz T.G. Masaryka: fakta, úvahy, souvislosti*, by Jiří Brabec et al. (Prague: Nakl. Lidové noviny, 2002), 115–16. Masaryk looked askance at Schopenhauer's assertion that an individual had no meaning as such; according to the latter, the individual's sole purpose was to perpetuate the nation and mankind; Masaryk, *Národnostní filosofie doby novější,*, 23. Concerning Masaryk's stand for individualism against collectivism from the philosophical viewpoint, see Zouhar, "Filozofie, metafyzika a pozitivní vědění," in Lakosilová, ed., *Cesta a odkaz T.G. Masaryka: fakta, úvahy, souvislosti*, 104.

113 Masaryk, *Česká otázka. Naše nynější krize. Jan Hus*, 15.

individualism was not seriously jeopardized by his skepticism about the adequacy of Empiricism and by his search for a religious dimension of individual and social life. As explained previously (in Chapter 4), in not taking Herder's *Humanität*, and the *Grand* Être of Comte literally (as metaphysical entities), Masaryk succeeded in avoiding ontic monism.[114]

---

114 The vagueness of Masaryk's references to the concept of Humanity was noted, for instance, by Kaizl, *České myšlenky*, 13. For a full discussion of Masaryk's philosophical relationship to Herder and Comte, as well as to Plato, see Chapter 4 of this book.

Chapter 6

National Languages

The issue of language was paramount for the leaders of the smaller nations of central and east-central Europe in the nineteenth century. Romantic notions, particularly under the influence of Johann G. Herder, stipulated the crucial role of a nation's own distinct language for its proper development as an organic entity. Masaryk considered language to be important, but neither as an indispensable mark of nationhood, nor as the dominant cultural value in society. Although hailing from a linguistically mixed background, he embraced the Czech language as a preferable cultural medium for the Czechs, and he personally employed it as the primary mode of expression in teaching and writing in general. Yet, for Masaryk, language remained only an instrumental medium for the rendering of substantive universal values that were esthetic, ethical, and religious, and that transcended national boundaries. Beyond that – as discussed in Chapter 5, contrary to the essentialist notions of the Romanticists and metaphysical Idealists – for him, the nation as such was not an ontic entity.

(That Masaryk should have so sharply differed from Herder on the role of national language is paradoxical, given that Masaryk otherwise assigned a highly positive role to Herder's intellectual influence on the Czechs. He saw the National Awakening and the subsequent political culture of Bohemia and Moravia as guided by Herder's ideal of service to Humanity. That issue is also addressed in this chapter.)

Masaryk's Linguistic Heritage

To some extent Masaryk's rejection of the ontic status of national tongues can be attributed to the complicated linguistic background of his family. In his childhood and youth, he encountered standard Czech, German, the Czech dialect of southeast Moravia, and Slovak. A particular fluidity in language and ethnicity was characteristic of his mother, Terezie, née Kropáčková. In his years of university studies, Masaryk declared bluntly that his mother was German.[1] He modified this view late in life in his conversations with Karel Čapek, stating about his mother: "She was a Moravian from the Haná area, but she grew up among Germans in Hustopeč, hence Czech caused her difficulties at the beginning."[2] Zdeněk Nejedlý, who devoted considerable time to probing Masaryk's genealogy, reached the conclusion that Masaryk's mother Terezie was not from the Haná region of north-central Moravia (as sometimes was mistakenly maintained), but a German woman from Hustopeč. Her great-grandfather Kropáček came from an area near Brno, but both her grandfather Tomáš and father Josef married German women.[3] Other biographers have likewise concluded that Terezie was, at least linguistically, more German than Czech.[4]

As for the language of communication within her family, Masaryk mentioned that his mother in her youth spoke better German than Czech but, after her marriage, conversed at home with her children only in Czech. Yet the children always prayed in German because their mother never learned her prayers in Czech, and to the end of her life she used a German prayer book printed in Gothic script. She never attempted to read Czech and her family always had to write to her in German.[5] Even though she spoke with her neighbors in the local Moravian dialect of Czech, Ma-

---

1   "... die Mutter ist eine Deutsche," cited from Masaryk's autobiography by Jaromír Doležal, *Masarykova cesta životem*, 2 vols. (Brno: Polygrafie,1920–1921), 2: 20.

2   Karel Čapek, *Hovory s T. G. Masarykem*, Spisy 20 (Prague: Československý spisovatel, 1990), 12.

3   Terezie was born August 4, 1813; see Zdeněk Nejedlý, *T. G. Masaryk*, 4 vols. (Prague: Melantrich, 1930–1937); 2nd ed., vols. 1–2, Sebrané spisy 31–32 (Prague: Orbis, 1949–1950), 1: 105.

4   She grew up in the strongly Germanized town of Hustopeč; see Stanislav Polák, *T.G. Masaryk*, 6 vols. (Prague: Masarykův ústav AVČR, 2000–2012), 1: 15. Terezie was a domestic servant, ten years older than her husband; by language, she was German, not Czech; see Roman Szporluk, *The Political Thought of Thomas Masaryk*, East European Monographs, 85 (New York: Columbia University Press, 1981), 11.

5   Doležal, *Masarykova cesta životem*, 2: 19.

saryk's mother still felt that German was the proper language of education, and supported Tomáš's studies at schools teaching in German.[6]

Masaryk's father Josef, who was born in Slovakia, spoke Slovak with
his children, and his Slovak was authentic. He never pronounced the
Czech "ř ", but always rendered it as Slovak "r", which was the characteristic distinction – a litmus test – between Slovak and the Czech dialect
of southeast Moravia.[7] Josef had also learned German in his service as a
coachman on noble estates in German-speaking areas, but Masaryk and
his brothers never spoke German with him.[8] Masaryk had other childhood contact with the Slovak people and their speech, since the Slovak
village of Podborov lay next to his native village of Čejkovice, and both
shared the church of a common parish.[9]

Masaryk's exposure to German began in a rudimentary way with his
mother teaching him to pray in that language, but in his childhood and
his early youth, he tells us, he was not as fluent in German as he was in
Czech or Slovak. At the age of six he could participate in taking German
lessons given to a son of the castle's manager.[10] In October 1861, his parents sent him to study at a German lower secondary school [*Hauptschule*]
in Hustopeč. He discovered that the German he had learned at home was
quite inadequate, and he had to memorize his lessons.[11] He was ridiculed by
teachers and classmates for his bad German, and his first attempt at writing
(retelling the story of Siegfried) came out poorly.[12] As a result, Masaryk acquired fluency in spoken and written German only during his gymnasium
and university studies in Brno, Vienna, and Leipzig.[13] At the age of thirteen, he started studying French, and, although he did not come in much
contact with French speakers prior to World War I, he eagerly followed

---

6   Alain Soubigou, *Thomas Masaryk* (Paris: Librairie Arthème Fayard, 2002), 27.
7   Also known as "Slovácko;" Doležal, *Masarykova cesta životem*, 2: 20; Jan Herben, *T. G. Masaryk*,
     3 vols. (Prague: Mánes, 1927–1928), 1: 12.
8   Doležal, *Masarykova cesta životem*, 2: 19.
9   Ibid., 2: 20.
10 Paul Selver, *Masaryk: A Biography*. London: M. Joseph, 1940, 16; Doležal, *Masarykova cesta
     životem*, 2: 9–10.
11 Selver, *Masaryk: A Biography*, 39.
12 Doležal, *Masarykova cesta životem*, 2: 21.
13 Thomas D. Marzik, "Masaryk's National Background," in *The Czech Renaissance of the Nineteenth
     Century*, ed. Peter Brock and H. Gordon Skilling (Toronto: University of Toronto Press, 1970),
     245–46; Eva Schmidt-Hartmann, *Thomas G. Masaryk's Realism: Origins of a Czech Political
     Concept*, Veröffentlichungen des Collegium Carolinum, 52 (Munich: Oldenbourg, 1984), 73–74.

French literature.[14] A tangential influence on Masaryk's concept of the subordinate role of language was the example of his American-born English-speaking wife Charlotte, née Garrigue, who made the transition from English to Czech after their settlement in Prague in 1882. Yet her views on music, emancipation of women, and religion, which affected Masaryk's opinions, remained the same, whether expressed in English or in Czech.[15]

As for his own definition of his nationality, Masaryk stated in 1892 that he felt himself to be Moravian to the bone, but he also stressed that he did not think that there was any substantial difference between the Bohemians (Czechs proper) and the Moravians.[16] At that time, he represented a district in Moravia in the Austrian *Reichsrat*. Later on in the 1920s, when he reflected on the founding of the state of Czechoslovakia, he added: "...by origin I [was] a Slovak and a Moravian...." [...*byl jem svým původem Slovák a Moravan.*].[17] Parenthetically, we may note the allegations that Masaryk's real father was not the coachman Josef, but the German speaking Jewish landowner Nathan Redlich, on whose estate Terezie Kropáčková worked as a cook prior to her marriage to Josef in a state of advanced pregnancy.[18] Even if true, however, these allegations would not have been likely to have had significant bearing on Masaryk's attitude toward nationality and national languages. As far as is known, he never reacted to these rumors.[19]

---

14 Tomáš G. Masaryk, *Světová revoluce za války a ve válce, 1914–1918*, Spisy 15 (Prague: Masarykův ústav AV ČR, 2005), 86.

15 On Charlotte Masaryk, see Polák, *T.G. Masaryk*, 2: 33–36, 269–271; Alice Garrigue Masaryk, *Alice Garrigue Masaryk, 1879–1966: Her life as recorded in her own words and by her friends*, ed. Ruth C. Mitchell and Linda Vlasak (Pittsburgh: Center for International Studies, University of Pittsburgh, 1980), 24.

16 Doležal, *Masarykova cesta životem*, 2: 65.

17 Masaryk, *Světová revoluce za války a ve válce*, 28.

18 The story was recently broached in Zbyněk Zeman, *The Masaryks: The Making of Czechoslovakia* (London, Tauris, 1976), 17, and repeated by Szporluk, *The Political Thought of Thomas Masaryk*, 170, n. 2, and by Josef Kalvoda, *The Genesis of Czechoslovakia* (New York: Columbia University Press, 1986), 17. Substantiation was offered in the form of recollection (in the early 1980s) by Gertrude, the second wife of Nathan Redlich's grandson Josef (1869–1936) in Roland J. Hoffmann, *T. G. Masaryk und die tschechische Frage* (Munich: Oldenbourg, 1988), 37, n. 4. Soubigou, *Thomas Masaryk*, 24–25, attempts a final refutation by citing the claim of Bernard Michel, *La chute de l'Empire austro-hongrois, 1916–1918* (Paris: Laffont, 1991), 283–84, that Josef Redlich denounced the allegations as baseless rumors. However, I could not find such a denial in Josef Redlich, *Schicksalsjahre Österreichs, 1908–1919: Das politische Tagebuch*, ed. Fritz Fellner, 2 vols. (Graz: Böhlaus, 1953–1954), vol. 2, from which Bernard Michel claims (without citing the exact page) to have taken the quote of Josef Redlich: "Son [Masaryk's] père était un simple cocher, sa mère une cuisinière. Une femme intelligente et énergique. On a dit que mon grand-père Nathan et elle ... Des rancontars!"

19 According to Stanislav Polák, *Masarykovi rodiče a antisemitský mýtus* (Prague: Masarykův ústav AV ČR , 1995), 9, the earlier circulating rumors were published for the first time by Willy Lorenz, "Die Sternstunde ging vorbei. Wer war Thomas Garrigue Masaryk?" *Monolog über*

Language as a Tool

In his lectures at the University of Prague in 1885, Masaryk already emphasized that language was important, but not the most important or even unique factor in the definition of nationality.[20] He also stressed that he did not view language as something sacred, but as an instrument or means that could be employed in the service of beneficent, as well as reprehensible, causes.[21] At the same time, Masaryk warned that the natural affection that an individual felt for his mother tongue could obscure its practical and instrumental character, and it might mislead him to assign to his tongue a higher value than the humble service status. He compared such an attitude to that of an avaricious person, who valued money for its own sake and forgot the purpose it should serve.[22] Along these lines, Masaryk decried what he considered a one-sided linguistic emphasis in Czech politics and public life, pointing out that the sheer number of speakers of a given language did not determine the worth of a nation.[23] Placing the matter into a historical perspective, Masaryk noted that respect for national languages was a modern phenomenon. Neither during Antiquity nor the Middle Ages did European societies show any notable interest in vernacular. Only after the Reformation ended the literary monopoly of Latin (imposed by the Roman Church), and established national churches was the way opened to a widespread use of local speech. Thus the use of the vernacular tongues began with the appearance of the individual Protestant denominations.[24]

To demonstrate the humble service function of language, Masaryk noted that since the eighteenth century, the study of nationality showed that the character of a nation was constituted by its entire cultural life, en-

---

Böhmen (Vienna: Herold, 1964), 112–21, following an anonymous appearance of his article as "Wer war Thomas Garrigue Masaryk?" *Die Furche*, 13, no. 37 (September 14, 1957). Polák maintains that Masaryk was at least aware of these rumors in the 1920s, but refused to make a public issue of them; ibid., 53, 73–74.

20   Tomáš G. Masaryk, *Praktická filosofie na základě sociologie,* in Univerzitní přednášky I, Spisy 4 (Prague: Masarykův ústav AV ČR, 2012), 219; see also Tomáš G. Masaryk, *Praktická filosofie na základě sociologie: Litografovaná příručka k přednáškám.* (Prague, [1885]), 405.

21   "Jazyk nepovažuji za svatý, ale za prostředek sloužící duchu za prostředek ve zlém i v dobrém." See Tomáš G. Masaryk, *Česká otázka. Naše nynější krize. Jan Hus,* Spisy 6, (Prague: Masarykův ústav AV ČR, 2000), 53.

22   "Many then of course see a value in the language as such, just as an avaricious person forgets the purpose to which money should serve." Masaryk, *Praktická filosofie na základě sociologie,* 221; [1885 ed., 409].

23   Tomáš G. Masaryk, "Čisté němectví," *Naše doba,* 4 (1895), 15.

24   Masaryk, *Praktická filosofie na základě sociologie,* 220–21; [1885 ed., 408, 410].

compassing a large inventory of components: literature and art, philosophy and scholarship, legislation and state, politics and administration, morals and religion.[25] A language, therefore, did not constitute a national character, which depended instead on the nature of the cultural program that the national community consistently carried on.[26] Moreover, the cultural programs of the various nations were not idiosyncratic. They were not dependent on, or restricted to, particular nationalities; instead they could be subsumed under a grand cosmopolitan objective of realizing the Ideal of Humanity. Therefore each nation was properly engaged in the same cultural task of humanization [*zlidštění*].[27] In connection with this principle, Masaryk invoked the name of Herder, with whom – as noted earlier – he carried on a complex intellectual relationship.[28]

Language not a factor in nation-building

Stressing further the limited role of language, Masaryk was convinced that language – unlike religion, for instance – could not supply the purpose of individual and social life.[29] Alone, therefore, its existence was not enough to give rise to a nation. In fact, there were nations which remained distinct despite speaking the same language, and other nations, the population of which spoke a variety of tongues. As an example of the first kind, Masaryk noted that the Americans and the English spoke one and the same language, but Americans felt themselves to be Americans, not English people. Their economic, cultural and historical memories were different from those of the English.[30] Masaryk also noted in 1908 that the Serbs and the Croats considered themselves two separate nations, although they shared the same speech.[31]

For Masaryk, the most striking example of the second category – a nation with more than one language – was Switzerland, where people speak-

---

25 Masaryk, *Světová revoluce za války*, 357–58.

26 Ibid., 355–56.

27 Tomáš G. Masaryk, *Karel Havlíček: Snahy a tužby politického probuzení*, Spisy 7 (Prague: Masarykův ústav AV ČR, 1996), 181; Masaryk, *Světová revoluce za války*, 374–75.

28 Tomáš G. Masaryk, *Parlamentní projevy, 1907–1914*, Spisy 29 (Prague: Masarykův ústav AV ČR, 2002), 170.

29 Masaryk, *Praktická filosofie na základě sociologie*, 224 [1885 ed., 412].

30 Masaryk, *Parlamentní projevy, 1907–1914*, 102; also Masaryk, *Praktická filosofie na základě sociologie*, 219 [1885 ed., 405].

31 Masaryk, *Parlamentní projevy, 1907–1914*, 102.

ing four different tongues formed a single nation.[32] A less felicitous of his examples was the status of Ukrainians in Russia. Masaryk argued in 1908 that, although it was possible to show that Ukrainians differed from the Russians on linguistic grounds, that difference alone was not enough to create a nation. Masaryk maintained that, after all, widely differing German dialects had also existed without giving rise to separate national entities.[33] Even in contemporary Germany language was not uniform; Masaryk cited a judicial case in Berlin, where the speech of two witnesses from Upper Bavaria could not be understood and the court had to appoint an interpreter.[34]

Even less felicitous, in view of the eventual denouement, was Masaryk's application of the concept of multi-lingual nations to the case of the Czechs and Slovaks. Speaking in the Austrian Parliament on May 25, 1908, he noted that the Slovaks separated themselves from the Czechs, although experts (with whom Masaryk agreed) considered Slovak to be a mere dialect of Czech.[35] In his *Slovenské vzpomienky* [Slovak Memories], written in 1917 during World War I, he noted that whenever he was negotiating about common interests with the Slovaks, he was determined that the language question should not be raised. His guiding principle was to let the Slovaks write as they wished, and to let them retain their own literary tongue as long as they considered it useful. The main objective was to achieve a political union, and the linguistic development could be left up to the future. The bottom line was that a distinct literary Slovak existed and it did not need, and should not, be a barrier to a common polity.[36]

Separability of political culture from language

Masaryk further elaborated the distinction between the linguistic and the more fundamental elements of nationhood, which consisted of standard ethical aspirations and principles that could seek expression in a variety

32 Masaryk, *Praktická filosofie na základě sociologie*, 219, [1885 ed., 405].
33 Masaryk, *Parlamentní projevy, 1907–1914*, 102.
34 Ibid., 165. Political, economic and social components were needed to create a nation; ibid., 102.
35 Ibid., 102.
36 Doležal, *Masarykova cesta životem*, 2: 23–24. Discussing the role of language in definition of a nation after World War I in 1919, Masaryk pointed out that neither President Woodrow Wilson, nor west-European democracies saw "nationality" simply in terms of language. Thus the peace treaty with Austria attributed to the Germans of Czechoslovakia "Czech nationality." Tomáš G. Masaryk, *Cesta demokracie I*, Spisy 33 (Prague: Masarykův ústav AV ČR, 2003), 161.

of tongues.[37] The guiding ethos, which was necessary for every nation – being universal – was in turn independent not only of language, but also of ethnicity or biological heritage.[38] In separating language from political culture, Masaryk adhered to the tenets of the empirical Austrian tradition in philosophy, which sharply contrasted with the essentialist concepts of nationalism taught by German Romanticists and metaphysical Idealists. In particular, he stood close to the prototypical figures of the Austrian tradition, Bernard Bolzano (1781–1848) and Franz Brentano (1838–1917), who considered language a mere instrument for expressing intellectual values that were inherently universal – namely, morality and humanity. According to these philosophers, there could never be an intrinsic connection between a system of ethics and a national tongue or ethnicity.[39] For Bolzano, in particular, differences among languages were entirely arbitrary; they merely used different words for the same concepts.[40] In this light, in his conversations with Čapek, Masaryk explained his political conflicts with the Young Czechs in Prague prior to World War I. He wished to base Czech politics on the moral principles of Humanity, and therefore clashed with those who placed linguistic interests above everything else.[41]

For Masaryk, as a philosopher and as a statesman, it was thus the ideological commitment to the Ideal of Humanity which defined the central purpose and aspiration of the Czech nation, independently of the Czech tongue. In a message to the National Assembly on December 22, 1918, he stated: "The creation of our state and its maintenance...., our Reformation and its ideals, the suffering caused to us by the violence of the Counter Reformation instigated by the Habsburgs..., our National Revival guided by the ideas of Humanity and the democracy that arises out of it – the whole fate of our nation is logically tied to the West and its

---

37 Masaryk, *Praktická filosofie na základě sociologie*, 224–25 [1885 ed., 412–13].
38 Cited from T. G. Masaryk, *Hus českému studentstvu*, 2nd ed. (Prague, n.d.), 1off. by Hoffmann, *T. G. Masaryk und die tschechische Frage* , 41–42.
39 See Masaryk, *Česká otázka. Naše nynější krize. Jan Hus*, 53–54. See also Zdeněk V. David, "Masaryk and the Austrian Philosophical Tradition: Bolzano and Brentano," *Czech and Slovak Culture in International and Global Context*, Selected Papers from the Twenty-Third World Congress of the Czechoslovak Society for Arts and Sciences, University of Southern Bohemia, České Budějovice, Czech Republic, June 24–July 2, 2006, ed. Miloslav Rechcigl et al. (České Budějovice: University of South Bohemia, 2008), 191–200.
40 Bernard Bolzano, *Über das Verhältniss der beiden Volkstämme in Böhmen* (Vienna: Wilhelm Braumüller, 1849), 44–48.
41 Čapek, *Hovory s T.G. Masarykem*, 87.

modern democracy."⁴² According to Masaryk, therefore, the core value of Czech nationhood – the commitment to the Ideal of Humanity – could be found, as discussed in Chapter 5, in the teaching of Hus, Jan Chelčický and – most specifically – the Unity of Brethren. The National Awakening appeared to Masaryk to be a continuation of the ideology of the Bohemian Reformation after the disruption caused by the Counter Reformation. The universal humanist appeal of the Czech ethos, on the one hand, and its linguistic independence, on the other, were, for Masaryk, clearly shown by the ideological migration at the onset of the Counter Reformation (in 1621) and after its demise (in 1781).⁴³ This dual truth was demonstrated through the survival of the Bohemian Reformation ethos in the German language milieu during the century and a half of hiatus of the Counter-Reformation. After the Josephist Enlightenment terminated the Counter-Reformation era and opened the door for the Czech National Awakening, the old ethos could be once more united with the Czech language.

As a more particular example of the separability of national culture from a language, Masaryk cited the case of František Palacký (1798–1876). The latter's *History of the Czech Nation* provided the core of modern Czech political consciousness by recalling the achievements of the Bohemian Reformation in the fourteenth through the sixteenth century. These memories were essential to the existence of Czech nationhood. Yet Palacký originally wrote the *History* in German, not in Czech.⁴⁴ Similarly, the pre-eminent Czech patriotic society of *Sokol* [Falcon] was founded in 1862 by Jindřich Fügner (1822–1865), who did not know Czech at all.⁴⁵

Masaryk also turned to areas outside Bohemia to illustrate the separability of culture from language. He pointed out that in nineteenth-century Russia, for instance, the higher civil service (which determined the Empire's political culture) was composed mainly of individuals who were not Russian speakers.⁴⁶ In particular, Masaryk cited the Jews as an example in order to show that historical memories were a crucial ingredient of the national culture, in which national language was a subordinate ele-

42 Masaryk, *Cesta demokracie I,* 25.
43 Milan Hauner, "The Meaning of Czech History: Masaryk versus Pekař," in *T. G. Masaryk, 1850–1937,* ed. Stanley Winters et al., 3 vols. (London: Macmillan, 1989–1990), 3: 27–28.
44 Masaryk, *Praktická filosofie na základě sociologie,* 220 [1885 ed., 407].
45 Ibid., 219 [1885 ed., 406].
46 Ibid., 219 [1885 ed., 405].

ment. For Masaryk, the continuity of the Jewish national consciousness was safeguarded thanks to the fact that its religious books were largely historical (not dogmatic) and despite the fact that the practical use of Hebrew was lost.[47] Thus – speaking from a rather Zionist point of view – Masaryk concluded that the Jews remained a distinct nation, even though they no longer spoke their own tongue, thus demonstrating that language was not the essential marker of nationality.[48]

Masaryk and Herder

As mentioned earlier, Masaryk's relationship to Herder was paradoxical. He admired Herder for advancing the Ideal of Humanity as the main purpose of individual and social existence, and for his role as a mediator between the Bohemian Reformation and the Czech National Awakening, but he firmly rejected Herder's view of the ontic status of nations and their languages. While lauding Herder's philosophy of Humanity,[49] he nevertheless disagreed with Herder's ontologically-based national pluralism, or the ontic status of collective mankind. On the one hand, Masaryk valued the German philosopher highly for his moralistic, non-dogmatic approach to religion with a focus on the Ideal of Humanity which, Masaryk thought, was virtually identical with the religious convictions of the Unity of Brethren. On the other hand, he entertained views that deprived national tongues of their Herderian metaphysical status.

Indeed, Herder's views in the linguistic area were sharply opposed to Masaryk's. According to him, a nation was endowed with a peculiar spirit [*Volkgeist*], which had to be protected from the effects of outside cultural influences in order to advance through the cultivation of its peculiar characteristics. Each *Volkgeist* could be expressed only through its peculiar speech.[50] Thus there was no universal culture, but each nation was to develop its own in all respects.[51] In a way, Masaryk deconstructed Herd-

---

47 Ibid., 220 [1885 ed., 407].
48 Masaryk, *Otázka sociální II*, Spisy 10 (Prague: Masarykův ústav AV ČR, 2000), 118.
49 Masaryk, *Parlamentní projevy, 1907–1914*, 170.
50 *Encyclopedia of Nationalism*, ed. Alexander Motyl, 2 vols. (San Diego, CA: Academic Press, 2001), 1: 172; see also Karl D. Bracher, *Die deutsche Diktatur: Entstehung, Struktur, Folgen des Nationalsozialismus*, 6th ed. rev. (Frankfurt/M: Ullstein, 1979), 9–10.
51 "Every nation carries within itself the central point of its own happiness, just as every ball

er and maintained that the Herderian self-realization of a nation through the service to the Ideal of Humanity was, in fact, a cosmopolitan undertaking independent of particular languages.

This linguistic independence of the service to Humanity was concretely demonstrated by Masaryk. He showed it by tracking in Czech history the influence of the Unity of Brethren, the teaching and practice of which was, for him, an example par excellence of the striving for realization of the Ideal of Humanity. The route by which this Ideal traveled from Bohemia and Moravia led first into Protestant Germany. After the Battle of the White Mountain in 1620, the members of the Unity carried their undogmatic ethically-oriented religion to Saxony and Brandenburg. There, the Brethren's teaching became an important ingredient in the healthy Enlightenment of Germany and England. The positive type of Enlightenment, particularly that in Germany, was in fact an extension of the sound and authentic spirit of the Bohemian Reformation.[52]

As noted in Chapter 5, relying heavily on the French historian Ernst Denis (1849–1920), Masaryk claimed that the religious and philosophical influence of the Bohemian Reformation on the positive religiously-oriented Enlightenment stemmed mainly from world-famous theologian and philosopher Jan Komenský [John Comenius] (1592–1670), the exiled bishop of the Unity of Brethren. Subsequently, the teachings of Komenský were passed on through Leibniz and Herder, who were both deeply influenced by his writings. To Masaryk, Komenský 's impact on Herder was particularly strong, and Herder in turn affected Josef Dobrovský (1753–1829) and Ján Kollár (1793–1852), the leading figures in the early phases of the National Awakening in Bohemia.[53] For Masaryk, Komenský spoke to the Czech Awakeners through Leibniz and Herder – as explained by Denis – first to Dobrovský and Jan Kollár, and then to Palacký, Pavel Šafárik (1795–1861) and Karel Havlíček (1821–1856), who formulated the Czech national program. Thus, the Ideal of Humanity was repatriated into Bohe-

---

contains its own center of gravity." Johann Herder, *Zur Philosophie der Geschichte*, vol. 1 (Berlin: Aufbau Verlag, 1952), 465, cited by Ivan T. Berend, *Decades of Crisis: Central and Eastern Europe Before World War II* (Berkeley: University of California Press, 1998), 54.

52 Masaryk, *Česká otázka. Naše nynější krize. Jan Hus*, 15. As discussed in the preceding chapter, Masaryk contrasted this type of positive Enlightenment with the French or Voltairean one, which he considered objectionable because of its anti-religious character.

53 Tomáš G. Masaryk, *Světová revoluce za války a ve válce, 1914–1918*, 391, 396, 399. See also in the English trans., Masaryk, *The Making of a State: Memories and Observations, 1914–1918*, ed. Henry W. Steed (New York: George Allen and Unwin, 1927), 424, 433.

mia, and the Czech Awakening was able to resume the aspirations of the Bohemian Reformation.[54]

The lesson which can be drawn from this ideological peregrination is that the ideology and practice of service to Humanity could appear as the core value and purpose of national life interchangeably in Czech or German linguistic garb. In a paradoxical way, Masaryk used Herder's Germanness against Herder's insistence that the essence of a nation had to be expressed only in its national tongue. According to Masaryk – after the expulsion of the national ethos from Bohemia, where it had been presented in the Czech language – the quintessential meaning of what had been the Czech national ideal was expressed in large part by Herder in German. Only afterwards, taken from Herder by Dobrovský, Kollár and their successors, did the Ideal of Humanity become the driving inspiration of the Bohemian Awakening in a Czech re-translation.

The sentimental and practical value of national languages

Although Masaryk denied that the national speech played an indispensable Herderian role in the formation of the national ideal or the historical or metaphysical destiny of a nation, he did not consider national languages insignificant. The latter had both a sentimental and a practical value. Early in his career he wrote to a friend in January 1877 that he was a Czech patriot who would never forget his language, which from his youth he regarded as his mother tongue. However, he went on stating, "except for the Czech patriotism I am a cosmopolite in Mill's sense, and that should say it all…"[55] Concerning sentimental value, Masaryk also proclaimed in an early lecture at the University of Prague (in 1885) that the mother tongue was to everyone the dearest of all others, stating further, "…memories of childhood happiness and its thorough knowledge make it precious…." Yet he cautioned that this natural affection should not be transformed into a political weapon against those who spoke another language.[56] Even earlier in 1877, Masaryk had privately declared in a letter to a friend: "…there

---

54   Masaryk, *Světová revoluce za války a ve válce*, 391, 396.
55   Polák, *T.G. Masaryk*, 1: 407, citing Miloslav Hýsek, "Masarykovy dopisy Leandru Čechovi," *Listy filologické*, 56 (1929), 143–44.
56   Masaryk, *Praktická filosofie na základě sociologie*, 221 [1885 ed., 409].

will not be a time in which I shall forget the language [Czech] which I have from youth considered to be my mother tongue."[57]

The other aspect – Masaryk's view of the practical utility of a national language – is illuminated by a conversation with Professor Gustav Fechner (1801–1887) which took place at the University of Leipzig. Masaryk was attracted to Fechner's non-dogmatic approach to religion (concerned instead with inner conviction and moral practice), and entered into friendly conversations with him in 1877, while a student in Leipzig.[58] In his diary, Fechner recorded discussions between himself and a young Thomas Masaryk during two visits that the latter paid him at his home. During the second visit on July 13, the two engaged in a discussion of the language situation in the educational institutions of Bohemia.

Masaryk stressed the problem arising from the fact that secondary schools (*Gymnasia* and *Real-schulen*) in Bohemia and Moravia were taught in Czech, but the University of Prague offered almost all courses in German. Hence, Czech students needed a year or two before being able to follow university lectures. He proposed that the half-German, half-Czech university be replaced with two different institutions: one solely Czech, and one exclusively German. Fechner worried that Czech students would be alienated from advanced science if they studied only in Czech at both the secondary school and the university level, since the main scientific sources were in German. He also wondered whether Czech had sufficiently developed a specialized vocabulary in philosophy to translate all the major philosophical works; and if not, if German terms would be acceptable. Masaryk retorted that those Czech students with higher academic ambitions could pursue their studies at a German university; most students, however, aimed at a practical profession in which the knowledge of Czech was more than sufficient.[59] He admitted that there was still a lack of Czech technical vocabulary, but Czech – as well as other Slavic languag-

---

57 Cited by Marzik, "Masaryk's National Background," 247, from Nejedly, I/2, 156.

58 This religious orientation stemmed from the Pietist tradition, and stressed the belief in a theistic God and in the immortality of human souls, but without the traditional Christian dogma. The intuitive approach to religion, replacing dogmatic theology, led to a sacralization of everyday life. See, for instance, Josef Táborský, *Reformní katolík Josef Dobrovský*, Pontes pragenses, 48 (Brno: L. Marek, 2007), 20. Masaryk found this orientation in Lagarde, as well as in Gustav T. Fechner; and it was foreshadowed for him by his first philosophical mentor, Friedrich A. Lange, see Chapters 1 and 2.

59 Wilhelm Wirth, "Eine Episode aus G. Th. Fechners Leben vor sechzig Jahren," in *Otto Glauning zum 60. Geburtstag*, ed. Heinrich Schreiber, 2 vols. (Leipzig: Hadl, 1936–1938), 2: 161.

es – was unable to accommodate German terms, which would appear unnatural and against the spirit of the language. Masaryk added that there was even a tendency to replace terms of Greek and Latin derivation with Czech equivalents in such fields as anatomy and chemistry.

Fechner was surprised by such purism, and wondered whether this was not just a transient fashion [*Stilgewohnheit*] as had been the case in Germany. Germans in the eighteenth century tended to use as many French words as possible, though later the fashion changed, and it became *de rigueur* to eliminate foreign words unless their use was absolutely necessary. If a certain anti-German feeling lurked behind the Czech purge, Fechner further wondered why it would be directed against French and Greek words, since the Czechs had no reason to dislike France or Greece. Masaryk denied that this purism was a matter of fashion and pointed out that the Czech language had a great facility to construct new words from its rich verbal thesaurus. He ventured the opinion, however, that anti-German feeling might play a role, and that this feeling might spill over into a certain dislike of foreign words in general.[60]

On these sentimental and practical grounds, Masaryk therefore insisted that the rights of national speech be respected. Consequently, he endorsed the demands to a full use of Czech and Magyar as literary and official languages during the National Awakening in Bohemia and in Hungary.[61] In this light, he lauded the Awakeners' resistance to the efforts under Emperor Joseph II (1780–1790) to replace Czech and Magyar with German in official dealings within the Habsburg Empire.[62] Likewise, he rejected the claim of Austrian Germans that as a "historical nation" their tongue had the right to dominate in the Habsburg Monarchy and become a state language. After all (Masaryk pointed out), the Czechs had a history stretching just as long as that of the Germans, and moreover the very concept of world-significant or historical nations was false and reprehensible. As an example, he insisted that the Ruthenes and the Slovenes, who could claim neither world-significance nor great historicity, had the same right to an official use of their languages as the Czechs and the Hungarians.[63]

Putting these principles into practice as President of Czechoslova-

---

60 Ibid., 2: 162.
61 Masaryk, *Světová revoluce za války a ve válce*, 435–36
62 Masaryk, *Praktická filosofie na základě*, 221 [1885 ed., 409–10].
63 Masaryk, *Parlamentní projevy, 1907–1914*, 170.

kia, Masaryk affirmed that all minorities had the right to preserve their languages and to attend elementary and secondary schools in their own tongues. Moreover, the Germans (who were the most numerous minority) were entitled to a German university and two technological institutes.[64] For the sake of reciprocity, in Bohemia and Moravia, Czech and Slovak secondary schools had to teach German as a language, and German secondary schools had to teach Czech as a language. Masaryk affirmed that in Slovakia, an analogous arrangement should apply to Slovak and Magyar, although perhaps to a lesser degree.[65] Elsewhere, in August 1922, responding to nationalist extremism of Karel Kramář, Masaryk stated that the Germans of Czechoslovakia should be Bohemicized intellectually, but freely retain their language.[66] Masaryk expressed his balanced view on the value of the national tongues succinctly when he traveled through the region of Lusatian Sorbs in Saxony, whose language was on the verge of extinction. On September 10, 1884, he wrote in the visitors' book of their central cultural institution *Matice Lužická* in Bautzen [Budyšín]: "It certainly can not be our main purpose to preserve our language, but we wish to be moral and educated and therefore we respect the language of our ancestors, because we do not have, for the expression of our aspirations, a better and dearer means than the mother tongue."[67]

An anti-Herderian view

Masaryk's position, therefore, once again differed diametrically – despite his great respect for Herder – from the German philosopher's concept of national languages. Indeed, Masaryk was convinced that ascribing a metaphysical status to languages could lead to violence among nations. He, who valued language only as a means of communication and education, would not be tempted to force his language on others. Such an imposition of words without thoughts could occur only on the perverse assumption that a language was the locus of the entire intellectual life and aspirations

---

64   Masaryk, *Světová revoluce za války a ve válce*, 355.
65   Ibid., 356.
66   "Dr. Kramáře 'Pět přednášek'," *Čas*, August 6, 1922, in Masaryk, Tomáš G., *Cesta demokracie II*, Spisy 34 (Prague: Masarykův ústav AV ČR, 2007), 324.
67   Vladimír Zmeškal, *T. G, Masaryk a Lužice: K osmidesátinám prvního presidenta Československé republiky* (Prague: Česko-lužický spolek Adolf Černý, 1930), 7, 9; Polák, *T.G. Masaryk*, 2: 65.

of human beings. Considering language only a means and nothing more, Masaryk tells us in his early lectures that he could not imagine wanting to impose it upon anybody else.[68] Masaryk's concept of national languages therefore did not agree with that of the integral nationalists of central and eastern Europe, such as the Polish thinker and statesman Roman Dmowski, who viewed language as the inherent foundation of the nation.[69]

It is also necessary to restate the fundamental distinction on the metaphysical level between Masaryk's and Herder's concepts of Humanity, which for Masaryk represented the core of the Czech national ethos stretching from the Unity of Brethren through Herder to the Czech National Awakeners. For Herder, the advancement and increasing perfection of humankind stood for a self-realization of divinity, which was ontologically of one substance with nature and history.[70] In other words, Herder embraced – like Hegel after him – the position of pantheism. As Masaryk explained in his conversations with Čapek, his position superficially resembled Herder's concept. He advanced the views that (1) mankind was fulfilling a divine plan on earth, (2) every human individual was to perform a role in the realization of this plan (that is, the full-fledged development of Humanity), and (3) hence a certain determinism was involved in history and in human life. Yet, there was a fundamental distinction between Herder's pantheism and Masaryk's ontological pluralism. For Masaryk, in the first place, individual human beings possessed an ontic identity; and in the second place, his God was theistic, that is, ontologically distinct from man and the rest of creation.[71]

For Masaryk, on the macro-level of society as a whole, the pursuit of Humanity involved, in the intellectual sphere, the spread of education and

---

68 Masaryk, *Praktická filosofie na základě sociologie*, 223–24 [1885 ed., 414].

69 As it is suggested, for instance, by Paul Latawski, "The 'Discrepancy between State and Ethnographic Frontiers': Dmowski and Masaryk on Self-determination," in *T. G. Masaryk, 1850–1937*, ed. Stanley Winters et al., 3: 86, 88.

70 Humanity was a part of Herder's "doctrine of vitalist pantheism," which subsequently became important for Schelling and Hegel. "Thus God is not an entity beyond the world, but the idea realized in history. Providence is not an 'external end', a supernatural plan imposed by God on nature, but an 'internal end', the ultimate purpose of history itself." Frederick C. Beiser, "Hegel's Historicism," in idem, ed., *Cambridge Companion to Hegel* (New York: Cambridge University Press, 1993), 271. See also *The Encyclopedia of Philosophy*, 2nd ed., Donald M. Borchert, 10 vols. (New York: Macmillan, 2006), 4: 333.

71 Čapek, *Hovory s T. G. Masarykem*, 249, 252. On Masaryk's view of individualism, see also František X. Šalda, "Těžká kniha," [*Rozhledy* 4 (1894–1895)] in Šalda, *Kritické projevy*, vol. 2 (Prague: Svoboda, 1950), 293–98.

increase of knowledge and, in the moral sphere, the expansion of freedom, tolerance, and democracy.[72] On the micro-level of individual responsibility, Masaryk at times treated the pursuit of "Humanity" simply as an ethical approach in which "one does not do unto others, what he would not want them do unto him."[73] In his conversations with Čapek, however, Masaryk amplified his idea of serving Humanity. The service did not involve preoccupation with all of mankind in the abstract, but rather activity on any scale in which an individual could be helpful. It could mean, for instance, aiding a suffering child or participating in public service to a community. In sum, it meant acting in a humane way – with justice and consideration.[74]

---

72   See, for instance, Miloš Havelka, "Masaryk ve sporu o smysl českých dějin," Jarmila Lakosilová, ed., *Cesta a odkaz T.G. Masaryka: fakta, úvahy, souvislosti* , by Jiří Brabec et al. (Prague: Nakl. Lidové noviny, 2002), 124. On the relationship between the pursuit of knowledge and the ideal of humanity, see also Šalda, "Těžká kniha," 289, 298.

73   Masaryk, *Karel Havlíček*, 181.

74   Čapek, *Hovory s T.G. Masarykem*, 342.

Chapter 7

Masaryk's Global Vision

Masaryk embraced the vision of a united mankind from early in his career as a philosopher. He based the idea of global unity on the philosophical concept of a single humanity, and he viewed the drive toward this goal as also exemplified by the Czech national tradition, which derived from the Bohemian Reformation. He saw an encouraging quantum leap toward world unification in the revolution of the massive spread of democracy that, as discussed in Chapter 8, resulted from World War I.

The Genesis of Cultural and Political Cosmopolitanism

Masaryk's cultural cosmopolitanism had its roots in the ancient classics. Jaroslav Opat traced the origins to Masaryk's special interest in Plato (see also Chapter 4). His doctoral dissertation of 1875 was on "Das Werden der Seele bei Plato" (The Being of the Soul in Plato), soon followed by a study of "Plato as a Patriot."[1] Masaryk outlined his belief in the coming unification of mankind in 1877 in his article "O pokroku, vývoji a osvětě" [On Progress, Development, and Enlightenment].[2] The concept of the general progress of humanity began its evolution thanks to the rise of Christianity, which taught that all people form a single whole without distinction of

---

1 In 1928 writing to Hugo Fischer concerning the origin of European thought, Masaryk stressed the role of the universal Roman Empire. Jaroslav Opat, "Masarykovo evropanství jako pojem a jako politický program," *Masarykův sborník* 8 (Prague: Ústav T. G. Masaryka, 1993), 36.
2 Tomáš G. Masaryk, "O pokroku, vývoji a osvětě," in Tomáš G. Masaryk, *Juvenalie: studie a stati, 1876–1881*, Spisy 16 (Prague: Ústav T. G. Masaryka, 1993), 48–67.

nationalities, and that all human beings are brethren. According to young Masaryk, the idea of cosmopolitanism, and with it, the idea of progress of the entirety of mankind, could only evolve gradually. Yet Christianity, being cosmopolitan, greatly contributed to the rapprochement of nations, and the concept of the unity of humanity eventually did appear. At the next stage of the eighteenth century, the idea of progress came to mean a general perfecting of humankind. This concept flourished, especially in France.[3] Finally, even if it could not be established that all mankind had descended from a single parental couple, or that all mankind stems from the same family tree, it was evident that all human beings were equal and there were no superior or inferior races.[4] As he wrote to his future wife Charlotte on December 10, 1877, he was inspired by Comte's proposal to regenerate society through a secularized Catholicism, an organization which would supervise the application of moral laws, and the unity of the moral authority would be accompanied "by a unity in the government of the world."[5] By the mid-1890s, Masaryk was becoming more critical of specific features of Comte's prediction of future "positive" culture, yet he did not doubt the idea of an eventual global cultural unification. He disagreed with Comte's idea that the culture of the future would consist of a particular combination of the characteristics of the elite nations: France would contribute its skill in philosophy and politics; England its penchant for reality and utility; Germany for consistent generalization; Italy the esthetic element; and Spain a sense for the worth of the individual and for common brotherhood. Masaryk maintained that the future culture could not be just a combination of diverse ingredients but, instead, it had to be an integral synthesis rooted in a common base.[6]

Aside from the universal trends pointing to the eventual unity of humanity, Masaryk discerned a special current in that direction in the Czech religious tradition, stemming from the Bohemian Reformation. A commitment to the Ideal of Humanity could be found in the teachings of Jan Hus, Petr Chelčický and – more specifically – the Unity of Brethren. The Czech National Awakening appeared to Masaryk to be a continuation of

---

3   Ibid., 50, 56.
4   Ibid., 65.
5   Cited by Stanislav Polák, *T.G. Masaryk: Za ideálem a pravdou*, vol. 1: 1850–1882 (Prague: Masarykův ústav AV ČR, 2001), 428 n21.
6   Tomáš G. Masaryk, *Moderní člověk a náboženství*, Spisy 8 (Prague: Masarykův ústav AV ČR, 2000), 65–66.

the ideology of the Bohemian Reformation after a disruption caused by the Counter Reformation (1622–1781).[7] Masaryk sought in particular to demonstrate the role of the Unity, because to him, the teaching and the practices of the Brethren were an example par excellence of the striving towards the realization of the Ideal of Humanity. Here Masaryk clung to his vision of the role of the Bohemian Reformation in European and world history. In tracking the worldwide intellectual contribution of the Unity, as discussed in Chapter 5, he pointed out that the route by which its Ideal traveled from Bohemia and Moravia first led into Protestant Germany. From there, through Leibniz and Herder, the Brethren's teaching became an important ingredient of the healthy Enlightenment of Germany and England. As we saw, before World War I Masaryk already tended to contrast this type of Enlightenment with the French or Voltairean one, which he considered objectionable because of its anti-religious character. According to Masaryk, the positive type of cosmopolitan Enlightenment, particularly in Germany, was in fact an extension of the sound and authentic spirit of the Bohemian Reformation.[8]

Focus on Europe in World War I

Nevertheless, the course of the war and its immediate aftermath brought on a temporary shift in Masaryk's public pronouncements to a stress specifically on Europe's integration. However, as will be discussed particularly in Chapter 10, this narrowing of the horizon from the world to Europe represented only a transient diversion – to stave off the charges of the "Balkanization" of Europe – rather than a real change in his ultimate vision that continued to embrace cultural and political unification of the entire world. The temporary narrowing of Masaryk's international vision from the cosmos to Europe derived from his preoccupation with the territorial and ideological transformation of Central Europe. In particular, the narrower focus was reflected in his articles in the journal *New Europe*, published in London in 1916 and 1917, before his departure from Lon-

---

7   See, for instance, Milan Hauner, "The Meaning of Czech History: Masaryk versus Pekař," in *T. G. Masaryk, 1850–1937*, ed. Stanley Winters et al., 3 vols. (London: Macmillan, 1989–1990), 3: 27–28.
8   Tomáš G. Masaryk, *Česká otázka. Naše nynější krize. Jan Hus*, Spisy 6 (Prague: Masarykův ústav AV ČR, 2000), 15.

don to Russia. In its pages, he stressed that Europe's regeneration after World War I "must be as much moral and spiritual as political." This, in turn, could only be carried out on a purely democratic basis, the foremost demand of which was "true equality – alike in the inward and outward sphere – an equality which extends to every citizen and to every nation."[9] In this context, Masaryk polemicized with the Hungarian proponent of a united Europe, Alfred H. Fried (1864–1921), in a review of Fried's book, *Restoration of Europe* (New York, 1916), in *New Europe* in early 1917. He considered Fried's analysis superficial because he judged all countries to be equally guilty in the outbreak of the war.

His accusation of the misuse of modern diplomacy and sovereignty really should only be directed against the countries partaking in the monarchist system. Masaryk likewise did not agree in contrasting Europe with the United States which, according to Fried, had developed a high degree of economic abundance because it had avoided the European arms race.[10] These strictures foreshadowed Masaryk's future problem with Coudenhove-Kalergi, who would borrow ideas, including the term *Paneuropa*, from Fried.[11] Masaryk expressed his views on the organization of Europe more systematically in his book *New Europe*, much of which he had written while traversing Russia on the Trans-Siberian railroad in the spring of 1918. The basic principle of organization was the self-determination of nations based on culture and history.[12] At the same time, the unification of Europe would be accompanied by a synthesis "of all cultural elements and components, elaborated by all nations" as a background for the spread of democracy. Masaryk pointed to his own experience of having studied German positive

9   Tomáš G. Masaryk, "'Sub specie aeternatis'," *The New Europe*, 1.10 (December 31, 1916), 305; also as "'Sub specie aeternatis'," Tomáš G. Masaryk, *Válka a revoluce: články, memoranda, přednášky, rozhovory, 1914–1916*, Spisy 30 (Prague: Masarykův ústav AV ČR, 2005), 315–38.
10   Tomáš G. Masaryk, "Herr Fried's Latest Book," *The New Europe*, 2.19 (February 22, 1917), 248–49; also in Tomáš G. Masaryk, *Válka a revoluce II: články, memoranda, přednášky, rozhovory, 1917*, Spisy 31 (Prague: Masarykův ústav AV ČR, 2008), 54–55. Fried was a founding member of the *Deutsche Friedensgesellschaft* in 1892 and editor of its journal *Fridens Warte* since 1899. He had received the Nobel Peace Prize in 1911 for envisaging a Pan-European Office (*Paneuropäische Bureau*), which would avert the movement toward a war. Franck Théry, *Construire l'Europe dans les annés vingt, l'action d l'Union paneuropéenne sur la scène franco-allemande, 1924–1932* (Geneva: l'Institut européen de l'université de Genève, 1998), 20–21.
11   Fried also had written a book devoted to Pan-America in 1911; Richard N. CoudenhoveKalergi, *Aus meinem Leben* (Zurich: Atlantis-Verlag, 1949), 85.
12   The book appeared in French and English in 1918, in Czech in 1920, and in German in 1922. Alain Soubigou, *Thomas Masaryk* (Paris: Librairie Arthème Fayard, 2002), 421–22.

cultural figures, such as Lessing and Goethe, and French and Anglo-Saxon culture, in addition to learning much from Russians, Poles, and South Slavs, and having knowledge of Italian and Scandinavian authors.[13]

More concretely, during his stay in the United States in 1918, Masaryk maintained contact with exile representatives of various European nations, mainly from Central Europe. He established the Mid-European Democratic Union, to which he was elected President, and secured the collaboration of the professor of sociology, Herbert Adolphus Miller of Oberlin College (1875–1951).[14] The Union's efforts culminated in a meeting in Philadelphia's Independence Hall on October 23–26, 1918. Altogether, eleven nations were represented in Philadelphia, although the Poles left the Union due to a disagreement with the Ukrainians. Professor Miller antagonized the United States government, and there was a danger that the State Department might repudiate the Union.[15] The crisis had developed around an October 3, 1918 luncheon in honor of the Union, at which William A. Phillips, United States Assistant Secretary of State, was to deliver the keynote speech. The event was derailed by a protest of the Italian Ambassador in Washington, Vincenzo Macchi di Cellere (1866–1919), who charged that the Union was a Slavic conspiracy to deprive Italy of annexations in the Balkan Peninsula that were promised by the Treaty of London (1915). This intervention caused the State Department to adopt a reserved attitude toward the Mid-European Democratic Union.[16]

In the end, Masaryk salvaged the situation by changing the emphasis from the formation of an inter-state union to a forum for bilateral discussion, aimed at minimizing territorial and other conflicts among the central European nations. The Union was also to be an answer to those who feared that the destruction of the Habsburg monarchy would usher in the "Balkanization" of the region. Masaryk wished the Union to prepare proposals

---

13   Citing from Masaryk's *Nová Evropa* (Prague, 1920), Opat, "Masarykovo evropanství jako pojem a jako politický program," *Masarykův sborník* 8, 41–42.

14   On Herbert A. Miller see also idem, "What Woodrow Wilson and America Meant to Czechoslovakia," in Robert J. Kerner, ed., *Czechoslovakia*. Berkeley, Cal.: University of California Press, 1945, 71–87; Negley K. Teeters, "Herbert Adolphus Miller, 1875–1951," *American Sociological Review* 16 (1951), 563–64.

15   Tomáš G. Masaryk, *Světová revoluce za války a ve válce, 1914–1918*, Spisy 15 (Prague: Masarykův ústav AV ČR, 2005), 197–98.

16   Only out of respect for Masaryk, the State Department was represented by Richard Crane. To avoid offending di Cellere, most European diplomats boycotted the luncheon. Arthur May, "H. A. Miller and the Mid-European Union of 1918," *American Slavic and East European Review*, 16 (1957), 480–81.

for a settlement in central Europe along the lines of his writings on the New Europe. This approach corresponded to the interest of Colonel Edward M. House, who was in charge of President Woodrow Wilson's brain trust to prepare for the peace negotiations.[17] The "Declaration of the Common Aims of the Central European Nations," annunciated in Philadelphia on October 26, 1918, essentially repeated the basic principles of democracy upon which future unification should be based. These basic tenets were likewise contained in the "Declaration of the Independence of the Czechoslovak Nation," authored by Masaryk in Washington, D.C. on October 18, 1918. The concluding principle was specifically advocated by President Wilson: it called for the creation of a League of Nations binding all countries to an effective cooperation to assure justice, and hence also peace, among nations.[18]

In a book, published in 1930, the German historian, Edmund von Glaise-Horstenau, claimed that Masaryk took advantage of Wilson's unfamiliarity with European affairs and kept him in ignorance about the large number of Germans in Bohemia and Moravia, allowing their inclusion in Czechoslovakia in violation of the principle of self-determination.[19] This charge was strengthened by a participant in the American Peace Delegation, Charles Seymour, who stated in 1951: "It was only on the *George Washington* [sailing to the Paris Peace Conference] that, to his surprise, he [Wilson] learned that there was a great mass of Germans in northern Bohemia. 'Why,' he said, 'Masaryk never told me that.'"[20] The assertions

---

17   Luboš Švec, "Herbert Adolphus Miller, psychóza útisku a středoevropská otázka," *Slovanský přehled* 93 (2007), 307–9; Dagmar Hájková, *'Naše česká věc': Češi v Americe za první světové války* (Prague: Lidové noviny, 2011), 127; May, "H. A. Miller and the Mid-European Union of 1918," 480. Edward H. House, *The Intimate Papers*, ed. Charles Seymour, 4 vols. (Boston: Houghton Mifflin, 1926–28), however, refers to Masaryk only once during the war years concerning a luncheon to discuss Russia on June 12, 1918: "Masaryk talked with more sense than most people with whom I have discussed the subject, and he knows Russia better." Ibid., 3:408. House's friend and colleague, David F. Houston, Secretary of Agriculture (1913–1920), immediately after the end of the World War, expressed his confidence that "Masaryk will be a powerful force for good in Europe." See David F. Houston, *Eight Years with Wilson's Cabinet, 1913–1920*, 2 vols. (Garden City, N.Y.: Doubleday, 1926), 1: 327.

18   Miloslav Bednář, "Filosofická východiska a politický význam Masarykova pojetí evropské identity, integrity a integrace," *Masarykův sborník* 10 (1996–98), Prague: Ústav T. G. Masaryka, 2000), 13–14. For the text of the declarations of October 18 and 26, 1918, see *Vznik Československa, 1918*, ed. Antonín Klimek et al. (Prague: Ústav mezinárodních vztahů, 1994), 317–320, and 330–32.

19   Edmund von Glaise-Horstenau , *The Collapse of the Austro-Hungarian Empire* (New York: Dutton, 1930), 219–20. As a further sign of Wilson's ignorance of European affairs, he cites the American President's surprise at the existence of the Treaty of London of 1915, voiced at of the Peace Conference in Paris in 1919, ibid.

20   Charles Seymour, *Geography, Justice and Politics at the Paris Peace Conference of 1919* (New York: American Geographical Society, l951), 9. Seymour's testimony is repeated in Margaret MacMil-

concerning Wilson's ignorance of the ethnic composition of Bohemia and Moravia, however, appear most dubious. In his textbook on comparative government, *The State*, originally published in 1889, Wilson had specifically pointed out that Bohemia and Moravia were not inhabited merely by the Czechs and, in addition, also demonstrated his knowledge of the numerical ratio of Magyars to other nationalities in pre-World War I Hungary. He wrote: "In Bohemia and Moravia the Czechs constitute considerably more than half the population; whilst in Hungary the Magyars, though greatly outnumbering any other element of the population, are less than half of the whole number of inhabitants."[21]

Thus it appears that Wilson was not unaware of the ethnic complexities of the Austro-Hungarian Empire, and he would not have needed Masaryk to inform him about the existence of Sudeten Germans in Bohemia and Moravia. According to D. Perman, the one recorded view of Wilson on the issue of Czechoslovak boundaries was a brief remark to an expert of the American Delegation, Allyn Abbott Young, during the same voyage on SS Washington in the winter of 1918. Another member of the Delegation, William C. Bullitt, recorded this statement in his diary as: "The President today said to Young that he thought it would be too complicated to draw any new boundary in Bohemia, even though there is a clear line which could and should be drawn eliminating two million Germans from Czechoslovakia."[22]

Return to globalization after World War I

In his World War I memoirs – returning to the global perspective – Masaryk maintained that the objective of humanity's development was now to organize not only Europe but the whole world in as unified a way as

lan, *Paris 1919: Six Months That Changed the World* (New York: Random House, 2002), 237. I am grateful to Michael Van Dusen for calling my attention to MacMillan's book.

21 Section "Austria-Hungary," subsection "Variety of Race," in Woodrow Wilson, *The State: Elements of Historical and Practical Politics.* 1st ed. (Boston: Heath, 1889), 337; rev. ed. (Boston: Heath, 1904), 336.

22 D. Perman, *The Shaping of the Czechoslovak State: Diplomatic History of the Boundaries of Czechoslovakia, 1914–1920* (Leiden: Brill, 1962), 139, cited from William C. Bullitt, "Diary on Board SS *George Washington* December 1918," entry of December 12, *William C. Bullitt Papers* in E. M. House Collection, Sterling Memorial Library, Yale University.

possible.[23] The destruction of the regimes based on theocratic absolutism accelerated the rise of democracy in the wake of the war.[24] The policy of enlightened and upright statesmen had to be formulated with an awareness of the history and the current situation of not only their own countries and Europe, but also of the rest of the world. That meant that there was a constant requirement for global politics.[25] In his public pronouncements after the war, he stressed the need to reorient intellectual life toward internationalism and cosmopolitanism (*mezinárodnost a všesvětovost*), as in his address to the delegates of the Congress of the International Organization of Free Thinkers on September 6, 1920.[26] In a message to the Zionist Organization of America, on August 5, 1920, Masaryk further stressed that all nations would be led to an international solidarity by the spirit of true democracy and humanity.[27]

Speaking at the inauguration of the Slavic Institute in Paris in October 1923, Masaryk drew a distinction between two ideals of unification contested in World War I. Germany with its Pangerman imperialism, emblematized by the Berlin-Baghdad axis, aimed at gaining dominance over Europe, Asia, and Africa. This was an old-fashioned approach to unification, perpetuating the ideals of the Roman Empire to which Germany in a sense was an heir. However, the contrary Western ideal of global unification, based on humanity in the broadest sense of the word prevailed. First Europe and America, and then the remaining continents became part of this global democratic union.[28] Somewhat earlier, in his endorsement of the monument to War Veterans in Paris in September 1923, Masaryk again linked democracy with humanity. He summed up his belief that as a result of World War I, democracy had scored world-wide victory; most civilized nations had joined the struggle against absolutism. Democracy was nothing less than "a political expression of the moral humanitarian ideal." The victory of the Allies was a victory of democracy and humanity, and

23 Masaryk, *Světová revoluce za války a ve válce, 1914–1918*, 375–76.
24 Tomáš G. Masaryk, *Cesta demokracie II*, Spisy 34 (Prague: Masarykův ústav AV ČR, 2007), 438.
25 Masaryk, *Světová revoluce za války a ve válce, 1914–1918*, 383–84.
26 Tomáš G. Masaryk, *Cesta demokracie I*, Spisy 33 (Prague: Masarykův ústav AV ČR, 2003), 337–38. International Organization of Free Thinkers [Internationale Freidenker-Verband], est. in Brussels in 1880; its Czech section was established in 1904. In 1907 its World Congress was also held in Prague. *Brockhaus Enzyklopädie*, 20 vols. (Wiesbaden: F. A. Brockhaus, 1966–1974), 5: 559.
27 Masaryk, *Cesta demokracie I*, 303.
28 Masaryk, Tomáš G., "Řeč prezidenta Masaryka při inauguraci Institutu pro slovanská studia," *Národní listy*, October 18, 1923, in idem, *Cesta demokracie II*, 467.

Masaryk hoped that yesterday's enemies would join today's victors in embracing these ideals. Masaryk saw no cogent arguments against the ideals of humanity and democracy, which for him had also become the twin guide posts toward global unity.[29]

The Twin Pillars of Global Unity: Democracy and Humanity

Once more Masaryk dwelt on the importance of democracy, this time for global unification. Democracy, according to him,[30] was not only a political system, but a thorough implementation of the ideals of liberty and equality in all areas. Since World War I, Masaryk's formulation of the idea of democracy was significantly influenced by the political and constitutional principles of the United States, in which he, likewise, saw the ideal pattern for global politics of the future. In a letter of September 7, 1918, addressed to President Wilson, he professed poignantly his own attachment to those principles:

> After arriving in the United States I paid my first visit to the Gettysburg Cemetery – after a year's sad experience in Russia I wished to collect my mind at this solemn place of America's great struggle for democracy and unity; – I read America's eternal message, cast in iron, that the government of the people, by the people, for the people, shall never perish from this Earth.

In the same letter, Masaryk went on to stress Wilson's role in seeking to apply the tenets of democracy from America's domestic experience to the world at large, thus illustrating Masaryk's view that democracy cre-

---

29 Masaryk's contribution for the memorial "Mémorial des Alliés" in Paris, written September 17, 1923, in Masaryk, *Cesta demokracie II*, 449.

30 Masaryk also offered this formal definition of democracy as "the form of state, based on the advanced organization of society, on the modern view of the world, on the modern man; democracy arises from a comprehensive view of life and the world, from a new view, a new angle of vision, a new method. Recognizing and putting into effect the equality of all citizens, acknowledging the freedom of every citizen, and adopting a humanitarian principle of fraternity both internally and externally – this is a new departure not only political, but also a moral one." Masaryk, *Světová revoluce za války a ve válce, 1914–1918*, 365; cited also by Soubigou, *Thomas Masaryk*, 267. The definition was criticized for vagueness by Bernard Michel, *La Mémoire de Prague* (Paris: 1986), 107.

ated for domestic purposes, governing internal relations, was destined to
enlarge its role to govern the relations among entire nations:

> At an historical moment ... Lincoln formulated these principles which
> were to rule the internal policies of the United States, – at a historical
> moment of world-wide significance you, Mr. President, shaped these
> principles for the foreign policies of this great Republic as well as
> those of the other nations: that the whole mankind may be liberated
> – that between nations, great and small, actual equality exists – that
> all just power of governments is derived from the consent of the gov-
> erned, these, you say, are the principles in which Americans have been
> bred, and which are to constitute the foundation of world-democracy.[31]

As for the other pillar of international solidarity – that of humanity –
it tended to exist in Masaryk's thought and writing from the beginning as
a somewhat vague, albeit important idea (see Chapter 5). Since World War
I, he sought to define the concept more precisely from moral, as well as
political and social points of view. Morally, it was a sympathy and respect
of every man for every other man. In a further refinement of this idea, the
Enlightenment of the seventeenth and eighteenth century embraced humanity as altruism, which, according to Masaryk, was a virtual synonym
of love for one's neighbor as taught by the Gospels. As with democracy,
Masaryk credited the French Revolution with the first application of the
humanist program to politics and statecraft.[32] Subsequently, the ideal of
human progress was generally applied in western Europe. Germany, however, went a separate way. The theocratic state was worshipped in Prussia,
which came to dominate the united Germany of Bismarck and Wilhelm
II. The humanitarian ideals of Lessing, Herder, Goethe, and Schiller were
replaced by Pan-German imperialism.[33]

---

31 These statements were contained in Masaryk's letter, expressing gratitude for the recent recog-
    nition of the Czechoslovak Army, National Council and the nation; Wilson, Woodrow, *The Pa-
    pers of Woodrow Wilson*, ed. Arthur S. Link et al., 69 vols. (Princeton, NJ: Princeton University
    Press, 1966–1994), 49: 485.
32 The French parliament declared the right of man, and the revolution proclaimed the program of
    freedom, fraternity, and equality. "Humanita, pacifismus a voják," *Naše vojsko*, October 15, 1928,
    in Masaryk, *Cesta demokracie III*, 312.
33 "Präsident Masaryk in Slawischen Institut," *Prager Presse*, October 18, 1923, in Masaryk, *Ces-
    ta demokracie II*, 467. It has been noted that, by the 1920s, Masaryk attributed the origin of the
    philosophy of humanity more to the French Enlightenment rather than to Herder's ideal of *Hu-*

The Czech tradition of democracy and humanity

After the establishment of Czechoslovakia, Masaryk often referred to the tradition of democracy and human universality as evident throughout Czech history.[34] In his first message to the National Assembly on December 22, 1918, he stated: "The creation of our state and its maintenance ..., our Reformation and its ideals, the suffering caused to us by the violence of the Counter Reformation instigated by the Habsburgs ..., our National Revival guided by the ideas of Humanity and the democracy that arises out of it – the whole fate of our nation is logically tied to the West and its modern democracy."[35] In his third message to the nation as president on March 7, 1920, Masaryk maintained that the new age of humanitarianism, ushered in by the "Great War," had been envisaged by Jan Kollár and, after him, by Pavel Šafárik and František Palacký. They all believed in the unity of humanity (*všelidskost*), not as a mere abstraction, but as a reality.[36] In the same year in a letter to the city of Amsterdam, Masaryk emphasized the international outlook pioneered by King George of Poděbrady, Bohemian Brethren, and especially Jan Amos Komenský.[37] In his introduction to Francis Luetzow's *Bohemia: An Historical Sketch* (1919), Masaryk noted the concern of Komenský and George of Poděbrady with all-human and all-European matters, and quoted Palacký's statement that "Bohemian Reformation contained in an embryonic state all the modern sciences and institutions." Masaryk also cited the French historian, Ernst Denis, that the cause of the Czechs was always related to worldwide issues.[38]

---

manität. For instance, Arne Novák, "Světová revoluce," *Lumír* 53 (1926) in Novák *Nosiči pochodní; kniha české tradice* (Prague: Literární odbor Umělecké besedy a Kruh českých spisovatelů, 1928), 222–23. Concisely, on Masaryk's use of the terms "humanity" and "democracy," see also Erazim Kohák, "Zdar a nezdar 'národní' filosofie: Patočka a Masaryk," *Filosofický časopis*, 55 (2007), 447 n18.

34   Jan Zouhar, "K filozofickému odkazu T. G. Masaryka," *T.G. Masaryk na přelomu tisíciletí, Sborník z VIII. ročníku semináře*, November 15, 2000 (Hodonín: Masarykovo muzeum, 2001), 6.

35   Masaryk, *Cesta demokracie I*, 25.

36   Ibid., 229. On the connection between Czech history and worldwide democracy and humanitarianism, see also Jan Zouhar, "Jan Patočka a Masarykovo pojetí dějin," *Filosofický časopis*, 55 (2007), 467.

37   Letter to the city of Amsterdam, on the occasion of laying the foundation stone for Komenský's memorial, November 14, 1920. Masaryk, *Cesta demokracie I*, 362. See also Dagmar Čapková, "Masaryk a Komenský," *Masarykův sborník* 8 (1993), (Prague: Ústav T. G. Masaryka, 1993), 11.

38   Tomáš G. Masaryk., "Introduction," in Francis Lützow, *Bohemia: An Historical Sketch* (London: Dent, 1919): Masaryk, *Cesta demokracie I*, 197.

During the 1920s, Masaryk repeatedly referred to the champions of human unity in the Czech past. On June 25, 1920, he praised the French Minister to Czechoslovakia, Fernand Couget, for mentioning King George's plans for uniting not just central Europe, but the entire Continent.[39] In October 1922, Masaryk restated to members of the diplomatic corps in Prague the mission of Czechoslovak politics, in which the nation had to remain faithful to its historical tradition, and conscientiously "labor with all means for the preservation of peace, and perform conscientiously and devotedly the great work for the renewal of Europe, especially Central Europe, to ensure this peace for a long time, if not forever, and thus to gradually realize the noble ideals of human civilization."[40] In 1922, he pointed out that it was, in fact, George of Poděbrady who launched a program of eternal peace among the nations after the devastation of the wars of the Bohemian Reformation.[41] On an official visit to France in 1923, Masaryk added Karel Havlíček Borovský (1821–1856) to Josef Dobrovský, Kollár, and Palacký as a champion of the Czech national ideal, aspiring to a unification of mankind.[42] In London, during the same journey, he focused on Komenský's internationalism.[43]

In his war memoirs (1925), Masaryk restated his favorite historical theory that the humanitarian outlook from the Bohemian Reformation returned to the Czech National Awakening, primarily through the influence of Komenský on the German Enlightenment of Leibniz and Herder.[44] During the tentative steps toward a European federation in 1927 under Aristide Briand and Gustav Stresemann (see Chapter 10) Masaryk pointed out that Palacký had already correctly grasped that the world was becoming increasingly cen-

39 Masaryk, *Cesta demokracie I*, 287. King George of Poděbrady has, in fact, received recognition as a precursor of the European Union, see. for instance, Achille Elisha, "Introduction," in *Aristide Briand: la paix mondiale et l'Union européenne*, ed. Achille Elisha, pref. René Cassin, 2nd ed. rev. (Louvain-la-Neuve: Academia-Bruylant, 2000), 36–41.
40 "Oslava 4. výročí republiky," *Čas*, October 30, 1922, in Masaryk, *Cesta demokracie II*, 363.
41 Tomáš G. Masaryk, "The Slavs after the War," *Slavonic Review* 1 (June 1922), 23.
42 "Präsident Masaryk in Slawischen Institut," *Prager Presse*, October 18, 1923, in Masaryk, *Cesta demokracie II*, 469. Endorsing Leibniz's concept of the unity of human culture, Havlíček wrote in 1846: "What can be more dignified than the idea of intellectually joining all of humanity into a single nation which would grasp by reason everything in the realm of speech, and would be able to think and communicate in the same purity the truth flowing out of the intellect." Karel Havlíček, "Leibniz a jeho idea," *Česká včela* 13 (1846), n. 55, 218.
43 "Pan president na londýnské radnici," *Venkov*, October 26, 1923, in Masaryk, *Cesta demokracie II*, 490. See also Bednář, "Filosofická východiska a politický význam Masarykova pojetí evropské identity, integrity a integrace," 9.
44 Masaryk, *Světová revoluce za války a ve válce, 1914–1918*, 391, 396.

tralized, and no state or nation could live without agreement and cooperation with other states.[45] In 1928, Masaryk credited Palacký with proclaiming
service to humanity as the Czech national program and finding its expression particularly in the teaching of the Unity of Brethren.[46]

Misconceived unification: Bolshevism and Panslavism

In 1920, Masaryk denounced Communist internationalism at the height
of its post-World War I influence inside Czechoslovakia in a series of articles, "Demokracie a bolševictví" (Democracy and Bolshevism). He pointed out that Lenin and the Bolsheviks did reject patriotism, stressing the
cosmopolitan character of their ideology, and that the life of Lenin and
his associates in foreign exile, indeed, increased their sense of internationalism (světovosti). According to Masaryk, however, Bolshevik internationalism and cosmopolitanism resulted in weakness. Lenin felt that
communism could not be established in Russia alone, but it had to be ushered in by a world revolution. In their pursuit of such a global conflagra-
tion, the Bolsheviks tried to interfere in a great variety of countries, and
thus frittered their energies.[47] Bolshevik internationalism was flawed not
just ideologically, but also organizationally. Its chief instrument was to be
the Communist, or Third, International; but – as Masaryk maintained –
the construction of global internationalism could not be directed from a
single center. The eventual organization of the international community would be democratic, not centralistic or absolutistic, because individual states would develop toward unity in parallel and autonomist ways.[48]

---

45 "Poselství prezidenta republiky," *Národní osvobození*, June 12, 1927, in Masaryk, *Cesta demokracie III*, 209–10. On the world centralization, see František Palacký, *Úvahy a projevy* (Prague: Melantrich, 1977), 87–91, 343. Palacký also described the phenomenon in "Předmluva k vlasteneckému
čtenářstvu," *Časopis českého musea* 11(1837), 7: "Now then let us spread, cultivate and perfect the various branches of knowledge, and let us bring pure and God-pleasing sacrifices not only on the altar
of our homeland, but also humanity. A time has surely begun in the world history, when all local
barriers in the intellectual life of individual nations are always further sinking and disappearing,
and when a free, constant and rapid exchange of thoughts, ideas, and sentiments occurs among
the advanced nations of Europe everywhere, establishing in this manner, although through divers
tongues, only one higher literature that is European and at times also universal."
46 "Humanita, pacifismus a voják," *Naše vojsko*, October 15, 1928, in Masaryk, *Cesta demokracie III*, 312.
47 "Demokracie a bolševictvi," 1920, in Masaryk, *Cesta demokracie I*, 329.
48 The incongruities of Bolshevism also included the superior even contemptuous way of dealing
with smaller states, shown by the Soviet Foreign Commissar, Georgii V. Chicherin; Masaryk,
Cesta demokracie I, 330–31.

With his interest directed toward the unification of Europe, albeit only as a part of the unification of all of humanity, Masaryk also rejected political Panslavism.[49] In particular, the idea of Panslavism as the ascendancy of Slav nations under Russia's leadership was discredited by World War I, which had opened much wider vistas.[50] As a general rule the individual nations ranked above Slavdom, and humanity ranked above the nations.[51] Masaryk did recognize that the Slav nations were closer to each other in languages than the speakers of Germanic and Romance languages; therefore, their kinship was deeper and more intimate.[52] Nevertheless, according to him, the Slavs held a cosmopolitan outlook, not a narrowly ethnic one. Thus Czech intellectual roots in the Reformation provided a historical connection with the west, especially England; the Poles tended to gravitate intellectually toward France; Russian society also had been open to French language and culture in the eighteenth century; and South Slavs were influenced by the Italians and the Greeks.[53] In fact, Masaryk suggested that instead of embracing ethnic parochialism, the Slavs may become the catalysts of the coming unity of Europe and the world. He touched upon this role specifically in his speech at the Slavic Institute in Paris in October 1923, where he stated: "Dostoevsky attributed to the Russians and the Slavs a special ability to penetrate the souls of other nations ... Perhaps he was correct to a certain degree."[54] Masaryk returned to the topic in his message to the First International Congress of Slavicists in Prague in October 1929 when he pointed out: "Slavic studies help to unite the Slavs culturally and the mission of the Slavs is to unite

49 Arcadie Joukovsky, "T. G. Masaryk et les Slaves d e l'Est," in *Thomas Garrigue Masaryk, européen et humaniste*, ed. VladimírPeška and Antoine Mareš (Paris: Etudes et documentation internationales: Institut d'études slaves, 1991), 173; Masaryk, "The Slavs after the War," 18. Concerning Masaryk's cautious and realistic approach to cooperation with other Slav nations prior to World War I, see Vratislav Doubek, *T. G. Masaryk a česká a slovanská politika, 1882–1910* (Prague: Academia, 1999), especially, 128–44. On Masaryk's critique of Russian Panslavism, see also Jaroslav Papoušek, "Masaryk und Slaventum," *Slavische Rundschau*, vol. 2, (1930), 179–81.

50 "Poválečné problémy Československa," dated July 9, 1932; in Tomáš G. Masaryk, *Cesta demokracie IV*, Spisy 36 (Prague: Masarykův ústav AV ČR, 1997), 293. Perhaps in the Balkans Yugoslavia and Bulgaria might join in a single state. Masaryk had felt already in 1913 that a rapprochement among all the South Slavs would useful; see "Thomas G. Masaryk Foresees Peace," *Christian Science Monitor*, March 12, 1926 in Masaryk, *Cesta demokracie III*, 130.

51 Papoušek, "Masaryk und Slaventum," 174–75.

52 Masaryk, *Světová revoluce za války a ve válce, 1914–1918*, 348.

53 "Präsident Masaryk in Slawischen Institut," *Prager Presse*, October 18, 1923, in Masaryk, *Cesta demokracie II*, 469.

54 Ibid., II. 470.

all nations: Slavic studies have an all-human mission (*poslání všelidské*)."[55] The cultivation of special ties among the Slavic nations due to their linguistic kinship was not a matter of politics, but of non-governmental and academic institutions.[56] Earlier in 1923, Masaryk had pointed out, as examples of such organizations, the Slav Institute in Paris and the Chair of Central European History in the School of Slavonic Studies in London, as well as the Ukrainian and Russian universities in Prague.[57]

Tangible Signs of Unification

Throughout the 1920s and into the very early 1930s, Masaryk identified several encouraging signs of trends toward the unification of Europe, and of the world, with the latter – as pointed out earlier – actually closer to his heart. In his 1922 article, "The Slavs after the War," he wrote that the World War and its aftermath obliged all European nations to mutual understanding, to solidarity, and to union, and he expressed a conviction that a United Nations of Europe was on the way to realization.[58] In his war memoirs, he similarly ventured the opinion that the "United States of Europe" was no longer merely a utopian ideal.[59] However, in Masaryk's vision of the future, expressed in "The Slavs after the War," the unification of Europe would logically be enlarged and completed only by the unification of humanity. This process advanced as the aftermath of World War I has brought together Europe with America and Asia; the Anglophone nations, in particular, established closer ties with the nations of East Asia. The countries became aware of their common fate, and the leaders of major nations embraced a program, aiming at the welfare of humanity that encompassed all people regardless of differences in language, nationality,

---

55   Prezident republiky o slavistice," *Lidové noviny*, October 15, 1929, in Masaryk, *Cesta demokracie IV*, 66.

56   "Prezident Masaryk o některých věcech," *Lidové noviny*, April 8, 1928, in Tomáš G. Masaryk, *Cesta demokracie III*, Spisy 35 (Prague: Masarykův ústav AV ČR, 1994), 272. See also Papoušek, "Masaryk und Slaventum," 188–89.

57   The two universities in Prague were the Ukrainian Free University (since 1921) and the Russian Popular University (since 1923), in addition to the Russian Law Faculty (1922). "Poselství prezidenta Masaryka," *Lidové noviny*, October 29, 1923, in Masaryk, *Cesta demokracie II*, 499.

58   Masaryk, "The Slavs after the War," 2–23.

59   Masaryk, *Světová revoluce za války a ve válce, 1914–1918*, 295–96. See also the reference to the coming brotherhood of European nations; in "Prezident Masaryk o budoucnosti Maďarska," originally printed in *Lidové noviny*, August 13, 1924, based on interview to Hungarian newspaper *Világ*, in Masaryk, *Cesta demokracie III*, 96.

or class. The unification of Europe and the world was not simply a matter of organization, which would be a mechanical process employing the existing instrumentalities. The task involved not only a need to organize, but also a need to create; namely, to replace old regimes and old statesmen with new regimes and new political leaders with a fresh vision. While economic and political structures were important, the unification also required a new intellectual infrastructure.[60] The war upset not only Europe, but the entire world; hence, this cataclysm should arouse a drive toward eternal peace for all nations and individuals.[61] It is important to stress at this point that Masaryk's vision located the European or World Federation – in the proper constitutional sense of the words – in a more or less distant future, although he did not rule out the possibility of a sudden leap, as mentioned later on. Under the existing circumstances, if he spoke of a "federation," as Peter Bugge has convincingly pointed out, Masaryk did not mean "surrender of national sovereignty."[62]

Masaryk stressed with great solemnity the relevance of globalism to Czechoslovakia's fate. Thus, in his "Third Message as President" on March 7, 1920, pursuing the universalist line, he noted that Czechoslovakia had a special interest in not just European, but global politics. He recalled that the origin of Czechoslovakia was due to nations of Europe, Asia, and America whose help Masaryk had solicited during the War. He also assiduously disseminated knowledge of the Czech idea of human universality and interdependence. Without the world community there would have been no Czechoslovakia.[63] At the same time, Masaryk emphasized that the global character of Czech politics harmonized with the overall political evolution of the world. Thus, on the tenth anniversary of Czechoslovak independence in October 1928, he restated with special force his conviction that World War I strengthened the feeling of an outright global

---

60   Masaryk, "The Slavs after the War," 22–23. Imperial Germany demonstrated great organizational skills, but without moral guidance, it did not lead to victory, ibid.

61   Masaryk, "The Slavs after the War," 22. On Masaryk's global vision, see also Bednář, "Filosofická východiska a politický význam Masarykova pojetí evropské identity, integrity a integrace," 12. For a comparison with Mazzini's idea of a world-wide federation of nations on the basis of democracy; see Francesco Leoncini, "Guiseppe Mazzini a Tomáš Masaryk jako průkopníci Evropské unie," *Masarykův sborník*, 14 (2006–2008, Prague: Ústav T. G. Masaryka, 2010), 402.

62   Peter Bugge, "Longing or Belonging? Czech Perceptions of Europe in the Inter-War Years and Today," *Yearbook of European Studies*, 11 (1999), 114; Peter Bugge, "České obrazy Evropy za první republiky," *Evropa očima Čechů*, Sborník ze symposia, Centrum Franze Kafky, 22.–23. října 1966, ed. Eva Hahnová (Prague: Nakladatelství Franze Kafky, 1997), 98–99.

63   Masaryk, *Cesta demokracie* I, 230.

internationalism, because the war was truly worldwide; it showed that all nations formed and should form a coherent whole.[64] Likewise, Masaryk called attention to the economic aspect of globalization, whereby the world market stimulated not only global politics, but also global agriculture, industry, and banking.[65]

The League of Nations

The League of Nations, in Masaryk's view, played a crucial role in the movement toward the unification of mankind. He gave a particularly warm endorsement of the League in his presidential message of March 1920, pointing out that over 85 percent of the countries in the world had joined the organization. He regarded this figure as statistical proof that humanity was becoming conscious of its collective identity and was beginning to think of its development as a whole.[66] Masaryk suggested that the League could provide a strong directing authority (promoting cultural inter-nationality) which Europe needed, especially after the War.[67] In his statement for Czechoslovak Independence Day on October 28, 1924, Masaryk sought to place the League into a historical perspective. He stressed the perennial longing for peace, which had been expressed, among others, by the great figures of Czech history, especially George of Poděbrady and Komenský. It was this historical yearning and need that had finally found an embodiment in the League of Nations. Masaryk noted that Jean-Jacques Rousseau had dreamed about such an organization, which was at last, fittingly, founded in his favorite city of Geneva.[68] In particular, Masaryk valued the establishment of a mechanism in the League for open diplomacy to replace the old bilateral diplomatic system that, in his

---

64 "Jubilejní poselství prezidenta Masaryka," *Lidové noviny*, October 30, 1928, in Masaryk, *Cesta demokracie III*, 325.
65 "Jubilejní poselství prezidenta Masaryka," *Lidové noviny*, October 30, 1928, in Masaryk, *Cesta demokracie III*, 330. As early as 1920, Masaryk had noted that a global economic reciprocity had represented already a degree of practical, existing internationality; "Demokracie a bolševictvi," 1920, in Masaryk, *Cesta demokracie I*, 330–31.
66 "Third Message as President" on March 7, 1920, in Masaryk, *Cesta demokracie I*, 229.
67 "Rozmluva s prezidentem Masarykem," *Čas*, June 13, 1920, Masaryk, Tomáš G., *Cesta demokracie I*, Spisy 33 (Prague: Masarykův ústav AV ČR, 2003), 280; see also "Demokracie a bolševictvi," 1920, in Masaryk, *Cesta demokracie I*, 329.
68 "Oslavy státního svátku u prezidenta republiky," *Národní listy*, October 29, 1924, in Masaryk, *Cesta demokracie III*, 81.

view, had led to international conflicts. Greatly disappointed by the absence of the United States from the organization, he hoped that the refusal to join might be reversed in the future. He also instructed Eduard Beneš, the Czechoslovak Foreign Minister, to support the League in every way and asked to receive a copy of every publication of the League.[69]

With Masaryk's full support, Beneš became actively involved in the work of the League, seeking to strengthen its effectiveness. He served as its president in 1920 and was one of the delegates who drafted the Geneva Protocol in 1924 that bound the contracting parties to have their conflicts resolved by arbitration of the League.[70] Masaryk kept a watchful eye on the operations of the League. On September 17, 1926, he congratulated Beneš on his election to the Council of the League,[71] and expressed satisfaction in December 1926 that the League had become a genuinely functioning international organ.[72] Two years later, he chided the Czech press for often not recognizing the importance of the League. Obviously it could not achieve its goals, such as disarmament, immediately. It was, however, important for Czechoslovakia, among others, as a platform to be in contact with the rest of the world, and to present and defend its interests.[73] In 1930, Masaryk paid a special tribute to the League of Nations as a kind of world parliament, the existence of which was the best justification for the policy of President Wilson. Masaryk went on to express his delight that Wilson's reputation was improving in the United States, not only among the Democrats, but also among the Republicans.[74]

Great and Little Entente

Masaryk, however, was not blind to the weaknesses of the League in enforcing its authority, and stressed that it had to rely on the support of the

---

69 Soubigou, *Thomas Masaryk*, 418.
70 The plenum of the League, however, did not accept the document; Soubigou, *Thomas Masaryk*, 420–21.
71 He also asked Beneš to convey his greetings to Briand, Chamberlain, Cecil, Stresemann, and Ninčić; see *Lidové noviny*, September 21, 1926, in Masaryk, *Cesta demokracie III*, 163.
72 "Prezident T. G. Masaryk *Právu lidu*," *Právo lidu*, December 25, 1926, in Masaryk, *Cesta demokracie III*, 174.
73 "Prezident Masaryk o některých věcech," *Lidové noviny*, April 8, 1928, in Masaryk, *Cesta demokracie III*, 273.
74 "Masaryk at Eighty," *New York Times Magazine*, March 2, 1930 in Masaryk, *Cesta demokracie IV*, 135.

great powers, especially France and Britain, on whom the security of the small European nations depended. In particular, he hoped that membership in the League would keep Britain involved in continental European affairs.[75] He repeatedly stressed the need to perpetuate the authority of the Entente in 1921,[76] and again in 1922 when he pointed out that he had always recognized the Entente as the necessary authority in post-war Europe and welcomed the efforts to enlist the United States to cooperate with Europe.[77] He took his message to France and Britain during his official visits there in October 1923, and exhorted President Alexandre Millerand in Paris and Minister of Foreign Affairs Lord Curzon in London to perpetuate the Entente, which had proved its worth during the war, and was currently necessary to ensure the effective functioning of the League of Nations.[78] In an interview with the Belgian journalist Robert Lerquin in 1925, Masaryk once again stressed that an entente between France and England must be the guarantor of the rapprochement of European nations under the auspices of the League of Nations.[79]

While emphasizing the crucial importance of the Great Entente – really the Franco-British alliance – for the League of Nations, Masaryk also regarded the Little Entente of Czechoslovakia, Romania, and Yugoslavia (formed in 1920–21) as a nucleus or an embryonic model for future European and world unification within the parameters of the League.[80] In addition, he viewed the Little Entente as a continuation of his work for New Europe, as defined in the Declaration of Common Interests of Independent States of Central Europe in Philadelphia on October 26, 1918.[81] He reminisced about a plan to ally mutually friendly states, which he had discussed in Paris in December, 1918 with the Romanian Foreign Minis-

---

75 Soubigou, *Thomas Masaryk*, 420–21.

76 "Oslavy národního svátku 28. října," Čas, October 29, 1921, in Masaryk, *Cesta demokracie II*, 156–57.

77 "Nový rok na Hradě: poselství prezidenta republiky," Čas, January 2, 1922, in Masaryk, *Cesta demokracie II*, 205–6.

78 "Millerand a Masaryk o nové Evropě," *Lidové noviny*, October 17, 1923, in Masaryk, *Cesta demokracie II*, 464; "Dr. Masaryk's visit," *Glasgow Herald*, October 24, 1923, in Masaryk, *Cesta demokracie II*, 485; "Odpověď pana prezidenta Masaryka Curzonovi," České slovo, October 25, 1923, in Masaryk, *Cesta demokracie II*, 489.

79 "Une journée chez le president de la République," *La Flandre Libérale,* September 26, 1925, in Masaryk, *Cesta demokracie III*, 112.

80 See, for instance, "Intervju med Masaryk," *Social-Demokraten*, April 7, 1923, in Masaryk, *Cesta demokracie II*, 410.

81 *Lidové noviny*, October 28, 1920, in Masaryk, *Cesta demokracie I*, 354.

ter, Take Ionescu, and the Greek Prime Minister, Eleftherios Venizelos.[82] The three attempted to organize a "United States of Eastern Europe" as a federation of thirteen states between Germany and Russia, reaching from Finland to Greece, to become the core of the future United States of Europe. The plan was submitted to the Peace Conference, but failed due to heightened nationalism in the area.[83] Subsequently, Masaryk expected that the Little Entente would be emulated by similar intimate political and economic agreements, likewise promoting integration under the auspices of the League. As specific possible examples, he cited Czechoslovak accords with Poland and Austria, the attempted accords between Poland and the Baltic states, the alliance among the countries of Transcaucasia, and an accord of Greece with Serbia.[84] Later, in 1924, Masaryk recalled that he would have liked to include Poland and possibly Greece in the Little Entente.[85]

Masaryk's enthusiasm for the Little Entente had a counterpart in his firm rejection of the projects for a Danubian Confederation. This attitude reflected Masaryk's qualms about reawakening the ghost of the former Habsburg Empire and possibly raising the specter of revisionism, which would come to the fore in connection with Coudenhove-Kalergi's concept of *Paneuropa* (see Chapter 10). Masaryk was frequently asked about the formation of the Danubian Confederation in the immediate post-War period, which evidently reflected a high level of concern about the Balkanization of central Europe due to the dismemberment of the Habsburg Monarchy. In at least five interviews between February 1919 and March 1920, Masaryk steadfastly fended off the idea of a Danubian Confederation on the grounds of the unacceptability of reestablishing political ties that might resemble the old Austro-Hungarian Empire.[86] In particular, during a visit by Austrian Chancellor Karl Renner, Masaryk firmly excluded the discussion of a confederation on the grounds that it was another version

---

82   "Prezident Masaryk o aktuálních otázkách," Čas, December 2, 1920, in Masaryk, *Cesta demokracie* I, 370.
83   Bednář, "Filosofická východiska a politický význam Masarykova pojetí evropské identity, integrity a integrace," 15–17.
84   Masaryk, "The Slavs after the War," 20.
85   "Rozhovor pro římský list Tribuna," April 2, 1924, in Masaryk, *Cesta demokracie III*, 389.
86   "Bohême: Une interview de Masaryk," *Le Temps*, February 2, 1919, in Masaryk, *Cesta demokracie I*, 82; "Das Schicksal der Deutschen in Tschechien," *Die Zeit*, August 1, 1919, in Masaryk, *Cesta demokracie I*, 153. "En Tchéco-Slovaquie," *Tribune de Gèneve*, August 20, 1919, in Masaryk, *Cesta demokracie I*, 156.

of the old Empire, a "restitutio in integrum."[87] Even a customs union with Danubian states was out of question at that time, because it might be the prelude to a political union.[88] After remaining dormant in the mid-1920s, the issue was revived in 1929 and into the early 1930s with the coming of the Great Depression. Masaryk argued that the rapprochement of the Danubian states to relieve the economic crisis would work best through bilateral economic agreements.[89] The problem militating against cooperation was the attitude of Hungary, which was not able to free itself of revisionist aspirations.[90] In any case, Masaryk did not see a special economic cogency for linking specifically the Danubian nations, because the river connection was no longer important for transport.[91]

Initiatives for World Harmony

As for concrete steps toward world harmony, Masaryk selected for special praise – in his article "Slavs after the War" (1922) – the international conferences in Washington in November 1921, in Cannes in January 1922, and finally the following April in Genoa (where Germany and Russia had recently signed an agreement).[92] He was particularly impressed by the Washington Conference convoked by President Harding that dealt with disarmament. He saw it as a good opportunity for statesmen from around the world to get to know each other. It was also a welcome sign for him that the United States was not entirely distancing itself from the problems of the outside world, despite the talk about isolationism. In addition to the emphasis on the Franco-British alliance, he noted, as early as 1921, that the crux of solidarity in Europe was the relationship between France and Germany. As for disarmament, Masaryk did not embrace pacifism –

---

87 "Die Unterredung mit Masaryk," *Prager Tagblatt*, December 25, 1919, in Masaryk, *Cesta demokracie I*, 204.
88 "Future of Czechoslovakia," interview with correspondent H. Robertson Murray for *Sunday Times*, March 14, 1920 in Masaryk, *Cesta demokracie I*, 245.
89 "Masaryk o světové hospodářské krizi," *Lidové noviny*, September 21, 1932, in Masaryk, *Cesta demokracie IV*, 302; "Masaryk o dnešní Evropě," originally published in *Berliner Tagblatt*, October 5, 1932, in Masaryk, *Cesta demokracie IV*, 310.
90 "Masaryk o evropském společenství," interview with Evelyn Wrench for *Daily Telegraph*, April 26, 1932, in Masaryk, *Cesta demokracie IV*, 260–61.
91 "Prezident Masaryk o Panevropě," *České slovo*, December 5, 1929, in Masaryk, *Cesta demokracie IV*, 88.
92 Masaryk, "The Slavs after the War," 20–21.

but he anticipated a change of political and moral climate initiating a truly cultured politics, which would reflect a worldwide friendship. Masaryk hoped that the Washington Conference would seek to implement its objectives through the League of Nations, and not weaken it by establishing separate organs.[93]

As addressed earlier, speaking at the inauguration of the Slavic institute in Paris in October 1923, Masaryk stressed that the German ideal of unification with its Pangerman imperialism was overcome in World War I by the contrary Western ideal of humanity in the broadest sense of the word. Masaryk undoubtedly had the League in mind for this grand design of world unification.[94] His faith in the League of Nations was subsequently bolstered by the Geneva Protocol of October 2, 1924, which provided for peaceful settlement of international disputes, attempting to strengthen the international machinery and overcome the weakness of the League structure. He gladly signed the Protocol himself.[95]

Masaryk continued to favor a reconciliation of Germany with the Entente powers, being convinced that post-War Germany had been cured of the curse of theocratic absolutism that had bedeviled the country under the Second Empire. In June 1924, he praised the policy of reconciliation pursued by British Prime Minister Ramsey MacDonald, in which the victors of World War I offered Germany a possibility to meet her obligations in an open and friendly way. Masaryk saw here an effective way to enhance international cooperation.[96] Likewise, he heartily approved the much more significant Locarno Conference and Treaties of October 5–16, 1925, praising Joseph A. Chamberlain's tact in presiding, and Briand's generous policy. He also accorded thanks to the German negotiators for their contribution.[97] A few days later on Czechoslovak Independence Day, he expressed satisfaction that the Locarno Treaties not only

---

93 "France need fear no aggression by future Germany," *New York World,* November 28, 1921, in Masaryk, *Cesta demokracie II,* 173–75.

94 Masaryk, Tomáš G., "Řeč prezidenta Masaryka při inauguraci Institutu pro slovanská studia," *Národní listy,* October 18, 1923, in idem, *Cesta demokracie II,* 467.

95 "Oslavy státního svátku u prezidenta republiky," *Národní listy,* October 29, 1924, in Masaryk, *Cesta demokracie III,* 81. The Protocol was eventually rejected by the British government, because of the Dominions' opposition, in March 1925.

96 "Pozitivní diplomacie," *Přítomnost,* June 26, 1924, in Masaryk, *Cesta demokracie III,* 50.

97 "Po skončení velkého díla," *Národní osvobození,* October 18, 1925, in Masaryk, *Cesta demokracie III,* 114.

confirmed the solidarity of the largest states of Europe, but also guaranteed the rights of smaller nations.[98]

Masaryk was more reserved toward the next major initiative of the League of Nations, which focused on disarmament. The League appointed the Preparatory Commission for a Disarmament Conference in 1925, with the participation of powerful outsiders: the United States and, from 1927, also the Soviet Union. Having held several sessions between May 1926 and December 1930, the Commission drafted a convention to be discussed at a Disarmament Conference called by the League for February 1932. Observing these steps, Masaryk had maintained his opposition to pacifism since at least 1920.[99] Although he considered the disarmament worthwhile,[100] he repeatedly distanced himself from Chelčický's and Tolstoy's doctrine of non-resistance to evil.[101] During the last gasp of the Disarmament Conference in September 1933, he did affirm his support for the League's initiative; he favored disarmament if it was gradual and simultaneously international.[102] In the meantime, however, the Disarmament Conference in 1932 and 1933 was ominously coming to an end over the French insistence on – and the German opposition to – preserving all the previous treaties, including the military clauses of Versailles.[103]

As Masaryk's twilight years approached, his vision of a united world community was increasingly challenged not only by the rise of the totalitarian powers, but also on the side of the democracies by the rise of European separatism. The Euro-centric challenge, which germinated since the start of the 1920s with Coudenhove's *Paneuropa*, continued to gain ground in the Briand Initiative of the late 1920s and early 1930s.

---

98 "Letošní 28. říjen," *Národní osvobození*, October 29, 1925, in Masaryk, *Cesta demokracie III*, 116.

99 "Third Message of President Masaryk, March 7, 1920," in Masaryk, Tomáš G., *Cesta demokracie I*, 231. See also "Armádě," August 14, 1923, in Masaryk, *Cesta demokracie II*, 438.

100 "Prezident Masaryk o některých věcech," *Lidové noviny*, April 8, 1928, in Masaryk, *Cesta demokracie III*, 273.

101 "Gespräch mit Masaryk," *Berliner Tagblatt*, September 29, 1929, in Masaryk, *Cesta demokracie IV*, 60; *Národní osvobození*, February 27, 1930, Masaryk, *Cesta demokracie IV*, 129; "Ist der Friede gefährdert?" *Prager Tagblatt*, September 30, 1930, in Masaryk, *Cesta demokracie IV*, 174.

102 "Masaryk o demokracii a diktatuře," originally in *Právo lidu*, October 1, 1933, [based on interview with French reporter for *Quotidien*] in Masaryk, *Cesta demokracie IV*, 376.

103 After Hitler came to power, Germany withdrew from the Disarmament Conference on October 14, 1933. The last futile meeting of the conference was held from May 29 to June 11, 1934.

Chapter 8

Masaryk's Perspective on and Participation in World War I

Masaryk's approach to the causes of World War I on the German side appears unusual in its focus on effect of philosophy on psychology.[1] Most interpreters who had sought the causes of World War I tended to stress, on the German side, political and economic factors rather than philosophical and psychological ones, as Masaryk does. The former approach goes as far back as Lenin, who in his 1917 treatise, *Imperialism as the Highest Stage of Capitalism,* combined the political and economic causes, deriving his inspiration to a considerable degree from John A. Hobson's *Imperialism* (1902).[2] Recent scholarship tended to perpetuate the exclusively political and economic approach. The famous interpretation by Fritz Fischer, launched in Germany in 1961 and remaining controversial for a quarter century, ascribed the cause of World War I to the desires of Germany's leaders for world power and for the perpetuation of the conservative social and political system, which grew out the Prussian tradition.[3]

---

1 Masaryk did not consider economic, imperialist, or nationalist causes as crucial; Arne Novák, "Světová revoluce," *Lumír* 53 (1926) in Novák, *Nosiči pochodní; kniha české tradice* (Prague, Literární odbor Umělecké besedy a Kruh českých spisovatelů, 1928), 215; Karel Vorovka, "Několik myšlenek o Masarykově filosofii a jeho *Světové revoluci*," *Ruch filosofický* 5 (1925), 265, questions the degree of influence of philosophy and high culture on German thinking.

2 Vladimir I. Lenin, *Imperialism: The Highest Stage of Capitalism,* in Lenin, Collected Works (Moscow: Progress Publishers, 1964), 22: 185–304; originally published as Lenin, *Imperializm kak noveishii etap kapitalizma* (Petrograd: Zhizn' i znanie, 1917); John Atkinson Hobson, *Imperialism; A Study* (New York: J. Pott & Company, 1902).

3 Fritz Fischer, *Germany's Aims in the First World War* (New York: Norton, 1967) [German original: *Griff an der Weltmacht* (Duesseldorf: Droste, 1961)]; idem, *War of Illusions: German Policies from 1911 to 1914* (New York: Norton, 1975) [German original: *Krieg der Illusionen* (Duessel-

Subsequent research has tended to stress the complexity of political issues and questions of military planning.[4]

At present it has become easier to confront Masaryk's interpretation with the German philosophical scene. While Masaryk himself had first-hand knowledge of German intellectual life before and during World War I, subsequently, the wartime views of German thinkers had been difficult to trace. Postwar reference works tended to fall silent about the writings and attitudes of German philosophers on war issues during 1914–1918. This appears to be true of the following discussed later in this paper: Rudolf Eucken, Willy Moog, Paul Natorp, Max Scheler, Heinrich Scholz, Werner Sombart, Ernst Troeltsch, Alfred Weber, Wilhelm Wundt, and Leopold Ziegler. Accounts of their writings and activities during the war are missing in the standard post-war German encyclopedias and biographic dictionaries.[5] The situation, however, has been improving at the turn of the twentieth century. This was due to the unearthing of the relevant information largely thanks to Kurt Flasch and H. Sebastian Luft,[6] although some beginnings were made in that regard by Fritz K. Ringer and Hermann Lübbe.[7]

In this chapter, Masaryk's derivation of German bellicosity will be traced to his explorations of Germany's intellectual, and particularly philosophical heritage. The results will be related to Masaryk's investigation of Dostoevsky's vision of a reciprocal connection, in the mentality of the modern man, between the subjective violence against the self and the objective violence directed against the others. Finally, the relevance of Ma-

---

dorf: Droste, 1969)]; idem, Fritz, *World Power or Decline: The Controversy Over Germany's Aims in the First World War* (New York: Norton, 1974) [German original: *Weltmacht oder Niedergang* (Frankfurt a/M: Europaeische Verlagsanstalt, 1965)]. For a review of the Fischer controversy, see *The Origins of the First World War: Great Power Rivalry and German War Aims*, ed. H. W. Koch, 2nd ed. (London: Macmillan, 1984).

4   See, for instance, Mark Hewitson, *Germany and the Causes of the First World War* (Oxford: Berg, 2004); Terence Zuber, *German War Planning, 1891–1914: Sources and Interpretations* (Rochester, NY: Boydell Press, 2004).

5   *Brockhaus Enzyklopädie*, 20 vols. (Wiesbaden: F. A. Brockhaus, 1966–1974); *Deutsche Biographische Enzyklopaedie*, 12 vols. (Munich: K. G. Sauer, 1995–2000); *Neue Deutsche Biographie*, 23 vols. (Berlin: Duncker & Humblot, 1953– [2006]).

6   Kurt Flasch, *Die geistige Mobilmachung: die deutschen Intellektuellen und der Erste Weltkrieg: ein Versuch* (Berlin: A. Fest, 2000); and H. Sebastian Luft, "Germany's Metaphysical War. Reflections on War by Two Representatives of German Philosophy: Max Scheler and Paul Natorp," in *Themenportal Erster Krieg* (2007), URL: http://www.erster-weltkrieg.clio-online.de/2007/Article'208.

7   Fritz K. Ringer, *The Decline of the German Mandarin: the German Academic Community, 1890–1933.* (Cambridge, MA: Harvard University Press, 1969); Hermann Lübbe, *Politische Philosophie in Deutschland: Studien zu ihrer Geschichte* (Basel: B. Schwabe [1963]).

saryk's interpretation will be tested through an examination of the attitudes of German philosophers, at the time of World War I, toward their intellectual tradition.

The Psychological Causes

In his initial writings, Masaryk tended to concentrate on man's violence against himself, that is, the question of suicide. In his 1881 inaugural dissertation (the so-called *Habilitationschrift*) at the University of Vienna, *Sebevražda hromadným jevem společenským moderní osvěty* (Suicide as a large-scale phenomenon in modern culture), he traced the root of the increased tendency toward suicides to the growing irreligiosity of the masses.[8] Monotheistic religions – whether Christianity, Judaism, or Islam – were not favorable to suicide. The idea of God as a loving Father and protector of the universe, especially of mankind, provided support for humanity in its travails and tribulations. Pantheism, on the other hand, tended to support the trend toward self-destruction; this was true of Buddhist pantheism and also of Stoic pantheism.[9] To highlight the difference in attitude, Masaryk pointed out that Blaise Pascal painted the meaninglessness of human life in even darker colors than Schopenhauer, yet he does not succumb to pessimism. The reason was that, unlike Schopenhauer, Pascal was a theist, and theism was never pessimistic, even if it did not value human life as highly as the Gospels did.[10]

Yet, already at this early stage Masaryk hinted at the suicide-murder syndrome and at the exceptional role that this psychological mechanism played in the mentality of contemporary Germany. He advanced the concept of Titanism, according to which modern man, who denied the existence of God, began to feel powerful and Godlike, and hence also as a master of life and death.[11] In Masaryk's opinion, the condition of irreligiousness was most pronounced in Protestant Germany where, since Kant,

---

8   Tomáš G.,Masaryk, *Sebevražda hromadným jevem společenským moderní osvěty*, Spisy 1 (Prague: Masarykův ústav AV ČR, 144, 180.

9   Masaryk, *Sebevražda hromadným jevem společenským*, 132.

10 Tomáš G. Masaryk, "Blaise Pascal: jeho život a filosofie," 1883 in Tomáš G. Masaryk, *Přednášky a studie z let 1882–1884*, Spisy 17 (Prague: Masarykův ústav AV ČR, 1998), 86.

11 Tomáš G. Masaryk, *Moderní člověk a náboženství*, Spisy 8 (Prague: Masarykův ústav AV ČR, 2000), 29. Originally published in 1896–98.

scholarship had become clearly anti-Christian. Even German theologians entered the campaign for discrediting traditional Christian orthodoxy. The first manifestation resulting from the new irreligiosity was the search for solace in morbid Romanticism, which sacrificed reason to emotion. A typical fruit of this mentality was Goethe's novel, *The Sorrows of Young Werther*. The most recent German intellectual current was pessimism, expressing modern weariness of life and a theoretical justification of suicide.[12]

The Philosophical Causes

Soon after his initial study of the causes of suicide, Masaryk turned specifically to an exploration of the philosophical roots of the intellectual and moral malaise in Germany's life. As discussed earlier,[13] he concluded that the subjective approach to knowledge and existence was a curse of the German philosophical tradition in his early work *Pokus o konkrétní logiku* [Essay of Concrete Logic] (1887).[14] In *Modern Man and Religion* (1896–98), Masaryk went on to point out that the Post-Kantian development of German philosophy revealed the great flaw of subjectivism whereby Hegel (as well as Fichte) had pushed Kant's view into a logical conclusion with their Absolute Idealism.[15] Much later, Masaryk restated his position in his conversations with Karel Čapek in the 1920s, as follows: Kant set modern philosophy on the wrong path and escaped radical subjectivism by postulating the unknowable thing-in-itself, the noumenon. Fichte overcame Kant's dichotomy by "Absolute Idealism," that is, solipsism. Against this Fichtean extreme, Hegel posited a – presumably comforting – Objective Idealism, in which the absolute subject was renamed "Objective Spirit," but it was, in fact, the same thing.[16]

---

12 Masaryk, *Sebevražda hromadným jevem společenským*, 158–59. Johann Wolfgang von Goethe, *The Sorrows of Young Werther,* trans. Michael Hulse (London and New York: Penguin, 1989).
13 See Chapter 1 in this book.
14 Tomáš G. Masaryk, *Pokus o konkrétní logiku; třídění a soustava věd*, Spisy 3 (Prague: Ústav T. G. Masaryka, 2001), 160, 221.
15 Masaryk, *Moderní člověk a náboženství*, 54. Jan M. Lochman noted that, for Masaryk, Hegel's dialectic undermined the existence of any permanent truths and values; Lochman, "Masaryk's Quarrel with Marxism," in *T. G. Masaryk, 1850–1937*, ed. Stanley Winters et al., 3 vols. (London: Macmillan, 1989–1990), 2: 121–122. See also Jan M. Lochman, "Masaryks Auseinandersetzung mit dem Marxismus," in *On Masaryk: Texts in English and German*, Studien zur österreichischen Philosophie, ed. Josef Novák, vol. 13 (Amsterdam: Rodopi, 1988), 231–32.
16 Karel Čapek, *Hovory s T. G. Masarykem*, Spisy 20 (Prague: Československý spisovatel, 1990), 234.

The extreme epistemological and metaphysical self-centeredness of the classical German Idealists (Kant, Fichte, Schelling and Hegel) led to what Masaryk called the 'Faust Complex' in German culture.[17] As pointed out in Chapter 1, Masaryk referred to this phenomenon as 'Titanism,' through which the modern man felt himself powerful or Godlike, as a master over life and death.[18] He saw in this phenomenon the roots of the modern man's inclination to self-destruction.[19] One way to escape the sense of psychological isolation and despair, resulting from this predicament, was to embrace pantheism. Hegel's pantheism – from the philosophical and sociological viewpoint – was an attempt to overcome "the illusion of individual consciousness" and especially "the illusion of sense perception." These "illusions" were to be ontically negated by "reason" – not an ordinary reason, but a higher "dialectical" reason, the World Spirit.[20] Taking umbrage under the World Spirit also had the unfortunate consequence of releasing the individual from his sense of personal moral responsibility.[21]

In a way, Masaryk preferred Schopenhauer and Nietzsche to the classical German Idealists. While the latter interpreted the world process as the unfolding of the universal reason and postulated a number of metaphysical stages and entities that parodied Christian dogmas, Schopenhauer and Nietzsche saw the world process more credibly as the austere unembellished manifestation of a Cosmic will. In the end, however, Masaryk also judged them severely. They intensified the despair of individual isolation, which derived from classical Idealism, by adding the putative Nihilism of the Cosmic will, and the visceral anger, which resulted from their pessimistic outlook.[22]

Schopenhauer's Nihilism sprang, according to Masaryk, from his metaphysical belief in a blind will aiming at nothing in particular. While

17 Masaryk, *Moderní člověk a náboženství*, 163. See also Zdeněk Nejedlý, *T. G. Masaryk*, 4 vols. (Prague: Melantrich, 1930–1937); 2nd ed., vols. 1–2, Sebrané spisy 31–32 (Prague: Orbis, 1949–1950), 3: 265.

18 Masaryk, *Moderní člověk a náboženství*, 29. On the concept of "Titanism," see, Milan Machovec, *Tomáš G. Masaryk*, 3rd ed. (Prague: Česká expedice, 2000), 150.

19 This was the theme of his first major philosophical work; see Masaryk, *Sebevražda hromadným jevem společenským moderní osvěty*.

20 Tomáš G. Masaryk, *Otázka sociální. Základy marxismu filosofické a sociologické*, 2 vols. Spisy 9–10 (Prague: Masarykův ústav AV ČR, 2000), 1: 144.

21 According to Masaryk, Tolstoy's pantheism partly had its source in Hegel, see Tomáš G. Masaryk, *Rusko a Evropa III*, Spisy 13 (Prague: Masarykův ústav AV ČR, 1996), 295.

22 Concerning Masaryk's view of Schopenhauer and Nietzche, see also Zdeněk V. David, "Masaryk on Schopenhauer and Nietzsche within the Austrian Philosophical Tradition," *Kosmas: Czechoslovak and Central European Journal,* vol. 23, no. 1, Fall 2009, 19–36.

this belief originated in his radical individualism, its consequence was an attitude of pervasive anger. Schopenhauer's outlook exemplifies an angry pessimism that was born from an excessive concentration on the self.[23] Therefore, the substance of Schopenhauer's pessimism was wrath and fury aimed at external violence, rather than a suicidal despair.[24] While subjectively, pessimism could lead man to a negation of life – in extreme cases to self-destruction – the objective pessimism in extreme cases led to murder. It was pessimism of critique, revolt, and defiance. This outwardly directed pessimist anger, in its societal manifestation, could lead to the embrace of socialist revolution, as it had done in Karl Marx.[25]

In the case of Nietzsche, Masaryk found the same heavy weight of a pessimistic outlook (as in Schopenhauer), which was ultimately traceable to the subjectivism of the German Idealists.[26] As a new interpretation, he attributed the anxiety that created a sense of egotistic isolation in Nietzsche to the influence of Max Stirner (1806–1856).[27] Furthermore, Masaryk advanced the poignant suggestion that Nietzsche experienced a distinct kind of pleasure from suffering.[28] In Nietzsche's case – as in the case of Schopenhauer – Masaryk was also concerned with the problem of Nihilism.[29] He attributed the roots of Nietzsche's Nihilism not only to a perception of the meaninglessness of the Cosmic will, but also to his rejection of all existing values which needed to be revised (transvalued). Moreover, Masaryk connected Nietzsche's Nihilism with anarchism and cultural Decadence rather than with the socialist revolutionarism in which he had seen the principal impact of Schopenhauer's nihilist outlook. In sum, the pessimism and Nihilism of Schopenhauer and Nietzsche, according to Masaryk – like the extreme subjectivism and self-centeredness of the classical German Ideal-

---

23   Jiří Olšovský, "Masaryk, Nietzsche a počátky diskuse o Nihilism," *Masarykův sborník*, 11–12 (1999–2003), 103; Robert P. Pynsent, "Masaryk and Decadence," in *T. G. Masaryk, 1850–1937*, ed. Winters et al., 1: 72.

24   Tomáš G. Masaryk, *Ideály humanitní a studie z let 1901–1903*, Spisy 24 (Prague: Ústav T. G. Masaryka, 2011), 55–56; Masaryk, *Sebevražda hromadným jevem společenským*, 63; Paul Selver, *Masaryk: A Biography* (London: M. Joseph, 1940), 68.

25   Masaryk, *Otázka sociální*, 2: 203.

26   Emil Ludwig, *Defender of Democracy: Masaryk of Czechoslovakia* (New York: McBride, 1936), 93; Masaryk, *Moderní člověk a náboženství*, 18.

27   Masaryk, *Moderní člověk a náboženství*, 58.

28   He saw the same kind of trait in the personality of Adolf Hitler; see Masaryk, "Masarykova recenze Hitlerovy knihy Mein Kampf," in Tomáš G. Masaryk, *Cestou demokracie IV*, Spisy 36 (Prague: Masarykův ústav AV ČR, 1997), 354.

29   Olšovský, "Masaryk, Nietzsche a počátky diskuse o nihilism," *Masarykův sborník*, 11–12, 101–103.

ists – produced a shaken, even deranged state of mind which might lead a man to killing himself, or to killing others, and above all to the catastrophe of war. To get rid of one's own life, or to deprive somebody else of life was nihilistic: a sudden appearance of nothing, death and nothingness.[30]

Dostoevsky's Paradigm

Masaryk in much of his writing stressed the similarity of his views to Dostoevsky's linkage of suicide and murder. However, as he tells us, he was not familiar with Dostoevsky's views when he wrote his first major work on the topic, his treatise on *Suicide* in 1881.[31] However, in early 1882, while still a private docent at the University of Vienna, Masaryk became acquainted with the Russian scholar and librarian Ernst L. Radlov, from St. Petersburg, with whom he had opportunities to discuss Russian literature, including the works of Dostoevsky.[32] Although he learned Russian during his university studies, he began to delve seriously into Russian literature and philosophy only in 1887 when – partly to refresh himself after the controversies about the false Czech manuscripts – he resolved to travel in Russia. He then reached a conclusion about the prominence of Dostoevsky's ideas and art and planned to write a history of Russian philosophy and intellectual life, centering on Dostoevsky's thought. In the end his *Russia and Europe* assumed another form, but he planned to append an extensive study of Dostoevsky as a third volume.[33]

---

30 Masaryk on the contrary, wished to base his philosophy on rational belief in God and human immortality. Olšovský, "Masaryk, Nietzsche a počátky diskuse o nihilism," *Masarykův sborník*, 11–12, 101.

31 Masaryk, *Sebevražda hromadným jevem společenským*, 12. See also Jan Patočka, "Kolem Masarykovy filosofie náboženství (1946)," idem, *Sebrané spisy* 12, (Prague: Oikoymenh, 2006), 395. Ironically, Masaryk's own interpretation of suicide had not been received favorably in Russia. Thus, Elena Likhacheva, in her article "O samoubiistve," *Otechestvennye zapiski*, no. 7 (1881), 21–53, referred on page 22 note 1 to Masaryk's *Der Selbstmord* (Vienna, 1881) as a work that had little to offer either by his interpretation (seeing the main reason for suicide in the decline of religion) or in the evidence that he presented.

32 Radlov also informed Masaryk that his family was of Czech origin and settled in Russia in the seventeenth century; Stanislav Polák, *T.G. Masaryk: Za ideálem a pravdou*, vol. 1: 1850–1882 (Prague: Masarykův ústav AV ČR, 2001), 331. See also, Vasil Škrach, "E. Radlow und Th. Masaryk," *Der russische Gedanke. Internationale Zeitschrift für russische Philosophie, Literaturwissenschaft und Kultur*," 1 (1929–1930), 208.

33 Masaryk, Tomáš G., *Světová revoluce za války a ve válce, 1914–1918*, Spisy 15 (Prague: Masarykův ústav AV ČR, 2005), 459.

Masaryk addressed the theme of Dostoevsky's treatment of suicide in his article "Spisy F. M. Dostojevského" (Writings of F. M. Dostoevsky), which appeared originally in 1892 in the newspaper *Čas*. Masaryk praised Dostoevsky's insight into the problem of self-destruction – coinciding with his own diagnosis – as the consequence of modern atheism which, having deposed God, had set man up onto God's judgment seat; and indeed man had made God out of himself. Consequently, this Man-God had the right to revise nature and history; he was a law-giver. [34] Masaryk pointed out that the ensuing syndrome of suicide-murder became, for Dostoevsky, a crucial problem of life. Dostoevsky had discoursed on the "right to murder" in *Crime and Punishment* and in *The Brothers Karamazov,* and had philosophized about suicide in *The Idiot* and *The Possessed,* as well as in *The Brothers Karamazov* and the article "The Judgment."[35]

Masaryk undertook a pointed analysis of Dostoevsky's paradigm in his major work, *The Social Question,* originally published in 1898. For Dostoevsky, like for Masaryk, suicide and murder were twin phenomena stemming from two kinds of pessimism. While subjective pessimism could lead man to negation of life – in extreme cases to suicide – objective pessimism in extreme cases led to murder. The objectively directed pessimism of critique, revolt, and defiance could also be called anarchism or Nihilism. Masaryk saw this attitude exhibited in "the poisoned souls" of characters in Dostoevsky's novels, such as Raskolnikov or Ivan Karamazov.[36] In Masaryk's opinion, Dostoevsky, in all his writings, novels, and articles, had grappled with this double issue in its several forms and variants. He was thus driven to understand the psychological, social and metaphysical problem of atheism, which led inwardly to despondency (tending to suicide) and outwardly to a revolutionary zeal (oriented to committing murder).[37] Subjective and objective pessimism were in an inverse relationship. There were fewer murders where there were many suicides, and vice versa. Subjectivism and objectivism were incompatible like melancholy and

---

34   Tomáš G., Masaryk, "Spisy F. M. Dostojevského," *Masarykův sborník* 2 (1926–1927), 21–33; originally: *Čas* 6 (1892). Recently, Dostoevsky's view of the relationship between atheism and suicide has been analyzed by Irina Paperno, *Suicide as a Cultural Institution in Dostoevsky's Russia* (Ithaca: Cornell University Press, 1997), 143; and Susan K. Morrissey, *Suicide and the Body Politic in Russia* (New York: Cambridge University Press, 2006), 3.

35   Masaryk, "Spisy F. M. Dostojevského," *Masarykův sborník* 2, 24.

36   Masaryk, *Otázka sociální,* 2: 203

37   Ibid., 2: 205, n8.

exaltation, "like tears and anger." Masaryk summed up Dostoevsky's view thus: "Suicide is a delirium of subjectivism, murder a delirium of objectivism. Both are rooted in egotism: One because he cannot love, the other because he hates."[38]

Masaryk returned to Dostoevsky's paradigm in 1907 when writing his large treatise, *Russia and Europe (Russland und Europa).* The large section on Dostoevsky, which originally was to be included in the book, ultimately was published only after World War I, as *Boje o Boha. Dostojevskij: filozof dějin ruského problému* (Struggles about God. Dostoevsky as a Philosopher of the History of the Russian Question) with chapter nine titled "Murder and Suicide."[39] At the start, Masaryk reiterated that his special interest in Dostoevsky arose because Dostoevsky was concerned by similar problems as he himself was, particularly in his treatise *Sebevražda.*[40] Dostoevsky saw the ultimate outcome of modern atheism in that the atheist kills himself or kills another.[41] Masaryk, however, also noted a certain differentiation that Dostoevsky made; he more often dealt with murder than with suicide. Only one story was entirely devoted to suicide: *Něžná* [*Netochka Nezvanova*]. He treated murder at length in *Crime and Punishment*; more briefly in *The Possessed, The Brothers Karamazov,* and *The Idiot.* Suicide reappeared in *The Possessed* (a double suicide), *The Adolescent* (suicide of Kraft), and in *The Brothers Karamazov,* as the death of Smerdiakov.[42]

Suicide and murder were sharply distinguished by Dostoevsky in *The Possessed.* Kirillov considered murder "the lowest manifestation of my free will", while suicide as the "highest manifestation." Verkhovensky, on the contrary, stated that, in order to show his free will, he would kill somebody else, rather than himself.[43] In this connection, Masaryk pointed out – not without a critical undertone – that Dostoevsky regarded the twin phenomenon of murder-suicide too starkly as a logical process.[44] Masaryk was openly critical of Dostoevsky's philosophical formula in *The Broth-*

---

38   Ibid., 2: 205.
39   Chapter 9: "Murder and Suicide," 95–102, in *Boje o Boha. Dostojevskij: filozof dějin ruského problému* in Masaryk, *Rusko a Evropa III,* 15–152.
40   Masaryk, *Rusko a Evropa III,* 9.
41   Tomáš G. Masaryk, *Rusko a Evropa* II, Spisy 12 (Prague: Masarykův ústav AV ČR, 1996), 95; Masaryk, *Rusko a Evropa III,* 348.
42   Masaryk, *Rusko a Evropa III,* 97.
43   Ibid., 98.
44   Ibid., 102. Zola in contrast attributes murder/suicide to passions and dispositions, springing from an atavism or inherited savagery; ibid., 97.

ers Karamazov. He felt that it was a mere play on words when Dostoevsky equated the suicide of the rich with the murder committed by the poor. According to this comparison, the rich, for their part, isolated themselves in their luxury and thus committed a spiritual suicide. Masaryk saw no equivalence here: the poor murdered physically and brutally, the rich killed themselves only "spiritually."[45] Eventually, however, Masaryk endorsed Dostoevsky's views without any reservations. In the preface to a new edition of the *Sebevražda* in 1926, he quoted, with approval, long passages from Dostoevsky's *The Possessed* (1871–72) and *The Diary of a Writer* (1876) to the effect that suicide becomes a logical necessity for a man who had lost faith first in the immortality of human soul and, second, in the existence of God. Masaryk again noted that he had not known of Dostoevsky's ideas when he wrote his own book originally, but subsequently discovered an amazing coincidence between them and his own.[46]

Dostoevsky and German Philosophy

Considering the role that German philosophy played in Masaryk's interpretation of the roots of modern man's metaphysical despair and epistemological predicament, it is rather paradoxical that prior to World War I, Masaryk did not try to link the influence of German philosophy in Russia with Dostoevsky's observations on the suicide/murder syndrome in Russia. Although he acknowledged the tremendous impact of German thought on the Russian intelligentsia,[47] he did not trace Dostoevsky's views or the views of his fictional characters to German ideas. Some commentators and historians, however, had sought influences of German philosophy on Dostoevsky's treatment of his characters, and some evidence has been cited concerning his interest in German thinkers, particularly in Kant and Hegel.[48]

---

45 Ibid., 99. On Masaryk's critique of Dostoevsky's concept, see also Patočka, "Kolem Masarykovy filosofie náboženství (1946)," 406–407.

46 Masaryk, *Sebevražda hromadným jevem společenským*, 12–14. Patočka questions the similarity between Masaryk's and Dostoevsky's views on murder and suicide, see Patočka, "Kolem Masarykovy filosofie náboženství," 396.

47 Masaryk, *Rusko a Evropa II*, 374.

48 Ironically, Masaryk's own work on suicide was not appreciated in contemporary Russia. Elena Likhacheva, "O samoubiistve." *Otechestvennye zapiski*, no. 7 (1881), 22 n1 referred to Masaryk's *Der Selbstmord* (Vienna, 1881) as a work that has little to offer either by its interpretation (seeing

While in exile in Siberia, Dostoevsky asked in 1854 for books, including Kant's *Critique of Pure Reason* and the works of Hegel, especially his *History of Philosophy*.[49] In November 1854, young Baron A. E. Wrangel, who knew Dostoevsky in Siberia, wrote to his father that he and Doestoevsky intended to translate Hegel's *Philosophy*.[50] Apparently the project did not proceed very smoothly since – according to Wrangel – Dostoevsky "did not know German and did not like the language."[51] According to Dmytro Chyzhevskyi, Dostoevsky gained some knowledge of Hegel through his cooperation with Nicholas Strakhov in the early 1860s. Appolinaria Suslova reminisced that during their joint travel in Italy, in discussing philosophy, Dostoevsky attempted to explain to her certain Hegelian ideas, especially the "reality of concept" [*Realtät des Begriffs*.].[52] Likewise, Chyzhevskyi claimed that Dostoevsky was enthusiastic about Herzen's articles from the 1840s on Hegel's philosophy, and still in 1872 recommended them as "the best philosophy" not only in Russia but also in Europe.[53]

As for reflections of German thought in Dostoevsky's literary characters, Irena Paperno has claimed that Kant's influence on Dostoevsky remains underestimated, especially the role of antinomies of pure reason, the dilemma of – on the one hand – the moral and religious truth of practical reason, and –on the other – the denial of this truth by pure reason. Facing the dilemma of Kant's antinomy, the moral necessity for God's existence and the empirical knowledge of God's absence, Kirillov in *The Possessed* attempted to resolve it by assuming the role of God: "If there is no God then I am God." Thus, this was another source of Dostoevsky's familiar dictum that suicide was a natural consequence of a Godless universe.[54] As for Hegel, in Kirillov's decision to commit suicide, Hegel's dictum "being and not being is the same" (*Sein und Nichtsein ist dasselbe*) had

the main reason for suicide in the decline of religion) or in the evidence that he presents. Cited by Paperno, *Suicide as a Cultural Institution*, 231.

49 Joseph Frank, *Dostoevsky: The years of ordeal, 1850–1859* (Princeton, NJ: Princeton University Press, c1983), 169. See also Edward H. Carr, *Dostoevsky, 1821–1881: A New Biography* (London: Allen and Unwin, 1931), 82.

50 A. E. Wrangel, *Vospominaniia o F. M. Dostoevskom v Siberii* (St. Petersburg, 1912), 66; cited in Frank, *Dostoevsky. The Years of Ordeal, 1850–1859*, 171.

51 Wrangel, *Vospominaniia o F. M. Dostoevskom*, 21; cited in Frank, *Dostoevsky. The years of ordeal, 1850–1859*, 171–72.

52 Dmytro Chyzhevskyi, *Hegel bei den Slaven* (Reichenberg: Stiepel, 1934), 349–50.

53 Ibid., 267.

54 Paperno, *Suicide as a Cultural Institution*, 145. See also Susan K. Morrissey, *Suicide and the Body Politic in Russia* (New York: Cambridge University Press, 2006), 222–23.

been a factor.[55] According to Edward H. Carr, the Hegelian postulate of thesis and antithesis inspired Dostoevsky's psychological theory, in which "the presence of the 'lower' as well as the 'higher' element was necessary in order to produce a synthesis."[56] Paperno saw the influence of Schopenhauer in Kirillov's assertion that a barrier to suicide was the fear of pain; otherwise, virtually everyone would seek self-destruction.[57]

As for Masaryk, he posited a link between the aberrations of Dostoevsky's characters and the effect of German philosophy on them only in his reflections subsequent to World War I. In his war memoirs, he pointed out that the problem of murder was analyzed intensively in Russian literature, with Dostoevsky playing a leading role. In *Crime and Punishment*, Dostoevsky probed the mentality of the young student Razkolnikov, who, having his mind confused by the European (but mainly German) philosophy of superman, ended up murdering a weak old woman. Another devotee of the philosophy of superman, Ivan Karamazov, insinuated the idea of parricide to his half-brother Smerdiakov. Masaryk further pointed out that it was his interest in Russian intellectual history that had led him to deal with the concept of murder and murderousness when analyzing the modern warfare, revolution, and terrorism.[58]

Masaryk on the Role of German Philosophy in World War I

In his war memoirs, Masaryk assigned the responsibility for the outbreak of World War I squarely to the radical nationalism with its roots in German history.[59] He argued that those principal characteristics of the Bismarckian Empire that distinguished Prussianized Germany from the liberal and democratic West – theocracy, militarism, amorality – were most clearly de-

---

55   E. Markov, "Kriticheskie besedy," *Russkaia rech*, 1 (June 1879), 197 n6.
56   Carr, *Dostoevsky, 1821–1881: A New Biography*, 255–56.
57   She refers to Schopenhauer's "On Suicide" in *Parerga and Paralipomena* [1851] see Arthur Schopenhauer, *Essays and Aphorisms*, trans. R. J. Hollingdale (Harmondsworth, England: Penguin Books, 1970), 79. Cited by Paperno, *Suicide as a Cultural Institution*, 143.
58   Masaryk, *Světová revoluce za války a ve válce*, 290.
59   Ibid., 413, 415. The passages dealing with the history of German thought were left out of the English translation of the war memoirs, which appeared as: Masaryk, *The Making of a State: Memories and Observations, 1914–1918*, ed. Henry W. Steed (New York: George Allen and Unwin, 1927). See also Zwi Batscha, *Eine Philosophie der Demokratie: Thomas G. Masaryks Begründung einer neuzeitlichen Demokratie* (Frankfurt: Surkamp, 1994), 31, 65.

rived from German philosophical tradition. The construction of the Prussian state as a theocracy, according to Masaryk, owed much to the secularization of German Lutheran theology. This occurred in the teaching of Hegel, as well as Fichte and Schelling, all of whom were originally trained as theologians.[60] Hegel in particular formulated the principles of Prussian theocracy through his pantheism and his tendency to fantasize, which led to the quasi-divinization of the state. Bismarck and Kaiser Wilhelm constantly referred to God, presumably embodied in the Prussian monarchy.[61]

In Masaryk's opinion, the German idealists were also the progenitors of Prussian militarism, which had already been anticipated by Kant's categorical imperative.[62] After Kant, German philosophy necessarily was mired in pessimism and egoism. An appeal to force – to realize the Pangermanic goals – was sanctified by philosophy, beginning with Kant and then Fichte and Hegel.[63] Hegel himself reacted to the subjectivism of Fichte and Schelling, which had led to moral isolation and bred nihilism and pessimism.[64] In the final analysis, modern militarism of the Prussian type represented an escape from suicidal inclinations.[65] Indeed, Masaryk asserted that Hegel declared not only the infallibility of the state, but also the redemptive value of war and militarism.[66]

Even German artistic culture reflected sharply the image of what Masaryk called "Titanic subjectivism with its egoism and isolationism."[67] Thus the artistic genre of Expressionism was pre-eminently German, representing an aspect of German self-centeredness, and therefore vitiated from the start. The Expressionists were nothing else but spokesmen for Kant and the neo-Kantians, or for the subjectivism à la Nietzsche. Masaryk called as a witness the Expressionist poet and critic Rudolf Paulsen

---

60 Masaryk, *Světová revoluce za války a ve válce*, 419. See also Ludwig, *Defender of Democracy: Masaryk of Czechoslovakia*, 79.

61 Masaryk, *Světová revoluce za války a ve válce*, 280, 381.

62 Ibid., 282. See also Nejedlý, *T. G. Masaryk*, 3: 175.

63 Masaryk, *Světová revoluce za války a ve válce*, 426. Patočka, however, considered simplistic and historically unproven Masaryk's claim that Hegel's absolute Idealism had served the authoritarianism of the Prussian state and had provided a justification for the theory and practice of the use of force; Jan Patočka, *Dvě studie o Masarykovi* (Toronto: Sixty-Eight Publishers, 1980), 59.

64 Masaryk, *Světová revoluce za války a ve válce*, 282. See also Nejedlý, *T. G. Masaryk*, 3: 175.

65 Masaryk, *Světová revoluce za války a ve válce*, 287.

66 Ibid., 282.

67 "...titanský subjektivismus, jeho egoismus a izolovanost...". Masaryk, *Světová revoluce za války a ve válce*, 475. See also William Preston Warren, *Masaryk's Democracy: A Philosophy of Scientific and Moral Culture* (Chapel Hill: University of North Carolina Press, 1941), 98–102.

(1883–1966), who had stated that the poet bears within himself "the fin-ished forms" (a Kantian term) out of which the whole world grows. Ma-saryk added: "This is subjectivism in all its violent absurdity. Paulsen also correctly states that Expressionism was in its essence German."[68] Further-more, Masaryk asserted that, without exaggerating, it was fair to say that during the war, German literature was more chauvinistic than any other, in quantity and quality, and that German publicists and journalists drove their people to war in Berlin, Vienna, and Budapest.[69] Masaryk did find a major exception in music. It was particularly Beethoven, who – in Ma-saryk's view – was free of Prussian influence. Prussianism, however, sub-sequently prevailed in Richard Wagner's music.[70]

Masaryk claimed that his perception of a combination of modern ten-dency to suicide with Prussian militarism in World War I was corrobo-rated by testimony from the German side. His witness was the historian Karl Lamprecht, who as early as 1904 had written about the era of "excit-ability," which both Bismarck and Kaiser Wilhelm exemplified. Masaryk added that in fact "the German superman, the Titan, was a nervous crea-ture," who sought relief from chronic excitement in death or war, either of which meant an even more acute excitement. While this psychological state of nervousness might have affected other nations, it was particularly true of the Germans. Masaryk explained that: "Their philosophers, artists and other active minds pushed subjectivism and individualism to the point of absurd egomania, with all its moral consequences. Nietzsche's superman, the Darwinian 'beast,' was to prove a remedy for the inhuman folly of solip-sism." The German philosophers, scientists, historians, and politicians, suf-fering from spiritual isolation, proclaimed German civilization and culture to be the culmination of history. With this arrogant sense of superiority, Prussian Pangermanism asserted its right to expand and to subjugate oth-ers by sheer force. Masaryk reemphasized that the Prussian State, its army, and its fighting spirit became antidotes to a pervasive morbid subjectivism.[71]

Although Masaryk recognized the role of the Prussian state and Ger-man army in the outbreak of the war, he ascribed the ultimate cause to

---

68 Masaryk, *Světová revoluce za války a ve válce*, 285.
69 Masaryk did acknowledge that there were exceptions among the writers, who embraced paci-fism, and names, among others, Eduard Stilgebauer and Fritz Unruh; Masaryk, *Světová revoluce za války a ve válce*, 285.
70 Ibid., 281.
71 Ibid., 289.

German intellectuals, especially philosophers. On his return to Prague from exile on December 23, 1918, he referred, this time, to the barbaric exhortations of Theodor Mommsen, Eduard Hartmann, Paul de Lagarde, and their followers against – among others – the Czech nation.[72] In his war memoirs, Masaryk added that Lagarde's view of German superiority was also evident in Marx, who held the same demeaning view of the Slav nations as Lagarde or Heinrich Treitschke.[73]

German Philosophers and the War

Let us then look at what German philosophers, as well as theologians, actually wrote about the war during World War I. There was, in fact, a tendency to connect the meaning of the conflict with earlier intellectual development in Germany, at times, strikingly similar to the intellectual paradigms suggested by Masaryk. First of all, there was an emphasis on the intellectual or spiritual causes of the war. Thus, Max Scheler (1874–1928) philosopher and a pupil of Rudolf Eucken, then an independent scholar, having previously taught as a privatdozent at the University of Munich until 1910, wrote in his book *Genius des Krieges und der Deutsche Krieg* (1915) that the meaning of the World War could not be economic or political; it could only be one of a psychological and/or moral cleansing (*Läuterungsinn*).[74] Scheler, also in *Genius des Krieges,* rejected the linking of war with either Marxian economic competition or the Darwinian struggle for existence. For him war was a purely human institution not connected with search for food or other economic or biological causes. He stated: "[War] is an indispensable part of the historical process impelling peoples to win their freedom, create cultures, establish values." It rested on the will to power and could not be reduced to a material motive; it was a cause sui generis. Max Weber (1864–1920) and Friedrich Naumann (1860–1919) had both advanced similar ideas in the 1890s.[75]

---

72 "Poselství prezidenta republiky," *Pražské noviny*, December 23, 1918, in Tomáš G. Masaryk, *Cesta demokracie I, 1918–1920*, Spisy 33 (Prague: Masarykův ústav AV ČR, 2003), 25.
73 Masaryk, *Světová revoluce za války a ve válce*, 413, 415.
74 Flasch, *Die geistige Mobilmachung*, 135.
75 Roland Stromberg, *Redemption by War: The Intellectuals and 1914* (Lawrence: Regents Press of Kansas, 1982), 79, also 215 n37. See also Max Scheler, *Genius des Krieges und der Deutsche Krieg* (Leipzig: Verlag der Weissen Bücher, 1915), 36.

As in Masaryk's paradigm, appeals to Kant and his Idealist successors became a standard staple in defining the country's destiny by German scholars after the outbreak of the World War. Rudolf Eucken (1846–1926), a philosopher and a professor in Jena since 1874,[76] writing in his book *Die Träger des deutschen Idealismus* (1915), declared that Kant, "for us Germans," had erected a specific Idealism which defined the nation's essence. It was an austere and powerful idealism, an idealism of the deed, which found its full development in the external world, but which also among the Germans released an ability to unfold this world in a new way. Thereby the German nation had received an inward empowerment and became sufficiently strong to defeat both external and internal foes. This idealism, which had constantly motivated the Germans, had also acquired – through Kant's liberating deed –a firm philosophical footing.[77] A philosophy professor in Marburg, Paul Natorp (1854–1924) in his book, *Deutscher Weltberuf* (1918) appealed to Kant's distinction between culture (*Kultur*) and mere civilization, and maintained that the meaning of the war was to defend the German *Kultur* against the outbreak of hatred on the part of the British and the nations speaking Romance languages.[78]

Ernst Troeltsch (1865–1923), Protestant theologian and professor in Berlin (1915),[79] affirmed in his *Deutscher Geist und Westeuropa* (1916) that the foundations of German identity had to be sought in the institutions of Prussia as well as "in the philosophical Idealist meaning of the state and history, which extend[ed] all the way to today's idealists from Kant, Fichte, and Hegel."[80] Troeltsch celebrated the spirit of the post-Napoleonic pe-

---

76   Previously, he had served as professor at the University of Basel since 1871, and had received the Nobel Prize in literature in 1908; *Brockhaus Enzyklopädie*, 5: 751.

77   "Uns Deutschen ... den eigentuemlichen Idealismus ausgebildet, auf den unser Wesen angelegt ist. Es ist ein herber und kraeftiger Idealismus, ein Idealismus der Tat, der die Welt um uns voller Verwicklung findet, der aber in uns das Vermoegen entdeckt, eine neue Welt zu enfalten, ... dabei auch eine innere Erhoehung erfaehrt und aus ihr stark genug wird, allen Gegnern draussen und drinnen zu trotzen. Dieser Idealismus, der von alters her in uns Deutschen wirkt, hat durch die Befreiungstat Kants auch einen festen wissenschaftlichen Boden erhalten." Rudolf Eucken, *Die Träger des deutschen Idealismus* (Berlin: Ullstein, 1915), 69. On Hegel's insistence on war as necessary for human progress, see Eucken, *Die Träger des deutschen Idealismus,* 207.

78   Paul Gerhard Natorp, *Deutscher Weltberuf, geschichtsphilosophische Richtlinien,* 2 vols. in 1 (Jena: E. Diederichs, 1918), "Die Seele des Deutschen," 2: 196. Cited by Lübbe, *Politische Philosophie in Deutschland,* 192.

79   Previously in Bonn (1892), then in Heidelberg (1894); *Deutsche Biographische Enzyklopädie*, 10: 91–92.

80   "... in der philosophisch-idealistischen Deutung von Staat und Geschichte, wie sie von Kant, Fichte und Hegel bis zu den heutigen Idealisten sich hinzieht." Ernst Troeltsch, *Deutscher Geist und Westeuropa* (Tuebingen: Mohr, 1925), 93.

riod in relation to the current war. The experience of 1914 resembled that of the year 1813, which in the very depth of the nation's soul ("im tiefen Inneren der Volksseele") had led to a re-thinking and a renewal ("zu einer Neubesinnung und Erneuerung gefuehrt habe"). At that time, it was the spirit of Kant, Romanticism, and Goethe that endowed the life struggle and the rebirth of the Prusssian state with the new form of the Gospel of the German national spirit of freedom ("die neue Form des Evangeliums des deutschnationalen Geistes der Freiheit..."). This spirit engendered the productive individuality and the originality of the metaphysical belief in the divine global destiny of Germandom ("die Urspruenglichkeit des metaphysischen Glaubens an die goettliche Weltbestimmung des Deutschtums"). Troeltsch continued to inventory the contributions of this fabulous era as "the autarky of the state, (as 'a closed commercial state'); the rebirth of a subjectivity from a degenerate cult of the self to a free and broad dedication to the national spirit; as well as the imbibing of the national spirit from the inner stream of the divine essence of the world." Finally, there was the sorting out of the several national characters among themselves (as mirrors of the Godhead), in brief, there arose the self-perception of the inherently creative and free Germandom as against the artificial, derivative, decorative and rationalistic essence of the Romance nations. These were the novel ideas of the era of Kant and his successors.[81]

Werner Sombart (1863–1941), a sociologist and economist in Berlin (since 1906),[82] maintained that no matter how much they may have differed in their particular views, all the notable German philosophers – Fichte, Schopenhauer, Hegel, Hartmann, Nietzsche – agreed on the cleansing and uplifting effect of war.[83] It was, however, Fichte who was singled out by German scholars as a symbolic figure of the war effort. Heinrich Scholz (1884–1956), a Protestant theologian and philosopher at the Uni-

81 "Autarkie des Staates als 'geschlossener Handelsstaat', Wiedergeburt der im Selbstkultus entarteten Subjekivitaet zur freien Hingabe an den Nationalgeist, Erfuellung des Nationalgeistes aus dem inneren Zuge des goettlichen Weltwerdens heraus, Anerkennung der Nationalgeister untereinander als des Spiegels der Gottheit, kurz Selbsterfassung des urspruenglich produktiven und freien Germanentums gegenueber dem kuenstlichen, abgeleiteten, dekorativen verstandesmaessigen Wesen des Romanentums: das waren damals die neuen Gedanken." Cited from Troeltsch, *Deutscher Geist und Westeuropa*, 33–34; Flasch, *Die geistige Mobilmachung*, 154–55.
82 Previously in Wrocław since 1890; *Brockhaus Enzyklopädie*, 17: 549.
83 Werner Sombart, *Händler und Helden: Patriotische Besinnungen.* (Munich and Leipzig: Duncker und Humblot, 1915), 95.

versity of Wrocław (Breslau) since 1917,[84] claimed in his *Das Wesen des deutschen Geistes* that in Fichte's philosophy the German spirit ascended into the boundless, without losing anything of its German character. In fact, in his exhortations, Fichte revealed the real German essence with a kind of overpowering rapture.[85] Alfred Weber (1868–1958), a philosopher of culture, a sociologist, and an economist at the University of Heidelberg since 1907,[86] maintained that Fichte, as "a man of the deed" [*Tatmensch*], was after all the only one whose words could express what the German nation truly felt in the current war.[87] Leopold Ziegler (1881–1958), a philosopher and a graduate from University of Heidelberg in 1905,[88] claimed that in Fichte's *Addresses to the German Nation* one could recognize the gigantic will of a man to create what had not existed – a nation.[89] Willy Moog (1888–1935), a philosopher and later a professor in Greifswald (since 1922), whose scholarly work focused on Kant, Fichte, Hegel and the Hegelian school, published an entire volume in 1917 on Fichte's philosophy of war.[90] Fichte's *Reden an die deutsche Nation* were reprinted several times during the war, including, for instance, an edition by Eucken.[91] Fichte's influence was institutionalized through the formation of the Fichte Society (*Fichtegesellschaft*) in 1916 with its own journal, *Deutsches Volkstum*.[92]

---

84   *Neue Deutsche Biographie*, 23: 454.
85   "In Fichtes Philosophie steigert sich deutsche Denkart ins Grenzlose; aber dies ist darum nicht weniger deutsch. Im Gegenteil, gerade in jenen Sätzen, die nicht unbedingt gültig sind, offenbart sich das deutsche Wesen in Fichte mit einer Art hin reissender Überkraft." Heinrich Scholz, *Das Wesen des deutschen Geistes*. (Berlin: Grote 1917), 29; cited by Lübbe, *Politische Philosophie in Deutschland*, 207. See also Scheler, *Genius des Krieges und der Deutsche Krieg*, 55.
86   Previously (since 1900) he had taught at the University of Berlin, then at the German University in Prague in 1904–1907, where he participated actively in German nationalist politics demanding the division of Bohemia into a German and a Czech part. In 1915, he entered war services and focused on an organization in Berlin that advocated a German dominated Central Europe and its extension into the East. *Deutsche Biographisches Enzyklopädie*, 12 vols. (Munich: K. G. Sauer, 1995–2000), 10: 349.
87   "Der einzige, der in Worten dem nachgekommen ist, was wir heute über das deutsche Volk fühlen, ist eben doch der Tatmensch Fichte." Alfred Weber, *Gedanken zur deutschen Sendung* (Berlin: S. Fischer, 1915), 87; cited by Lübbe, *Politische Philosophie in Deutschland*, 207.
88   He then lived as a private scholar in Karlsruhe, and since 1925 in Überlingen am Bodensee; *Deutsche Biographische Enzyklopädie*, 10: 656.
89   "In den 'Reden' Fichtes spürt man den ungeheueren Eigensinn eines Mannes, der das erschaffen will, was nirgends ist: das Volk." Leopold Ziegler, *Der deutsche Mensch* (Berlin: S. Fischer, 1915), 10. Cited by Lübbe, *Politische Philosophie in Deutschland*, 207.
90   Willy Moog, *Fichte über den Krieg* (Darmstadt: Falken-Verlag, 1917). See also *Brockhaus Enzyklopädie*, 12: 778.
91   Johann G. Fichte, *Fichtes Reden an die deutsche Nation*, ed. Rudolf Eucken (Leipzig: Insel, 1915); Flasch, *Die geistige Mobilmachung*, 71–72.
92   Lübbe, *Politische Philosophie in Deutschland*, 207.

The role of Nietzsche in inspiring German national warlike consciousness was not as systematically emphasized by the German philosophers as the role of the classical Idealists. Yet, there were journalistic reports claiming that a typical German soldier carried in his knapsack Nietzsche's *Zarathustra* together with the Bible.[93] Likewise, Sombart, celebrated the war of 1914 as Nietzsche's war (*Krieg Nietzsches*). According to Sombart's flowery language, Nietzsche was "the bard and the visionary, who had descended from heaven to deliver us the tidings that from us a son of God would be born, whom in his manner of speaking, he named the Superman." [94] Sombart also eulogized Nietzsche as a "crown witness" [*Kronzeuge*] for the transvaluation of values. In the process of transvaluation, in particular, the word "fanaticism" no longer had a negative connotation but stood for "a powerful surge of the will to action" (*Hochspannung des Willens zur Tat*), without which any kind of Idealism would soon be emasculated.[95] In his war memoirs, Masaryk was particularly critical of Sombart, who extolled German militarism in the spirit of Hegel and "prided himself with the Fausts and Zarathustras" fighting in the trenches.[96]

At the other side of the ledger, German philosophers tended to deprecate empiricism, realism, and individualism, which they considered typical of the West European, especially British, prosaic outlook, and as the reverse of the German attachment to Idealism and metaphysics. Thus the famous Wilhelm Wundt (1832–1920), philosopher and psychologist at the University of Leipzig since 1875,[97] decried "the shallowness" of British ethical theories as well as that of common sense realism and of empirical epistemology since Locke. Likewise, he denounced the "egotistical utilitarianism" and "pragmatism" of the Anglophone philosophical and social thought.[98] Wundt traced the origin of the English attachment to empiricism and aversion to philosophical generalization all the way back to me-

---

93   Flasch, *Die geistige Mobilmachung*, 72; Arne Novák, "Světová revoluce," *Lumír* 53 (1926) in Novák *Nosiči pochodní; kniha české tradice* (Prague: Literární odbor Umělecké besedy a Kruh českých spisovatel, 1928), 201.

94   "Nietzsche sei der Sänger und Seher gewesen, der, vom Himmel hoch dahergekommen, uns die Mär verkündet hat, das aus uns der Gottessohn geboren werden soll, den er in seiner Sprache den Übermenschen nannte." Sombart, *Händler und Helden*, 53.

95   Ibid., 58, 111.

96   Masaryk, *Světová revoluce za války a ve válce, 1914–1918*, 287.

97   Previously, professor in Heidelberg since 1864, and in Zurich in 1874; *Brockhaus Enzyklopädie*, 20: 504.

98   Wilhelm Wundt, *Die Nationen und ihre Philosophie: Ein Kapitel zum Weltkrieg*. 2nd ed. (Leipzig: Kröner, 1915), 37–41, 46–49; see also Ringer, *The Decline of the German Mandarins*, 185.

dieval scholasticism, particularly the teaching of Duns Scotus and William of Ockham.[99]

While admitting that German thinking had been affected to some extent by Locke and Rousseau, Troeltsch considered these contributions marginal at best. They did not serve as the foundation of German intellectual and social development, which had to be sought in the institutions devised by Prussian statesmen like vom Stein and Scharnhorst, as well as in the historical and social theories advanced by Kant, Fichte, and Hegel, and their followers and successors.[100] Sombart denounced the English ethics stressing political individualism, which focused not on collective life ("life per se, supraindividual life"), but –in a mundane way – on particular lives. He found especially abhorrent the goal of the utilitarians – the happiness of the greatest number of individuals.[101] Even the rather moderate Friedrich Meinecke (1862–1954), philosopher of history at the University of Berlin since 1914,[102] rejected in 1915 the English and French ideal of universal humanity, and – appealing to Fichte – he forecast that European nations would welcome a German victory that would encourage the nations' ontic individualities. In other words, a victory of the Entente would usher in homogenizing globalization, a victory of Germany, on the contrary, would favor vigorous nationalisms, promoting a high degree of differentiation and diversification within humanity.[103]

Challenges to Masaryk's Diagnosis of the German Problem

The influence of German philosophy in Europe

Masaryk's idea of German philosophy's responsibility for World War I has not gone unchallenged. It could be pointed out that German philosophers

99 Wundt, *Die Nationen und ihre Philosophie: Ein Kapitel zum Weltkrieg*, 29.
100 Troeltsch, *Deutscher Geist und Westeuropa*, 93; see also Flasch, *Die geistige Mobilmachung*, 166, 416 n60.
101 Sombart, *Händler und Helden*, 19–20, 143–44. For special stress on Fichte and Nietzsche as opponents of English ethical theories, see ibid., 55–56. See also Ringer, *The Decline of the German Mandarins*, 184.
102 Previously at the University of Strasbourg since 1901, and the University of Freiburg in Breisgau since 1906; *Brockhaus Enzyklopädie*, 12: 352.
103 Friedrich Meinecke, *Deutsche Kultur und Machtpolitik im englischen Urteil* (Berlin: C. Heymann, 1915), 25–27. See also Ringer, *The Decline of the German Mandarins*, 186.

were popular not only in Germany, but also in other European countries before World War I. This was especially plausible to argue in the case of Schopenhauer and Nietzsche, since the setting of their philosophy could be detached from the German historical and social context. It was more difficult to do for the classical German Idealists, from Kant to Hegel. Even Hegel, however, was popular outside of Germany in the nineteenth century, especially in Italy and Russia. In Italy, Benedetto Croce (1866–1952) and Giovanni Gentile (1875–1944) were fascinated by Hegel's philosophy of history as a rational dialectical process.[104] The appeal of Hegelianism affected almost all the luminaries of Russia's nineteenth-century intellectual firmament, including Petr I. Chaadaev, Ivan V. Kireevskii, Mikhail Bakunin, Vissarion G. Belinskii, Alexander Herzen, Nikolai G. Chernyshevskii, and Georgii V. Plekhanov.[105] However, in Italy, Hegelianism was diverted into Fascism and in Russia into Marxism, neither of which was directly relevant to the outbreak of World War I.

The metaphysics of a dominant Cosmic will was fairly fashionable in most of Europe, although it was initiated by Schopenhauer and Nietzsche.[106] Nietzsche's influence in fact spread throughout the Continent with its appeal of radical individualism and artistic culture.[107] He was particularly popular in France,[108] where, for instance, famous author Romain Roland (1866–1944) expressed his great admiration for Nietzsche in the period before World War I.[109] Nietzsche was also important to Andre Gide in France, William Yeats in Ireland, Franz Kafka in Bohemia, Gabriele d'Annuzio in Italy, and Dmitii Mrezhkovkii in Russia.[110] Nietzsche's West-European influence, however, primarily focused on his esthetics within the movement of artistic Decadence, while his metaphysics of the Superman had little effect outside of Germany.

---

104 Stromberg, *Redemption by War*, 74, 104, 190.
105 Dmytro Chyzhevs'kyi, *Gegel' v Rossii* (Paris: Dom knigi, [1939]), especially, 12–31, 210–26, 260–65; Tomáš G. Masaryk, *The Spirit of Russia: Studies in History, Literature, and Philosophy*, tr. by Eden and Cedar Paul, and W. R. and Z. Lee, 2nd ed., 3 vols. (London: Allen & Unwin, 1961–67), 1: 149–50, 217, 222; Boris V. Jakovenko, *Ein Beitrag zur Geschichte des Hegelianismus in Russland* (Prague: Bartl, 1934).
106 Stromberg, *Redemption by War*, 62.
107 Ibid., 20.
108 Ibid., 60.
109 Romain Rolland, *Mémoires, et fragments du Journal* (Paris: A. Michel [1956]), 106–7.
110 Stromberg, *Redemption by War*, 62,102.

Subjectivism and dynamism in French philosophy

A particularly strong challenge to Masaryk's diagnosis, however, was a trend toward subjectivism and dynamism in French philosophy itself, represented above all by Henri Bergson. Bergson's "élan vital" resembled Schopenhauer's Will to Live and Nietzsche's Will to Power, which in Germany had superceded the cosmic reason of Hegel's Absolute. In addition, Bergson wrote with some enthusiasm about the war as bringing about a moral regeneration of Europe.[111] In an address to the Academy of Moral and Political Sciences in Paris on December 12, 1914, he portrayed the German mentality – in contrast to his own philosophy of freedom, vitalism, and spontaneity – as believing in "brute force" and as burdened (rather bizarrely from Masaryk's point of view) by a mechanistic and materialistic view of the world.[112] German philosophers, for their part, tried to utilize Bergson for their propaganda purposes. For instance, Kurt Riezler (1882–1955), a diplomat writing on philosophical subjects,[113] attempted in 1914 to use Scheler's ideas to combine Bergson's philosophy with Nietzsche and Treitschke.[114] In addition, Troeltsch suggested that Bergson, as well as his teacher Emile Boutroux (1845–1921), were in many ways indebted to German philosophy for their Idealist metaphysics.[115]

Concerning Bergson, Masaryk noted in his war memoirs that in modern French philosophy a revolt had indeed occurred, aimed against abstract intellectualism and positivism. The prime example was Bergson's intuitionism with the concept of a cosmic "élan vital." Masaryk conceded that such an orientation seemed to be affected, more than the French would be willing to admit, by German psychology with its activism and emotionalism from Kant to Nietzsche.[116] During a visit to Paris in 1923,

---

111 Stromberg, *Redemption by War*, 2; H. Sebastian Luft, "Germany's Metaphysical War. Reflections on War by Two Representatives of German Philosophy: Max Scheler and Paul Natorp," in *Themenportal Erster Krieg* (2007), URL: http://www.erster-weltkrieg.clio-online.de/2007/Article'208, 1 n3.

112 Henri Bergson, *The Meaning of the War: Life and Matter in Conflict* (London: Unwin, 1915), 32–33. See also Stromberg, *Redemption by War*, 143.

113 *Neue Deutsche Biographie*, 21: 618–19.

114 Flasch, *Die geistige Mobilmachung*, 236, 248. Kurt Riezler, [pseud. J. J. Ruedorffer], *Grundzüge der Weltpolitik in der Gegenwart* (Suttgart and Berlin, 1914), 11, 232. See also Ringer, *The Decline of the German Mandarins*, 337–38.

115 Troeltsch, *Deutscher Geist und Westeuropa*, 71.

116 Masaryk, *Světová revoluce: Za války a ve válce*, 88. Just before World War I Masaryk referred to Bergson's "evolution créatrice" in his criticism of Georges Sorel; see Tomáš G. Masaryk,

asked by the French newspaperman his opinion of Bergson's philosophy, Masaryk answered diplomatically that Bergson's élan resembled voluntaristic concepts in German philosophy, especially those of Schopenhauer and Nietzsche. Bergson, however, expressed the concept more precisely as an emotion or volition that opposed intellectualism, positivism, and criticism. Masaryk said he would have expressed the concept differently namely, as "internal experience." According to Masaryk, Bergson eventually did begin to speak of "internal experience" in his book *Matière et mémoire*.[117] Later in his conversations with Karel Čapek, he expressed himself more critically, saying that Bergson's intuition was close to the concept of revelation, as found in the writings of modern philosophers.[118] For Masaryk, revelation was epistemologically an unacceptable source of real knowledge.

In general, Masaryk admitted that some of the spiritual malaise of modern man affected also other nations, but it was especially acute among the Germans.[119] Only in Germany did the murderous desire to escape from sickly subjectivism prevail and did spark the war conflict in 1914. As mentioned earlier, Masaryk, however, did note some exceptions from suicidal subjectivism and Prussian militarism in German culture. Most importantly, he expected that World War I would also liberate Germany from its old regime. This free Germany would be rid of its previous spiritual isolation, it would overcome the immoral Bismarckianism, and would return to the humanistic ideals, particularly of Herder and Beethoven.[120] One may add in conclusion that Masasryk's optimistic prognosis came one war too early.

"Syndikalismus a demokracie," in idem *Politika vědou a uměním, 1911–1914*, Spisy 28 (Prague: Masarykův ústav AV ČR, 2011), 326–27.

117 "Une heure avec Masaryk," *Nouvelles Littéraires*, 2 (1923), in Tomáš G. Masaryk, *Cestou demokracie II*, Spisy 34 (Prague: Masarykův ústav AV ČR, 2007), 477. Masaryk referred to Henri Bergson's *Matière et mémoire, essai sur la relation du corps a l'esprit*, 8th ed. (Paris: F. Alcan, 1912).

118 Čapek, *Hovory s T. G. Masarykem*, 228.

119 Masaryk, *Světová revoluce za války a ve válce*, 292–93.

120 Ibid., 296.

Chapter 9

Democracy and Totalitarian Regimes

In his writings, especially after World War I, Masaryk maintained that the objective of mankind's development was now to attain "internationalism" and "inter-statism" [*mezistátnost*], that is, an effort to organize not only Europe but the entire world in as unified a way as possible. He suggested that an era of cultural synthesis was arriving, which would bring together the cultural elements of different nations.[1] This denouement was made possible by the rise of democracy in the wake of the war. He stressed that the global conflict had destroyed three regimes based on theocratic absolutism (in Russia, Prussia, and Austria), and in their place republics and democracies emerged, which could and would jump-start new principles in international politics. [2]

Masaryk took very seriously the need – on the way of replacing theocracy by democracy – to abolish the mainstay of theocracy, namely, the concept of governments, the power of which was allegedly based on their possession of divine rights. Early on, he urged that the elimination of theocratic governmental principles be embodied in the peace treaties ending World War I. Thus in his recommendations for a German Peace Treaty, he wrote the U.S. Secretary of State, Robert Lancing on October 29, 1918:

---

1   Tomáš G. Masaryk, *Světová revoluce za války a ve válce, 1914–1918*, Spisy 15 (Prague: Masarykův ústav AV ČR, 2005), 375–76.

2   Even the armies became more democratic as a result of World War I. With the old militarism no longer sufficient, it became clear that "not only the high commander, but every officer and soldier has to think [for himself]... The army became democratized also in strategic and tactical area." Masaryk, Tomáš G., *Cesta demokracie II*, Spisy 34 (Prague: Masarykův ústav AV ČR, 2007), 438.

Constitutional reforms in Germany and Prussia are not sufficient; the constitution of the component states must be democratized. The position of the Kaiser, as well as all three Kings and the rest of the smaller twenty dynasts must be clearly changed, so that they derive their power from the people and not by divine grace. The same holds good for Austria-Hungary (and Turkey). Prussianism, dynastical absolutism in Germany emanates not only from the Emperor but from the twenty-three dynasties.[3]

Masaryk clung to his thesis that replacement of theocracy by democracy was the main purpose of the sacrifices in World War I, despite severe criticism from those seeing the crux of victory in the cause of national liberation.[4]

Democracy, which originated as an internal political system of individual countries, could be applied, after World War I, in external affairs as well, and thus it rose from the level of a domestic actor to that of an international one. Masaryk particularly focused on the League of Nations, which had acquired an institutional reality, and the program of which was endorsed by all modern, truly democratic politicians and statesmen. However, his post-World War I optimism about the prevalence of democracy was challenged in the inter-war period by the rise of the totalitarian dictatorships.[5] Although the course of events ran counter to his expectations that the new democratic era in Europe would include even Germany, he found a consolation in that the modern European dictatorships, whether Stalin's, Mussolini's, or Hitler's, were affected by democracy at least to the extent of paying lip-service to democratic principles. They eschewed any tendency of returning to the principles of the "ancient regimes" with their divine-rights monarchies and the prerogatives of hereditary nobility.

---

3   Wilson, *The Papers of Woodrow Wilson* , ed. Arthur S. Link et al., 69 vols. (Princeton, NJ: Princeton University Press, 1966–1994), 51: 508.
4   For instance, Arne Novák, "Světová revoluce," *Lumír* 53 (1926) in Novák, *Nosiči pochodní; kniha české tradice* (Prague, Literární odbor Umělecké besedy a Kruh českých spisovatelů, 1928), 215–17, 220.
5   For recent literature on totalitarianism, see Sheila Fitzpatrick and Michael Geyer, *Beyond Totalitarianism: Stalinism and Nazism Compared* (Cambridge: Cambridge University Press, 2008); John Connelly, "Totalitarianism: Defunct Theory: Useful Word," *Kritika* 11 (2010), 819; Ronald R. Suny, "Reading Russia and the Soviet Union in the Twentieth Century: How the 'West' Wrote Its History of the USSR," in *Cambridge History of Russia*, 3 vols (Cambridge: Cambridge University Press, 2006), 3: 22–28.

Vladimir I. Lenin

Masaryk first took notice of Lenin in his magisterial work *Russland und Europa* (Russia and Europe), originally published in 1913. He called attention to the Marxist Russian Social Democratic Party, which by 1891 had taken over the leadership of the Russian working class from the previously influential Populists [*Narodnaia volia*], who advocated terrorism and immediate revolution. Masaryk traced the public appearance of Lenin to the year 1895, when he associated Lenin with the political and activist faction of the Social Democrats (together with Vera Zasulich, L. Martov, and others) in contrast to the theoreticians, including Plekhanov, Mikhail I. Tugan-Baranovskii, and Sergei N. Bulgakov.[6] Masaryk noted that the Social Democrats were weakened in 1900 by the defection of the moderates, labeled as Economists and Revisionists, which led to the strengthening of the Social Revolutionaries, heirs of the Populists' revolutionary tradition of the *Narodnaia volia*. Masaryk traced the subsequent efforts of the Social Democrats to define themselves against the Social Revolutionaries,[7] and particularly focused on the party's formal split at its Second Congress in London in 1903, which left Lenin in charge of the Bolshevik majority, and Martov of the Menshevik minority. In Masaryk's opinion, Lenin performed a volte-face and led the Bolsheviks to emulate the ultra-radical Social Revolutionaries. Masaryk charged that Lenin embraced the tactics and the goals of the *Narodnaia volia*, envisioning a revolution as an immediate possibility, as well as the outcome of a centralized dictatorship, led by an elite of revolutionaries.[8]

As a professional philosopher, Masaryk expressed a low opinion of Lenin's philosophical erudition and skill in *Russland und Europa*. Lenin, just like Plekhanov, derived his philosophical, especially epistemological foundation not directly from Marx, but from Engels and his treatise *Anti-Dühring* which, according to Masaryk, was nothing more than "a na-

6 Masaryk, Tomáš G., *Rusko a Evropa II*, Spisy 12 (Prague: Masarykův ústav AV ČR, 1996), 241. Curiously, in his review of Masaryk's *Russland und Europa* in 1914, Leon Trotsky blames the author for – among other errors concerning Russian Marxism – underrating Lenin's role in the organizational and journalist activities of the Bolsheviks; see Trotsky, Leon, "Profesor Masaryk o Rusku," *Masarykův sborník* 1 (1924–1925), 83–84. Originally published as N. Trotzky, "Professor Masaryk über Russland," *Kampf, sozialdemokratische Monatschrift*, 7 (1914), no. 11–12, 519–27.
7 Particularly in the political journal *Iskra* (1901–1905), and the theoretical one, *Zaria* (1901–1902).
8 Masaryk, *Rusko a Evropa II*, 243–44.

ïve explanation of a naïve realism."[9] Thus, Lenin's defense of Marx's materialism in his treatise on Empiriocriticism, according to Masaryk, was disappointing. Lenin found in Avenarius, Mach, and their Russian adherents nothing but the disguised solipsism of Fichte and Berkeley. According to him, this subjectivism shook one's conviction of sound reason in the objective lawful world and thereby tended to strengthen religious proclivities (which, in turn, were among the pillars of bourgeois dominance). This philosophy was, therefore, reactionary. Masaryk gives Lenin credit for witty sarcasms, but he stresses that philosophically he had not advanced beyond Engels.[10]

Comments on the Revolution

Masaryk had little to say in his public pronouncements about Lenin, although he was present in Russia at the time of the Bolshevik Revolution (May 1917–March 1918), and his name would be linked with Lenin's both in the inter-war period and during the Cold War. After the March Revolution, in June 1917, he commented on the ease of the overthrow of Tsarism, adding: "Even the extremist partisans of Mr. Lenin show little energy." The best explanation is that the Tsarist system was so rotten that it fell apart by itself.[11] At that time, he was mainly concerned about Lenin's embrace of defeat for the sake of the Bolshevik cause, urging "a peace without annexations and contributions." Masaryk saw Lenin's "defeatism" as a threat to the successful prosecution of the war by the Allies.[12] He warned Czech legionnaires in Russia to beware of Lenin's party and its peace policies.[13] Immediately after the Bolshevik Revolution in December 1917 and January 1918, he published in English in the journal *New Eu-*

9   Masaryk, *Rusko a Evropa II*, 277.
10 Masaryk, *Rusko a Evropa II*, 279. See also Vladimir I. Lenin, *Materialism and Empirio-Critism: Critical Comments on a Reactionary Philosophy* in idem, *Collected Works* 4th ed. 38 vols. (Moscow: Foreign Languages Publishing House, 1961–1962), 14:17–388; Vladimir I. Lenin, *Materializm [i] empiriokrititsizm: kriticheskie zametki ob odnoi reaktsionnoi filosofii* (Moscow: Zveno, 1909) in idem, *Sochineniia*, 4th ed. 45 vols. (Moscow: Izd. politicheskoi literatury, 1950–1967), 14: 5–343.
11 "Professor Masaryk on Russia. What the Allies May Expect. Legacies of Tsarism," *The Times*, June 5, 1917 in Tomáš G. Masaryk, *Válka a revoluce II: články, memoranda, přednášky, rozhovory, 1917*, Spisy 31 (Prague: Masarykův ústav AV ČR, 2008), 120.
12 Ibid., 121.
13 "Organizovat politické strany?" *Čechoslovák*, July 3, 1917 in Masaryk, *Válka a revoluce II: články, memoranda, přednášky, rozhovory, 1917*, 141.

rope excerpts from his book, *Russland und Europa* (1913), on Bakunin and Chernyshevskii as precursors of the revolution.[14]

A consistent and comprehensive indictment of Lenin's regime was delivered by Masaryk on October 28, 1919, when he devoted about a quarter of his annual statement as President of the Republic in the National Assembly to the topic. First, Lenin was wrong in declaring his Communist program real Marxism. In reality, Lenin's Bolshevism, according to Masaryk, was more a revolutionary anarchism in the style of Bakunin. Second, Lenin's Bolshevism was authoritarian and brutal. According to Masaryk, if Marx juxtaposed the proletarian mass against the bourgeoisie, he posited a democratic majoritarian system. Lenin embraced the concept of the dictatorship of the proletariat as a small clique ruling in the name of the workers. Third, Lenin's Bolshevism did not overcome Russian Tsarism, and his tactics resembled those of Ivan the Terrible.[15]

Masaryk added to his criticism of Lenin's regime in early March 1920, when he noted how mistaken Lenin was, when at the start of his rule he incorrectly assumed that a social revolution could be carried out in a short time of several months. He soon realized his error, and now he estimated that the social revolution would not occur for another thirty years. His other great mistake was that the socialist revolution could be carried out by the subjugation of the bourgeoisie, if the proletariat was ignorant of modern methods of economics and production. Thus Lenin was led to recommend that his followers study the American Frederick W. Taylor, who is considered a quintessential teacher of capitalist methods.[16]

Escalation of criticism

Masaryk's critique of Lenin's Bolshevism escalated from the fall of 1920 to the spring of 1921.[17] It was provoked by the direct intrusion of Lenin-

---

14 Tomáš G. Masaryk, "Forerunners of the Russian Revolution," *The New Europe*, "Bakunin" 5.63 (December 27, 1917), 345–52; "II. Bakunin and Marx: Anarchy and Socialism," 5.64 (January 3, 1918), 373–76; "III. Chernyshevskii," 6.67 (January 24, 1918), 55–58.

15 "Statement of the President of the Republic in the National Assembly, October 28, 1919," Masaryk, Tomáš G., *Cesta demokracie* I, Spisy 33 (Prague: Masarykův ústav AV ČR, 2003), 174–75. On Masaryk's questioning Lenin's Marxism, see also Antonie van den Beld, *Humanity: The Political and Social Philosophy of Thomas G. Masaryk* (The Hague: Mouton, 1975), 148.

16 "Third Message of President Masaryk, March 7, 1920," in Masaryk, *Cesta demokracie* I, 232.

17 Initially, Masaryk had not expected the assertion of Bolshevik Communism in Czechoslovakia.

ism in Czech politics when, in September of 1920, the left faction of the Czech Social Democratic Party asked for acceptance, by the party, of the Communist International's twenty-one conditions for membership, and at the same time launched an unsuccessful attempt to seize the headquarters of the Social Democrats.[18] Masaryk reacted initially in a series of articles under the title "Soviet Russia and We," published in the newspaper Čas between September 5 and 23, 1920.[19] He stressed that in Russia, a small organized party of the Bolsheviks could seize power thanks to the fact that most of society was not organized. Czech socialists had an entirely different tradition of mass organization and parliamentary orientation. Their goal was to be achieved through parliamentary work, as a nonviolent revolution.[20] The mass of the Russian people were illiterate, hence accustomed to obey teaching and preaching from above. This explains the elitist character of the Russian revolution with leaders, like Lenin, coming from the aristocratic, educated circles. On the contrary, the Czech workers were literate and skeptical about dictatorial methods from above.[21]

According to Masaryk, Lenin's strength was that of a tactician who sternly reminded Russian and German Communist radicals that rigid abstract programs were not enough – real leaders had to offer concrete plans that were realizable. Likewise, he prided himself on the ability to compromise and opportunistically change directions. For tactical reasons, he recommended participation in parliaments, trade unions, and recognition of the Versailles treaty. He warned in the interest of socialism that reckless attempts at coups d'états had to be avoided. Only experienced leaders

---

In an interview in September 1919, he had expressed confidence that social reforms have stifled Marxist radicalism. See Masaryk, *Cesta demokracie* I, 158.

18 Victor S. Mamatey and Radomír Luža, eds. *A History of the Czechoslovak Republic, 1918–1948* (Princeton, NJ: Princeton University Press, 1973), 103–4. Established in March 1919, the Second Congress of the Comintern, was held in July and August. 1920. see Ivan Avakumovic, "Comintern," in *Modern Encyclopedia of Russian and Soviet History*, ed. Joseph L. Wieczynski 60 vols. (Gulf Breeze, FL: Academic International Press, 1976–2000), 7: 177. On the crisis in the fall on 1920, see also Beld, *Humanity: The Political and Social Philosophy of Thomas G. Masaryk*, 149–51; Antonie van den Beld, "La morale et l'humanté de Masaryk et le problème de la violence politique," in Vladimír Peška, and Antoine Mareš, eds., *Thomas Garrigue Masaryk, européen et humaniste*. Paris: Etudes et documentation internationales: Institut d'études slaves, 1991, 58; Alain Soubigou, *Thomas Masaryk* (Paris: Librairie Arthème Fayard, 2002), 272–73; 402–3; Mary Heimann, *Czechoslovakia: The State That Failed* (New Haven: Yale University Press, 2009), 70. On the historical background of Czech socialism, see Zdeněk Kárník, *Socialisté na rozcestí: Habsburk, Masaryk či Šmeral*, 2nd ed. (Prague: Univerzita Karlova, 1996).

19 Masaryk, *Cesta demokracie* I, 304–36.

20 Ibid., 305.

21 Ibid., 306.

of the proletariat in each country should be followed.[22] Masaryk sought
to illustrate Lenin's perfidious skill as a tactician through the attitudes he
displayed at the Ninth Congress of the Russian Communist Party, meeting from March 29 to April 4, 1920.[23]

Masaryk's concern with Lenin's Bolshevism culminated in the winter of 1920–1921, when the left wing of the Social Democratic Party of
Czechoslovakia sought to precipitate a revolutionary situation by calling
for a general strike in December 1920. The strike collapsed on December
15, but the crisis led to the foundation of the Czechoslovak Communist
Party in May 1921.[24] Masaryk reacted in the midst of the December disturbances with the article *"Revoluce a bolševici"* [The Revolution and the
Bolsheviks] in *Lidové noviny* of December 24, 1920.[25] He concentrated on
drawing a contrast between Lenin's violent revolutionary Bolshevism and
the evolutionary approach of most European Social Democrats, who had
by and large embraced the parliamentary route toward their goal of social
justice.[26] Masaryk portrayed Lenin's deviation from Marx in even starker
terms than hitherto, depicting Lenin as an opponent of Marx and Engels.
In 1895, Engels, shortly before his death, and in his legacy to the German
proletariat, advised giving up armed revolution for a revolution through
the ballot box. Similarly, Masaryk noted that, as early as 1872, Marx himself – addressing a socialist meeting in Amsterdam – stated that at least
in countries like Netherlands, England, and the United States, the social
transformation could occur peacefully without a revolution.[27] Aside from

22 Ibid., 309–10.

23 Ibid., 310–14. On the Ninth Congress of the Russian Communist Party, see John S. Reshetar,
     A Concise History of the Communist Party of the Soviet Union (New York: Praeger, 1960), 165–70;
     Jerry F. Hough and Merle Fainsod, *How the Soviet Union is Governed* (Cambridge, MA: Harvard
     University Press, 1979), 98, 126–27; P. N. Pospelev, ed., *Vladimir Il'ich Lenin: Biografiia.* (Mos-
     cow: Institut Marksizma-Leninizma pr TsK KPSS, 1960), 455–56.

24 Its admission into the Third International was delayed until October 1921; see Mamatey and
     Luža, eds. *A History of the Czechoslovak Republic, 1918–1948*, 105–6. Masaryk amnestied the par-
     ticipants in the Communist putsch of December 1920 in February 1922, "Amnestie účastníkům
     komunistického puče," Čas, February 15, 1922, Masaryk, *Cesta demokracie II*, 246.

25 "Revoluce a bolševici," in *Lidové noviny*, December 24, 1920, in Masaryk, *Cesta demokracie I*, 380–
     85. On Masaryk's reaction see Jacques Rupnik, "Masaryk and Czech Socialism, *"T. G. Masaryk,
     1850–1937*, Stanley Winters et al., eds., 3 vols. (London: Macmillan, 1989–1990), 1: 140–42; Jaro-
     slav Opat, "Rusko a Evropa. Zkušenosti XX. Století v optice Masarykovy filosofie dějin," in Ja-
     roslav Opat, *TGM: Evropan světoobčan* (Prague: Masarykův ústav AV ČR, 1999), 68–69.

26 "Revoluce a bolševici," in *Lidové noviny*, December 24, 1920, in Masaryk, *Cesta demokracie I*, 380.

27 Ibid., 381. On Masaryk's criticism of Lenin's Bolshevism as non-Marxist, see also Jaroslav Krejčí,
     "La philosophie de l'histoire de Masaryk à la lumière de notre époque," in Peška and Mareš, eds.,
     Thomas Garrigue Masaryk, européen et humaniste. 90–91; Miroslav Novák, "T. G. Masaryk, cri-

questioning its necessity, Masaryk emphasized the exceptional brutality
– reflecting Russian primitiveness – of Lenin's revolution. The Bolsheviks delighted in wasting lives. Masaryk had a chance to observe the hor-
rid acts of the revolutionaries, reflecting barbarian coarseness, even bes-
tiality. The special moral horror stemmed from the obvious arbitrariness
of their choice of victims.[28]

In the next newspaper article, which followed closely on January 1,
1921, Masaryk returned to emphasize the un-Marxist character of Lenin's
concept of the dictatorship of the proletariat. Marx and Engels, in their
romantic period, envisaged the dictatorship only as a brief phenomenon
exercised by the overwhelming majority in the interest of the majority.
Marx thought of the dictatorship of the proletariat in a benign sense as
better than the capitalist state; it could even assume a parliamentary form.
Lenin developed an uncritical and mystical theory of the relationship between leaders and the proletariat. Lenin maintained that the decision of
a leader must be followed in order to attain proper ends, but at the same
time it must be assumed that the objectives of the leader express the will
of the proletariat.[29] Marx and Engels expected the proletariat to be highly cultured, trained in science, and in possession of administrative skills.
Lenin decided to carry out "the final socialist revolution" with an unedu-
cated, illiterate mass.[30] In conclusion, Masaryk reiterated the baneful influence of Russian tradition, including the doctrines of revolutionaries like
Bakunin, and the Tsarist absolutism, as an inspiration of Bolshevik terrorism.[31] Still, in July 1921, Masaryk returned to the disastrous economic
consequences of Lenin's rule, caused by the lack of administrative, technological, and scientific skills in the country.[32] As a coda, in a polemic with
the Communist journal *Rudé právo*, in October 1921, Masaryk stated concerning the contemporary Russia:

tique du marxisme," in Peška and Mareš, eds., *Thomas Garrigue Masaryk, européen et humaniste,* 131–38.

28   "Revoluce a bolševici," in *Lidové noviny,* December 24, 1920, in Masaryk, *Cesta demokracie I,* 384–85.

29   "Prezident republiky o tak zvané diktatuře proletariátu," first published in Čas 31 (January 1,
1921) no. 1, 1–4, in Masaryk, *Cesta demokracie II,* 15–17.

30   Ibid., 17–18.

31   Ibid., 19–21.

32   He also noted conflicts developing between Lenin and Trotsky; see "Aus Sowjetrussland," *Prager
Presse,* July 14, 1921, in Masaryk, *Cesta demokracie II,* 65–66. In 1922, in a confidential memorandum, Masaryk favored economic assistance to Lenin's Russia, if it were accompanied by greater
respect for the liberty and the lives of Soviet citizens, see "Pomoc Rusku Evropou a Amerikou",
written in January and February 1922, in Masaryk, *Cesta demokracie II,* 236.

Today it is not unknown to anybody that Russia is neither a Soviet nor a Communist state, but a large cemetery, in which there rest thousands upon thousands of victims unnecessarily and, therefore, barbarically attacked and murdered. That cemetery, of course, also contains a section of buried illusions and fantasies.[33]

Retrospective view

Masaryk's concern with Lenin's Bolshevism diminished when the likelihood of a Communist seizure of power in Czechoslovakia was averted, and the call for World Revolution was toned down by Lenin after 1920.[34] Gradually, Masaryk's attitude further softened during the concessions of the New Economic Policy (NEP) in Soviet Russia which began in 1921, and especially after Lenin's death on January 21, 1924. In an interview with Dorothy Thompson, for the *Philadelphia Ledger* in March 1925, he even foresaw at least an unintentional service of the Soviet system to democracy. When asked about the future of democracy in Europe – considering that the foremost figures of the political scene, Lenin and Mussolini, have been opponents of parliamentarianism – Masaryk responded that such enemies would benefit the cause of democracy by demonstrating how detrimental the opposite system was.[35] Finally, in an interview for *Christian Science Monitor*, dated March 12, 1926, Masaryk expressed hope in the gradual evolution of the Soviet system, stating: "Bolshevism will be changing, and Russia will need at least fifty years to recover."[36]

By October 1932, he thought that Russia had become a virtually capitalist country, except that the administration of capital was more concentrated than elsewhere in Europe.[37] Asked further about his view of Trotsky's denunciation of Stalin, and specifically about the claim that Lenin had warned against Stalin in his last testament, Masaryk respond-

33 "Kritika nekritické kritiky," *Čas*, October 30, 1921, in Masaryk, *Cesta demokracie II*, 162.
34 Tomáš G. Masaryk, *Les Slaves après la guerre* (Prague: Orbis, 1923), 39.
35 "Prezident Masaryk o Dunajské federaci," *Neue Freie Presse*, March 8, 1925, in Masaryk, *Cesta demokracie III*, 103.
36 *Christian Science Monitor*, March 12, 1926, in Masaryk, *Cesta demokracie III*, 130.
37 As for the future, bolshevism was developing in the direction of economic individualism; "Masaryk o dnešní Evropě," originally published in *Berliner Tagblatt*, October 5, 1932, in Masaryk, Tomáš G., *Cesta demokracie IV*, Spisy 36 (Prague: Masarykův ústav AV ČR, 1997), 308.

ed cautiously that, as far as he knew, Lenin was not particularly satisfied with Trotsky either, and that such judgments had to be assessed according to the particular situation.[38] The Czechoslovak Communists, however, did not appreciate the softening of Masaryk's attitude toward the Soviet Union, vociferously adopting the slogan "Not Masaryk, but Lenin," during the Czechoslovak presidential elections of 1934.[39]

Masaryk's later problems with Lenin

It was after Lenin's death and Masaryk's attitude toward Soviet Russia had softened that the figure of the Bolshevik dictator came to haunt him. The case involved Masaryk's dealings during the Russian Civil War with Lenin's opponent, a prominent leader in the Social Revolutionary Party, Boris Savinkov (1879–1925).[40] Masaryk met with Savinkov in Moscow from March 2 through 5, 1918, at the time of the signing of the Treaty of Brest-Litovsk, and prior to his own departure for Siberia in April (and on his way through Japan to the United States). Masaryk's note, written at the time, indicates that he had asked treasurer František Šíp to pass on to Savinkov 200,000 rubles through Jiří Klecanda (1890–1918), secretary of the Russian Section in the National Czechoslovak Council.[41] Subsequently, Savinkov was credited with engineering the assassination of V. Volodarskii, Commissar for the press in June 1918; the assassination of the German Ambassador Count Wilhelm Mirbach in Moscow in July 1918; and an at-

---

38 "Masaryk o dnešní Evropě," originally published in *Berliner Tagblatt*, October 5, 1932, in Masaryk, *Cesta demokracie IV*, 308.

39 Jacques Rupnik, "Masaryk et le socialisme tchécoslovaque," in Peška and Mareš, eds., *Thomas Garrigue Masaryk, européen et humaniste*, 155; see also Anna Gašparíková-Horáková , *U Masarykovcov. Spomienky osobnej archivárky T. G. Masaryka*. Bratislava: Academic Electronic Press, 1995, 229.

40 On Savinkov see Scott B. Smith, *Captives of Revolution: The Socialist Revolutionaries and the Bolshevik Dictatorship, 1918–1923* (Pittsburgh, PA: University of Pittsburgh Press, 2011); John Biggart, "Savinkov, Boris Viktorovich, 1879–1925," in *Modern Encyclopedia of Russian and Soviet History*, ed. Joseph L. Wieczynski, 60 vols. (Gulf Breeze, FL: Academic International Press, 1976–2000), 33: 113–16. The post-1990 Czech historiography appears to have largely shied away from Masaryk's involvement in the Savinkov affair; for instance, the matter is not mentioned in the monumental biography of Stanislav Polák, *T.G. Masaryk* 6 vols. (Prague: Masarykův ústav AV ČR, 2000–2012).

41 The note also indicates that Savinkov had received 7,000 rubles for the assassination of Grand Duke Sergei Aleksandrovich Romanov (1857–1905), and 30,000 rubles for the assassination of Viacheslav K. Plehve (1846–1904); Soubigou, *Thomas Masaryk,* 232–33.

tempted anti-Bolshevik uprising in the city of Iaroslavl. Finally, on September 30, 1918, Fanny Kaplan shot three times at Lenin from a revolver, allegedly furnished by Savinkov.[42] Subsequent revelations from the French archives showed that, in supporting Savinkov, Masaryk actually acted in harmony with French interests and policies. Savinkov, an important politician under the Provisional Government, remained committed to fighting the Germans after the Bolshevik Revolution and the Bolsheviks' negotiation of a Peace Treaty with Germany. Hence Savinkov was attractive to the Entente. The French Ambassador Joseph Noulens gave Savinkov 2,500,000 rubles in July 1918. Masaryk's interests then clearly coincided with those of the French.[43]

While the French role was not known, Masaryk's dealing with anti-Soviet groups came to public attention in the 1920s. In February 1923, Masaryk responded to allegations in a book, published by a Russian émigré in Shanghai in 1921 that before leaving Russia in 1918, he provided funds to an anti-Bolshevik organization, *Soiuz zashchity rodiny i svobody*.[44] The situation became more pressing in August 1924 on the occasion of Savinkov's trial. Savinkov escaped from Russia and became an agent of British Intelligence. He crossed into the Soviet Union secretly in the summer of 1924 and was captured almost immediately. At his trial, he stated that Masaryk gave him money to assassinate Lenin. He was sentenced to ten years imprisonment, but allegedly died of suicide in May 1925.[45] Masaryk was questioned by Communist deputies in the Czechoslovak Parliament about his relations with Savinkov. The President issued a statement that he barely knew Savinkov and met him only once, when he talked with him philosophically about the moral value of terrorism. He returned to

---

42 Ibid., 234.

43 It was desirable to stop the Bolsheviks from making peace with Germany, which might jeopardize the separation of Czechoslovakia from Austria, hence as a political realists Masaryk had reasonable motivation to aid Savinkov's activities and strategic objective; Soubigou, *Thomas Masaryk*, 239–41. On the financing of Savinkov's group by the French military mission, see also René Girault and Marc Ferro, *De la Russie à l'URSS, histoire de la Russie de 1850 à nos jours* (Paris: Nathan, 1983), 129. On French and British support of Savinkov, see also George Kennan, *Soviet-American Relations*, vol. 2, *The Decision to Intervene*. Princeton, N.J.: Princeton University Press, 1958, 430–31, 435–36.

44 The book by Anatolij Gan (Gutman), *Rossia i bolsheviki* (Shanghai, 1921), 241, alleged that the group in question had urged Masaryk to turn the Czechoslovak legionnaires against the Bolsheviks. Masaryk responded that he dealt with a number of groups, although he could not specifically remember the *Soiuz zashchity rodiny i svobody*, he doubted that he gave it any money. He considered the whole episode insignificant. Soubigou, *Thomas Masaryk*, 234–35.

45 Ibid., 235.

the Savinkov case once more in October 1931, claiming that he just asked Klecanda to give Savinkov two to three hundred rubles to support his literary activities. [46]

After a considerable hiatus, the question of Masaryk's involvement in the Savinkov affair would acquire new life in Czechoslovakia after the Communist seizure of power in February 1948. The Communist campaign in the 1950s to discredit Masaryk (together with the democratic regime in inter-war Czechoslovakia), publicized the contents of Masaryk's 1918 note on his dealings with Savinkov, as well as Savinkov's statements at his trial in 1924 concerning the plot to assassinate Lenin.[47] The second propaganda wave that utilized the Savinkov affair against Masaryk followed the failure of the Prague Spring in 1968 and was orchestrated directly from Moscow. Once more the records of Savinkov's trial were cited to show that the French Ambassador Noulans and Masaryk sought in the spring of 1918 to overthrow the Soviet power by way of an armed uprising and terrorist acts against members of the worker-peasant government. Masaryk specifically authorized a subsidy of 200,000 rubles for Savinkov to organize the assassination of Lenin and others.[48]

It is clear that in supporting Savinkov's revolutionary activities, Masaryk acted in accord with the intention of his French allies to re-establish a military front against Germany. As for the initiative to assassinate Lenin, which has not been proved, one can safely assume that Masaryk regarded Lenin as a war criminal who – as he repeatedly stated – was responsible for murders of thousands upon thousands of innocent individ-

---

46 Soubigou questions discrepancies in Masaryk's notes of 1918 and his written notes of 1931, in which he claimed that he gave money to Savinkov for literary activities, not terror, and the amount he gave was merely 200–300 rubles, while in 1918 notes had listed 200,000 rubles. Soubigou, *Thomas Masaryk*, 236–37. On the other hand, Masaryk's interest in Savinkov as an intellectual is indicated by his pre-World War I mention that as a novelist (under the pseudonym P. Ropshin) Savinkov portrayed Russian anarchists as devotees of Nietzsche. See Masaryk, *Rusko a Evropa II*, 352–53.

47 Václav Král, *O kontrarevoliutsionnoi i antisovetskoi politike Masarika*, trans. M. M. Khazanov (Moscow: Izdatel'stvo innostrannoi literatury, 1955), 79–80. For an overview of the allegations against Masaryk, published in the 1950s in Czechoslovakia, see Karel Hulička, "The Communist Anti-Masaryk Propaganda in Czechoslovakia," *American Slavic and East European Review*, 16 (1957), 160–74; and Jaroslav Dresler, "Masaryk und die Kommunisten," *Osteuropa* 10 (1960), 663–68.

48 Vasilii Ardamatskii, *Vozmezdie. Povest* (Moscow: Molodaia gvardiia, 1968); on Boris Savinkov, see 566–91, especially, 567–68; see also M. Shiriamov, "Whose Interests Did President Masaryk Defend?" *Current Digest of the Soviet Press*, 20 (1968), n. 19, 8–9, citing from *Sovetskaia Rossiia*, May 14, 1968, 3.

uals.[49] While in the twenty-first century war criminals are not normally executed,[50] the situation was different earlier in the twentieth century.[51] Moreover, one may add, that, as President of the Czechoslovak Republic, Masaryk was not reluctant to approve capital punishment in particularly monstrous cases which "demanded expiation."[52]

Nevertheless, Masaryk's attitude toward Lenin during the war was ambiguous with the shifts of the volatile situation in the Bolshevik area, and the corresponding shifts in the attitude of the French allies. Soon after Masaryk's dealings with Savinkov, it appeared that the Bolsheviks might resist the German advance eastward despite the Treaty of Brest-Litovsk. French diplomats in Moscow began to offer assistance to Trotsky on March 19, 1918, and continued to do so until early April.[53] In the meantime, Masaryk traveled across Siberia to Japan, and upon arriving in Tokyo on April 15, in line with French intentions, he voiced his support for the Allies' assistance to Lenin. In a case of the right hand not knowing what the left one was doing, the report of Masaryk's statement created consternation in Paris, where the Minister of Foreign Affairs, Stephen Pichon, favored an anti-Bolshevik intervention in Russia by the Allies.[54] Even upon Masaryk's arrival in the United States on May 29, 1918 the French Am-

---

49   For instance, see "Poselství prezidenta Republiky československé," *Národní listy*, October 29, 1919, in Masaryk, *Cesta demokracie I*, 175; "Revoluce a bolševici," in *Lidové noviny*, December 24, 1920, in Masaryk, *Cesta demokracie* I, 384–85. On Masaryk's view of Lenin's criminality, see also Jacques Rupnik, "Masaryk et le socialisme tchécoslovaque," in Peška and Mareš, eds., *Thomas Garrigue Masaryk, européen et humaniste*, 151.

50   Except for the case of Bin Ladin in May 2011. On the legal and legitimate character of this operation, see Nigel Inkster, "The Death of Osama bin Laden," *Survival*, 53.3 (June–July 2011), 6–7.

51   At the Nuremberg War Crimes Trials, involving twenty-four leading Nazis, from November 20, 1945 to October 1, 1946, for crimes against humanity, death sentences were imposed on twelve defendants. At the Tokyo International Tribunal, sitting from May 3, 1946 to November 4, 1948, of the twenty-five defendants, seven were given death sentences. As late as 1961, death sentence was imposed on Adolf Eichmann for war crimes by the High Court of Israel. *Encyclopedia Americana*, 30 vols(Danbury, CT: Grolier, 1994), 28: 336–38.

52   Emil Ludwig, *Defender of Democracy: Masaryk of Czechoslovakia* (New York: R. M. McBride, 1936), 193–94. See also Otakar A. Funda, *Thomas Garigue Masaryk: Sein phiosophisches, religiöses und politisches Denken* (Bern: P. Lang, 1978). During Masaryk's presidency in 1923–1935, altogether eleven sentences of capital punishment were carried out in Czechoslovakia; see Jiří Plachý and Ivo Pejčoch, *Masarykovy oprátky. Problematika trestu smrti v období první a druhé Československé republiky, 1918–1939* (Cheb: Svět křídel, 2012), 206.

53   The overtures to Trotsky were made by Captain Jacques Sadoul, a French military assistant, and after March 29 by Ambassador Joseph Noulens; see Kennan, *Soviet-American Relations*, vol. 2, *The Decision to Intervene*. 112–14, 122; Victor M. Fic, *Bolsheviks and the Czechoslovak Legion* (New Delhi: Abhinav, 1978), 11.

54   Antoine Mareš, "Masaryk vue par les Francais," in Peška and Mareš, eds., *Thomas Garrigue Masaryk, européen et humaniste*, 238.

bassador Jean Jusserand informed Pichon in a telegram from Washington that Masaryk insisted on the need to cooperate with the Bolsheviks in an interview with the *New York Times* on May 27, 1918, claiming that they were growing increasingly anti-German. [55]

It was only in July 1918 that Masaryk became completely disillusioned with the idea of enlisting the Bolsheviks for a renewed struggle against the Germans. In a note to Wilson, dated July 20, 1918, he called attention to a report from the Czechoslovak legion in Siberia (dated July 14, 1918), indicating that the Bolsheviks were turning pro-German and were organizing detachments of German and Hungarian prisoners of war to fight the Czechoslovaks. Masaryk therefore wanted to ask for Allied help to rescue the Czechoslovak Legion from Siberia. On the previous day he had submitted a memo to the same effect Frank L. Polk.[56] As for the wider issue of restoring an anti-German front in Russia, with the Bolsheviks turning pro-German and the White Russians no longer able to organize sufficient forces, an armed assistance from the Allies would be necessary for that task.[57]

Adolf Hitler

Whereas Masaryk dealt with Lenin early in his presidency, he apparently mentioned Adolf Hitler for the very first time in March 1925, when he referred retrospectively to Hitler's Putsch of November 8–11, 1923, in which the future Führer – together with the German war hero, General Erich Ludendorff – attempted to overthrow the Bavarian government. In 1925, Masaryk retrospectively dismissed the event as a minor crisis that would not hinder Europe's progress in the direction of democracy, disarmament, and parliamentarianism.[58] After a considerable lapse of time, he became seriously concerned about Hitler's ideas and activities in early 1932, when he started collecting substantive information. Hitler appeared to him as a

---

55 He opposed intervention and favored industrial and economic aid; see Wilson, *The Papers of Woodrow Wilson*, 48: 202.

56 Ibid., 49: 44. Frank L. Polk was Counselor to the State Department (1915–1919).

57 Ibid., 49: 45–46. By September 21, 1918, Masaryk definitely disparaged any expectations of reestablishing an anti-German front in Russia in his discussion with U.S. Secretary of State Robert Lansing; Wilson, *The Papers of Woodrow Wilson*, 51: 86–87.

58 Interview with Dorothy Thompson, for *Philadelphia Ledger*, published as "Die politischen Probleme des neuen Staates," *Neue Freie Presse*, March 8, 1925, in Masaryk, *Cesta demokracie III*, 102. Hitler was sentenced to five years in prison for his part in the event.

"nobody" [*nimand* (sic!)] without any constructive ideas, but with an ability to throw Europe back a hundred years.[59] In an interview with an Austrian correspondent in April 1932, Masaryk considered the aspirations of Hitler's supporters purely negative, based on a bitterness of those who considered themselves slighted.[60] In Masaryk's opinion, Hitler's followers were supported, as similar groups elsewhere in Europe, "by reactionaries of all sorts and by political illiterates."[61] On December 7, 1932, Masaryk recalled the statement of Hitler's disgruntled former associate, Gregor Strasser (1892–1934), that the former was characterized by "Habsburg mendacity and shameless ignorance."[62]

Until the very moment of Hitler's actual seizure of power, Masaryk continued to cling to the idea that World War I had cured Germany's earlier psychological and political ills and set the country on a healthy political course. Still, in October 1932 – a mere three months before Hitler's political victory – Masaryk stated in an interview that having studied Hitler's speeches and his book, *Mein Kampf,* he felt that Hitler was a German problem, which the Germans would resolve correctly. He found it difficult to imagine that they could pronounce his name with the same respect and affection as the names of Kant, Goethe, and Beethoven.[63] In an even later interview with the editor of *Vossische Zeitung,* Werner Hegemann, on December 17, 1932, Masaryk once more referred to the great benefit for Germany from her defeat in World War I, comparable to the benefit accrued to Prussia during the Napoleonic Wars, thanks to the defeat in the battle of Jena in 1806, which freed the country from its obsolete political institutions.[64]

---

59   Gašparíková-Horáková, *U Masarykovcov,* 183.
60   "They denounced the Jews, the French, the Poles, the Czechoslovaks;" see "Gespräch mit Masaryk," *Neue Freie Presse,* April 17, 1932, in Masaryk, *Cesta demokracie IV,* 264.
61   In Czechoslovakia, Masaryk referred to the extreme nationalists around Jiří Stříbrný (1880–1955); "Z politické periferie," *Národní osvobození,* April 24, 1932, in Masaryk, *Cesta demokracie IV,* 267.
62   At that time Masaryk assembled a collection of some 100 photographs of Hitler; Gašparíková-Horáková, *U Masarykovcov,* 183.
63   "Gespräch mit Masaryk," *Berliner Tagblatt,* October 5, 1932, in Masaryk, *Cesta demokracie IV,* 308–9.
64   "President Masaryk in Gespräch," *Vossische Zeitung,* January 22, 1933, in Masaryk, *Cesta demokracie IV,* 333–34; see also Antoine Mareš, "Masaryk vue par les Francais," in Peška and Mareš, eds., *Thomas Garrigue Masaryk, européen et humaniste,* 250. The Battle of Jena in October 1806 marked a crushing defeat of the Prussians by Napoleon. The shock caused the Prussian government to seek wide-ranging reforms from 1807 on, and a modernization of the decrepit political structure that had dated to the time of Frederick the Great. The king relied on Karl von Hardenberg and Karl vom Stein. See James J. Sheehan, *German History, 1770–1866* (Oxford: Clarendon Press, 1989), 296–298.

Critique of *Mein Kampf*

Almost immediately after Masaryk's interview appeared in *Vossische Zeitung* (on January 22 and 29, 1933), Hitler was appointed German Chancellor on January 31, and the Enabling Act of March 23 established the basis of Nazi dictatorship.[65] Masaryk then had to take the German *Führer* very seriously and prepared a penetrating review of *Mein Kampf*, dated April 18, 1933.[66] At the start, Masaryk pays Hitler a compliment for his stylistic skills, which combined folksy expressions with formulating the basic demands of his program and the basic viewpoints clearly and precisely. In that respect, Hitler could serve as an example to political and other popular leaders.[67] The rest of Masaryk's review consisted of scathing criticism, which may be analyzed under the headings of Pan-Germanism, dictatorship ("Teutonic democracy"), expansionism (*Drang nach Osten*), anti-Semitism, and racism.

Pan-Germanism, Teutonic democracy, and the *Drang nach Osten*

Beginning with Pan-Germanism, Hitler claimed to be especially influenced by the Austrian, Georg von Schönerer (1842–1921), but Masaryk noted that he also could have pointed to German precursors such as Treitschke, Lagarde, Mommsen, and Hartmann. These ideologues of Pan-Germanism advocated the use of unscrupulous force against the Slavs, such as "the cracking of skulls" and extermination. Masaryk asked, rhetorically, why a soldier from the front of World War I, such as Hitler, should be more humane or sentimental than the advocates of Pangermanism, who in addition were receiving the approval of priests and pastors of contemporary German churches.[68] Like Schönerer, a fellow Austrian, Hitler despised the Habsburg Monarchy, as well as political parliamentarianism.[69]

---

65 On October 14, 1933, Nazi Germany withdrew from the League of Nations.
66 Tomáš G. Masaryk, "Masarykova recenze Hitlerovy knihy *Mein Kampf*," in Masaryk, *Cesta demokracie IV*, 348–55. The review is based on Adolf Hitler, *Mein Kampf*, 7th ed., 2 vols. in 1 (Munich: Verlag Eger, 1931). Extensive reports appeared in *Prager Presse*, April 30, 1933, and in České.slovo, May 3, 1933.
67 "Masarykova recenze Hitlerovy knihy *Mein Kampf*," in Masaryk, *Cesta demokracie IV*, 348.
68 Ibid., 348, 355.
69 Ibid., 349–50.

According to Masaryk, Hitler was in favor of democracy – but only the new National Socialist one. Parliament could exist, but not the old one, which was an arena for intellectual mediocrities and retards. It could exist only as a consultative assembly. The spiritus movens of old parliamentarian democracy was the Jews; it was the antithesis of the ancient Teutonic democracy.[70] The latter freely chose the Leader, who was responsible to the community even at the risk to his life and property. Only the Leader made decisions, not the traditional majority of the merely consultative parliament. In this ideal order, obedience to the Leader was the duty of citizens. The Teutonic democracy was aristocratic and, properly speaking, monarchic–hence the absolutism of the Leader. It was also heavily militaristic, the army was the school of life. Hitler condemned pacifism as cowardice, and was not afraid of war. Finally, the Teutonic democracy did not permit the establishment of multiple parties; parties meant splitting up the nation, while the Teutonic ideal was a single, all-embracing weltanschauung.[71]

Masaryk also addressed Hitler's plans for Germany's expansion. According to Hitler, Aryan and Teutonic Germandom could find its fulfillment only in a National Socialist state. Hence, all Germans of Central Europe had to be united in the new Reich. For the time being, Hitler definitely demanded union with Austria. He made no specific mention of other disputed territories, such as Alsace-Lorraine, Switzerland, or Czechoslovakia except for a general claim that all Germans should be brought together. Masaryk, however, observed that Hitler's associate Gottfried Feder (1883–1941), spoke specifically of the annexation of Danish, Polish, Czechoslovak, Italian, and French inhabitants of German nationality.[72] On a broader scale, the proper space for German expansion was not, according to Hitler, in overseas colonies, but on the European continent. The need for an eastward advance was a crucial claim of the Führer's book. Ultimately, he aimed at Russia, which, according to him, was

---

70 Ibid., 349–50.
71 Ibid., 349.
72 "Masarykova recenze Hitlerovy knihy *Mein Kampf*," in Masaryk, *Cesta demokracie IV*, 350; Gottfried Feder, *Der deutsche Staat auf nationaler und sozialer Grundlage*, 6th ed. (Munich: F. Eher Nachf., 1932), 42; Gottfried Feder, *Das programm der N.S.D.A.P. und seine weltanschaulichen Grundgedanken* (Munich: F. Eher Nachf., 1931). Ferder was initially Hitler's teacher, and after 1924 he was considered the leading theoretician of the Nazi Party prior to 1933, when he fell into disfavor; see *Brockhaus Enzyklopädie*, 20 vols., 17th ed. (Wiesbaden: Brockhaus, 1966), 6: 103; see also Ditrich Orlow, *The History of the Nazi Party, 1919–1933* (Pittsburgh: University of Pittsburgh Press, 1969), 64, 264, 294–95.

organized as a state by the Germans and inhabited by inferior Slavs; the nearer targets were Poland and Ukraine.

Hitler was aware that allies were needed in the south and the west to accomplish his foreign policy's eastern objectives, and he focused on Italy and England. While he viewed France as a mortal enemy, he saw a natural ally in Mussolini's Italy, and thought that England was also antagonistic to France. In Masaryk's opinion, although Hitler claimed interest in history, he disregarded the lessons of the past. Especially with respect to Italy, he overlooked the age-old antagonism generated by the efforts of the German Empire to dominate the Italian Peninsula. Also, the Pangerman program traditionally called for an expansion into the Mediterranean, in particular via the control of Triest. Hitler spoke more reticently with respect to England, but showed a special fondness for Lloyd George. Masaryk pointed out that specifically according to Hitler's racial philosophy, George could not be considered a typical Englishman, since he was a Celt and regularly delivered sermons in Welsh.[73] Moreover, on the racial front, Hitler was willing incongruously to sacrifice the Germans of South Tyrol to Italy for the sake of alliance with Mussolini. Hitler justified this stand by maintaining that in foreign policy there was no place for "sentimentality."

Masaryk observed that Hitler's assertion of an "unsentimental" approach to foreign affairs provided a clue to his lack of humaneness on the domestic scene. This reflected Masaryk's conviction that a moral approach to the external world reflected the moral approach to the internal society.[74] A politician who was not "sentimental" in foreign policy, could not be "sentimental" in domestic policy. This was confirmed, according to Masaryk, by Hitler's *Mein Kampf,* in which he threatened domestic scoundrels (*Lumpen*) and traitors with merciless death.[75]

Anti-Semitism and racism

Hitler recognized two principal enemies: the external one was France; the internal one was Marxism. Paying relatively little attention to the

73 "Masarykova recenze Hitlerovy knihy *Mein Kampf,*" in Masaryk, *Cesta demokracie IV,* 350–51.
74 For instance, Masaryk, *Světová revoluce za války a ve válce, 1914–1918,* 375–76.
75 Such as those who suppressed his Putsch of November 8, 1923; "Masarykova recenze Hitlerovy knihy *Mein Kampf,*" in Masaryk, *Cesta demokracie IV,* 351, 354.

West, he concentrated in his book on Marxist socialism. In turn, his attitude toward Marxism was inextricably tied up with his anti-Semitism. He was adamantly opposed to the program and weltanschauung of Social Democracy, which for him was synonymous with Marx and Marxism. Marx was of Jewish origin and the National Socialists were dedicated to a struggle against the Jews and any form of Judaization. Hitler drew his invectives against the Jews from the notorious *Protocols of the Elders of Zion* and presented himself as an outright anti-Semite. According to him, the National Socialists wished to counter Judaization, and would not hesitate to decisively weaken and incapacitate the Jews in every respect.[76] Masaryk pointed out that in his anti-Semitism Hitler was contradicted by the views of such German national paragons as Goethe, Lessing, and Herder. It could also be countered by pointing to the global success of Jesus, a Jew, and his teaching. The Pangermans' theories that Christ was an Aryan could not be taken seriously. Likewise, the cultural role of the Old Testament in Christianity had been defended by outstanding German authors, such as Emil Kautzsch (1841–1910).[77]

Inasmuch as Hitler claimed to be a socialist, Masaryk highlighted the paradox of the Führer's facile dismissal of Marxism, the dominant doctrine of socialism, for being Jewish in origin and materialistic in philosophy. The idea that Marxism was Jewish was not only simplistic, but evidently false. It was certainly incorrect since the principal teachers of Marx were the German gentiles, Feuerbach and Hegel, and the Englishman Ricardo. Hitler's condemnation of Marxism for its materialist ontology was also specious, since the new weltanschuung that Hitler propagated was nothing else, but materialism. Materialism was not just the historical metaphysics of Marxism – postulating that history was determined by economics – but every movement which used force and compulsion for its application. Hitler's all-powerful blood was no less material than Marx's economic conditions. Compulsive force attained its goals mechanically or materialistically.[78]

According to Masaryk, Hitler also derived his emphasis on race from pre-World War I Pan-Germanism, which had taught that the Germans must think and act in full awareness of their Aryan and Teutonic racial

76 Ibid., 348–49.
77 Ibid., 351–52.
78 Ibid., 351–52, 355.

origins. Masaryk could proudly state that he had argued against the racist views of the Pan-Germans and others since the beginning of his academic career. As early as 1877, he had maintained that there were no pure races in Europe,[79] and in his university lectures in Prague in 1885 he again targeted racism, focusing on Joseph R. Gobineau's *Essai sur l'inegalité des races*.[80] In 1933, he once more encountered, in Hitler's National Socialism, the view that "the pure Aryan blood was the German Grail, this blood was the motor of history and the desired ideal." Therefore, Hitler saw the ultimate reason for Germany's collapse in 1918 in the failure to understand the racial problem.[81] In Masaryk's opinion, the claim of the Germans' Teutonic or Aryan racial purity was simply a fiction. He reemphasized that scientific anthropology and ethnography of Germany showed that the German population east of Elbe was Slav and in East Prussia – Baltic Prussian. Even the Bavarians, whom Hitler extolled, had much Slavic and Celtic blood. Simply said, pure races were not found anywhere in Europe, or anywhere in the world.[82]

In his concluding assessment, Masaryk found Hitler's principal concepts lacking in clarity to the point of obscurity, and his political orientation burdened by amoral fanaticism. Firstly, he failed to explain the relationship between race and the national program, namely, how the program could rise from German blood.[83] Secondly, Hitler dwelt on the decline of contemporary culture and civilization, especially in his favorite subjects of modern architecture and modern art, a development which he attributed mainly to Jewish influences. In Masaryk's opinion, he failed to distinguish between temporary crises, and a real decline or decay.[84]

---

79 Tomáš G. Masaryk, "O pokroku, vývoji a osvětě," in Tomáš G. Masaryk, *Juvenalie: studie a stati, 1876–1881*, Spisy 16 (Prague: Ústav T. G. Masaryka, 1993), 48–67. See also Milan Jelínek, "Masarykův vztah k cizím národům a jejich jazykům," *T.G. Masaryk na přelomu tisíciletí*, Sborník z VIII. ročníku semináře, November 15, 2000 (Hodonín: Masarykovo muzeum, 2001), 89.

80 Tomáš G. Masaryk, *Praktická filosofie na základě sociologie: Litografovaná příručka k přednáškám.* Prague, [1885], National Library, Prague, call no. 54 D 7938. See also Jaroslav Opat, "Kritik rasismu," in Jaroslav Opat, *Masarykiana a jiné studie II* (Prague: Masarykův ústav AV ČR, 2006), 51.

81 "Masarykova recenze Hitlerovy knihy *Mein Kampf*," in Masaryk, *Cesta demokracie IV*, 349.

82 Ibid., 352.

83 Thus Friedrich Burgdörfer in his book *Volk ohne Jugend* calculated that the German population would sink to 50 million by the end of the century. Hitler for the purpose of population expansion proposed racial hygiene, such as early marriages, and a struggle against prostitution and venereal decease. "Masarykova recenze Hitlerovy knihy *Mein Kampf*," in Masaryk, *Cesta demokracie IV*, 352–53; Burgdörfer, Friedrich, *Volk ohne Jugend; Geburtenschwund und Überalterung des deutschen Volkskörpers* (Berlin-Grunewald: K. Vowinckel, 1932).

84 "Masarykova recenze Hitlerovy knihy *Mein Kampf*," in Masaryk, *Cesta demokracie IV*, 354.

Masaryk suggested that conceptual opaqueness was combined in Hitler's mind with almost pathological hubris, mendacity, and cruelty. The Führer displayed an absolute self-confidence in the abilities of his own leadership, convinced that Germany would have won World War I if he had been in charge. He believed in his own supernatural mission, and the program of his party was to be treated as a sacred covenant. Likewise, Hitler taught an extreme, even religious-like fanaticism in the attachment to the nation. He explicitly endorsed a lack of objectivity in denouncing other nations, which were perceived as inimical.[85] Hitler's fanaticism was combined with a rejection of what he called "sentimentality;" he was both unscrupulous and heartless. According to Masaryk, one might even say that "this pride à la Nietzsche had a distinct trait of a certain pleasure in suffering." He felt, however, that this aspect of Hitler's personality was best left for psychoanalysts to explore.[86]

Hitler in power, 1933–1934

Masaryk continued to follow developments in Nazi Germany during the rest of 1933 and into 1934, focusing on issues of anti-Semitism, Pan-Germanism, and German dictatorship. Interviewed on the occasion of the Zionist Congress in Prague in August 1933, he declared his support for the Jews, who were being deprived of their civil rights and possibility of earning a living in Nazi Germany. He expected the League of Nations to provide the victims with relief in the places of their resettlement. He still thought that the situation would improve, evidently considering the Nazi campaign as an expression of the traditional and familiar Austrian anti-Semitism.[87]

In an interview with a French reporter in September 1933, Masaryk returned to his analyses of the movement of the *"Alldeutsch pangermanismus"* before and during World War I. At that point it was more a theory,

---

85   Ibid., 353–54.
86   Ibid., 354.
87   "Keine interne Frage Deutschlands," *Prager Abendzeitung*, August 25, 1933, in Masaryk, *Cesta demokracie IV*, 368. Masaryk, however, declined with reference to his advisors (as unpolitic), the suggestion of Coudenhove-Kalergi that he deliver a series of lectures aimed at listeners in Germany in favor of freedom to counteract the Nazi propaganda; see Richard N. CoudenhoveKalergi, *Aus meinem Leben* (Zurich: Atlantis-Verlag, 1949), 179.

but in the1930s it received a practical application. It became known as National Socialism or racism, but its foundation was still the views of Schönerer, Lagarde, and others.[88] Masaryk rejected the idea that some nations were more worthy than others, in particular the ideas of the Nazi publicists, who believed in the superiority of the "Nordic" race. It was true that some nations developed culturally faster than others, but that had no importance in the long run. The Russian peasants still led a primitive existence, but Russia produced outstanding authors such as Pushkin, Gogol, Turgenev, Tolstoy, Dostoevsky, and Gorky, who were at least as skilled as the writers of western Europe.[89]

With his assertion of the basic kinship between old Pan-Germanism and Hitler's National Socialism, Masaryk was, however, forced to revise his earlier view of Germany's ideological redemption through World War I. The Weimar constitution was written on paper, but not into the soul of the German nation. The Social Democrats came to power where previously Army officers issued orders, which represented a drastic swing of the pendulum. In 1933, the pendulum swung the other way. The Germans could not imagine that the Prussian system, which had won the wars of 1864, 1866, and 1870, could lose the greatest of wars in 1918, and blamed democracy for the defeat. Yet, in reality the war was lost by "a dictatorial-style monarchy," not by democracy.[90]

As long as his health permitted, Masaryk studied and commented on German issues into 1934.[91] In January, he stated privately that – as much as he could – he followed the literature on Hitler. What Hitler himself wrote or spoke indicated a semi-educated person with the typical horizon of a non-commissioned military officer [*vachmajstr*].[92] Masaryk exhibited a special zest for the refutation of racist doctrines. When a Jewish doctor from Karlovy Vary, a certain Dr. Zollschan, proposed to organize an in-

88 "Masaryk o demokracii a diktatuře," *Právo lidu*, October 1, 1933, [based on an interview with a French reporter for *Quotidien*] in Masaryk, *Cesta demokracie IV*, 374.
89 Ibid., 375.
90 "Democracy Still Lives," *New York Times,* Magazine, November 12, 1933, in Masaryk, *Cesta demokracie IV*, 386.
91 In early May 1934, he was partly disabled by a stroke, which affected his left eye, and right arm and knee. It was said that he found it difficult to express himself in Czech, and preferred to speak in English. Although he did not abdicate the presidential office until December 2, 1935, his activities were severely limited. Gradually, giving interviews and writing articles virtually stopped. See also Soubigou, *Thomas Masaryk,* 438–39.
92 Conversation on January 20, 1934, see Gašparíková-Horáková, *U Masarykovcov*, 217.

ternational anthropological congress, which would prove objectively and scientifically that it was impossible to distinguish human races, Masaryk endorsed this project enthusiastically. He urged the doctor to be sure to invite representatives of German science so that their views expressed before a world-wide audience could be judged independently of their political setting.[93] In the spring of 1934, Masaryk supported the publication by the Czech Academy of Arts and Sciences of a volume on the equality of European races.[94] The introductory chapter rejected the idea of pure races, and deplored Hitler's fascination – apparently under the influence of Houston Chamberlain – with the Aryan race and his fierce denunciation of the Jews in the *Mein Kampf.* The chapter also opposed the ideas of the National Socialists that the "Nordic" race was destined for world rule, and the German nation should be purged from all racial admixtures.[95]

On the whole, Masaryk seemed to minimize the threat that Hitler's dictatorship might pose for Europe. In May 1934, he thought that Hitler was not serious about wishing to annex all areas with German-speaking populations, pointing out that Hitler had declared to the French newspaper *Le Matin* that Germany had given up its claims to Alsace-Loraine.[96] A month later, Masaryk expressed an optimistic view on avoidance of war in Europe. He did not think that any European country, including Germany, had sufficient means to engage in an armed conflict in the midst of the deep economic depression. As for Hitler's bellicosity, in his opinion, the Führer's radicalism was bound to diminish after the seizure and consolidation of power.[97] In July, Masaryk commented with unexpected sarcasm on the brutal suppression of Ernst J. Röhm (1887–1934) and the SA only a

---

93 "Masaryk o současných problémech," *Morgenzeitung* (Ostrava), May 9, 1934, in Masaryk, *Cesta demokracie IV*, 417–18.

94 Karel Weigner, ed., *Rovnocennost evropských plemen a cesty k jejich ušlechťování* (Prague: Nákl. České akademie věd a umění, 1934), and a German translation appeared a year later, as Karel Weigner, ed. *Die gleichwertigkeit der europäischen rassen und die wege zu ihrer vervollkommnung* (Prague: Tschechische akademie der wissenschaften und künste, in generalkommission Verlag Orbis, 1935). See also Jaroslav Opat, "Kritik rasismu," in Opat, *Masarykiana a jiné studie II*, 54–55.

95 Weigner, ed., *Rovnocennost evropských plemen a cesty k jejich ušlechťování,* 15–16.; idem, ed., *Die gleichwertigkeit der europäischen rassen und die wege zu ihrer vervollkommnung,* 25–27. See also Eugen Fischer (1874–1967), *Der Begriff des völkischen Staates biologisch betrachtet*; Rede bei der Feier der Erinnerung an den Stifter der Berliner Universität, König Friedrich Wilhelm III. in der Alten Aula am 29. Juli 1933 (Berlin: Preussische Druckerei- und Verlags-Aktiengesellschaft, 1933).

96 "Rozhovor s panem prezidentem Masarykem," May 24, 1934, talk with American journalist K. Werzos, in Masaryk, *Cesta demokracie IV*, 419–20.

97 The interviewer remarked that Masaryk was expressing a hope rather than a conviction. "Bude válka v Evropě," *Lidové noviny*, June 10, 1934, in Masaryk, *Cesta demokracie IV*, 428.

few months after Hitler had praised them as the mainstays of the regime, whom he had personally indoctrinated. Now accused of sexual perversion and self-serving epicurean behavior, "they were deprived of their command insignia by the same hand that shortly before had eulogized them."[98]

The last platform on which Masaryk could comment in a comprehensive way on Hitler's Germany was provided by the book of interviews with Emil Ludwig completed exactly in 1934.[99] In characterizing National Socialism, as well as Italian Fascism, Masaryk saw them as attempts to endow with political reality Nietzsche's philosophical construct of the Superman. The Will to power was the cardinal point of either system, and according to this voluntarist orientation, instinct became the infallible authority and the ultimate criterion for the understanding of human motivations and actions. Although Fascism rejected the racial theory, which animated the ideology of Nazism, it endorsed expansionism, just as the Pan-Germans endorsed the *Raumpolitik*.[100] Democracy did not prove durable in Germany, collapsing after a mere fourteen years. The Germans had the Prussian spirit drilled into them for a long time, which militated against democracy. Aristocratic Prussian monarchism, supported by the army, was in its very essence different from modern democratic governments. Generally on the European continent countries had been ruled into the eighteenth century by monarchs who claimed to be sustained by divine right. The French and the American revolutions, however, put an end to the old regime by undermining the principles on which it was based.[101] If Mussolini and Goebbels described their political systems as pure democracies, these statements were not completely meaningless, at least to the extent that they both opposed monarchies.[102] Nevertheless, in their

---

98 "Úder proti úderníkům," [Strike Against the Shock Troops] *Národní osvobození*, July 8, 1934, in Masaryk, *Cesta demokracie IV*, 430. Ernest J. Röhm (1887–1934), SA Chief of Staff, arrested June 30, 1934, on the orders of Hitler for high treason and moral turpitude, was shot in a prison in Munich the next day, after refusing to commit suicide. 2000 SA leaders were punished, of whom 87 executed; see *Neue Deutsche Biographie,* [23 vols.] (Berlin: Duncker & Humblot, 1953– [2006]), 21: 714. The motives for the purge still remain obscure, see Eleanor Hancock, "The Purge of the SA Reconsidered: 'An Old Putschist Trick'?" *Central European History*, 44 (2011), especially, 680–83.

99 Emil Ludwig (1881–1948), a German novelist and journalist, lived in exile in Switzerland since 1932.

100 Ludwig, *Defender of Democracy*, 216–17. On December 20, 1934, when reviewing Masaryk's interview with Ludwig, Eduard Beneš suggested that Masaryk should make clear the difference between Lagarde's Pangermanism and Hitler's ideology. Gašparíková-Horáková, *U Masarykovcov*, 237.

101 Ludwig, *Defender of Democracy*, 220.

102 Ibid., 223.

expansionism, their imperialism, they were the contradiction of democracy. Nazi imperialism was exemplified by Alfred Rosenberg (1893–1946) and his old German mythology, while Fascist expansionism was exemplified by Julius Evola (1898–1974) with his heathen imperialism. They stood for Caesar, not for Jesus. Here Masaryk resorted to one of his favorite metahistorical dichotomies. While Jesus taught expansionism, it was one of morality to be preached all over the world; Nazi and Fascist expansion was one of military domination – a throwback to Caesar.[103]

Defense of Democracy

With totalitarianism on the rise in the early 1930s, and with the dynamic Hitler regime joining the older Soviet and Fascist dictatorships, Masaryk was frequently asked, especially by journalists, his opinion about the survival of democracy, which was under attack: first, on the Right, that it was unable to sufficiently assure the state's authority, and second, on the Left, that it was unable to abolish social inequalities. Masaryk's response was invariably optimistic. Surprisingly, he seemed to underrate the threat of the totalitarian dictatorships. To explain this at times striking equanimity, it is possible to point out two factors: first, a firm belief in the international order that emerged from World War I; and second, a rather antiquated, but visceral dislike for the "old regimes," based on divine-right monarchies, and hereditary aristocracies.

Democracy, young and yet persistent

In two interviews with reporters for German newspapers on what proved to be the eve of Hitler's rise to power in October and December 1932, Masaryk maintained that Fascism, just like Communism, would prove to be ephemeral phenomena of the transitional age through which the entirety of Europe was passing. Everything was in transition: politics, econo-

---

103 Ludwig, *Defender of Democracy*, 217. Masaryk referred to Alfred Rosenberg, *Der Mythus des 20. Jahrhunderts. Eine Wertung der seelisch-geistigen Gestaltenkämpfe unserer Zeit,* 5th ed. (Munich: Hoheneichen-Verlag, 1934); and to Julius Evola, *Rivolta contro il mondo moderno* (Milano: Ulrico Hoepli, 1934).

my, art, literature, science. This era started with the beginning of modern history, connected with the French Revolution, when freedom became the central political concept. This transitional age gave rise after World War I also to Fascism and Bolshevism.[104] Masaryk remained convinced of the final victory of democracy despite so-called successes of dictatorships from the right and the left. In its advance, democracy still encountered rear-guard actions of the regimes which it was replacing. Since its earlier advance had undermined the old theocratic monarchist regimes, it could also handle the new challenges.[105]

After Hitler's ascension to power, Masaryk expressed his conviction in newspaper interviews between July and November 1933 that democracy was sound and would eventually prevail everywhere.[106] After all, democracy was still a young institution; it began only with the American and French Revolutions of the late eighteenth century, while authoritarian regimes were as old as the world; the Greeks and the Romans had a certain form of democracy, but it was based on slavery. While not perfect, democracy was stronger than the "old regimes," since it had succeeded in overthrowing them. Thus, the authoritarian government was weaker, not stronger than democracy, and it was therefore false to maintain that democracy was doomed to yield to a dictatorial system. If democracy had its faults, modern dictatorships had even worse ones. World War I had aroused fierce emotions, as had the current economic depression, hence some sought salvation in dictatorship.[107]

In his newspaper interviews in the first half of 1934, Masaryk continued to deal with the issue of dictatorships in Europe. He retained his conviction that dictatorships were short-lived, and added a new stress on the differences among countries in their readiness to establish and maintain democratic regimes. The dictatorships that were springing up were likely only transitory stages for countries which had lost the status of mon-

---

104 "Masaryk o dnešní Evropě," *Berliner Tagblatt*, October 5, 1932 in Masaryk, *Cesta demokracie IV*, 308.
105 "Masaryks Bekenntnis zur Demokratie," *Der Wiener Tag*, December 8, 1932, in Masaryk, *Cesta demokracie IV*, 478.
106 "Prezident Masaryk o demokracii a diktaturach, first published as Edgar A. Mowrer, "Masaryk, Sage of Prague," *Chicago Daily News*, 58 (1933), 6 n.157, July, 5, in Masaryk, *Cesta demokracie IV*, 363.
107 Mowrer, "Masaryk, Sage of Prague," *Chicago Daily News*, July 5, 1933, in Masaryk, *Cesta demokracie IV*, 363; "Masaryk o demokracii a diktatuře," originally in *Právo lidu*, October 1, 1933, in Masaryk, *Cesta demokracie IV*, 374–378; "Democracy Still Lives," *New York Times*, Magazine, November 12, 1933 in Masaryk, *Cesta demokracie IV*, 387.

archies, but had not yet succeeded in creating a truly democratic regime.[108] When a reporter quoted to Masaryk Mussolini's statement that within ten years the entirety of Europe would be Fascist, Masaryk restated that most of the thirty-five European countries were republics or constitutional monarchies. While some dictatorships sprang up, Masaryk predicted that they would not last more than ten or fifteen years. Democracies, though young, have lasted longer: France – withstanding the stress of World War I – had lasted sixty years (as the Third Republic). Other democracies, such as England, Holland, Switzerland, and Norway were older still.[109] Asked by an American correspondent about the future of democracy in Europe, Masaryk responded that preparedness for democracy had differed among the various countries. Thus, Germany had a strong and active monarchy, hence feelings for democracy were relatively weak. The Czechoslovaks, on the contrary, were historically predisposed toward democracy, because (1) they lacked their own dynasty; (2) lacked their own army; and (3) lacked a noble aristocracy.[110] To another American reporter, Masaryk stated on May 24, 1934, that real democracies, such as in west European countries, Czechoslovakia or Switzerland, did not show any desire to follow the example of those states that had established dictatorships.[111]

Democratic elements in modern dictatorships

In a way, more surprising than Masaryk's belief in the persistence of democracy was his conviction that even the modern dictatorships contained democratic elements. Shortly after Hitler's assumption of power in December 1932, Masaryk stated that if the Fascist and the Soviet dictatorships were juxtaposed to democracy, it would be important to note that

108 "Prezident Masaryk o našich stycích s Francií," May 1, 1934, Masaryk, *Cesta demokracie IV*, 415.
109 "Masaryk o současných problémech," *Morgenzeitung* (Ostrava), May 9, 1934, in Masaryk, *Cesta demokracie IV*, 419.
110 "Rozhovor s panem prezidentem Masarykem," May 24, 1934, talk with American journalist K. Werzos, in Masaryk, *Cesta demokracie IV*, 420.
111 "Democracy Will Outride Storm," *Christian Science* Monitor, May 24, 1934, Masaryk, *Cesta demokracie IV*, 423. On a previous occasions Masaryk had found the existing number of democracies reassuring. In addition to Switzerland, which was the oldest, they included France, England, Belgium, Spain, Holland, the Scandinavian lands, and also Czechoslovakia. "Masaryk o demokracii a diktatuře," *Právo lidu*, October 1, 1933, in Masaryk, *Cesta demokracie IV*, 375; "Demokracie neselhala," published as "There be no New War," *Morning Post* (London) October 9, 1933, in Masaryk, *Cesta demokracie IV*, 380–81.

even the Fascists and the Soviets had made certain concessions to democracy. The Fascists had to grant some rights to the parliament in Italy, and the Soviets flaunted their imitations of parliamentarianism.[112] Three months later he repeated the same claim about Fascist Italy.[113] With Hitler firmly established in power in May 1933, Masaryk astonished a Swiss journalist with his willingness to see in the New Germany a distinct form of democracy, not a sympathetic one, but nevertheless a form of democracy. The Swiss observed that, as a fighter against the Habsburg monarchy, Masaryk stated almost passionately that there was no reaction, no restoration, no "anti-democracy." The reporter asked whether from the hatred and the lack of spirituality in which the new democracy was being born, there would awaken a more humane, cultured, and peace-loving democracy. Masaryk responded that "[we] have to hope so." He also thought to find an excuse for what he considered a temporary setback for democracy: "The Germans are schooled, but not educated." Masaryk perceived a lack of intellectual cultivation not only in Hitler's system, but also in the ideology of Mussolini. Wondering whether Masaryk's relatively mild judgment of dictatorships was not just a matter of diplomatic tact, the Swiss reporter was assured by a high official in the Czechoslovak Foreign Ministry, Kamil Krofta, that the President often spoke in such an unrestrained and open way that experienced diplomats shook their heads in disbelief; he could not be kept within the confines of diplomatic caution.[114]

In his subsequent statements in the summer of 1933, Masaryk continued to stress the democratic features that he counterintuitively discerned in modern dictatorships. He pointed out that Hitler, "who was accepted by his nation, is not a king, but a man like the others." The same could be said of Mussolini. In the fact that they were acclaimed as leaders by their nations, Masaryk saw a certain form of democracy, although it was not the form he cherished. Above all, he did not expect Germany to return to monarchic principles, which were so fully discredited.[115] Along the same

---

112 "Masaryks Bekenntnis zur Demokratie," *Der Wiener Tag*, December 8, 1932, in Masaryk, *Cesta demokracie IV*, 478.

113 "Prezident Masaryk o věcech evropských a o sobě," *Lidové noviny*, March 19, 1933 in Masaryk, *Cesta demokracie IV*, 343.

114 Rozhovor s Masarykem," originally published in ["*Gespräch mit Masaryk*"] *Neue Züricher Zeitung*, May 28, 1933. in Masaryk, *Cesta demokracie IV*, 482.

115 "Prezident Masaryk o vývoji demokracie," *Lidove noviny*, June 20, 1933 in Masaryk, *Cesta demokracie IV*, 360.

lines, Masaryk claimed to an American reporter, on June 3, 1933, that he was not worried about the future of democracy. First, the new leaders, Hitler, Mussolini – and this time he included Stalin – needed support from the nation with each of them stemming from the common (non-aristocratic) people and, second, none of the totalitarian rulers sought to restore the old monarchic regime.[116] Their authority was based neither on Providence, nor on genealogy.[117]

Against monarchism and aristocracy

As the Swiss reporters surmised in 1933, the root of Masaryk's relatively indulgent (but unexpected) attitude toward the rising European dictators most likely lay in the political thought and experience of his remote younger years.[118] Masaryk's negative attitude toward the old monarchy and the nobility continued to surface at the time of the rise of the new dictatorships. For instance, on the eve of Hitler's seizure of power, Masaryk pointed out to the editor of the prominent German newspaper, *Vossische Zeitung,* in an interview printed on January 22, 1933, that the Habsburgs carried out the barbaric persecution by which three quarters of the land in Bohemia and Moravia was confiscated, and some of the best citizens of the country (like the world-renowned philosopher, Jan A. Komenský) were forced into exile. The post-World War I Land Reform in Czechoslovakia was to correct the results of this lawless deed; together with the land reform, the titles of nobility were abolished.[119] Masaryk also had a personal grievance against the old order of aristocratic preference. As he told Karel Čapek during the interviews in the 1920s, before graduating from the *gymnasium* in Vienna in 1872, he wished to enter the Oriental Academy, a school for diplomats, but discovered that only nobles were admitted to the

---

116 "Prezident Masaryk o demokracii a diktaturach," Edgar A. Mowrer, "Masaryk, Sage of Prague," *Chicago Daily News*, July, 5, 1933 in Masaryk, *Cesta demokracie IV*, 363.

117 "Masaryk o demokracii a diktatuře," *Právo lidu*, October 1, 1933, in Masaryk, *Cesta demokracie IV*, 375–76.

118 *"Gespräch mit Masaryk,"* Neue Züricher Zeitung, May 28, 1933. in Masaryk, *Cesta demokracie IV*, 482. The same observation is made by Jaroslav Krejčí , "La philosophie de l'histoire de Masaryk à la lumière de notre époque," in Peška and Mareš, eds., *Thomas Garrigue Masaryk, européen et humaniste*, 93.

119 "President Masaryk o Německu," *Vossische Zeitung*, January 22, 1933, Masaryk, *Cesta demokracie IV*, 332.

academy and to diplomatic service.[120] Later, still under the old monarchy, he felt resentment at having to deal with public officials appointed because of their noble status, such as the Governor of Bohemia (1896–1911), Karl Maria Count Coudenhove.[121] Likewise, Masaryk mentioned that Francis Count Thun-Hohenstein, Governor of Bohemia (1911–1915), in conversation with him in the building of the Bohemian Diet stated about the Czechs: "The Czech is either a boor (*hulvát*), or a hand-kisser."[122] Masaryk still dwelt on the unsavory character of the Bohemian and Moravian nobility in an interview for a French newspaper, *Excelsior*, in March 1934. He explained that noble status was abolished in Czechoslovakia since by and large the nobility was not national, but Habsburg, and he again referred to the large-scale confiscations, which the Habsburgs carried out after the battle of the White Mountain, offering no compensation.[123]

Yet, once the titles of nobility were abolished and the noble estates were cut in size by the land reform shortly after World War I, Masaryk's attitude became more indulgent to the chastened nobles, especially, if they showed willingness to work in the interest of the new Czechoslovak state. Some of such former aristocrats found new opportunities to engage in politics, diplomacy or in the social and economic sphere.[124] Masaryk even tried to modify the land reform, especially in cases of unfairness of compensation for land confiscated from noble estates.[125] After retirement from the presidential office, in 1935 to 1937, he asked the scion of a former aristocratic family, Zdeněk Bořek-Dohalský, now a newspaperman on the staff of *Lidové noviny* and a friend of Karel Čapek, to come to see him weekly to discuss current domestic and international affairs.[126] This development went so far that in his old age Masaryk was ready to make allowance for nobility but only on the basis of moral distinction, rather than political or social privilege. In his conversation with Karel Čapek, he even suggest-

---

120 In preparation he had taken courses in spoken Arabic; see Karel Čapek, *Hovory s T. G. Masarykem*, Spisy 20 (Prague: Československý spisovatel, 1990), 54.

121 Soubigou, *Thomas Masaryk*, 430–31.

122 "Čech je buď hulvát, nebo...líbá ruku." See Čapek, *Hovory s T. G. Masarykem*, 120.

123 "Les sort des Familles historiques de l'ancien empire austro-hongrois," *Excelsior*, March 13, 1934; Masaryk, *Cesta demokracie IV*, 411.

124 Such as Maximilian Lobkowicz, Jindřich Kolowrat-Krakowský, František Schwarzenberg, and brothers, František, Antonín and Zdeněk Bořek Dohalský. Zdeněk Hazdra, Šlechta ve službách Masarykovy republiky: Mezi demokracií a totalitními režimy (Prague: Lidové noviny, 2015), 13.

125 Hazdra, Šlechta ve službách Masarykovy republiky, 43, 94–95.

126 Ibid., 166, 168. Another noble, with whom Masaryk cultivated friendly relations the late 1920s and early 1930s was Maximilian Prince Lobkowicz (1888–1967), ibid., 204–5.

ed the possibility that his own children on their mother's side might have been of noble, or perhaps royal, origin – from the aristocracy of southern France, partly from Capetians, on the Garrigue side, and from the New England elite on the grandmother's side. He hoped that these forebears were individuals of moral excellence, significantly adding that such paragons of virtue could be, of course, found also among ancestors from the peasantry or the industrial working class.[127]

Special indulgence for the Soviets

It was noted earlier that after the replacement of War Communism with the New Economic Policy in the Soviet Union, and after Lenin's death in January 1924, the special bitterness of Masaryk's critique of Bolshevism diminished. In the beginning of the 1930s, he treated the Soviet system as part of the same political syndrome as Italian Fascism and German National Socialism. As noted earlier, by June 1933 he included Stalin with Hitler and Mussolini among leaders who had to show at least some obeisance to democracy by seeking the support of the common populace.[128] In October 1933, Masaryk failed to respond when a correspondent raised the question of Stalin's brutal suppression of his policy's opponents.[129] Somewhat earlier, he had pointed out to a Swiss reporter that Bolshevism turned out to be "nothing else but state capitalism," and, elsewhere, that the Soviet dictatorship, like the Fascist one, had to introduce at least a pseudo-parliamentary system as a gesture toward democracy.[130]

Even more remarkably, by 1934 Masaryk's attitude toward the Soviet Union had grown almost entirely friendly. At this point, despite the earlier mentioned assurances of the Czechoslovak Foreign Ministry, Masaryk was most likely swayed by diplomatic considerations. Following

---

127 Čapek, *Hovory s T. G. Masarykem*, 82.
128 The interview took place on June 3, 1933. "Prezident Masaryk o demokracii a diktaturach," Mowrer, "Masaryk, Sage of Prague," *Chicago Daily News*, July, 5, 1933 in Masaryk, *Cesta demokracie IV*, 363.
129 "Demokracie neselhala," published as "There be no New War," *Morning Post* (London) October 9, 1933, in Masaryk, *Cesta demokracie IV*, 380.
130 "Gespräch mit Masaryk," *Neue Züricher Zeitung*, May 28, 1933, in Masaryk, *Cesta demokracie* IV, 482; "Masaryks Bekenntnis zur Demokratie," *Der Wiener Tag*, December 8, 1932, in Masaryk, *Cesta demokracie IV*, 478.

Soviet overtures for alliances with France and the Little Entente in 1933, the French and Czechoslovak governments began negotiations with the Soviets in that direction in 1934.[131] Under these circumstances, Masaryk stated in an interview, published in May 1934 that he has always felt empathy toward the Russians, even toward the Bolsheviks. He was convinced that eventually the Russians would advance on the basis of their post-war experiences to an acceptable social arrangement. He would, of course, wish to spare his own nation such terrible experiences.[132] When the rapprochement with the Soviet Union led to the establishment of diplomatic relations, President Masaryk received the new Soviet Ambassador, Sergei Aleksandrovskii, in July 1934, with a warm welcome. He assured the ambassador that increasing effective international cooperation was the objective of both countries, and this common goal would lead to growing closeness between them. A detailed program of cooperation and mutual contacts between the two countries was favored by the tradition of mutual sympathies between the two countries. The President and the Ambassador agreed that these sympathies had already accompanied the Czechoslovak struggle for independence. Masaryk assured Aleksandrovskii that he could rely on an implementation of the Czechoslovak-Soviet cooperation "with readiness, and friendly and loyal support of [his] government and [his own] personal one."[133] Perhaps Masaryk could relate – in this newly found friendly tone towards the Soviet Union – to his much earlier encouragement of Allied cooperation with the Bolsheviks in the spring of 1918.[134] As in April and May 1918, so again in July 1934, the considerations of international security prevailed over those of political ideology. [135]

---

131 Bilateral treaties between Soviet Union, and both France and Czechoslovakia would be signed in 1935. See Mamatey and Luža, eds., *A History of the Czechoslovak Republic, 1918–1948*, 229.
132 "Masaryk o současných problémech," *Morgenzeitung* (Ostrava), May 9, 1934, in Masaryk, *Cesta demokracie IV*, 417.
133 "Nástupní audience sovětského vyslance," *Národní osvobození*, July 19, 1934, *Lidové noviny*, July 19, 1934, in Masaryk, *Cesta demokracie IV*, 431. Subsequently, however, Masaryk was not spared reports of Stalinist atrocities, particularly of the Ukrainian genocide. Louise Weiss records that Ms. Rodzianko, a close relative of an earlier President of the Russian Duma, who was one of two of Masaryk's nurses in 1937, provided eyewitness accounts of "the extermination of the kulaks of the Ukraine by the commissars of the Kremlin." Louise Weiss, *Mémoire d'une Européenne.* 3 vols. Paris: Payot, 1968–1970, 2: 42.
134 Noted earlier in this chapter.
135 See earlier in this chapter and Wilson, *The Papers of Woodrow Wilson*, 48: 202.

The Failure of Intellectuals, and Divine Providence

Masaryk made his most profound observations concerning his faith in democracy in interviews with American and French reporters in the summer of 1933. He was asked whether he did not believe that the new dictators would lead their nations into civic slavery and a new war. Masaryk responded that he did not believe that they would start a new war. He felt that the populace submitted to the leaders because of the economic crisis, which affected the middle class most heavily. The rise of new leaders was partly due to the abdication of constructive leadership by intellectual elites in democratic societies who failed to address the needs of the general public. Democracy also needed leaders to keep generating ideas toward social cohesion. Society needed a common faith and the intellectuals did not supply one. They had no unified political agenda, but a hundred truths. Hence the masses deserted to representatives of a single dogma, no matter how primitive, which had the virtue of simplicity. For successful democratic leadership one had to understand the material and intellectual concerns of the common man.[136] The interviewer asked if the new leaders simply enticed the common man with impossible promises and nonsensical demagoguery, did not that mean a mortal danger for democracy. Masaryk retorted that it did not in the long run; it simply meant that there were no short cuts to democracy.

It was Masaryk's view that the dictators would stay in power only as long as they could satisfy human needs. Once they no longer could, they would be removed. To the interviewer's objections that such a denouement might last years, even decades, Masaryk counseled patience, and cautioned

---

136 "Prezident Masaryk o demokracii a diktaturách," first published as Edgar A. Mowrer, "Masaryk, Sage of Prague," *Chicago Daily News*, July, 5, 1933, in Masaryk, *Cesta demokracie IV*, 363. Masaryk's thinking here appears to run parallel with Julien Benda, 1867–1956, *La trahison des clercs*; introd. André Lwoff (Paris: B. Grasset, [1975]). In this book, Benda castigated contemporary thinkers and writers, including the professionals and intellectuals. "The treason of the intellectuals, according to Benda, is that in the twentieth century they abandoned critical thinking and became advocates of political hatreds. No longer seekers after truth, the intellectuals became rationalizers of modern politics." See, Gale Stokes, "The Clerks," in *From Stalinism to Pluralism*, ed. Gale Stokes (New York: Oxford University Press, 1991), 137. Earlier in 1931, Masaryk evidently had in mind Benda, when he referred to "a French philosopher recently noted a betrayal by the intellectuals." See "Poselství prezidenta republiky," *Lidové noviny*, October 29, 1931, Masaryk, *Cesta demokracie IV*, 223. Masaryk had noted this defect of the intelligentsia even earlier in October 1927; see "Projev prezidenta republiky," *Lidové noviny*, November 2, 1927, in Masaryk, *Cesta demokracie III*, 237–38.

that history showed how periods of liberty were brief and applied to only limited geographic areas, yet eventually democracy was inevitable.[137] In another interview at this time, Masaryk reaffirmed his faith in the future of democracy, referring ultimately to a providential design of the universe. In his view, civilization zigzagged in the long run – sometimes even backtracking slightly – but on the whole, it moved forward. The period of the 1930s was one of a particular crisis, but that was only a transitional condition. The time would be eventually ripe for further advancement and, therefore, patience and sang-froid were needed in the meantime. Finally, Masaryk tipped his hand in a spiritual direction. He stated that it was his firm belief that God, who created the world and its inhabitants, would not allow his artifact to perish.[138] Thus, despite his overt opposition to traditional Churches – whether Protestant, Catholic, or Orthodox – Masaryk revealed his residual faith in a theistic religion.[139] Earlier in 1925, Dorothy Thomson – with only mild irony – compared Masaryk's faith in democracy, disarmament, and parliamentarianism (despite the challenge of the dictators) to that of "a Christian convinced that all the adversities of life were but tests, posed by a loving heavenly father."[140] In fact, in October 1928, Masaryk stated on the occasion of the tenth anniversary of Czechoslovakia: "We have our own state in order to try to establish the best conditions in it – I would say, a Kingdom of God; I believe that, often unwittingly, we are led there by destiny; by Providence."[141]

---

137 If people preferred a permanent tyranny, oppression, and intolerance, then he has been mistaken; "Prezident Masaryk o demokracii a diktaturách, first published as Mowrer, "Masaryk, Sage of Prague," *Chicago Daily News*, July, 5, 1933, in Masaryk, *Cesta demokracie IV*, 364.

138 Here a rare instance of Masaryk's revealing the basis of his ultimate hope in the durability of democracy. "Prezident Masaryk o vývoji demokracie," first published in *Lidove noviny*, June 20, 1933, in Masaryk, *Cesta demokracie IV*, 360. Based on an interview with J. Nedel, reporter for the newspaper *L'Intansigeant*.

139 On New Year's Day 1922, Masaryk declared to the representatives of the Evangelical Church of Bohemian Brethren: "I believe with you, that the lives of both the individual and the nations are not governed by chance, but by a providential plan; I have acted on this faith during the war and I do now." See "Nový rok na Hradě: poselství prezidenta republiky," *Čas*, January 2, 1922, Masaryk, *Cesta demokracie II*, 214.

140 "Prezident Masaryk o Dunajské federaci," *Národní listy*, March 9, 1925, also in *Neue Freie Presse*, March 8, 1925, based on an interview with Dorothy Thompson for the *Philadelphia Ledger*, see Masaryk, *Cesta demokracie III*, 102.

141 "Jubilejní poselství prezidenta Masaryka," *Lidové noviny*, October 30, 1928, in Masaryk, *Cesta demokracie III*, 324.

Chapter 10

The Challenge of United Europe, 1918–1934

While encouraged in his expectation of the cultural and political uni-fication of the world – mainly thanks to the League of Nations and its multi-faceted activities in the 1920s and early 1930s (described in the preceding chapter) – Masaryk also encountered complications due to the narrowly European-focused unification schemes. These projects, Aristide Briand's initiative and particularly Richard Coudenhove-Kalergi's *Paneuropa* scheme – in their defensive Euro-centrism and the exclusion of the outside world, especially the United States – clashed with the President's global vista. In the case of Briand's Initiative, however, Masaryk could adopt an indulgent view, seeing it (despite its current limitation to Europe) more as a preliminary move toward a likely greater – even global – inclusiveness. His attitude toward Coudenhove-Kalergi's project was much more equivocal, seeing it as sharply exclusivist in its ultimate goal and, moreover, burdened with undesirable historical baggage. These complicat-ing detours, however – even in the last period of his active intellectual life in 1933–1934 – did not discourage his anticipation of a united world based on democratic and humanitarian principles, despite the fact that National Socialism in Germany had crowned the rise of totalitarian governments in Russia, Italy, and Japan.

The Briand Initiative, 1928–1932

Launched in 1929, the Briand Plan – perhaps the most significant inter-war move toward a European unification – was unfolding while the Disar-mament Commission was active. As a prelude to this momentous step, it is important to note Masaryk's reactions to the Kellogg-Briand Pact (the Pact of Paris), signed on August 27, 1928, and to the Hague Conference in August 6– 31, 1929. The Kellogg-Briand Pact, which criminalized aggres-sive wars and was implemented as a general act by the League of Nations, was greeted by Masaryk as – together with the existence of the League – the first steps toward the unification of mankind.[1] On a more modest Eu-ropean scale, Masaryk endorsed the Hague Conference as proof that re-construction and pacification could proceed in Europe, and no conflict was so intractable that it could not be resolved by negotiation like those that had taken place at the Hague.[2]

Although first presented in 1929, Briand's plan itself had a fairly long genesis. As early as February 23, 1923, as a member of the French Chamber of Deputies, Briand cited the example of the United States and suggest-ed the need to find a formula for "a federal union of Europe." Becoming Minister of Foreign Affairs in 1925, during the time of Locarno he started talking about Europe and European values. There was an evident connec-tion between the Locarno Treaties of 1925 and the proposal for a Europe-an federation in 1929. [3] Masaryk soon commented with approval on Bri-and's moves toward a federal Europe. He noted at the time of Locarno that

---

1   "Ist der Friede gefährdert?" *Prager Tagblatt*, September 30, 1930, in Tomáš G. Masaryk, *Cesta de-mokracie IV*, Spisy 36 (Prague: Masarykův ústav AV ČR, 1997), 174. Eventually, the famous mil-itary tribunal in Nuremberg in 1945–46 used the Pact to establish the criminality of aggressive warfare; see *Brockhaus Enzyklopädie*, 20 vols. (Wiesbaden: Brockhaus, 1970), 10: 77.

2   "Masaryk at Eighty," *New York Times Magazine*, March 2, 1930, in Masaryk, *Cesta demokracie IV*, 134. For agreeing to the Young plan for reparation, the Germans were rewarded in Hague by a promise of an evacuation of Rhineland before June 30. For Briand's praise of the Hague Perma-nent Court of International Justice at League of Nations on September 11, 1930, see Aristide Bri-and, *La paix mondiale et l'Union européenne*, ed. Achille Elisha, 2nd ed. rev. (Louvain-la-Neuve: Academia-Bruylant, [2000]), 297.

3   Jacques Bariéty, "Aristide Briand: les raisons d'un oubli," in *Le Plan Briand d'Union fédérale européenne: perspectives nationales et transnationales, avec documents: actes du colloque international tenu à Genève du 19 au 21 septembre 1991*, ed. Antoine Fleury and Lubor Jílek (Bern and New York: Lang, c1998), 8. The year 1929 seemed propitious to advancing the cause of peace: following the Locarno Pact, Briand-Kellogg Pact, adoption by the League in 1928 of "General Act for Peace-ful Resolution of International Conflicts." Economic conditions, on the other hand, became dif-ficult, plagued by protectionism; Antoine Fleury, "Avant-propos," in *Le Plan Briand d'Union fédérale européenne*, x.

Briand did not hesitate to publicly adhere to the ideal of the United States of Europe, which he himself had formulated as an ideal and objective of Czechoslovak policy several years earlier.[4] A year later Masaryk returned to the topic, stating that the plans for a federal Europe had moved in the right direction. According to Masaryk, the plans of idealists could be realized sooner than the skeptics would consider them practicable.[5] Thus, in 1913 it would have appeared utopian if somebody had described the arrangement of Europe as it would actually be in 1918. As a case of such an early epiphany, Masaryk evidently had in mind the precedent of Briand's endorsement, on February 3, 1916, of his own plan for Bohemia's independence and the reconstruction of central Europe.[6] As for Briand's visionary tendency, Jacques Bariéty refers to Briand's powerful Celtic imagination as *"la puissante imagination de Celte."*[7]

Briand presented his plan on September 5, 1929 at the sixth plenary session of the League of Nations. He highlighted the need for federal ties among the nations of Europe because of their close geographic grouping. These ties should enable them to be in constant contact, discuss their interests, make joint resolutions, and maintain ties of solidarity in the face of grave concerns, should they arise.[8] Masaryk expressed his support for Briand's plan in short order.[9] According to Masaryk, the meaning of Briand's call was to spread mutual understanding in Europe to the point of creating a common European mentality; in other words, to promote Europeanization. He had envisaged something like this in his own war memoirs [*Světová revoluce*]. Masaryk went on to defend Briand against sceptics who saw in his initiative nothing more than a diplomatic trick to distract from more immediately pressing problems in Europe.[10]

---

4   According to Masaryk, "Letošní 28. říjen," *Národní osvobození*, October 29, 1925, in Tomáš G. Masaryk, *Cesta demokracie III*, Spisy 35 (Prague: Masarykův ústav AV ČR, 1994), 116.

5   "Thomas G. Masaryk Foresees Peace," *Christian Science Monitor*, March 12, 1926, in Masaryk, *Cesta demokracie III*, 130.

6   Briand had become prime minister on October 28, 1915. Tomáš G. Masaryk, *Světová revoluce za války a ve válce, 1914–1918*, Spisy 15 (Prague: Masarykův ústav AV ČR, 2005), 78–79.

7   Bariéty, "Aristide Briand: les raisons d'un oubli," 7. On the way to Geneva to deliver the September 5, 1929, speech, Briand confided to his associates that since France was abandoning her military positions, it had to assume moral positions. Hence he was launching the idea of a United States of Europe. Bariéty, "Aristide Briand: les raisons d'un oubli," 13.

8   Briand, *La paix mondiale et l'Union européenne*, 265.

9   "Gespräch mit Masaryk," Berliner Tagblatt, September 29, 1929, in Masaryk, *Cesta demokracie IV*, 60.

10 "Prezident Masaryk o Panevropě," *České slovo*, December 5, 1929, in Masaryk, *Cesta demokracie IV*, 87.

Masaryk also sided with Briand on the primacy of political over economic concerns. All the questions of an economic union would be entirely and more effectively solved within the framework of the proposed federal Europe. The union, of course, would not come quickly and would require a preliminary agreement among the large countries (France, Germany, England, and Italy). The most important factor was an understanding between France and Germany, which Czechoslovakia was particularly eager to foster.[11]

A Memorandum, sent from Paris on May 2, 1930 to twenty-seven European governments, concretely outlined Briand's proposals. The heart of the document envisaged an operating structure under a "European Conference," which would have ties with the League and include all League members in Europe. It would also establish an executive organ, a "Permanent Political Committee," which could occasionally invite to its deliberations extra-European League members or representatives of countries that were not League members. The memo also proposed the creation of a Secretariat to provide an administrative infrastructure for the Conference and the Committee.[12] The discussions of the French Memorandum in Geneva, however, led to the emasculation of the proposed organizational structure, allegedly out of fear of duplicating the League's institutional organs. Instead, on a British proposal, a toothless "Commission of Study for the European Union" [Commission d'étude pour l'Union européenne] was appointed to further consider the project, with Briand as president and Britannique Drummond (Secretary of the League) as secretary.[13] The Commission held six meetings in 1931 with non-members of the League admitted, but gradually even Briand's idea of the priority of political over economic issues was abandoned.[14] Masaryk was undoubtedly disappointed by the outcome of Briand's Memorandum. Yet, he had been impressed by the opportunity for all European countries to present their desiderata, and he had looked forward to the establishment of organs or offices that

11 "Prezident Masaryk o Panevropě," in Masaryk, *Cesta demokracie IV,* 89; "Hablando con el Presidente Masaryk," *El Sol,* June 5, 1930, in Masaryk, *Cesta demokracie IV,* 153.

12 These organs should be located in Geneva. See *Le Plan Briand d'Union fédérale européenne,* 574–77.

13 Fleury, "Avant-propos," in *Le Plan Briand d'Union fédérale européenne,* xiii.

14 Fleury, "Avant-propos," in *Le Plan Briand d'Union fédérale européenne,* xiii. In the meantime, the very prospects of Franco-German cooperation – on which the federal project depended – were becoming dim with Gustav Stresemann's death on October 3, 1929, and the Reichstag election of September 14, 1930, in which Hitler's party won 107 seats.

would permanently devote themselves to European issues that he considered imperative.[15] He continued to maintain a degree of optimism.[16]

In particular, Masaryk clung to the irenic vista of Briand's policy of accommodation with Germany.[17] Speaking with a British journalist in March 1932, Masaryk stated that his foreign policy was based on the conviction that France and Germany had to come to an agreement; Europe could not exist as it did before World War I with two blocs of mutually hostile nations. Europe needed a federal system, which had to rest on a Franco-German agreement with the support of Britain and Italy.[18] In July 1932, Masaryk returned to a focus on the role of the Czech nation in fostering a federation and democratic harmony. He dwelt on Bohemia's early attainment of the religious Reformation, which gave rise to Petr Chelčický's doctrine of pacifism, King George of Poděbrady's principle of eternal peace, and above all, Komenský's adherence to international humanity, peace, and justice. This program was suitable not only for Czechoslovakia, but also for all the small nations of Europe; its pursuit was not only a question of ethics, but also of political prudence.[19]

Czechoslovak foreign policy consistently supported Briand's plan and subsequently the resulting *Commission d'étude pour l'Union européenne*, until its demise in 1933.[20] Up to the very edge of the precipice – Hitler's appointment as German Chancellor on January 30, 1933 –Masaryk main-

15 "Prezident Masaryk o mírové Evropě," *Právo lidu*, June 18, 1930. in Masaryk, *Cesta demokracie IV*, 156.
16 Asked by a Spanish visitor, Artemisio Prercioso, about his opinion of European union, he stated that aside from the efforts of individuals there was in Europe an obvious desire of nations and states to unite, interpenetrate, and cooperate. Those who only yesterday were enemies now shake hands. There is a tendency for practical fraternization without undue sentimentality; there is the aim of mutual understanding. "Velké osobnosti evropské," June 19, 1931, in Masaryk, *Cesta demokracie IV*, 213. On Briand's death on March 7, 1932, he sent an official note of condolences, addressed to the President of France; see "Prezidentův soustrastný projev k úmrtí Aristida Brianda," dated March 8, 1932, in Masaryk, *Cesta demokracie IV*, 249.
17 Masaryk's letter to J. S. Machar, March 13, 1932, in Masaryk, *Cesta demokracie IV*, 256. Actually, the policy of rapprochement with Germany cost Briand popularity in France in the aftermath of World War II. It did not help that in mid-1930s a wreath was laid at his monument at Quai d'Orsey with the inscription "Aristid Briand in Dankbarkeit, Adolf Hitler" [For Aristid Briand in Gratitude, Adolf Hitler]; see Maurice Baumont, *Aristide Briand, Diplomat und Idealist* (Göttingen, Frankfurt, and Zurich: Musterschmidt, 1966), 86.
18 "Masaryk o evropském společenství," interview with Evelyn Wrench for *Daily Telegraph*, April 26, 1932, in Masaryk, *Cesta demokracie IV*, 263.
19 "Poválečné problémy Československa," dated July 9, 1932; in Masaryk, *Cesta demokracie IV*, 292–293.
20 Bohumila Ferenčuhová, "L'accueil du Plan Briand dans les milieu politiques tchèques et slovaques," *Le Plan Briand d'Union fédérale européenne*, 206–7.

tained his optimism, especially as to French and German reconciliation. He told the *Berliner Tagblatt* in October 1932 that he endorsed Briand's search for a rapprochement with Germany and was pleased that a segment of German public opinion received the French statesman's overtures positively. This German receptivity showed the possibility of all nations coming to an agreement.[21] In an interview conducted on December 17, 1932 and printed in the *Vossische Zeitung on* January 29, 1933, Masaryk spoke in a similar vein, describing his impression that in the younger generation of Germans, the dangerous antagonism toward France had been overcome and a positive sense of improving relations might prevail.[22]

The Issue of Coudenhove's *Paneuropa*

As a distinct issue, Masaryk's relationship to Richard Coudenhove-Kalergi (1894–1972) is of special interest because of the latter's notable role in pioneering the idea of a European Union. In fact, this relationship can serve as a prism through which to view the nuances of Masaryk's attitude toward European unification. Coudenhove came from a family with roots in Brabant, a province in the Low Countries. Raised in Bohemia, he received a Ph.D. in philosophy from the University of Vienna in 1917.[23] The shock of the World War, including the dismemberment of the Habsburg Empire and the loss of aristocratic privileges, caused him to reassess the European situation, in particular Franco-German hostility, which he considered suicidal for European civilization.[24] His first meeting with Masaryk took place at the Prague Castle on November 12, 1920. Masaryk evidently did not think Coudenhove very knowledgeable and instructed his secretary, Vasil Škrach, to provide his young visitor with literature on the history and geography of Czechoslovakia. According to Coudenhove, Masaryk stated that the United States of Europe would become a reality, but the time was not yet ripe. He referred to his own attempt to forge a union of states situated between Russia and Germany from Finland to Greece,

---

21   "Masaryk o dnešní Evropě," originally published in *Berliner Tagblatt*, October 5, 1932, in Masaryk, *Cesta demokracie IV*, 309.
22   "O vojenské službě a miličním systému," originally published in *Vossische Zeitung*, January 29, 1933, in Masaryk, *Cesta demokracie IV*, 338.
23   He combined his Greek grandmother's name Kalergi with his own in 1903.
24   Alain Soubigou, *Thomas Masaryk* (Paris: Librairie Arthème Fayard, 2002), 422.

but the idea failed due to nationalism. Coudenhove consoled himself by attributing Masaryk's notable reticence to the President's advanced age. Subsequent developments would shed further light on the inability of the two to see eye to eye.[25]

Coudenhove further discussed his ideas about a united Europe in newspaper articles in 1922, and in the spring of 1923 he published his book *Pan-Europa* in German in Vienna (translated into English and Czech in 1926, and into French in 1927), that proposed a loose confederation more than a tight federation. In November 1922, Masaryk had sent him a German edition of his own *New Europe*, published as *Das Neue Europa*, by which Coudenhove may have been influenced.[26] In April 1924, a *Pan-European Manifesto* was issued in Vienna, and a *Program of the Pan-European Union* was published in Vienna in September of the same year.[27] In the early 1920s Masaryk facilitated contact between Coudenhove and the French journalist Louise Weiss (1893–1983), who was Masaryk's friend and was influential in certain French governmental circles. In Paris since 1919 she had published a journal *L'Europe nouvelle*, in a way a continuation of *New Europe*.[28] She helped Coudenhove meet the politicians who, in the second half of the 1920s, directed French politics (*Cartel des gauches*) and free masons.[29]

In particular, Masaryk introduced Coudenhove to Beneš, who initially did several favors for Coudenhove. Yet they were not particularly close, and the contacts were more a matter of diplomatic politeness on Beneš's part.[30] By September 19, 1926, Beneš, in fact, warned Masaryk in a letter from Geneva not to accept the honorary presidency of the *Paneuropa* Congress in Vienna, scheduled for October, 4–6, 1926. In line with Masaryk's less parochial objectives, he suggested that the President may write a letter expressing in general terms that Coudenhove's movement helped build cooperation and peace in Europe, and that the goal of Czechoslovak pol-

25 Coudenhove thought that Masaryk still preserved a youthful spirit, but did not have his old energy. Richard N. Coudenhove-Kalergi, *Aus meinem Leben* (Zurich: Atlantis-Verlag, 1949), 87–88; Soubigou, *Thomas Masaryk,* 424– 25.
26 Soubigou, *Thomas Masaryk* , 425–26.
27 Franck Théry, *Construire l'Europe dans les annés vingt, l'action d l'Union paneuropéenne sur la scène franco-allemande, 1924–1932* (Geneva: l'Institut européen de l'université de Genève, 1998), 157–60, 28 Louise Weiss, *Mémoire d'une Européenne,* 3 vols. (Paris: Payot, 1968–1970), 1: 244; 2: 339.
29 Soubigou, *Thomas Masaryk,* 427.
30 Soubigou, *Thomas Masaryk,* 428; see also on sporadic contacts with Masaryk, in Richard N. Coudenhove-Kalergi, *Aus meinem Leben,* 102–3, 136.

icy was to gradually consolidate his and similar initiatives "into a singular great world movement." It was better to avoid specifics, Beneš advised
Masaryk, because Coudenhove's projects contained a number of impracti-
cal suggestions with which it was not possible to agree.[31] Masaryk in fact
sought to minimize his contacts with Coudenhove and kept him at a distance, claiming that at his age he lacked the stamina to devote himself
specifically to the cause of Coudenhove's *Paneuropa*, and that an involvement in Coudenhove's private enterprise might be inconsistent with his
role as a head of state.[32]

Eventually, Coudenhove planned to promulgate a constitution of twenty articles as a *Projet de Pacte paneuropéen* at a *Paneuropa* Congress scheduled for Berlin on February 25, 1930.[33] By this time the disconnect between
Masaryk's and Coudenhove's visions of European unification had become
quite clear. In any case, Masaryk remarkably never mentioned Coudenhove
in his writings or statements, nor in his conversations with Karel Čapek
or Emil Ludwig.[34] The reasons for Masaryk's displeasure can be best discussed under the following five rubrics: the monarchism and aristocracy
nexus; revisionism; the shadow of Mitteleuropa; the exclusion of Britain;
and the assertion of Europe against the outside world.

The nexus of monarchism and aristocracy

In the first place, there was Masaryk's deep distaste for what he considered the combined power of monarchism and aristocracy in the Habsburg
Empire. He reiterated his feelings clearly in a letter to President Woodrow Wilson on November 1, 1918 when he wrote of eight non-German nations "oppressed and exploited [in the Habsburg Empire] by a degenerate

31 Masaryk, however, could make a financial contribution. See Jana Čechurová and Jaroslav
    Čechura, *Edvrad Beneš: diplomat na cestách* (Prague: Karolinum, 2000), 163.
32 Václav Veber, *Dějiny sjednocené Evropy: od antických počátků do současnosti,* 2nd ed. (Prague:
    Lidové noviny, 2009), 128.
33 Théry, *Construire l'Europe dans les annés vingt, l'action d l'Union paneuropéenne sur la scène franco-
    allemande, 1924–1932,* 160–77.
34 Coudenhove saw Masaryk on several occasions during the rest of the 1920s; in 1930 and 1935
    he published laudatory articles on the occasion of Masaryk's birthdays in his monthly Jour-
    nal *Paneuropa,* see Soubigou, *Thomas Masaryk,* 427. See also Richard N. Coudenhove-Kalergi,
    "Präsident Masaryk," in *Festschrift Th. G. Masaryk zum 80. Geburtstag,* ed. Boris V. Jakovenko, 2
    vols. (Bonn: F. Cohen, 1930), 2: 379–80.

dynasty and inconsiderate aristocracy...."[35] Masaryk harbored a personal grievance in that regard; as noted in Chapter 9, in his youth he aspired to enter the imperial diplomatic service only to discover that it was a preserve of Austrian aristocracy. This episode must have left a particularly bitter memory, since he later recounted the slight in his conversations with both Ludwig and Čapek.[36] When settling into the presidential country residence, the chateau of Lány in 1920, Masaryk considered the furnishings too much to the nobility's taste, and had his favorite architect Josip Plečnik replace them.[37] Equally telling were his comments on the new direction of secondary schooling in Czechoslovakia in August 1923 when he maintained that democracy was "a victory of physical and mental work over the aristocratic ideal of indolence and domination."[38] In his conversation with Ludwig, Masaryk repeated his charges against the Habsburgs, whose choices of persons for high offices, such as Cabinet Ministers, were based on aristocratic status, not on ability or training. In that sense, even the Prussian rulers were more competent than the Habsburgs. Masaryk also denounced the Bohemian nobles, whose prosperity was essentially based on theft, ultimately deriving from the usurpations of properties from domestic exiles after the Battle of the White Mountain.[39] In March of 1934, Masaryk returned to the subject, pointing out that the Habsburg monarchy rested on aristocracy, which in Bohemia consisted of foreign nobility and benefitted from confiscated lands.[40]

Coudenhove-Kalergi's family was a representative par excellence of the Habsburg aristocracy that Masaryk so strongly detested. His father, Heinrich Coudenhove (1859–1906), served as a diplomat during the 1890s in Japan, where he married a Japanese woman, who later became Richard's mother in 1894. The family had played an important role in the administrative apparatus of the Habsburg Empire, and specifically in Bo-

35 Letter from Masaryk to Wilson, November 1, 1918, Archiv TGM, XV/25, cited by Miloslav Bednář, "Filosofická východiska a politický význam Masarykova pojetí evropské identity, integrity a integrace," *Masarykův sborník* 10 (1996–98), (Prague: Ústav T. G. Masaryka, 2000), 14.
36 Emil Ludwig, *Defender of Democracy: Masaryk of Czechoslovakia* (New York: R. M. McBride, 1936), 114; Karel Čapek, *Hovory s T. G. Masarykem*, Spisy 20 (Prague: Československý spisovatel, 1990), 54. See also Masaryk, *Světová revoluce za války a ve válce, 1914–1918*, 267.
37 Jana Croÿ, *Zámek Lány: 600 Years of History* (Prague: Správa Pražského hradu, 2007), 102–3.
38 "List Mezinárodnímu sjezdu středoškolských profesorů," August 24, 1923, in Tomáš G. Masaryk, *Cesta demokracie II*, Spisy 34 (Prague: Masarykův ústav AV ČR, 2007), 440.
39 Ludwig, *Defender of Democracy: Masaryk of Czechoslovakia*, 109–10.
40 "Les sort des Famillies historiques de l'ancien empire austro-hongrois," *Excelsior*, March 13, 1934, in Masaryk, *Cesta demokracie IV*, 411.

hemia. Richard's uncle, Maxmilian Coudenhove (1865–1928), was the last Habsburg governor of Bohemia from 1915 to 1918. Another uncle, Karl Maria Coudenhove (1855–1913), had occupied the same post from 1896 to 1911. Moreover, Masaryk had to deal with the troublesome question of Maxmilian Coudenhove's negotiations with local Czech politicians in Prague in October 1918 before his own return to Bohemia.[41]

While maintaining his strictures against the aristocracy, Masaryk, however, needed to modify his position vis-à-vis the monarchy. Ludwig pointed to a seeming inconsistency that, despite his dislike of monarchs, he referred occasionally to the tradition of the old Bohemian kings. Masaryk responded that he was pleased to cite St. Wenceslas, Charles IV, and George of Poděbrady, but that it was not his main point of reference in Czech past.[42] He explained earlier that while in the theocratic empires of Central and Eastern Europe, monarchy and aristocracy were bound together, in the west the monarchies were democratic.[43] Towards the end of the eighteenth century, France and the United States became republics while Britain (and France temporarily) became constitutional monarchies; thus democracy developed in diverse forms and degrees.[44] Although he preferred the republican form of state, Masaryk considered constitutional monarchies, like the British one, to also be praiseworthy. Only absolute monarchies belonged to the past and their collapse in World War I confirmed their obsolescence.[45]

Revisionism

Turning to revisionism, Coudenhove had a remarkably cavalier attitude toward the post-World War I peace treaties, leaving open the possibility of revision, while for Masaryk the treaty settlements of 1919–20 had a basic

---

41 "Protilegionářská zeď národní demokracie zříceninou," *Národní osvobození*, July 13, 1924, in Masaryk, *Cesta demokracie III*, 59–60; see also "Demokracie je diskuse," Masaryk, *Cesta demokracie III*, 66. Coudenhove position based on the book of Karl Friedrich Nowak, *Chaos* (Munich: Verlag für Kulturpolitik, 1923), 34–44, 285–87. Masaryk returned to the Coudenhove negotiations in *"Doslov k diskusi o 28. říjen"* [Epilog of the Discussion about October 28]; see *Národní osvobození*, November 1, 1924, in Masaryk, *Cesta demokracie III*, 85.

42 Ludwig, *Defender of Democracy: Masaryk of Czechoslovakia*, 111–12.

43 "Prezident Masaryk v Belgii," *Lidové noviny*, October 22, 1923, in Masaryk, *Cesta demokracie II*, 482.

44 "Präsident Masaryk in Slawischen Institut," *Prager Presse*, October 18, 1923, in Masaryk, *Cesta demokracie II*, 466.

45 "Masaryk o dnešní Evropě," originally published in *Berliner Tagblatt*, October 5, 1932, in Masaryk, *Cesta demokracie IV*, 311.

importance, guaranteeing the democratic world revolution that he cherished as an outcome of the War.[46] Coudenhove, in fact, considered the existing borders untenable, and felt that the possibility of a friendly revision had to be maintained.[47] There were troubling signs of Coudenhove's popularity among the Sudeten Germans during his rallies in Liberec in October 1926 and in Carlsbad in August 1927. Masaryk, as well as Beneš, had reason to suspect that Coudenhove felt a special sympathy for his Sudeten countrymen.[48] Even more ominous were his statements concerning the frontiers of Hungary, established by the Treaty of Trianon, which he viewed as historically, economically, and geographically unjust.[49] In late 1930, Coudenhove openly asserted that the key to the Franco-German reconciliation was the revision of treaties. He deemed half-way measures like the Young Plan and evacuation of the Rhineland insufficient. It was necessary to invalidate all treaties that "contradicted the principle of equality" and perpetuated the antagonisms of the World War.[50] At a meeting of the *Paneuropa* Chapter in Bratislava in January 8, 1932, Prince Karl Anton Rohan also openly advocated the revision of peace treaties. Similar revisionist ideas characterized the Paneuropean Congress in Basle in October 1932.[51]

To understand Masaryk's sensitivity to the issue of revisionism, it should be noted that the idea of an adjustment of Hungary's border had caused him embarrassment on at least two occasions. On March 15, 1923, in an interview with E. Pályi, reporter of the *Budapesti Hirlap*, Masaryk talked about reconciliation with Hungary. Subsequently, in 1927, Pályi published a pamphlet, in which he claimed that Masaryk conceded the possibility of population exchanges and eventual territorial changes. Masaryk denied making any such promises.[52] In the second instance, in an in-

46 Ferenčuhová, "L'accueil du Plan Briand dans les milieu politiques tchèques et slovaques," *Le Plan Briand d'Union fédérale européenne*, 184.
47 Richard Coudenhove-Kalergi, " Zum paneuropäschen Locarno," *Paneuropa* 8 (1927), 16–17, cited in Martin Posselt, "Die deutsch-französischen Beziehungen und der Briand-Plan im Spiegel der Zeitschrift *Paneuropa*, 1927–30," in *Le Plan Briand d'Union fédérale européenne*, 36.
48 Richard Nicolaus Coudenhove-Kalergi, *Ein Leben für Europa: meine Lebenserinnerungen* (Cologne: Kiepenheuer & Witsch, 1966), 146.
49 Ferenčuhová, "L'accueil du Plan Briand dans les milieu politiques tchèques et slovaques," *Le Plan Briand d'Union fédérale européenne*, 188–89.
50 Posselt, "Die deutsch-französischen Beziehungen," *Le Plan Briand d'Union fédérale européenne*, 49–50.
51 Ferenčuhová, "L'accueil du Plan Briand dans les milieu politiques tchèques et slovaques," *Le Plan Briand d'Union fédérale européenne*, 205.
52 See Anna Gašparíková-Horáková, *U Masarykovcov* (Bratislava: Academic Electronic Press, 1995), 82. Correct text published in "Prezident Masaryk o našem poměru k Maďarům," *Zahraniční politika*, 4 (1923) pt. I, 504–5, in Masaryk, *Cesta demokracie II*, 408–9.

terview for the *Prager Tagblatt* in September 1930, Masaryk stated that he could understand Hungary's desire to modify the current boundary line, but it would have to happen with the agreement of the Czechoslovak parliament, as well as with the consent of the Little and the Great Entente. At the same time, the exchange could not be one-sided –Czechoslovakia would have to receive new territory as compensation.[53] The first version of the interview, published in the Viennese *Neue Freie Presse* on September 28, 1930 as "Patriotismus und Pacifismus," which presented Masaryk as a friend of revisionism, provoked deep resentment in Czechoslovakia. The Czechoslovak government issued an official clarification.[54] Subsequently, Masaryk expressed himself more cautiously, stipulating conditions which virtually excluded revisions.[55] In the early 1930s, Masaryk became particularly adamant in stressing the inviolability of all the existing peace treaties. If a change should be made, it had to be done with the agreement of all who had signed the documents.[56]

The shadow of Mitteleuropa

A related retrospective aspect of Coudenhove's project, which ran contrary to Masaryk's global vision, was the limitation of his Paneuropa to continental western and central Europe, excluding both Britain and Russia.[57] It was thus also reminiscent of the older German concept of Mitteleuropa formulated by Friedrich Naumann (1860–1919) in 1915, which would have placed most of continental Europe under German hegemony.[58] Long dis-

---

53   "Ist der Friede gefährdert?" *Prager Tagblatt*, September 30, 1930, in Masaryk, *Cesta demokracie IV*, 175.

54   "Prohlášení vlády o interview prezidenta Masaryka," *Národní osvobození*, October 3, 1930, in Masaryk, *Cesta demokracie IV*, 176–78.

55   Asked by American correspondent John MacCormac about the possibility of concessions in the Magyar areas, he responded that it was not just an issue between two states. The matter concerned a lot of countries that had signed the treaties after World War I: France, England, Italy, Germany, Romania, and Yugoslavia; see "Masaryk at Eighty," *New York Times Magazine*, March 2, 1930, in Masaryk, *Cesta demokracie IV*, 134–35.

56   "Smlouvy nejsou cár papíru," *Lidové noviny*, December 13, 1931, in Masaryk, *Cesta demokracie IV*, 231. He did not rule out minor corrections, but any substantial changes were excluded. "Prezident Masaryk of Maďarech," *Lidové noviny*, December 18, 1932, in Masaryk, *Cesta demokracie IV*, 324.

57   Jaromír Nečas, *Spojené státy Evropské* (Prague: Čin, 1926), 46.

58   Henry C. Meyer, "Mittleuropa in German Political Geography," *Annals of the Association of American Geographers* 36, 3 (1946), 179, 185–89.

trustful of this concept, Masaryk condemned it during World War I as one of Germany's illegitimate war aims. The journal *New Europe* – which he edited in London during World War I –was intended to be an answer to Mittleuropa, and – as Masaryk wrote to Wilson on November 1, 1918 – the Democratic Mid-European Union was to be a positive alternative to the plan for German hegemony in Central Europe.[59] Due to its resemblance to Mitteleuropa, Coudenhove's *Paneuropa* aroused an opposition in the Czech press as early as 1926.[60] Moreover, Coudenhove's campaign – receiving a subsidy from the Hamburg banker Max Warburg to the tune of 60.000 gold marks – appeared to have a rather Germanic tinge. Above all, the *Paneuropa* Central Committee was headquartered in the Hofburg, the ancient Habsburg palace in Vienna, with the support of the Catholic Chancellor of Austria, Ignaz Seipel (who accepted the presidency of the Austrian committee, and his successors did so as well until 1938).[61] It was these elements, when combined, which created the impression that either the old Germanic dream of Mitteleuropa was being resurrected, or a restoration of the Habsburg Empire was being attempted. The French Foreign Ministry – especially the group around Jacques Seydoux (chief of the cabinet of the Minister of Foreign Affairs) – was apprehensive in that regard. [62] It did not help matters when in 1930, the sections of *Paneuropa* in Vienna, Dresden, Brno, and Budapest actually tended to identify the project with the 1915 *Mitteleuropa* of Naumann.[63] Independently, interest in

---

59 Jaroslav Opat, "Masarykovo evropanství jako pojem a jako politický program," *Masarykův sborník* 8 (1993, Prague: Ústav T. G. Masaryka, 1993), 40. Masaryk and Robert W. Seton-Watson launched the journal *New Europe* in part against the concept of *Mitteleuropa,* see Henry C. Meyer, *Mitteleuropa in German Thought and Action, 1815–1945* (Hague: Najhoff, 1955), 4, 215, 250, 340. It did not help matters that some of Masaryk's political opponents in Bohemia, especially Bohumil Šmeral and František Udržal, had expressed interest in Naumann's project in 1915, see ibid., 189.

60 For instance, Viktor Dyk, "Paneuropa a nebezpečné probuzení," *Národní listy*, January 10, 1926, cited in Ferenčuhová, "L'accueil du Plan Briand dans les milieu politiques tchèques et slovaques," *Le Plan Briand d'Union fédérale européenne*, 187.

61 Théry, *Construire l'Europe dans les annés vingt, l'action d l'Union paneuropéenne sur la scène franco-allemande, 1924–1932*, 32–33.

62 Elisabeth Du Réau, *L'idée d'Europe au XXe siècle : des mythes aux réalités* (Bruxelles: Editions Complexe, c1996), 82, about French diplomatic concerns, citing from Laurence Badel, *Itinéraires culturels franco-allemands, l'entourage européen de Briand,* Mémoire de maitrise (Paris: université I, 1989), 72–75.

63 Ferenčuhová, "L'accueil du Plan Briand dans les milieu politiques tchèques et slovaques," *Le Plan Briand d'Union fédérale européenne*, 194. On the relationship between Coudenhove's plan and Mittleuropa, see Reinhard Frommelt, *Paneuropa oder Mittleuropa: Einigungsbestrebungen im Kalkül deutscher Wirtschaft und Politik* (Stuttgart: DVA, 1977), 11–16, 73–78, 105–6.

the project of *Mitteleuropa* was rising in Germany between 1927 and 1933, and *Mittleuropa* institutes were established and published studies in Vienna, Dresden, and Leipzig.[64]

A particularly sensitive topic along these lines, from Masaryk's point of view, was the idea of an Austro-German unification, or the *Anschluss*. Coudenhove had a long history of advocating a customs union between Germany and Austria as the beginning of the unification process.[65] Masaryk, on the contrary, early voiced his skepticism about such a union. In August 1922, he responded to the argument of Chancellor Ignaz Seipel that Austria needed to lean politically on a neighboring country. If circumstances forced a tie of Austria with another country, Masaryk favored its connection with Czechoslovakia rather than Germany or Italy.[66] In Masaryk's view, Austria was capable of separate existence and had much to offer Germany if it remained politically independent.[67] From an even broader angle of vision, Masaryk maintained in 1929 that Austria had a valuable cultural role to play on its own, and thus, it would be a loss for humanity if it were to dissolve in a Germanic sea. Anyway, nothing prevented Austria from having close normal relations with Germany under the current circumstances.[68]

Masaryk focused attention on the issue even more after 1931–32, when Coudenhove openly came out in favor of a union of Austria and Germany, and even suggested calling a conference to revise the peace treaties that prohibited the *Anschluss*.[69] In an interview for the *Deutsche Allgemeine Zeitung* in June 1931, Masaryk stated that he did not consider the unification of Austria with Germany to be inevitable – and if it did happen, Aus-

64 Meyer, "Mittleuropa in German Political Geography," 190. On the interest of German historians and economists in this topic at the time, see Paul Sweet, "Recent German Literature on Mitteleuropa," *Journal of Central European Affairs*, 3 (1934–1944), 1–24.
65 The project was abandoned under French pressure on September 3, 1931, and invalidated by the World Court, September 5, which held it in violation of peace treaties stipulating Austria's independence. Posselt, "Die deutsch-französischen Beziehungen und der Briand-Plan im Spiegel der Zeitschrift Paneuropa, 1927–30," in *Le Plan Briand d'Union fédérale européenne*, 49–50.
66 "Otázka Rakouska," August 29, 1922, in Masaryk, *Cesta demokracie II*, 331.
67 Resorting to a historical perspective, Masaryk noted that Germany and Austria had not united during the previous thousand years, which indicated that there was something artificial in the idea of the *Anschluss*; see "Thomas G. Masaryk Foresees Peace," *Christian Science Monitor*, March 12, 1926, Masaryk, *Cesta demokracie III*, 131.
68 "Prezident Masaryk o Panevropě," *České slovo*, December 5, 1929, in Masaryk, *Cesta demokracie IV*, 88.
69 Ferenčuhová, "L'accueil du Plan Briand dans les milieu politiques tchèques et slovaques," *Le Plan Briand d'Union fédérale européenne*, 205.

tria would be most disappointed. The German reporter interpreted Masaryk's aversion to the *Anschluss*, as well as to the Danubian federation, as a fear that such eventualities would create political dependence of Central Europe on Germany and/or lead to the restoration of the old Habsburg conditions.[70] In a conversation with an Austrian correspondent, Masaryk pointed out that a cultural mutuality had been achieved among individual segments of the German speaking population, including that in Switzerland and the Sudetenland.[71] Still, in October 1933, Masaryk expressed his conviction that Austria rightly sought to preserve its independence and repeated that he saw no reason why Austria should obliterate itself after so many centuries of existence.[72]

The exclusion of Britain

Coudenhove's proposed exclusion of Britain from the Pan-European space was particularly contradictory to Masaryk's vision of the future. Coudenhove excluded Britain on the grounds that her overseas ties, especially in the dominions (Australia, Canada, and South Africa), created interests alien to continental Europe. This stand challenged Masaryk's profound Anglophilia. Having spent the war years mainly in London, he learned to admire the British character.[73] He was particularly impressed by the English sense of diplomacy and tactfulness. In his introduction to the Czech edition of Henry W. Steed's memoirs (1924), he noted that Steed often found himself in awkward situations when his own views differed from those of official British policy, but in those cases, Steed "knew how to combine extreme tactfulness with adherence to his principles." He was not only Masaryk's helper in London during the war, but also his mentor.[74] Above all, Masaryk felt strongly that Britain had to remain involved

70 "Prezidentův rozhovor pro *Deutsche Allgemeine Zeitung*," June 10, 1931, in Masaryk, *Cesta demokracie IV*, 473.
71 Austria would play a demeaningly subordinate role in Germany; "Gespräch mit Masaryk," *Neue Freie Presse,* April 17, 1932, in Masaryk, *Cesta demokracie IV*, 264.
72 "Masaryk o demokracii a diktatuře," originally in *Právo lidu*, October 1, 1933, [based on interview for French reporter for *Quotidien*] in Masaryk, *Cesta demokracie IV*, 376.
73 Soubigou, *Thomas Masaryk*, 431.
74 "Třicet let novinářem," Masaryk, *Cesta demokracie III*, 74–75. Refers to H. W. Steed, *Třicet let novinářem* (Prague: Orbis, 1924), 7–8. The English original: Henry W. Steed, *Through Thirty Years, 1892–1922: A Personal Narrative*, 2 vols. (Garden City, NY: Doubleday, Page & Company, 1924).

in Continental European affairs on the side of France in order to maintain the post-World War I order.[75]

Masaryk was not troubled by the British monarchy or imperialism. In any case, democracy was better understood and developed in the West, mainly in England and in the United States, than elsewhere in Europe. The Anglophone countries rejected the divinization of the state that had been common in Germany and Austria. These countries functioned on a higher cultural plane than Germany and Austria. Their democracy was a political system based on morality, not on force, thus exemplifying Masaryk's favorite precept: "Jesus, not Caesar."[76] Masaryk was convinced that British statesmen could solve sensitive issues within the empire in a manner that was both effective and fair. Thus Canada received her autonomy and remained loyal. The British government practiced the art of politics with an understanding of what was attainable, and it knew when and how to retreat in time.[77] More broadly, to counteract the charge of British imperialism, Masaryk pointed out that Britain was federalizing her Empire after World War I, citing as a particular example the decision to grant autonomy to Ireland.[78] Speaking to an English correspondent in March 1932, he predicted that British policy would adjust to changing conditions in Africa and Egypt, and when the time came it would accommodate the desire of Asian nations (he had been asked his opinion about India) "to the growing desire of the Asian population for independent control over its destinies."[79]

On his official visit to England in 1923, Masaryk stated that he never felt as free as he did during his two year stay in London during World War I. He felt at home in the midst of English culture. He added that, of course, his own family was partly English, or – to be more exact – American.[80] At times, he corresponded even with Czech friends in

75 "Britain and Europe," *Daily Telegraph*, August 6, 1925, in "Jubilejní poselství prezidenta Masaryka," *Lidové noviny*, October 30, 1928, in Masaryk, *Cesta demokracie III*, 397.

76 "Řeč při promoci na doktora Husovy bohoslovecké fakulty evangelické," May 24, 1923, in Masaryk, *Cesta demokracie II*, 426.

77 "Prezident Masaryk o věcech evropských a o sobě," *Lidové noviny*, March 19, 1933, in Masaryk, *Cesta demokracie IV*, 344.

78 "Organizace Evropy problém centralizace a autonomizace. Tak zvaná balkanizace Evropy," February 8, 1922, in Masaryk, *Cesta demokracie II*, 242.

79 "Masaryk o evropském společenství," interview with Evelyn Wrench for *Daily Telegraph*, April 26, 1932, in Masaryk, *Cesta demokracie IV*, 263.

80 "Pan president na londýnské radnici," *Venkov*, October 26, 1923, in Masaryk, *Cesta demokracie II*, 490.

English,[81] and he tended to speak in English with family members, especially his daughter Alice.[82] In May 1934, Masaryk endorsed English as the international language and showed an interest in C. K. Ogden's *The System of Basic English*. Likewise, he favored a reform of Czechoslovak secondary schools to augment the teaching of English.[83]

Masaryk also had a high opinion of English literature, which he strongly expressed in his war memoirs.[84] The depth of his interest is indicated by the reviews he wrote of novels by twelve British and American authors in the journal *Přítomnost* in 1927, and of an additional four novels by British authors in 1928 in the same journal. [85] In September 1930 in an interview with German book publisher Robert Freund, co-owner of the Piper Publishing House in Munich, Masaryk stated that – as far as belles lettres were concerned – he read primarily English and American authors. Asked whether he was familiar with the works of Virginia Woolf, he said that he was very favorably impressed by her treatment of the "women question" and had conveyed to her some of his own ideas on the topic.[86] Four years

---

81   For instance, answering congratulations from his friend, evangelical clergyman Ferdinand Císař (1850–1932), for his 72nd birthday, March 15, 1922, he wrote in English: "Many and many nights are devoted to thinking about the future; it is the age that brings me to it." Masaryk, *Cesta demokracie II*, 259.

82   Masaryk liked to speak English, also when he was very old and sick. His daughter Alice recorded her conversation with him after dinner on August 27, 1934: "I might die – I am not afraid at all." "You can trust Jenda and Beneš absolutely." "I would like to say a few ideas. Very short and absolutely honest and not have it published." "I am tired." "I am very sick Eliško, you know that – it may be death." "My wish is to have Beneš my successor. Real democracy. I have some…" He could not speak any further; Gašparíková-Horáková, *U Masarykovcov*, 232. Again he spoke in English, "I am lost," when unable to concentrate on receiving the loyalty oath of the new cabinet of Milan Hodža in the spring of 1935; ibid., 256. According to his secretary, Vasil Škrach, in August 1934 Masaryk found it easier to pronounce English than Czech; Michaela Košťálová, *Rodokmen a soukromí T. G. Masaryka* (Prague: Petrklíč, 2013), 142.

83   At present Germany enjoyed something of a privileged position due to geographic and administrative considerations. See "Democracy Will Outride Storm," *Christian Science* Monitor, May 24, 1934, in Masaryk, *Cesta demokracie IV*, 423. See also Charles Kay Ogden, *The System of Basic English* (New York: Harcourt, Brace, [c1934]).

84   Masaryk, *Světová revoluce za války a ve válce, 1914–1918*, 89–91. Subsequently, in February 1926 he warmly welcomed the series of translations from English and American literature, launched by Aventinum, the publishing house of Otakar Štorch-Marien in Prague; see "Vydavatelstvu Anglo-americké knihovny," Masaryk, *Cesta demokracie III*, 125.

85   *Přítomnost*, 4 (1927), 426–28, 474–76, 782–84, in Masaryk, *Cesta demokracie III*, 218–28, 245–49; *Přítomnost*, 5 (1928), 73–74, 218–19, 248–49, 267–68, 280–81, 361–62, in Masaryk, *Cesta demokracie III*, 263–65, 275–79 284–85, 292–95, 304.

86   "Literarische Unterredung mit Masaryk," *Prager Tagblatt*, September 7, 1930, in Masaryk, *Cesta demokracie IV*, 164. Woolf thanked Masaryk for his interest, but she was evidently not prepared for a lengthy literary discussion; see, letter of Virginia Woolf to Tomáš G. Masaryk, Prague, Masarykův ústav - Archiv Akademie věd České republiky (MSÚ - A AV ČR), April 7, 1930, in *Korespondence II*, 80, 713.

later, Masaryk again referred to his continuing warm interest in English and American novels. He thought that women were especially outstanding as Anglophone writers. He sent several unique letters to Willa Cather, indicating that she was his favorite author.[87]

In addition to his fondness for the English language and literature, Masaryk also preferred to dress in the English manner. In March 1930, a *New York Times* correspondent described Masaryk as dressed in a "Prince Albert [coat] and a broad-brimmed soft black hat" so that he appeared like "a Kentucky gentleman of the old school."[88]

Not only the exclusion of Britain, but also that of Russia under Coudenhove's *Paneuropa* project, ran against Masaryk's convictions. There were even intimations that Coudenhove not only considered Russia culturally different from Europe, but also favored military intervention against the Soviet Union.[89] Masaryk firmly opposed any type of interventionist policy in Russia. Although he wished to see Russia democratic and consolidated, this task, in his view, had to be performed by the Russians themselves. Beyond that he believed that Russia had been basically European in culture, and its foremost intellectual representatives had always been oriented toward the West.[90] It should be a part of Europe.

---

87 "Democracy Will Outride Storm," *Christian Science* Monitor, May 24, 1934, in Masaryk, *Cesta demokracie IV*, 423. Willa Cather (1873–1947) wrote novels about immigrant life in the American West; in "My Antonia" (1918) she dealt with a Czech immigrant family in Nebraska. *Enc. Americana*, vol. 6, 16. Masaryk wrote to Willa Cather that although as a rule he did not prefer short stories – "I like the whole drama of life" – he appreciated "Neighbor Rosicky" and could quote the last page of "Old Mrs. Harris." Phyllis C. Robinson, *Willa, the Life of Willa Cather* (Garden City, NY: Doubleday, 1983), 261, citing from Tomáš Masaryk to WC, 1932, in Willa Cather Pioneer Memorial, Red Cloud, Nebraska (see 308). See also *The Selected Letters of Willa Cather*, ed. Andrew Jewell and Janis Stout, (New York: Knopf, 2013), 364–66, 369, 472–73, 504–5, 642. Cather responded to Masaryk's literary interests in several letter in 1923–1925, see Letters of Willa S. Cather to Tomáš G. Masaryk, in Prague, Masarykův ústav - Archiv Akademie věd České republiky (MSÚ - A AV ČR), December 1, 1923, in Korespondence II, 41, 706; February 14, [1924] in Korespondence II, 41, 706; September 23, [1924], in Korespondence II, 227, 738; February 2, 1925, in Korespondence II, 57, 708. She wrote to him twice in 1935–1936, when he was no longer able to respond personally; see Letters of Willa S. Cather to Tomáš G. Masaryk, in Prague, Masarykův ústav - Archiv Akademie věd České republiky (MSÚ - A AV ČR), February 14, 1935, and December 1, 1936, Korespondence II, 94, 717.

88 John MacCormac, "Masaryk, at Eighty, Toils on at his Task," *New York Times,* March 2, 1930, 3. "Prince Albert" is defined as "a long, double-breasted frock coat." See also Soubigou, *Thomas Masaryk*, 431.

89 For instance, on the part of the French Foreign Ministry in June 1932, see Laurence Badel, "Les promoteurs français d'une union éonomique et douanière de l'Europe dans l'entre-deux-guerres," in *Le Plan Briand d'Union fédérale européenne*, 25.

90 Masaryk, *Světová revoluce za války a ve válce, 1914–1918*, 352.

Euro-centrism

Coudenhove's Paneuropa clashed with Masaryk's view of the coming unification of mankind, not only by excluding Britain and Russia, but even more blatantly by juxtaposing the truncated *Paneuropa* to the rest of the world. Coudenhove proposed the formation of five blocks: Pan-European, British, Pan-American, Sino-Japanese, and Russian. The Paneuropa was to assert the European cultural values vis-à-vis the other global components.[91] As a corollary, Coudenhove projected a skeptical attitude, if not outright hostility toward the League of Nations. According to him, the League was burdened by the legacy of the war; it was weak, inarticulate, and unreliable. Because it aspired to be everything to everybody, it turned out to be nothing to anybody.[92]

While Coudenhove aimed to preserve Europe's peculiarity against the external world and deprecated the League of Nations, Masaryk envisaged Europe's union with all the countries of the world on the basis of democratic regimes, and the starting point of this fully global union was to be the League of Nations. In turn, the League was thus a broader, more perfect and higher forum than what *Paneuropa* could aspire to be. It stood for incontestably higher ideals, because they were explicitly universal.[93] In 1932, Masaryk reemphasized that the special value of the League was its inclusion of not only European, but also extra-European nations, since the realization of democracy and justice was a global project.[94] Two years later, he again stressed the need to cultivate an all-human feeling, a feeling of universality. This should start with the school children, who should learn about foreign lands in order to realize that even in China and Africa people had the same needs and concerns.[95]

Masaryk found it particularly uncongenial that Coudenhove's assertion of Europe's metapolitical distinctiveness drew an intrinsic line of separation between the Old Continent and the United States, which Couden-

---

91 Soubigou, *Thomas Masaryk*, 423; Nečas, *Spojené státy Evropské,* 49–51.

92 Nečas, *Spojené státy Evropské,* 54; Veber , *Dějiny sjednocené Evropy: od antických počátků do současnosti,* 129.

93 Ferenčuhová, "L'accueil du Plan Briand dans les milieu politiques tchèques et slovaques," *Le Plan Briand d'Union fédérale européenne,* 184.

94 "Až se změní naše srdce, bude věčný mír," České slovo, November 18, 1932, in Masaryk, *Cesta demokracie IV,* 315.

95 "Vidět, vnímat, pozorovat," *Lidové noviny,* March 7, 1934, in Masaryk, *Cesta demokracie IV,* 406.

hove moreover regarded as Europe's potential competitor.[96] Right after his return to the newly independent Czechoslovakia Masaryk sent a telegram to Wilson from Prague on January 2, 1919, expressing thanks to Wilson for his role in making the independence of Czechoslovakia possible, in the following words:

> Our nation will never forget that it was you Mr. President who by his kind sense of freedom and justice has brought about the disruption of the immoral state combination called Austria Hungary and it was you who with his knowledge of our right in the most critical moment has made possible the revolution which brought us our national independence. We greet you the spokesman of the political ideals of the great American Republic .... These ideals are one with the ideals of our nation and will always find an enthusiastic defender in the free Czecho Slovak Republic.[97]

Wilson responded on January 10, 1919 with equal warmth: "It is deeply gratifying to me that the Czecho-Slovak peoples should recognize in me their friend and the champion of their rights and I beg you to believe that I shall be always happy to serve the Nation in any way that it is in my power to serve it."[98]

Ironically, in the early 1920s, Masaryk's vision of a close association between Europe and the United States suffered a notable setback with the rise of American isolationism.[99] His personal relation with Wilson grew warmer during the latter's retirement from office in March 1921. In their exchanges of correspondence, they began to address each other as "My dear Friend."[100] Especially poignant was Masaryk's reply to Wilson's condolences on the death of his wife Charlotte dated May 19, 1923. On June 15, 1923, Masaryk wrote: "My wife was a real American, living up to the best & loftiest American ideas; I shared her views & accepted her Ameri-

96 Veber, *Dějiny sjednocené Evropy: od antických počátků do současnosti*, 129.
97 Woodrow Wilson, *The Papers of Woodrow Wilson*, ed. Arthur S. Link et al., 69 vols. (Princeton, NJ: Princeton University Press, 1966–1994), 53: 590.
98 He concluded: "I hope that you will let me know from time to time what service of counsel or action you think I could render it. I rejoice in its establishment and hope for its permanent prosperity." Wilson, *The Papers of Woodrow Wilson*, 53: 711.
99 "Interview pro americký list *Boston Advertiser*," March 26, 1923, in Masaryk, *Cesta demokracie II*, 431.
100 Wilson, *The Papers of Woodrow Wilson* , 68: 364, 386, 481.

canism & that brought me to you in 1918. I believed in the American ideals as you expressed them.[101] On the occasion of Wilson's death in February 1924, Masaryk expressed a deep admiration for him as the American author of the League who – like himself – was a believer in "humanitarianism and humanity."[102]

In 1929, Masaryk openly opposed attempts to keep a future United States of Europe at a distance from the United States of America. He maintained that the relations between Europe and America should not remain merely economic and external; they were destined to become ideological and internal (moral and cultural). The cultural relationship between Europe and America was constantly deepening. Masaryk was following, as much as possible, American belles lettres and philosophical, historical, and sociological literature. In all these areas, America influenced European thought, and the Americans were paying more attention to intellectual developments in Europe.[103] Masaryk repeatedly pointed out that it was particularly World War I which had brought Europe and the United States closer together. The Americans had crossed the ocean for Europe. "For the first time in history nations of the entire world discovered that they were a single entity."[104] A linkage with the United States was part of the process of world unification. If voices in the United States called for separation from Europe, the actual course of events belied such an assertion. There were not just common economic interests, but above all general civilizational ties.[105]

In a particularly poignant statement broadcast by radio to the United States on George Washington's two hundredth birthday in February 1932, Masaryk referred to the connection between America and Europe during

---

101 Ibid., 68: 386; see also ibid., 364. In the same year Wilson repeated assurances of friendship and respect for Masaryk, as well as of his concern for the welfare of the Czechoslavak nation in his letters of January 3, April 18, and November 23, 1923; see Wilson, *The Papers of Woodrow Wilson*, 68: 263, 337, 481.

102 "Projevy k úmrtí W. Wilsona," February 4, 1924, in Masaryk, *Cesta demokracie III*, 13. On Masaryk's relation with Wilson, see Herbert A. Miller, "What Woodrow Wilson and America Meant to Czechoslovakia," in *Czechoslovakia*, ed. Robert J. Kerner (Berkeley: University of California Press, 1945), 77–87.

103 Interview for *Cosmopolitan*, May 14, 1929, in Masaryk, *Cesta demokracie IV*, 37.

104 "Rozmluva prezidenta Masaryka s anglickým novinářem," October 10, 1929, in Masaryk, *Cesta demokracie IV*, 62.

105 "Poselství prezidenta republiky," *Lidové noviny*, October 29, 1931, in Masaryk, *Cesta demokracie IV*, 223. On Masaryk's fondness for the United States, see also: Peter Bugge, "Longing or Belonging? Czech Perceptions of Europe in the Inter-War Years and Today," *Yearbook of European Studies*, 11: 119.

the American Revolution and during World War I as proof that the United States was a natural continuation and extension of Europe. Europe and America were bound together, and they penetrated each other; America was Europeanized, and Europe was Americanized. These phenomena were but two aspects of the same process. He himself experienced the process of Americanization, learning intensively from the United States, a land for which he had a great appreciation.[106] The United States reciprocated Masaryk's fondness: in May 1935, he received a medal from the Woodrow Wilson Foundation "in recognition of his tireless struggle for human rights and against tyrannical oppressors." [107] (See the Preface).

Coudenhove and Briand

Although Masaryk's position was much closer to Briand's than Coudenhove's, even Briand's project – in Masaryk's eyes – did not remain untainted by Euro-centrism and anti-Americanism. Ironically, Masaryk, with Beneš's assistance, actually helped to bring the Frenchman and the Austrian together. It was on their recommendation that Briand, as Foreign Minister, received Coudenhove in Paris in March 1925.[108] Attracted by then to the idea of Franco-German rapprochement, Briand agreed to serve as an honorary president of the *Paneuropa* Congress in Vienna in October 1926.[109] When the Central Council of Paneuropa held meetings in Paris in April 29 – May 2, 1927, Briand accepted the honorary presidency of the Paneuropean Union.[110] The Second Paneuropa Congress in Berlin in May 1930 received a telegram from Briand who praised the

---

106 "T. G. Masaryk o Jiřím Washingtonovi," *Národní osvobození*, February 23, 1932, in Masaryk, *Cesta demokracie IV*, 247.

107 See the Preface in this volume. The citation was signed by Hamilton Fish Armstrong (1893–1973), president of the foundation. Other recipients of the medal included Viscount Cecil of Chelwood (Lord Robert Cecil, 1864–1958), Colonel Lindbergh, Senator Elihu Root, and the League of Nations; see "Masaryk vyznamenán Wilsonovou medailí," in Masaryk, *Cesta demokracie IV*, 444.

108 Posselt, "Die deutsch-französischen Beziehungen," in *Le Plan Briand d'Union fédérale européenne*, 31–32.

109 The relationship was paradoxical from the start; Briand was not a radical revisionist. Although Briand was not in power during the negotiation of the peace treaties, he never opposed them and never wished to see them revised. Bariéty, "Aristide Briand: les raisons d'un oubli," 6.

110 Posselt, "Die deutsch-französischen Beziehungen," in *Le Plan Briand d'Union fédérale européenne*, 32–33.

work of Paneuropa as preparing European minds for a federal organization. French delegate Louis Loucher brought a copy of Briand's famous memorandum of May 2, 1930, which in fact was launched at the Congress.[111] Soon afterwards, however, on May 20, 1930, Beneš – speaking for Masaryk – warned the French Ministry of Foreign Affairs against the political aspects of the Congress and advised steering clear of the Paneuropa organization, which saw the center of the federal Europe in Berlin and Vienna.[112] Paradoxically, the German Foreign Office, on the contrary, considered the Congress under Coudenhove's leadership too pro-French, because it did not pay sufficient attention to the German need for the revision of treaties, and to the special relation with Soviet Russia, which Germany had developed in the 1920s.[113] Hence, while Masaryk viewed Coudenhove's attitude toward the peace treaties as too revisionistic, the German government did not consider it revisionist enough.

Even more significant, from Masaryk's point of view, was the Euro-centric and anti-American bent in the genesis and character of Briand's European federation, which had a curious starting point in the negotiations of the Kellogg-Briand Pact of August 1928. Aware of French weakness in Europe, Briand had negotiated with the Secretary of State, Frank B. Kellogg, in hopes of engaging the United States on the European scene. In particular, he wished to receive guarantees of French security, and of American support for the maintenance of the peace treaties, all of which had been originally promised at Versailles, but aborted by the American refusal to sign the Treaty of Versailles and join the League of Nations. When Kellogg rejected direct United States involvement in European security and insisted only on a multilateral proclamation, Briand felt compelled to seek an alternate arrangement for French safety through the isolationist European federation in a rapprochement with Germany.

111 *Le Plan Briand d'Union fédérale européenne,* 46–47. In preparation for the Second Paneuropa Congress that was to meet on May 17, 1930, in Berlin, Coudenhove published his own private proposal for a Paneuropäische Pact; see Posselt, "Die deutsch-französischen Beziehungen," in *Le Plan Briand d'Union fédérale européenne,* 45–46.

112 Ferenčuhová, "L'accueil du Plan Briand dans les milieu politiques tchèques et slovaques," *Le Plan Briand d'Union fédérale européenne,* 200.

113 Bernhard Büllow (1885–1936), state secretary in the Foreign Ministry (1930–33), recommended adopting a reserved attitude toward the Congress, noting that Coudenhove in the last years increasingly supported French interests. See Posselt, "Die deutsch-französischen Beziehungen," in *Le Plan Briand d'Union fédérale européenne,* 47.

At the same time, the new scheme in his mind acquired an anti-American tinge. Europe would coalesce around its own economic interests against the United States and its high tariffs. Paradoxically, the German Foreign Ministry was apprehensive about being drawn into an anti-American position through a European front or the League; American assistance was seen as valuable to Germany in confronting the French system of alliances.[114] Briand was unaware of the German attitude until June 1929, when the German Chancellor Stresemann pointed out to him in Madrid that Germany could not afford to antagonize the Americans; it could not break its financial solidarity with the United States. Briand was not discouraged, instead, in his speech on September 5, 1929, and in the memorandum of May 17, 1930, he left out any references to America.[115] This Euro-centric aspect of Briand's initiative evidently explains Masaryk's evasiveness in answering Ludwig's question about the French statesman's projected European Union.[116]

The Twilight Years, 1933–1934

Even in the last period of his active intellectual life in 1933–1934, Masaryk continued to expect the arrival of a united world based on humanitarian and democratic principles, despite the rise of totalitarian powers in Europe and Asia. He retained his convictions about the power of democratic politics and the seminal role of the League of Nations.

A federated world

In fact, Masaryk made some of his most powerful pronouncements about the coming of a federated world around this time. In a statement for the American press in July 1932, within a broad discussion of Czechoslovak and European affairs, Masaryk spoke of the political organization of the world. He traced a series of misguided attempts at political unification, proceeding in the West from the ancient Roman Empire to the medieval Holy Roman one, which, in turn, had its heirs in Germany and Austria-

---

114 Bariéty, "Aristide Briand: les raisons d'un oubli," 10–11.
115 Ibid., 11–12.
116 Ludwig, *Defender of Democracy: Masaryk of Czechoslovakia*, 249–50.

Hungary. In the East, the Byzantine part of the Roman Empire found its continuity in Russia. The imperial idea, with its centralism and absolutism, was destroyed in Europe in World War I so that the old structure was replaced by a universal federation of states and nations (Masaryk presumably had, again, in mind an idealized view of the League of Nations). Masaryk welcomed this post-war principle of federation, which brought into harmony the interests of all nations and states – political, economic, and cultural – along with the principles of freedom and democracy, which rejected the old regimes and the system of aristocratic superordination. What the Mediterranean had meant for the concentration of the ancient world, the Atlantic had already assumed in the modern world after the United States had come to the rescue of Europe in World War I. In what may be considered an uncanny anticipation of the future rise of the BRICS nations, Masaryk added: "and even the Atlantic might become replaced by the Pacific as the focus of world civilization."[117] A federalization, inter-nationality (*mezinárodnost*) in all regions was stimulated by the multiplication of smaller states not only in Europe, but also in Asia (especially Russian Asia).[118]

As to the organizational arrangement of the future world, Masaryk remained convinced that a federal (not a unitary) constitutional system was essential. Observation of world politics had persuaded him that the world could not be governed by a single center. Its multitudinous forms required a degree of autonomy among the uniting countries. Democracy in interstate relations was just as important as in intra-state ones.[119] He did not advocate speed or compulsion. Having probably in mind the United States' federalism, Masaryk maintained that each state would have a large sphere of autonomy. Mutual economic and political agreements or treaties would organize political and economic activities. Perhaps a directorium would be created, such as existed on the federal level in Switzerland.[120] Masaryk

---

117 "Poválečné problémy Československa," dated July 9, 1932, in Masaryk, *Cesta demokracie IV*, 292. Masaryk had, in fact, some first-hand knowledge of the Pacific region, having stayed in Japan and crossed the Pacific from Japan to the western coast of the United States in the summer of 1918.

118 "President Masaryk o Německu," *Vossische Zeitung*, January 22, 1933, in Masaryk, *Cesta demokracie IV*, 335.

119 "O vojenské službě a militním systému," interview on December 17, 1932, printed originally in *Vossische Zeitung*, January 29, 1933, in Masaryk, *Cesta demokracie IV*, 337–38.

120 "Prezident Masaryk o věcech evropských a o sobě," *Lidové noviny*, March 19, 1933, in Masaryk, *Cesta demokracie IV*, 344–45.

noted that paradoxically even the war alliances of 1914–1918 advanced the work of rapprochement since "the world was organized in two camps; two great Internationals confronted each other." The need for cooperation in war had cultivated common interests.[121]

During his twilight years, Masaryk had not lost any of his belief in democracy as the road to a unified world. On the negative side, democracy removed all aristocratism, an artificial inequality among human beings, which led to strife in education, religion, and social relations.[122] On the positive side, democracy fostered morality, akin to the Christian precept of "Love thy neighbor." In democracy, personal morality projected itself into the social and political arenas. Conversely, a social and political conviction would also express itself in personal moral behavior. [123] Moreover, Masaryk saw no distinction between personal morality and the moral principles governing domestic and international politics; once these principles were applied, nations would live in peace.[124] Hence in his critique of Hitler's *Mein Kampf*, in March 1933 – looking at the reversal of this relationship – he pointed out that the Führer's proclaimed brutality in external relations would necessarily lead to a brutality in domestic relations as well.[125] Masaryk noted the important role that the schools and the press had in teaching democratic ideals.[126] Ultimately, in his conversations with Čapek, he raised the realization of democracy into the eschatological realm, and reaffirming his attachment to the ontic principle of love, he declared: "True democracy, based on the love and respect for one's neighbor and for all neighbors, is a realization of the divine order on earth."[127]

---

121 "Prezident Masaryk o výchově," *Lidové noviny*, September 6, 1933, in Masaryk, *Cesta demokracie IV*, 371.

122 Ibid.

123 "Na záchranu dětí," *Lidové noviny*, January 28, 1934, in Masaryk, *Cesta demokracie IV*, 397; "Rozhovor prezidenta s novinářkou Betty Rossovou," June 21, 1933, in Masaryk, *Cesta demokracie IV*, 485.

124 "Rozhovor prezidenta s novinářkou Betty Rossovou," in Masaryk, *Cesta demokracie IV*, 485; Masaryk's contribution, dated January 11, 1930, for *Pax mundi:livre d'or de la paix* (Geneva: Société Pax unis, 1932). See Masaryk, *Cesta demokracie IV*, 123.

125 Tomáš G. Masaryk, "Masarykova recenze Hitlerovy knihy *Mein Kampf*," dated April 18, 1933, in Masaryk, *Cesta demokracie* IV, 351.

126 "Eidický princip u T.G. Masaryka," *Národní osvobození*, May 12, 1934, in Masaryk, *Cesta demokracie IV*, 406. "Rozhovor prezidenta s novinářkou Betty Rossovou," in Masaryk, *Cesta demokracie IV*, 485.

127 Čapek, *Hovory s T.G. Masarykem*, 335.

The League of Nations

Masaryk never abandoned his belief in the destiny of the League of Nations as the catalyst for the unification of the world. In early 1933, he stated that the League signified a new stage in the realization of politically organized peace and friendship among nations.[128] The international organization was still in the early years of its existence; therefore, it was not surprising that it encountered problems.[129] It was above all a place for representatives of all nations to meet and get to know each other. Its lessons were learned in war; from cooperation in combat there sprang cooperation for peace.[130] In his conversations with Ludwig, Masaryk likewise expressed his support for the League as an instrument for humanity's progress.[131] Masaryk's belief in the League's credibility remained unshaken even after Germany's withdrawal from the international organization on October 23, 1933. Shortly before then, on August 25, he had argued that the League of Nations should make up for German misdeeds, and in particular should organize help for the Jewish people, who were deprived of civil rights and lost the possibility of earning a living in Nazi Germany.[132] In December 1933, he reemphasized the role of the League as the guardian of the post-War world and of the peace treaties.[133] As late as May 24, 1934, Masaryk maintained his confidence in the League, despite the current crises.[134]

As for assisting the League in its work of the federalization of Europe and the world, Masaryk continued to present the Little Entente as an exemplary instrument in helping to implement this great task.[135] In August 1933, Masaryk was still convinced that the *Anschluss* would not be a desir-

---

128 "Prezidentův příspěvek do alba pařížské společnosti *Les Amitié Internationales*," January 25, 1933, in Masaryk, *Cesta demokracie* IV, 340.

129 "Democracy lives" *New York Times Magazine*, November 12, 1933, based on interview of August 22, 1933, in Masaryk, *Cesta demokracie IV*, 387.

130 "Demokracie neselhala," published as "There will be no New War," *Morning Post* (London) October 9, 1933, in Masaryk, *Cesta demokracie IV*, 383.

131 Ludwig, *Defender of Democracy: Masaryk of Czechoslovakia*, 249.

132 "Keine interne Frage Deutschlands," *Prager Abendzeitung*, August 25, 1933, in Masaryk, *Cesta demokracie IV*, 368

133 "Prezidentovo vánoční poselství," *Národní osvobození*, December 19, 1933, in Masaryk, *Cesta demokracie IV*, 393.

134 "Rozhovor s panem prezidentem Masarykem," May 24, 1934, talk with American journalist K. Werzos, in Masaryk, *Cesta demokracie IV*, 421. The crises apparently referred to the recent problems of the Disarmament Conference and the World Economic Conference.

135 "Prezident Masaryk o vývoji demokracie," first published in *Lidové noviny*, June 20, 1933, in Masaryk, *Cesta demokracie IV*, 359.

able solution for Austria with its centuries-old tradition of distinct identity. As a more plausible solution, he suggested that Austria might join
in a system of commercial agreements among independent states, mod-
eled after the Little Entente.[136] As late as June 6, and again on October
24, 1935, when receiving respectively the French and the Yugoslav ambas-
sadors, Masaryk stressed the forward-looking harmony between the Little Entente and the principles of the League of Nations.[137]

The Four-Power Pact

In a case of misplaced optimism, Masaryk welcomed the Four Power Pact
between Britain, France, Italy, and Germany, concluded on July 15, 1933.
When the pact was under preparation, Masaryk greeted the Treaty ex-
pecting that the agreement of the four large countries would, together
with the Little Entente, form an off-shoot of the League of Nations. Masaryk also anticipated that France would play the dominant role among
the treaty partners.[138] Despite his uneasiness that it might sharpen the issue of small versus great nations,[139] Masaryk felt that the Pact would become a means of unifying Europe, not an instrument of aggrandizement
by particular signatories.[140] Actually, the Four-Power Pact was inspired in
March 1933 by Mussolini, who aimed at replacing the influence of small
countries in the League with a bloc of major powers. In practice the Four-
Power Pact proved moribund from the start.[141]

Curiously, however, this still-born entity would acquire a quasi-life five
years later on September 29, 1938 to promulgate the Munich Agreement,
which – concluded by the same four powers – would strip Czechoslovakia
of much of its territory in favor of Hitler's domain. Masaryk, of course,

136 "Democracy lives" *New York Times Magazine*, November 12, 1933, based on interview of August 22, 1933, in Masaryk, *Cesta demokracie IV*, 387.
137 "Nový francouzský vyslanec P. E. Naggiar přijat panem prezidentem," *Pražské noviny*, June 6, 1935, in Masaryk, *Cesta demokracie IV*, 445; "Nástupní audience nového jugoslávského vyslance," *Národní osvobození*, October 24, 1935, in Masaryk, *Cesta demokracie IV*, 450. It is, however, likely that be-cause of his poor health, these two statements were not actually written by Masaryk himself.
138 "Prezident Masaryk o vývoji demokracie," first published in *Lidové noviny*, June 20, 1933, in Masaryk, *Cesta demokracie IV*, 359.
139 "Prezident Masaryk o výchově," *Lidové noviny*, September 6, 1933, in Masaryk, *Cesta demokracie IV*, 371.
140 "Democracy lives" *New York Times Magazine*, November 12, 1933, based on interview of August 22, 1933, in Masaryk, *Cesta demokracie IV*, 387.
141 Raymond J. Sontag, *A Broken World, 1919–1939* (New York: Harper & Row, 1971), 247–49.

had not had the benefit of the twenty-first century's hindsight on the denouement of the 1930s. In any case (after three years of virtual incapacity since mid-1934[142]), he was not alive to witness the event in Munich, having passed on September 14, 1937 into – as he had firmly believed that he would – posthumous immortality.

Critique of Masaryk's Globalism

As a coda, it needs to be pointed out that Masaryk's globalism did not escape criticism at home either during his lifetime or subsequently. Masaryk was chastised, for instance, in 1926 by the eminent Czech scholar and public intellectual, Arne Novák, for looking to all-human humanitarian motives (not those of national liberation) in both *Česká otázka* [Czech Question] and *Světová revoluce* [World Revolution]. Masaryk envisioned the soldiers of all nations fighting for abstract ideals of democracy and humanity, while actually, according to Novák, they struggled and died for tangible national interests.[143] More recently, at an emblematic conference on Masaryk's idea of democracy and contemporary Europeanism [*T. G. Masaryk, Idea demokracie a současné evropanství*] in the millennial year 2000, Václav Klaus (later President of Czech Republic, 2003–2013) stated accusingly: "Masaryk [advanced] normatively construed European and global visions and concepts, and these were supported ... by popular and influential journalists and writers... As a result, national interests remained virtually unguarded...."[144]

During his lifetime, in 1924, Masaryk had to defend himself from the accusations of right-wingers, especially in the National Democratic Party, that by positing humanity as a goal, he was neglecting the nations. He pointed out that in his *New Europe* he had explicitly stated that human-

---

142 As pointed out earlier, a stroke on August 31, 1934, impaired Masaryk's physical and mental faculties, although he continued formally as president until his abdication on December 14, 1935. See Soubigou, *Thomas Masaryk*, 438–39; Dagmar Hájková, "Constructing National Unity: Commemorations of Tomáš Masaryk's Death," *Střed* 1 (2012), 33–34.

143 Arne Novák, "Světová revoluce," *Lumír* 53 (1926), in Novák, *Nosiči pochodní; kniha české tradice* (Prague: Literární odbor Umělecké besedy a Kruh českých spisovatelů, 1928), 216–17. A shift occurs as a result of World War I in attributing the humanitarian aspects of the victorious ideology to French Enlightenment rather than to Herder; see ibid., 222–23.

144 Václav Klaus, "Projev předsedy Poslanecké sněmovny Parlamentu ČR," in *T. G. Masaryk, idea demokracie a současné evropanství*, ed. Emil Voráček, Sborník mezinárodní vědecké konference Praha, 2. - 4. března 2000, 2 vols. (Prague: Filosofia, 2001), 1: 17–18.

ity and nationality do not exclude each other.[145] The tendency toward inter-nationalism and inter-statism was inherent in world affairs and had always existed to some extent because complete economic and cultural autarky was impossible. Earlier historical examples were the Roman Empire with its *ius gentium*, and the attempt of the Roman church to unite Europe and the world religiously.

Concerning specifically the Czech side, he could again turn in 1933 to his favorite thesis (see Chapter 9) that, throughout history, Czech politics always gravitated toward internationalism. Among the most inspiring examples, was the initiative of George of Poděbrady, who negotiated in the fifteenth century with the French King for a league of Christian sovereigns for the preservation of peace. As another example, the Unity of Brethren spread all over the world and preached the ideal of international harmony. In addition, the Unity's famous Bishop, Jan Komenský, advocated the idea of the internationally-oriented education of peaceful citizens, and he tried to apply this pedagogy worldwide – in Hungary, Poland, Germany, England, and even among American Indians.[146]

Looking at the other side of the equation, Masaryk pointed out that the Czech nation owed its independence and statehood to the international community, represented by the Entente.[147] Moreover, Masaryk recalled that the Czechoslovak independence was, in fact, born on the soil of the United States, the oldest democracy in the world, and its paragons were the great figures of American history as well as the noble ideas of President Wilson.[148] Therefore, the politics of the Czech nation and the Czechoslovak republic had to be global [*světová*].[149] Finally, Masaryk illustrated the harmony between local and global values with the character of Bedřich Smetana's music, which was perfectly national, and – because of that – was also truly international and thus accepted worldwide.[150]

---

145 "Filozofie v politice," *Přítomnost*, February 28, 1924, in Masaryk, *Cesta demokracie III*, 18. Masaryk responded to the charges voiced in František Mareš, *Otázky filozofické, národní a sociální v politice* (Plzeň: Česká národní demokracie, 1923).
146 "Prezidentův příspěvek do alba pařížské společnosti *Les Amitié Internationales*," in Masaryk, *Cesta demokracie* IV, 340.
147 Tomáš G. Masaryk, *Cesta demokracie* I, Spisy 33 (Prague: Masarykův ústav AV ČR), 230.
148 "Nástupní audience amerického vyslance," September 8, 1933, in Masaryk, *Cesta demokracie IV*, 484.
149 Politika národa musí být světovou," *Národní osvobození*, August 15, 1933, in Masaryk, *Cesta demokracie IV*, 365.
150 "T. G. Masaryk o Smetanovi," *Lidové noviny*, May 10, 1934, in Masaryk, *Cesta demokracie IV*, 416.

III
Legacy

Chapter 11

Masaryk's Legacy:
The Criticism of Jan Patočka
and the Globalism of Václav Havel

In tracing the legacy of Masaryk's vision of the united democratic world, one first encounters a drastic setback that followed the optimism engendered by the outcome of World War I and symbolized by the establishment of the League of Nations. The discouragement emanated from the rise of totalitarian regimes, which led to the outbreak of World War II and the ensuing division of the world into two hostile camps during the Cold War from 1948 to 1989. From the viewpoint of this disheartening situation an especially illuminating critique of Masaryk's philosophy and politics was offered by Jan Patočka (1907–1977), probably the most prominent twentieth-century Czech philosopher.

Patočka was educated in the era of Masaryk's Czechoslovakia and later championed the principles of democracy and human rights under the Czechoslovak Communist regime, which was established by the coup d'état of February 1948 and later reaffirmed after the demise of the liberal interlude of the Prague Spring (1967–1969). In the latter period of so-called Normalization, he served as a spokesman for the dissident group Charter 77, and eventually succumbed to police persecution, dying after a lengthy interrogation in 1977. The dramatic denouement of his intellectual life and political activism endowed his views with an aura of special significance. Prior to the Prague Spring, Patočka's attitude toward the teaching of Masaryk, was distinctly critical, as he reacted to Masaryk's views in philosophy, theology, politics, and history. While much of the criticism stemmed from Patočka's perception of Masaryk's unwarranted political and historical optimism, there were also major differences in their philosophical starting points, stemming from Patočka's devotion to Edmund Husserl, and Masaryk's to Franz Brentano and Paul A. de Lagarde.

The Interlude of People's Democracy, 1945–1948

Epistemology: perception of the real world

Patočka disagreed with Masaryk on the basic issue of learning to know the external world. Where Masaryk followed Plato and considered sense perceptions as simply real without any additional philosophical speculation, Patočka, to the contrary, followed Edmund Husserl's phenomenology that regarded sense perceptions as mere phenomena, which needed validation through the process of subjective transcendence.[1] Masaryk, in turn, resolutely opposed both phenomenalism and subjectivism. Auguste Comte's phenomenalist epistemology was one of the principal reasons for Masaryk's parting of the ways with the French philosopher. As we saw, he condemned even more sharply subjectivism in epistemology on ethical grounds, especially in German philosophical Idealism, as a root of evil in German traditional philosophy and politics.

While Patočka considered rather outdated Masaryk's acceptance of the normally perceived world as real, he also condemned Masaryk's rejection of the subjective channel to the discovery of reality. He claimed that Masaryk erroneously advanced the misconception of "Titanism" as a megalomania produced by the German Idealist philosophy, which led to the intellectual crisis of modern humanity. Moreover, Masaryk wrongly claimed that "the focus on the self" produced an intellectual and moral isolation, which drove the affected individual to a self-destruction or to an external destruction, in other words, to suicide or murder.[2]

---

1   Erazim Kohák, ed., *Jan Patočka: Philosophy and Selected Writings* (Chicago: University of Chicago, 1989), 13.
2   Jan Patočka, "Pokus o českou národní filosofii a jeho nezdar (1946)," idem, Sebrané spisy 12 (Prague: Oikoymenh, 2006), 365; Jan Patočka, "Kolem Masarykovy filosofie náboženství (1946)," idem, Sebrané spisy 12 (Prague: 2006), 402 n416.

Aside from the question of subjectivism in the perception of the real world, the other major epistemological issue that Patočka criticized was Masaryk's concept of a comprehensive science that would provide an integrating umbrella for all the particular sciences. Masaryk proposed the discipline of "concrete logic" as the form of this integrating universal science. According to Patočka, Masaryk (following Comte) thus proposed a futile search for an a priori logical system of sciences that were still in the process of development.

Metaphysics: free will and providence

In his critique of Masaryk's metaphysics, Patočka focused on the relationship between determinism and free will. He pointed out that Masaryk held contradictory beliefs, on one hand, in man's free will, and, on the other, in a teleological purpose, which governed both in history and in the world. Patočka's critics, in turn, have viewed his strictures of Masaryk's metaphysics as excessively pedantic. For instance, Erazim Kohák has maintained that he inappropriately attempts to fit Masaryk's thought into the rigid frame of a strict logic and unambiguous definitions, instead of understanding Masaryk's propositions as humanistic (not as scientific) statements from the viewpoint of informal logic (or *fuzzy logic*).[3] A more probing view of Patočka's objection to Masaryk's unreconciled dichotomy might point to the fact that Patočka did not share Masaryk's Herderian optimism that both nature and history supported the "ideal of humanity."[4]

Theology: theistic God and European "Theoria"

Patočka sided with his teacher Husserl against Masaryk on the issue of the intellectual and moral crisis that afflicted the contemporary, modern western man. Both Masaryk and Husserl saw the principal cause of this phenomenon in the lack of religious belief. Masaryk, however, identified the key symptom of the crisis in the spread of suicides, Husserl in a decline of

---

3   Erazim Kohák, "Zdar a nezdar 'národní' filosofie: Patočka a Masaryk," *Filosofický časopis*, 55 (2007), 446.
4   Kohák, ed., *Jan Patočka: Philosophy and Selected Writings*, 40–41.

the philosophy that accompanied the decline of religion.[5] Masaryk advocated a solution of the predicament by the acceptance of a rational theism with a personal God and immortality of the human soul. Husserl expected a solution from the renewal of Europeanism (*evropanství*) as a renewal of rationality under the label of "Theoria."

Masaryk's solution was unacceptable to Patočka. He resolutely rejected Masaryk's idea of God, which for him was essentially derived from medieval scholasticism.[6] Specifically, he doubted that Christianity offered a plausible cure for suicides.[7] Not surprisingly, Patočka found Husserl's solution for the crisis of the modern man more palatable.

Politics: the nature of democracy

Patočka, like Masaryk, thought of philosophy as having a practical purpose to serve as a guide to politics. In the language of phenomenology, politics provided a path to the essence of authentic life, in other words, to the natural world. During the interlude of People's Democracy (1945–1948), Patočka positively assessed Masaryk's concept of politics in two main respects. First, democracy as an embodiment of the humanitarian outlook had a deep ethical core. Second, Masaryk's concept of democracy included a warning against the manifestations of human hubris that raised its ugly head whenever man succumbed to self-satisfaction and selfishness.[8]

In tracing the roots of these ethical principles, Patočka located the quintessence of Masaryk's democratic ethics – rather imaginatively – in American Puritanism. Where Puritanism imposed inner discipline on man, it became possible to have political freedom. Members of society would not misuse this freedom to oppress each other, but instead they would seek to protect the freedom of every individual.[9]

5   Jan Patočka, "Masarykovo a Husserlovo pojetí duševní krise lidstva, 1936," idem, *Češi I*, Sebrané spisy 12 (Prague: Oikoymenh, 2006), 25.

6   Patočka, "Masarykovo a Husserlovo pojetí duševní krise lidstva, 1936," 31–32. Karel Čapek, *Hovory s T. G. Masarykem*, Spisy 20 (Prague: Československý spisovatel, 1990), vol. 3, 24 points.

7   Patočka, "Kolem Masarykovy filosofie náboženství (1946)," idem, Sebrané spisy 12 (Prague: Oikoymenh, 2006), 408.

8   Patočka, "Masaryk a naše dnešní otázky 1946," in Sebrané spisy 12 (Prague: Oikoymenh, 2006), 89, 91.

9   Patočka, "Pokus o českou národní filosofii a jeho nezdar (1946)," idem, Sebrané spisy 12 (Prague: 2006), 349, 355.

Historiography

In Patočka's opinion, Masaryk went on to graft the democratic ideal, derived from the American experience, onto the mentality of the Czech National Awakening, improperly claiming that this democratic mentality was an intellectual heritage from the Bohemian Reformation. Next, according to Patočka, Masaryk went on to link the allegedly autochthonous Czech democracy with American democracy from which, according to Patočka's assertion, Masaryk —in a case of circular reasoning – had derived (perhaps unwittingly) the historically-rooted concept of Czech democracy, in the first place.[10]

Next Patočka challenged Masaryk's meta-historical interpretation of the First World War. For Masaryk, the war was a contest between theocracy and democracy. Democracy replaced theocracy in all fields of life. In particular, the entry of the United States into the War transformed the conflict into a struggle for democracy. Not surprisingly, the illusion of a historically based Czech democracy fitted perfectly into this historical scheme.[11] Actually history proved Masaryk's grand interpretation of World War I wrong. In less than twenty years, the world democracy found itself in a great crisis. In Patočka's eyes, Masaryk was no more successful in his attempt to develop a national philosophy of Czech history and to make it an integral part of a global historical movement.[12] The very idea of such a philosophy had been an anachronism. In actuality, a national history tended to be a discontinuous process.

What particularly touched a raw nerve in Patočka was Masaryk's theory of the interplay between subjectivism (Idealism) and objectivism (Realism) in history, with specifically the philosophical, subjectivism, playing the role of villain.[13] As we saw, for Patočka, to the contrary, philosophical subjectivism (in line with Husserl) was the path whereby the philosopher could reach the real world and the authentic Being.

---

10 Ibid., 355.
11 Ibid., 349, 355.
12 Josef Zumr, "Patočka a Masaryk," *Filosofický časopis*, 39 (1991), 453.
13 Patočka, "Kolem Masarykovy filosofie náboženství (1946)," 395, 406–7.

The Effect of the Prague Spring

The Prague Spring of 1968 and its aftermath affected Patočka's thought significantly.[14] He especially called attention to the study of Masaryk's concept of the democratic character of Czech and Slovak politics, which was manifest by Czechoslovakia's political regime that was distinct from those of its Central European neighbors.[15]

Against his previously harsh judgments of Masaryk's philosophy of Czech history, Patočka softened his attitude in the 1970s. According to him, in criticizing Masaryk's historical interpretation, Pekař and his colleagues failed to realize that Masaryk's idea of Czech history was his personal ideal which was created not for the past, but for the future. Pekař and his allies had nothing to offer for the future, all he could do was just to research the past.[16]

Perhaps the most remarkable shift from the mid-1940s to the mid-1970s in Patočka's views on Masaryk's political theory and historiography was on the relationship between Anglophone Puritanism and the Bohemian Reformation in the rise of the Czech tradition of democracy. In 1974, Patočka was ready to recognize that there had existed a similarity between the ethos of Puritanism and that of the Unity of Brethren.[17] It is relevant to speculate that Patočka's latter-day emphasis on the kinship between American Puritanism and the teaching of the Unity of Brethren owed much to his immersion into the study of John A. Comenius during the mid-1950s.[18] After all, the Puritans' interest in the Brethren had led to the story, possibly apocryphal, that the presidency of Harvard College in New England's Massachusetts was offered to Comenius in the 1640s.[19]

---

14 Kohák, *Patočka: Philosophy and Selected Writings*, 106–7.
15 Jan Patočka, "O potřebě obnovit činnost Ústavu T. G. Masaryka," 1968, in his *Češi II*, Sebrané spisy 13 (Prague: Oikoymenh, 2006), 251.
16 Patočka, "Vzpomínka a zamyšlení o Rádlovi a Masarykovi," 1974, in his *Češi II*, Sebrané spisy 13 (Prague: Oikoymenh, 2006), 327; Jan Patočka, "České myšlení v meziválečném období (Koncept přednášky)," [1974] in his *Češi II*, Sebrané spisy 13 (Prague: Oikoymenh, 2006), 348, 368.
17 Patočka, "České myšlení v meziválečném období (Koncept přednášky)," [1974], 351–52, 379–80.
18 While he was barred from university teaching, see Patočka, *Komeniologické studie I*, Sebrané spisy 9 (Prague: Oikoymenh, 1997), 7.
19 Samuel E. Morison, *The Founding of Harvard College* (Cambridge, MA: Harvard University Press, 1935), 243–45. On the ties between the Brethren and American Puritans, see also Zdeněk V. David, *Finding the Middle Way: The Utraquists Liberal Challenge to Rome and Luther* (Washington, D.C. and Baltimore, 2003), 367.

Post-1970 Criticism

Despite the adoption of a more benign attitude toward Masaryk's teaching, during the Prague Spring, Patočka maintained a markedly critical attitude, especially upon the onset of the Communist "normalization." This critique ranged widely across Masaryk's philosophy, political theory (national state and theocracy), historiography (Nietzschean re-interpretation) and epistemology (asubjective phenomenology).

Philosophy

Even in the 1970s Patočka's general assessment of Masaryk as a philosopher remained distinctly low. He appeared skeptical about the overall value of Masaryk's philosophy, asserting that he had not introduced even a single new speculative idea or principle. Surprisingly, he called Masaryk basically a metaphysician.[20] He does so in rebutting those who claimed that Masaryk adhered to existentialism, and presents Masaryk as a metaphysician, presumably for his adherence to ontic realism, an essentialist (that is, metaphysical) position which was inconsistent with the existentialist outlook.[21] Patočka also called attention to Franz Brentano's assertion that Masaryk was mostly interested in the practical effect of philosophical doctrines and in their political consequences, but not in the doctrines themselves. Specifically, this led Masaryk to the study of Marxism and its impact on Russian politics.[22]

Patočka was critical of Masaryk's *Sociální otázka* (The Social Question), while giving Masaryk credit that he interpreted Marxism as a philosophy, and endorsing Masaryk's stress that socialism could not exist without democracy. At the same time, he asserted that Masaryk identified Marx's teaching excessively with that of Engels, while neglecting the specificity of Marx's views.[23]

---

20   Patočka, "České myšlení v meziválečném údobí (Záznam přednášky)," [1974] in his *Češi II*, Sebrané spisy 13 (Prague: Oikoymenh, 2006), 353, 355.
21   Patočka, "Vzpomínka a zamyšlení o Rádlovi a Masarykovi," [1974] in his *Češi II*, Sebrané spisy 13 (Prague: Oikoymenh, 2006), 332. See also Milan Machovec, *Tomáš G. Masaryk* (Prague: Melantrich, 1968), 50; Milan Machovec, *Tomáš G. Masaryk* (Prague: Riopress, 2000), 39–40.
22   Patočka, "České myšlení v meziválečném údobí (Záznam přednášky)," [1974], 358.
23   Patočka, "O potřebě obnovit činnost Ústavu T. G. Masaryka," [1968], 249; Patočka, "České myšlení v meziválečném údobí (Záznam přednášky)," [1974], 358, 378.

Politics: the multinational state

The failure of the intellectual liberation and of the democratic optimism, engendered by the Prague Spring, led Patočka to express serious concern with the multinational character of Czechoslovakia, which was apparently sharpened by the assertion of Slovak nationalism in the Prague Spring and its aftermath. Masaryk, according to him, erred in basing the idea of the Czechoslovak state on the concept of the nation as defined by Herder and Palacký, such a concept was untenable in a multinational country which could exist only as a civic state, not a national one. [24] Especially in view of the large German population Patočka maintained that Czechoslovakia should have become a civic state.[25] The failure to achieve an agreement among equal national components violated Masaryk's cherished principle of following "Jesus not Caesar," and ultimately Czechoslovakia as a national state could be considered a "lie/falsehood" (lež).[26]

On the other hand, Patočka admitted at that time that Masaryk's blaming of German subjectivism for the war in *Světová revoluce* (The World Revolution) had a deep connection with his early views that he had expressed starting with his book on Suicide (*Sebevražda*) in 1881. Although this point of view turned out to be a very effective propaganda for the Allied cause, in the case of Masaryk the invective was not just an ad hoc propagandistic tool, but a result of previous philosophical and sociological reflection.[27]

Nevertheless, even in the 1970s, Patočka resumed his criticism Masaryk's view of World War I as a world revolution. He was particularly dubious about Masaryk's concept of theocracy, applied to the quasi-absolutistic regimes of the Austrian, German and Russian empires. According to him, the derivation of governing power from divine grace had lost its theological meaning and had become an empty formula by the start of the twentieth century. Above all, Patočka scored Masaryk's optimism about the final victory of democracy in the world in 1918.[28] Returning to his critique of Masaryk's Czechoslovakia as a national state, Patočka rath-

---

24 Patočka, "Vzpomínka a zamyšlení o Rádlovi a Masarykovi," 328.
25 Patočka, "České myšlení v meziválečném údobí (Záznam přednášky)," [1974], 366.
26 Ibid., 380, 381.
27 Ibid., 352–53.
28 Jan Patočka, "Co jsou Češi?" [-1973] in his *Češi II*, Sebrané spisy 13 (Prague: Oikoymenh, 2006), 318–19.

er startlingly maintains that Czechoslovakia, as a civic democracy, might have withstood the challenge of Munich, and even if it succumbed, the country would have gathered moral credit for the future as a model of a multinational state.[29]

Historiography: Nietzschean interpretation

The reference to Munich, deploring the lack of military resistance to Germany in 1938, signaled Patočka's latter-day Nietzschean turn[30] that he developed with respect to Czech history in a series of letters to his German friend, Hildegard Ballauff, in the early 1970s .[31] In outlining his fresh concept of Czech historical destiny in his letters "What are the Czechs?" Patočka expressed regret that unlike the Germans, the Poles, and the Magyars, the Czechs lacked a gentry class and consequently strong, self-confident leadership.[32]

As Erazim Kohák points out, Patočka then in his historical interpretation shifted "from Masaryk's ideal of nurturing human growth to Nietzschean-like assertion of greatness."[33] The Czech greatness lay neither in the Bohemian Reformation nor in the humanistic philosophy of the Czech national awakening, but in the thrusts to empire building under the medieval rulers, King Přemysl Otakar II (1253–1278) and Emperor/ King Charles IV (1346–1372).[34] The Bohemian Reformation, in fact, led to a wasteful scattering of national assets and thus undermined the greatness of the proper Czech political design.[35] As for the National Awakening, it involved a rise of hitherto obscure plebian classes that retained Czech language, but lacked any aspiration to greatness. It was a community of "liberated lackeys" (osvobozených sluhů).[36]

---

29 Ibid., 321.
30 Erazim Kohák, "Patočka: A Philosophical Biography," in idem, ed., *Patočka: Philosophy and Selected Writings* (Chicago: University of Chicago, 1989), 111–12.
31 Kohák identifies Hildegard Ballauff as the widow of Patočka's German colleague and a friend; Kohák, "Patočka: A Philosophical Biography," 111. Miloslava Holubová in her memoirs touching on Patočka, *Necestou cestou* (Prague: Torst, 1998), 362, 365, 368, states that Hildegard, whom she identifies as "paní B," eventually returned to her husband after the end of her friendship with the Czech philosopher.
32 Patočka , "Co jsou Češi?" [-1973], 13, 259
33 Kohák, "Patočka: A Philosophical Biography," 111–12.
34 Patočka, "Co jsou Češi?" [-1973], 269–72.
35 Ibid., 275–76.
36 Ibid., 303; Kohák, "Patočka: A Philosophical Biography," 111–12.

As for Masaryk himself, his own greatness – according to Patočka's reinterpretation – was not in his humanistic philosophy, but in his aspiration to a Nietzschean like aristocratic daring expressed in his foundation of a state.[37] Patočka extolled Masaryk's courage in his campaign against the superstition of ritual murder, which aroused deep public hostility, causing him to abandon establishment of his own political party and was disrupting his university lectures.[38] Finally, Masaryk appeared as a veritable Nietzschean superman in Patočka's laudatory assessment of him, as he emerged from World War I: "Masaryk was brave, decisive, after deep consideration a man acting with consistency and according to principles." He was highly exceptional within the constrained and limiting Czech conditions.[39]

Epistemology: a subjective phenomenology

Originally, Patočka had advocated Husserl's phenomenalist subjectivism which he had embraced in opposition to Masaryk's realist objectivism. After the failure of the Prague Spring by 1970, Patočka intensified his critique of the subjectivism of Husserl's phenomenology.[40] According to Patočka, Husserl could not free himself from the grasp of the phenomena as something immanent even in transcendence. Hence the identity of what is manifested in the phenomena remained hidden. [41] In this dilemma, Patočka turned to Martin Heidegger for help, according to whom the phenomenon was not constituted subjectively, but the subjective self could discover its potential through an exploration of the phenomena.[42] Hence Patočka wished to determine the phenomenological field, which provided the setting for the manifestation of being that emanated from the subjective self. He wished to make transparent the process of the manifesta-

---

37 Kohák, "Patočka: A Philosophical Biography," 111–12.
38 Patočka, "Co jsou Češi?" [-1973], 322. Patočka had previously described Masaryks action against the anti-Jewish superstition in great detail in his study of early 1950s: "Masaryk v boji proti antisemitism," [1950–54], in his *Češi II*, Sebrané spisy 13 (Prague: Oikoymenh, 2006), 33–112.
39 Patočka draws a contrasting non-Nietzschean image of Eduard Beneš, who was "an ambitious, diligent and loquacious average individual." Patočka, "Co jsou Češi?" [-1973], 318.
40 Kohák, "Patočka: A Philosophical Biography," 106–8.
41 I. Šrubař, "Asubjektivní fenomenologie, přirozený svět a humanismus," *Filosofický časopis*, 39 (1991), 407. On the topic, see also Katarzyna Slowiková, "Patočkův projekt revize Husserlovy fenomenologie," *Filosofický časopis,* 55 (2007) , 511–36.
42 Šrubař, "Asubjektivní fenomenologie, přirozený svět a humanismus," 407–8.

tion of being (synonymous with the natural world), whereby it becomes a phenomenon.[43]

Toward the end of his life, however, Patočka execute a sharp turn in epistemology which brought him close to Masaryk's view of one of the two major epistemological channels through which to reach the ultimate reality.[44] According to Patočka's latter-day view, the way to attain to ontic reality need not lead through the exploration of phenomena in the individual's mind in the tedious process based on asubjective phenomenology. Instead the road led more directly through erotic ecstasy. In his essay, "Husserlova idea evropské racionality," (1974), Patočka came to maintain that "the dream of happiness" was a way to reach the real world through love. In the erotic rapture a human being forgot his own self in the feeling of acceptance by another being, which aroused and nourished that ecstatic yearning.[45]

Critical Scrutiny and Restoration

Despite Patočka's at times sharp criticism of Masaryk's philosophy, in the final analysis what bound them together was stronger than what separated them. Patočka had thorough knowledge of the philosophical work of Thomas Masaryk, and he was fully aware of the intellectual connections among Brentano, Masaryk and Husserl within the framework of the Austrian philosophy.[46] In addition, Erazim Kohák points out that the stress on the influence of Husserl on Patočka tended to obscure the strength of Masaryk's role.[47]

Patočka's severe critique of Masaryk's philosophy of history and its theologically based optimism was largely derived from the contemporary situation of international relations. It was especially after the collapse of the Prague Spring that this critique crescendoed, when all democratic and optimistic perspectives seemed to collapse. The bitterness of disappointment largely accounted for the Nietzschean turn in Patočka's philosophy

43 Ibid., 409.
44 Treated in Chapter 4.
45 Patočka, "Husserlova idea evropské racionality," (1974) *in Péče o duši III,* Sebrané spisy 3 (Prague: Oikoymenh, 2002), 178–79. This view might have been generated by his love affair with the German friend, Hildegard Ballauff, for whom he had written his essays "Co jsou Češi?" On that relationship see note 31 in this chapter.
46 Balázs Mezei, "Patočkovo místo v klasické fenomenologii," in Ivan Chvatík, ed., *Myšlení Jana Patočky očima dnešní fenomenologie.* Prague: Filosofia and Oikoymenh, 2009, 51, 60–61.
47 Kohák, "Patočka: A Philosophical Biography," 10, also 10 n9.

of history. Only the arrival of the Velvet Revolution a dozen years after Patočka's death opened new perspectives for the realization of Masaryk's bright vision of a global victory of democracy, and enabled Václav Havel to resume Masaryk's political legacy.[48]

Consequently, the influence of Masaryk's philosophy on politics did not end with the destruction of the state of Czechoslovakia, which he inspired and which retained a democratic form of government in the interwar period of 1918–1938, while its neighbors in central and eastern Europe adopted authoritarianism, if not totalitarianism.[49] After five decades of totalitarian regimes imposed by the National Socialist Germany and the Communist Soviet Union (relieved only by the two brief respites of "the People's Democracy," 1945–1947, and of the Prague Spring, 1967–1969), Masaryk's political style once again reappeared toward the end of 1989 as the philosophical inspiration of the statehood of Czechoslovakia, and after 1992 that of the Czech Republic due to the leadership of Václav Havel.

Havel on Masaryk: the period of dissent

Havel's intellectual engagement with Masaryk came early in life. In his interviews with the journalist Karel Hvížďala in the mid-1980s, Havel recalled that, already as a ten-year-old, he began reading the works of Masaryk and his followers Karel Čapek and Ferdinand Peroutka in his family's library at home.[50] In a discussion group with his student friends while

48 Jaroslav Opat, *Slovanský přehled,* 3/1990, cited by Zumr, "Patočka a Masaryk," 454.
49 On democracy in Czechoslovakia, 1918–1938, see R.J.W. Evans: "For years Czechoslovakia, by contrast with the surrounding states, conducted its affairs in a broadly orderly and stable way. It sustained real parliamentary procedures and an open and multinational cultural life," in "Introduction," *Czechoslovakia in a Nationalist and Fascist Europe, 1918–1948,* ed. Mark Cornwall and R.J.W. Evans (New York: Oxford University Press, 2007), 1. See also Josette Baer, "Imagining Membership: The Conception of Europe in the Political Thought of T. G. Masaryk and Václav Havel," *Studies in East European Thought,* 52 (2000), 204–5; Sharon L. Wolchik, "Czech Republic," *Encyclopedia of U. S. Foreign Relations* (New York: Oxford University Press, 1997), 1: 401; Stefan Auer, *Liberal Nationalism in Central Europe* (London; New York: Routledge Curzon, 2004), 107–13. On the Czech side, Eva Broklová has advanced an even more significant claim for modern Czech political culture, as a variant of the American and West European tradition, in contrast to the political cultures prevalent in Central and Eastern Europe, including Germany; see Eva Broklová, *Politická kultura německých aktivistických stran v Československu, 1918–1938* (Prague: Karolinum, 1999); see also the review by Eagle Glassheim in *Kosmas* 16/1 (Fall 2002): 110–11. Recent revisionist literature does little to alter the image of Masaryk's Czechoslovakia; see Andrea Orzoff, *Battle for the Castle: The Myth of Czechoslovakia in Europe, 1914–1948* (New York: Oxford University Press, 2009); Mary Heimann, *Czechoslovakia: The State That Failed* (New Haven: Yale University Press, 2009).
50 Václav Havel, *Dálkový výslech,* [1985–86], in idem, *Spisy,* 8 vols. (Prague: Torst, 1999–2007), 4: 717.

still a teenager, he viewed himself as Masaryk's disciple in the field of ethics, which he sought to combine with a concept of socialism and with a Hegelian pantheism in metaphysics.[51] In the November–December 1953 issue of a typewritten journal of the same group, young Havel published an article, "Hamletova otázka," [Hamlet's Question]. There he discussed Masaryk's famous treatise on suicide and agreed that taking one's life expressed a contempt for all of creation or for the entire universe, an attitude, for which a certain brand of modern philosophy was largely responsible.[52] On a more practical level, later he saw the dissident activities of Charter 77 as an example of Masaryk's "non-political politics" [nepolitická politika]. He used it to express in a semi-metaphoric way the meaning of the dissidents' actions which could not directly enter into real politics as an arena of power, but which undoubtedly had a political effect.[53]

With the Czechoslovak Communist regime showing signs of a final deterioration in the late 1980s, Havel focused on a revival of interest in Masaryk's teaching in Czechoslovakia. In his message for the seventieth anniversary of Czechoslovakia's independence, broadcast by Radio Free Europe in September 1988, Havel deplored the Communist government's suppression of information about the nation's history. As a result, young people knew very little about winning their country's freedom, in particular about Masaryk's enormous work in exile during World War I.[54] Havel proclaimed that the time had come to take Masaryk's teaching seriously once again including, for instance, his exhortation to small deeds toward education and enlightenment in order to overcome the existing apathy engendered by the oppressive Communist regime. In order to propagate Masaryk's ideas once more, Havel appealed for republication of important classics of Czech democracy, such as Masaryk's Světová revoluce [The World Revolution], or Peroutka's Budování státu [The Building of a State].[55]

On his father's admiration for Masaryk, see also John Keane, Václav Havel: A Political Tragedy in Six Acts (London: Bloomesbury, 1999), 36.
51 Václav Havel, "Po roce sochařské práce," August 1953 in idem, Spisy 3: 15.
52 Václav Havel, "Hamletova otázka," in Spisy 3: 36. He had presumably in mind the line of philosophy stemming from Schopenhauer.
53 Václav Havel, "Ztráta paměti," Prague, September 13, 1994, in idem, Spisy 7: 270. See also Keane, Václav Havel: A Political Tragedy in Six Acts, 275–76.
54 Václav Havel, "Pozdrav k 70, výročí vzniku Československa," September 1988, [text intended for a commemorative program by Svobodná Evropa October 27, 1988], in idem, Spisy 4: 1082.
55 Ibid., 4: 1083–84.

After the Velvet Revolution

During the state reconstruction following the Velvet Revolution, Havel tended to cite Masaryk's principles frequently.[56] In the first place, it was the relationship between politics and ethics. In his first major speech after assuming the presidency of Czechoslovakia in January 1990, Havel reminded his listeners that Masaryk grounded politics in morality, and that the renewed Czechoslovak Republic should follow this approach. Politics should spring from a desire to contribute to the benefit of the community and not to misuse or harm the community's interests.[57]

In the second place, Havel emphasized Masaryk's commitment to Truth as the guiding principle of social and political life. Havel did so, when he delivered his major address on Masaryk during the commemoration of the 140th anniversary of Masaryk's birth in Hodonín on March 7, 1990. He referred to John F. Kennedy's book, *Profiles in Courage,* to draw a parallel with Masaryk's taking stands, which he held to be true, even if they ran against public opinion and were almost certain to cause him a loss of popularity. Havel cited two such instances. The first one was Masaryk's challenge to the authenticity of the manuscripts of Zelená Hora and Dvůr Králové [rukopisy zelenohorský a královédvorský], which were considered some of the greatest cultural treasures of the Czech nation. In 1886, Masaryk was convinced that these documents were forgeries, and he joined a campaign to discredit them. He maintained that even a good cause should not be supported by a lie. The second time Masaryk severely challenged public opinion was by arguing in 1899 against the accusation that Leopold Hilsner had committed a Jewish ritual murder. Thus, he met head on a widespread undercurrent of anti-Semitism in Czech society.[58]

In the third place, Havel dwelt on Masaryk's global vision. He emphasized the international character of Masaryk's legacy when he addressed the Council of the Conference on Cooperation and Security in Europe

---

56 According to Whipple: "Havel has cast himself in Masaryk's mold of the intellectual and liberal statesman who guarantees stability by remaining above the domestic political fray." See Tim D. Whipple, ed., *After the Velvet Revolution: Václav Havel and the New Leaders of Czechoslovakia Speak Out* (New York: Freedom House, 1991), 37.

57 Václav Havel, "Novoroční projev," January 1, 1990, in idem, *Spisy* 6: 15.

58 Václav Havel, "Výročí narození T. G. Masaryka," Hodonín, March 7, 1990, in idem, *Spisy* 6: 91–92; Jiří Kovtun, *Tajuplná vražda. Případ Leopolda Hilsnera* (Prague: Sefer, 1994), 478–89. The reference is to John F. Kennedy, *Profiles in Courage* (New York: Harper, 1956).

that met in Prague on January 30, 1992. He reminded the audience that Masaryk called the changes resulting from World War I "a world revolution," that, by sweeping away the theocratic regimes [governments based on the divine rights of rulers] in Germany, Austria, and Russia, opened up the way to a universal spread of democracy. It was in this setting that the independence of Czechoslovakia became possible.[59] Havel commented that the downfall of the Soviet Communist camp in Europe could again be called a world revolution. The old order had collapsed and a new democratic one was being built in an international setting.[60]

Along the lines of Masaryk's global vision, later in the 1990s Havel entertained an ambitious hope to transform Prague into a Mecca radiating moral and humanitarian ideas (according to Masaryk's example) to Europe and the world. A more modest, scaled down operation in this regard was the establishment of the Forum 2000 in 1997, which would gather annually in Prague distinguished minds of the world to consider problems crucial to global society.[61]

The United States, Germany, and Russia

On a more specific level, Havel shared Masaryk's conviction about the paramount need of their country's friendship with the United States, as the Czech people proceeded on the road toward integration with the rest of humanity. Thus Masaryk never associated in the 1920s and early 1930s with the call of Count Richard Coudenhove-Kalergi for a *Paneuropa*, and later with Aristide Briand's European federation, both of which stressed Europe's peculiarity that would isolate the continent from the United States, regarded as Europe's potential competitor.[62] Havel highlighted Masaryk's friendship with the United States, particularly his relationship with Woodrow Wilson. In what was among his last public appear-

---

59 Václav Havel, "2. Zasedání Rady ministrů KBSE," Prague, January 30, 1992, in idem, *Spisy* 6: 633.

60 Václav Havel, "Státní svátek České republiky," October 28, 1999 in idem, *Spisy* 8: 19–20.

61 Martin C. Putna, *Václav Havel: Duchovní portrét v rámu české kultury 20. století* (Prague: Knihovna V. Havla, 2011), 303–4. The twentieth annual meeting of Forum 2000 will take place October 16–19, 2016 in Prague.

62 See Chapter 10 in this volume; see also Václav Veber, *Dějiny sjednocené Evropy: od antických počátků do současnosti,* 2nd ed. (Prague: Lidové noviny, 2009), 129; Jacques Bariéty , "Aristide Briand: les raisons d'un oubli," in *Le Plan Briand d'Union fédérale européenne : perspectives nationales et transnationales, avec documents : actes du colloque international tenu à Genève du 19 au 21 septembre 1991* (Bern and New York: Lang, c1998), 10–11.

ances, during the restoration of Wilson's monument in Prague on October 5, 2011, Havel deplored the ingratitude shown by the Czech public in objecting to the American missile shield on the territory in 2008. He was disappointed by such an act of ingratitude, which caused skepticism about an alliance with a country that took, but did not give back. He hoped that the restored Wilson monument would remind the Czech public that debts should always be repaid, and concluded by saying, "I believe that we owe more than one memorial to the United States of America."[63]

In addition, Havel, like Masaryk, was naturally concerned with the Czechs' large neighbors, the Germans and the Russians. In the case of Germany, it was the issue of militarism and imperialism. Speaking in Prague in 1995 he addressed veteran fighters against Nazi Germany in World War II. He stated that after the Allies had won over Germany, it could be said fifty years later that Germany had also won over Germany, namely, the democratic and liberal Germany over the nationalistic, and subsequently also the Communist, Germany.[64] In another statement, Havel reaffirmed that Germany itself was victorious over its Nazi past in World War Two, and had become an essential part of the democratic and uniting Europe. It had forsaken its nationalist and expansionist tradition.[65]

Somewhat ironically, Masaryk had presented an assessment of Germany of the 1920s and early 1930s that was strikingly similar to Havel's in the 1990s. Until the very time of Hitler's actual seizure of power, Masaryk continued to cling to the idea that World War I had cured Germany's earlier psychological and political ills and set the country on a healthy political course.[66] The major difference on this issue, between Masaryk and Havel, of course, was that Masaryk saw the German transformation one war too soon.

In the case of Russia, the question for Masaryk and Havel was the issue of belonging to Europe. Paradoxically, Masaryk believed in the essentially European character of Russia and its culture, although he was a deci-

63 Václav Havel, "The Legacy of Wilson and Masaryk Today, Part I," *Slovo* (Cedar Rapids, IA), 12, 2 (2011), 18.

64 Václav Havel, "Gézskámedaile," Vlaardingen, March 13, 1995," in ibid., *Spisy* 7: 379.

65 Václav Havel, "Projev k veteránům druhé světové války," Prague, May 8, 1995, in idem, *Spisy* 7: 464.

66 "Gespräch mit Masaryk," *Berliner Tagblatt*, October 5, 1932, in Tomáš G. Masaryk, *Cesta demokracie IV*, Spisy 36 (Prague: Masarykův ústav AV ČR, 1997), 308–9.

sive opponent of the Communist regime, especially during Lenin's lifetime. Coudenhove-Kalergi' exclusion of Russia from his *Paneropa* was an additional reason for Masaryk's disagreement with the Count's unification project.[67] Masaryk believed that, before 1917, Russia had been basically European in culture, and its foremost intellectual representatives had always been oriented toward the West.[68] Eventually, it should be again a part of Europe.

Although he was no longer faced with a Communist Russia, Havel – contrary to Masaryk – maintained that Russia had entirely different historical tradition and lived in another intellectual milieu. It should stay outside the Euro-Atlantic cultural sphere, although – like all the other cultures – it should maintain a peaceful and cooperative relation to Europe as another civilizational sphere.[69] He restated before the Canadian Parliament in April 1999 his view that Russia and the Euro-Atlantic area could not merge, nor should Russia join NATO, which was to remain an exclusive domain of the Euro-Atlantic sphere. Russia had some traits similar with the Euro-Atlantic civilization, but at the same it was different, just like Africa, Latin America, or the Far East were.[70]

The nature of the global civilization

Havel, like Masaryk, envisaged that the world moved toward a harmonious coexistence of all humanity on earth. He differed, however, from Masaryk in assuming that this goal as a prerequisite demanded a general adoption by humankind of a sense of the "transcendent," a semi-mystical concept, which he derived from one of his mentors, the philosopher

---

67 For instance, on the part of the French Foreign Ministry in June 1932, see Badel, Laurence, "Les promoteurs français d'une union éonomique et douanière de l'Europe dans l'entre-deux-guerres," in *Le Plan Briand d'Union fédérale européenne : perspectives nationales et transnationales, avec documents : actes du colloque international tenu à Genève du 19 au 21 septembre 1991* (Bern and New York: Lang, c1998), 25.

68 Tomáš G. Masaryk, *Světová revoluce za války a ve válce, 1914–1918*, Spisy 15 (Prague: Masarykův ústav AV ČR, 2005), 352.

69 "Konference SHAPEX '95," Mons, April 27, 1995, in Václav Havel, *Spisy* 7: 459. On the issue of Russia's cultural exclusion from Europe, Havel went along with his compatriot Milan Kundera, with whom he has had otherwise serious disagreements about the direction of dissent under Communism, see Baer, "Imagining Membership: The Conception of Europe in the Political Thought of T. G. Masaryk and Václav Havel," 212; Zdeněk V. David, "Patočka, Milan Kundera, and Václav Havel: Effect of the Prague Spring," *Comenius: Journal of Euro-American Civilization*, 3 (2016), 9–26.

70 Společné zasedání obou komor kanadského parlamentu," Ottawa, April 29, 1999, in Václav Havel, *Spisy* 7: 862–63.

Jan Patočka.[71] Masaryk more prosaically expected the happy denouement to come with the universal acceptance of the principles of democracy and humanitarianism.

Looking at the concept of "civilization" from the technological and administrative viewpoint, separated from the cultural and religious aspects, Havel was able to maintain that by the end of the twentieth century only a single global civilization was in existence. The planet earth was by then interconnected through thousands of economic, commercial, and monetary relations, which constituted an integral system.[72] Nevertheless, individual cultures or civilizational spheres [*civilizační okruhy*] – as he liked to call them – persisted.[73] Conflicts among them could be prevented by a universal adoption of Western values that included the idea of democracy, human rights, civil society, and the free market. The obstacle to such a world-wide endorsement was the lack of a spiritual foundation for those political principles in the West.[74]

Therefore, after the stage of creating a political framework, acceptable to all existing cultures, according to Havel, it was necessary to proceed beyond what he called "meta-politics," to another stage, which would fill the existing spiritual void. Humanity within an all-embracing civilization needed to develop a relationship with the transcendent reality in order to fulfill its overarching responsibility in the stewardship of the earth. Coexistence, peaceful life together, and creative cooperation in the contemporary multicultural world had to rest on what was the common starting point and the common ground of all cultures. This source was transcendence, which was much more deeply implanted in the human hearts and minds than any political opinions, sympathies, and antipathies.[75]

According to Masaryk, global civilization depended on two pillars, namely democracy and humanitarianism, both of which were products of

---

71 For the teaching on the transcendent, see Patočka, *Přirozený svět jako filosofický problém,* in his *Fenomenologické spisy* vol. 1/ *Sebrané spisy* vol. 6. (Prague: Oikoymenh, 2008), 148–50. On relation between Havel and Patočka concerning transcendence, see also Roger Scruton, "Masaryk, Patočka and the Care of the Soul," in Josef Novák, ed., *On Masaryk: Texts in English and German,* Studien zur österreichischen Philosophie, Bd. 13. (Amsterdam : Rodopi, 1988), 119–21.

72 "Cena Indíry Gándhíové," Delhi, February 8, 1994, in Václav Havel, *Spisy* 7: 199–200.

73 "Cena Jacksona H. Ralstona," Stanford, September 29, 1994, in Václav Havel, *Spisy* 7: 284–85.

74 Ibid., 7: 288–89.

75 "Medaile svobody," Philadelphia, July 4, 1994, in Václav Havel, *Spisy* 7: 267. See also Edward F. Findlay, "Classical Ethics and Postmodern Critique: Political Philosophy in Václav Havel and Patočka," *Review of Politics,* 61 (1999), 403.

Western civilization and were entirely adequate to the task of creating an international community world-wide. Democracy, according to Masaryk,[76] was not only a political system, but also a thorough implementation of the ideal of liberty and equality in all areas. Its advance against aristocratism was the most important trend in the nineteenth and into the twentieth century.[77] Democracy promoted friendly relations among states and nations, unlike absolutist regimes, such as the old Habsburg Monarchy, which tried to maintain control by encouraging national rivalries and hostilities.[78] If democracy was applied in internal politics, its application in external relations should naturally follow.[79]

For Havel, as for Masaryk, the unification of Europe and the world was not simply a matter of organization, which would be a mechanical process employing the existing instrumentalities. The task involved not only a need to organize, but also a need to create, namely to replace old regimes and old statesmen with a new regime and new political leaders. While economic and political structures were important, the unification also required a fresh intellectual infrastructure.[80]

Religious views

The differences in their outlook as to the viability of Western politics and culture as the framework of global civilization reflect, to a large extent, differences in their religious views. In contrast to the quasi-mystical transcendent of Havel, Masaryk believed in an empirically inferred theistic God of the Enlightenment in order to understand the operation of the universe; and in the Gospels of Jesus to provide practical moral guidance.

---

76 For a full definition of democracy, see Tomáš G. Masaryk, *Světová revoluce za války a ve válce, 1914–1918*, Spisy 15 (Prague: Masarykův ústav AV ČR, 2005), 365; cited also by Alain Soubigou, *Thomas Masaryk* (Paris: Librairie Arthème Fayard, 2002), 267.

77 The process was still continuing; see "Präsident Masaryk über kulturelle Zeitfragen," *Bohemia*, January 30, 1927, in Tomáš G. Masaryk, *Cesta demokracie III*, Spisy 35 (Prague: Masarykův ústav AV ČR, 1994), 189.

78 "28. říjen na Hradě," *Národní osvobození*, October 29, 1926, in Tomáš G. Masaryk, *Cesta demokracie III*, 166. In conversation with a French reporter, Masaryk called for "democratization" of foreign policy: too much of the prewar spirit and methods left. *L'Intransigeant*, June 28, 1921, in Tomáš G. Masaryk, *Cesta demokracie II*, Spisy 34 (Prague: Masarykův ústav AV ČR, 2007), 61.

79 Tomáš G. Masaryk, *Světová revoluce za války a ve válce, 1914–1918*, Spisy 15 (Prague: Masarykův ústav AV ČR, 2005), 295–96.

80 Imperial Germany demonstrated great organizational skills, but without moral guidance, it did not lead to victory; see "President Masaryk in Gespräch," *Vossische Zeitung*, January 22, 1933, in Masaryk, *Cesta demokracie IV*, 333–34.

His religious views were deeply affected by the undogmatic Unitarianism of his American-born wife Charlotte.[81]

Havel balanced his references to Christianity by references to non-Christian religions, like Buddhism. Thus in his New Year message of 1990, he promised to invite both the Pope and Dalai Lama to Prague. His concern with the Dalai Lama was not accidental, but rather related to the theosophic interest of his parents and grandparents. Later, he enlisted the help from the Dalai Lama in planning the Fórum 2000 and supplied a preface to the Tibetan *Book of the Dead*.[82] Havel differed from Masaryk's austere Unitarianism that did not value the traditional church rituals. Havel's family saw in old religious rites valuable traces of cosmic insights.[83] During his visit to the Pope in March 1994, Havel disclosed the wide range of his religious interests. He told John Paul II that he had had the recent opportunities of visiting the sacred sites of various religious faiths: Islam, Buddhism, Hinduism, and Judaism , and he always carried away the impression that at the core of all these faiths was the idea of toleration, understanding one's neighbor, and helping one's neighbor – simply said, the idea of good that God expected from human beings.[84]

Masaryk, to the contrary, was not particularly impressed by Oriental spirituality. To the extent that he commented on Asian religions, he was disturbed by Schopenhauer's praise of Buddhism, although he disagreed with his assertion that Buddhism was atheistic. According to Masaryk, Buddha taught pantheism that however – in contrast to monotheistic faiths – was a religion of suicide par excellence.[85] He confided during his conversations with Karel Čapek that – although he could appreciate the Oriental wisdom of resignation, the Christian wisdom of effective love, for him, was much higher.[86]

81   Such as outlined in the sermon "Unitarian Christianity," preached by William Ellery Channing (1780–1842) in Baltimore in 1819. On Channing, see *American National Biography* (New York: Oxford University Press, 1999), 4: 680–81.

82   Putna, *Václav Havel: Duchovní portrét v rámu české kultury 20. století* , 289–91.

83   Ibid., 291.

84   "Návštěva u papeže," Vatican March 7, 1994, in Václav Havel, *Spisy* 7: 217.

85   Tomáš G. Masaryk, *Sebevražda hromadným jevem společenským moderní osvěty*, Spisy 1 (Prague: Masarykův ústav AV ČR, 2002), 174. Masaryk regretted that Schopenhauer's claim that Buddhism was an atheistic religion was not clarified in Nisikanta Chattopadhyaya, *Indische Essays* (Zurich, 1883), *Atheneum*, 1 (1883–1884), in Tomáš G. Masaryk, *Z počátků Athenea, 1883–1885*, Spisy 18 (Prague: Masarykův ústav AV ČR, 2004), 304.

86   Čapek, *Hovory s T. G. Masarykem*, 265–66.

Kinship and continuity

Thus, Havel and Masaryk did not fully agree on the source of the spiritual purpose governing humanity and the universe, yet they both affirmed the existence of such a power and saw its global manifestation in democracy and humanitarianism. Havel's approach was more ontological, Masaryk's empirical. However, Havel's ontology was not essentialist; it did not envisage reaching hard conceptual realities, but rather saw philosophy as a journey of existential questioning, relying on subjective insights to reach the "transcendent." In dispensing with the Platonic-Hegelian metaphysical model, Havel was prepared – in the words of Richard Rorty – to substitute groundless hope for theoretical insight. In this sense, although a disciple of Patočka's phenomenology, he approached Masaryk's empiricism.[87]

As much as we can distinguish the philosophical differences between the two men, we can also see them linked together in a long historical continuum. If it was Masaryk's place in history to be the initiator of Czech independence, it was Havel's destiny to be its revivifying force. Above all, both of them saw their crucial mission in using their high office to proclaim the ideals of universalism, democracy, and humanitarianism, and to seek a realization of these ideals in the world community. In that respect, Madeleine Albright, the former United States Secretary of State, declared in October 2011, that Havel in her judgment embodied "more thoroughly than anyone else, the spirit and character of T. G. Masaryk."[88]

87 Robert Pirro, "Václav Havel and the Political Uses of Tragedy," *Political Theory*, 30 (2002), 228–29; Rorty, Richard, "The End of Leninism, Havel, and Social Hope," in his *Truth and Progress* (Cambridge: Cambridge University Press, 1998), 231, 236, 239.
88 On October 5 at the unveiling of the restored monument to President Woodrow Wilson in Prague; Madeleine Albright, "The Legacy of Masaryk and Wilson Today, Part II," *Slovo* (Cedar Rapids, IA), 12, 2 (2011), 19.

Epilog

The crucial issue in Masaryk's philosophical teaching was the juxtaposition of idealism and empiricism, which had a seminal effect on his approach to politics. In politics, the monistic ontology of idealism tended to promote collectivism, while the pluralistic assumptions of empiricism favored individualism. Masaryk's often-expressed negative view of German Idealist philosophy was one of the main leitmotifs of his teaching (as discussed in Chapter 1). In his ontological preference, he definitely gravitated to realistic empiricism, characteristic of the Austrian philosophical tradition (see Chapter 2). Masaryk's preference for empiricism was nevertheless combined with a reluctance to embrace whole-heartedly the stark empiricist epistemology, represented by Franz Brentano, the paragon of the Austrian philosophical school. A residual yearning for the religious dimension would continue to affect his philosophical and political views. He found the empirical concept of reality deficient in that – focusing solely on the detached sensory experience – it was thereby inherently programed to discount the religious and ethical meaning of life and culture.[1] Hence, morality and social policy, based on empiricism (as in the French Enlightenment and in nineteenth-century liberalism) were deficient in philosophical depth, and the liberals, according to Masaryk, tended to lack a moral, and especially a religious, basis for politics.[2] As shown

---

1   Tomáš G. Masaryk, *Česká otázka. Naše nynější krize. Jan Hus*, Spisy 6 (Prague: Masarykçv ústav, 2000), 315; on the anti-religious tenor of German nineteenth-century liberalism see also Tomáš G. Masaryk, *Otázka sociální. Základy marxismu filosofické a sociologické*, 2 vols., Spisy 9–10 (Prague: Masarykův ústav AV ČR, 2000), 2: 121.
2   Masaryk, *Česká otázka*, 316–17.

in Chapter 3, the way to resolve this dilemma was to add a moral dimension to the epistemology of empiricism, and a guide to this solution came to him through the teaching of the revisionist theology of German Lutheranism. This approach added an overtone of faith to the sensory perceptions without involving metaphysical concepts of idealism or recourse to revealed knowledge of conventional religion. In the long run Masaryk finally argued for supplementing the sensation of faith by an ontic emotion of love (Chapter 4). Ultimately the gap between the realistic epistemology and the ontic goal of moral purpose of the Universe was bridged by the ontic powers and insights of faith and love.

Applied to the realms of politics and social relations, Masaryk's philosophical teaching supported the conditions of individual freedom and militated against the ideological underpinnings of collectivism. Eventually, his political legacy underwent a fascinating dialectical process. Prevalence of Nazism and even longer one of Communism seemed to negate his optimism about worldwide democracy and humanitarianism. This negative phase produced the somber commentary of Jan Patočka (Chapter 11). It was, however, followed after the downfall of Communism in 1989 by a new third era in which the achievement of worldwide democracy and humanitarianism appeared on a higher plain of probability than was the case in the first era in the aftermath of the Allied victory in World War I.

One hundred years after the outbreak of World War I in which he played a significant and distinguished role, Thomas Masaryk's plans for the future of humanity required considerable modification without distracting from their original high mindedness. It was his disciple and successor, Václav Havel, who produced suitable adjustments for the Post-Colonial and the Post-Communist eras at the threshold of the twenty-first century.

In the first place, it turned out that Masaryk overestimated the power of Western (Euro-Atlantic) culture on the global scale. The European mastery over all of Africa and much of Asia from mid-nineteenth to mid-twentieth century had created the illusion that the entire world would adopt not only the political, but also the cultural values of the West. With the vanishing of colonial rule, it turned out that – while the political democracy may be suitable for the entire world – the cultural/religious values were not likely to disappear. Here Havel envisaged a solution that would have the non-Western world embrace the political values of the principles of democracy, while retaining its distinctive religious and cultural values. The global unity would embrace several cultural or "civilizational spheres."

In the second place, Masaryk evidently underestimated the possibilities – despite its ethnic differentiations – of a political harmony of Europe. Again his views were (mis)shaped by the rampant nationalism of European nations, growing throughout the long nineteenth century and eventually producing the gruesome slaughters of the World War. It, however, turned out that the consequences of another great war in mid-twentieth century would tame the demons of the nationalist malady and the precondition for a European economic and political unity would arise. In particular, the trend towards unification would not be directed against the United States – like the Coudenhove and Briand plans of the interwar period – that Masaryk opposed with his intellectual attraction for American culture and politics fortified by his American-born wife Charlotte and eventually by his friendly contacts with Woodrow Wilson during the peace settlement of World War I and its aftermath. Rather than being excluded, America, on the contrary, would prove to be the midwife in the birth of the new European unity in launching the Marshall Plan in 1947. Moreover, the redeemed Europe would be linked with the nations of North America by the framework of the North Atlantic Treaty Organization. Within the new European ambiance nations regardless of their size could feel secure and this condition rendered obsolescent Masaryk's idea of a unitary Czechoslovak statehood.

Once again Havel was able to welcome this new geopolitical denouement and rejoice in the emergence of a Euro-Atlantic cultural entity as an associate, though not integral part, of the global human community. At the same time, however, he introduced a notable modification into Masaryk's vision of the anticipated world order by detaching Russia from the Euro-Atlantic entity and placing it on par with other civilizational circles such as Africa, East Asia, and Latin America. Havel's appreciation of non-European cultures (or civilizational circles) and their distinct contributions to the emerging global culture, evidently owed much to Jan Patočka, his other philosophical mentor and fellow dissident during the Communist totalitarianism in the 1970s.[3]

---

3   "The Influence of Jan Patočka's Philosophy on Václav Havel's Political Thought," *Kosmas: Czechoslovak and Central European Journal*, vol. 29, no. 1 (Fall 2015): 37–50.

Masaryk's political and ideological mission, however, was essentially resumed by Václav Havel. As much as we can distinguish the philosophical differences between the two men, we can also see Havel linked with Masaryk together in a long historical continuum. Like Masaryk, Havel distinguished himself as an exemplary political leader of the Czech nation and, above all, he proclaimed as his guiding principle in using his high office to proclaim Masaryk's ideals of universalism, democracy, and humanitarianism, and to seek a realization of these ideals in the world community. As noted earlier, Madeleine Albright, the former United States Secretary of State, declared in October 2011 that in her judgment Havel had embodied the spirit and character of T. G. Masaryk more thoroughly than anyone else.[4]

Nevertheless, it has become necessary to end this study on a note of caution. Since Havel's death in December 2011 and the centennial of World War I, the project of world unification has suffered challenges that indeed starkly resembled the clashes of civilizations that Havel had ruled out. Even on the provincial scale of European integration the beneficial institution of the European Union – evidently embodying the aspirations of Masaryk and Havel – has undergone stresses of disharmonies in the financial sector, and challenges in the rise of assertive nationalism and populism, especially (but not exclusively) in the countries of the former Communist bloc. Thus far this disturbing situation culminated in the Brexit of June 2016[5]. It is to be hoped that by the arrival of the centennial of World War II the interfering disturbances would subside, and the global and the Euro-Atlantic scenes would come closer to the visionary views of Thomas Masaryk, of his fellow idealist, Woodrow Wilson, and of his disciple, Václav Havel.

---

4   On October 5, 2011, at the unveiling of the restored monument to President Woodrow Wilson in Prague; Madeleine Albright, "The Legacy of Masaryk and Wilson Today, Part II," *Slovo* (Cedar Rapids, IA), 12, 2 (2011): 19.

5   See Igor Lukeš, "The Hamlet of Central Europe: Czechs between East and West," *Comenius: Journal of Euro-American Civilization*, 3 (2016): 215–222; and the collection of eight articles "Explaining Eastern Europe," *Journal of Democracy*, vol. 29, no. 3 (2018): 24–128, as well as Jroslav Pánek, "Europe at a Crossroads," *Selected Papers from the Twenty-Sixth World Congress of the Czechoslovak Society of Arts and Sciences,* 2 vols. (New York: The Publishing House of the Society, 2013), 1: 37–55.

Chronology of Masaryk's Life and Accomplishments

Childhood and Student Years, 1850–1879

1850s
- Born (March 7, 1850) in Hodonín in southern Moravia.
- Czech elementary school.

1861–1863
- German lower secondary school in Hustopeče.

1863–1864
- Successive apprenticeships: locksmith in Vienna, blacksmith in Čejč, teacher's aid in Čejkovice.

1865–1869
- German Gymnasium in Brno, supported by tutoring the son of Anton LeMonnier, the police chief of Brno.

1869–1872
- German Gymnasium in Vienna, continued as private tutor in the LeMonnier family.

1872–1876
- Study at the University of Vienna; first registering in classical languages, but soon shifting permanently to philosophy, under the influence of Franz Brenatano and Robert Zimmermann.

1876
- Awareded Ph. D. in philosophy on the basis of his thesis on Plato's concept of the soul.

1876–1877
- A year of study at the University of Leipzig, where he established friendship with Edmund Husserl and also met and became engaged to an American music student, Charlotte Garigue.

1878
- Married to Charlotte in Brooklyn, New York.
- Returned to Vienna to work on his Habilitation thesis.
- Early Career, 1879–1890

1879

· His Habilitation thesis *Sebevražda hromadným jevem společenským* [Suicide as a Mass Social Phenomenon] accepted. Appointed *Privatdozent* in philosophy at the University of Vienna.

1880

· Left the Catholic Church and was formally received into the Reformed Protestant Church in southern Moravia.

1882

· Named Professor of Philosophy in the Czech University of Prague (*Univerzita Karlova*).

1883

· Established the leading Czech scholarly review, *Atheneum.*

1885

· Published his first major philosophical work, *Základové konkretné logiky: třídění a soustava věd* [Foundations of Concrete Logic: Classification and System of Sciences], heavily influenced by Comte.

1886–1888

· Together with Jan Gebauer, Jaroslav Goll, and Otakar Hostinský, engaged in a bitter public controversy to prove the alleged medieval manuscripts of Dvůr Králové and Zelená Hora to be modern forgeries.

1887–1888

· Two journeys to Russia, establishing contacts with Leo Tolstoy and other Russian intellectuals.

1889

· Joined a small political group of Realists, including Josef Kaizl and Karel Kramář, around the review *Čas.*

1890

· Adhered to the Party of the Young Czechs.
· Mature Scholar and Politician, 1890–1914

1891–1893

· Served as deputy of the Young Czechs in the Austrian *Reichsrat* in Vienna.

1894

· Established a new scholarly review, *Naše doba* [Our Time].

1895–1896

· Published *Česká otázka* [The Czech Question], *Jan Hus*, and *Karel Havlíček.*

1898

· Published *Otázka sociální. Základy marxismu filosofické a sociologické* [The Social Question: Philosophical and Sociological Foundations of Marxism].

1899–1900

· The Hilsner Affair, attack on anti-Semitism and the superstition of ritual murder.

1900
· Established the Popular (Realist) Party.

1902
· Second visit to the United States.

1907–1914
· Serving again in the *Reichsrat* this time as deputy of the Realist Party.

1907
· Third visit to the United States.

1909
· Intervention in the *Reichsrat* during the Zagreb and the Friedjung trials against the persecution of the Serbs.

1910
· Masaryk's high reputation attested by the publication of an international *festschrift* for his 60th birthday [*T. G. Masarykovi k 60. Narozeninám* (1910)].
· Third visit to Russia.

1912
· Three visits to Belgrade.

1913
· *Russland und Europa* published [Russia and Europe, English translation: *The Spirit of Russia,* 1919] (Masaryk, Tomáš G., *Rusko a Evropa*, Spisy 11–13, 3 vols. (Prague: Masarykův ústav AV ČR, 1996).
· War and Presidency, 1914–l937

1914
· In November traveled to Rome and henceforth remained in exile.

1915
· In January moved to Geneva, Switzerland.
· In April traveled to Paris and London submitting to governments his memo on *Independent Bohemia.*
· In July in Zurich and in Geneva he declared war on Austria-Hungary in the name of the Czechs and the Slovaks.
· Settled in London, while Beneš stayed in Paris.

1916
· In February 1916 French Prime Minister Aristide Briand expressed support for
· Masaryk's objectives of dissolving the Austro-Hungarian monarchy.
· In London obtained teaching position at the University of London and with Robert Seton-Watson began publishing the journal *New Europe.*
· September 16, England and France recognized the Czech (later Czechoslovak) National Council Headed by Masaryk

1917
· In May, fourth journey to Russia to organize Czechoslovak legions.
· After the November Revolution attempted to deal with the Soviet government.

1918
- During March and April undertook his fourth journey to the United States through Siberia, Japan, and across the Pacific Ocean.
- During his stay in Washington from May to October, Masaryk secured a recognition for the National Council as legitimate representation of Czechoslovakia, from France and Britain (June 29) and from the United States (September 3).
- October 28, the independence of Czechoslovakia was proclaimed in Prague.
- December 22, Masaryk installed as President of the Republic.

1920
- Re-elected President on the adoption of the new constitution.

1923
- May 13, the death of Charlotte Garrigue Masaryk.
- October official visits to France, Belgium and Britain.

1924
- Treaty of French-Czechoslovak alliance signed.

1927
- Voyage to Egypt, Israel (Palestine), and Greece.
- Reelected President for the third time.

1928–1932
- Friendship with Oldra Sedlmayerová.

1934
- The Czechoslovak-Soviet Pact signed.
- In the late spring, Masaryk suffering a stroke, seriously limiting his activities.
- Re-elected President for the fourth time.

1935
- Abdicated in December.

1937
- Died on September 14.

Bibliography

Baer, Josette. "Thomas Masaryk: Democracy as Czech Humanism." In Josette Baer, *The Slavic Thinkers or the Creation of Polities: Intellectual History and Political Thought in Central Europe and the Balkans in the 19th Century*, 15–42. Washington, D.C: New Academis, 2007.

Peška, Vladimír, and Antoine Mareš, eds. *Thomas Garrigue Masaryk, européen et humaniste*. Paris: Etudes et documentation internationales: Institut d'études slaves, 1991.

Soubigou, Alain. *Thomas Masaryk*. Paris: Librairie Arthème Fayard, 2002.

Glossary of Philosophical Terms

A priori: Knowledge that does not depend on evidence from sensory experience; non-empirical knowledge.

The Absolute: Ultimate reality regarded as uncaused, unmodified, unified, and complete, timeless.

Analytical Sentence (Kant): Proposition necessarily true on purely logical grounds; self-evident.

Collectivism: The practice or principle of giving a group priority over each individual in it.

Deism: Doctrine that God created the world and its natural laws, but does not take any further part in its functioning,

Ding an sich: Absolute state of being, independent of human perception

Egocentric Predicament: an epistemological presumption that "a knower is unable to get outside his own mind because all that the knower can know is what is present to his own mind."

Elan vital: In Bergsonian philosophy, the original vital impulse which is the substance of consciousness and nature.

Empiricism: A theory that the only source of knowledge is sense experience,

Epicureanism: Belief that pleasure or happiness is the sole or chief good in life.

Epistemology: The study of the derivation and the character of knowledge.

Hume's skepticism: Hume's scepticism derived from the egocentric predicament (q.v.)

Idealism, Absolute: Same as Solipsism.

Idealism, Objective: Stands for the unconditional reality that is considered the spiritual ground of all things.

Idealism, Platonic: Based on the metaphysics of ideas, often contrasted with Aristotelian Realism, based on the metaphysics of perceptions

Materialism: A doctrine holding that matter is the ontic reality.

Mental and Verbal Truths (Locke): Ideas and Words, or mental and verbal propositions

Metaphysics: Study of the real ultimate existence

Monism: Doctrine that there is only one ultimate substance whether mind (idealism) or matter (materialism) in contrast to dualism and/or pluralism.

Nihilism: A doctrine, particularly in Russia (1860-1917), that existing political, social, and economic institutions must be destroyed as a prerequisite for new ones.

Noumenon: A thing in itself in Kant's philosophy, unable to be known through perception, but serving as an intellegible ground of phenomenon.

Ontic: Having the status of real and ultimate existence.

Ontology: Same as Metaphysics

Pangermanism: The doctrine of German cultural and military superiority, and eventual world domination by stages of imperial expansion.

Pantheism: A doctrine that God and cosmos are identical.

Positivism: Philosophical school, basing knowledge solely on the data of sense perceptions, and rejecting speculation about the ultimate origins of phenomena.

Prussian Absolutism: Masaryk's characterization of the political system of Germany from Frederick the Great (1740-1786) to William II (1888-1918)

Slavophilism: A doctrine in nineteenth-century Russia, claiming cultural and religious superiority of Orthodox lands over Catholic and Protestant Western and Central Europe.

Solipsism: The theory that nothing is real or exists but the self

***Sturm und Drang*:** An early romantic movement in eighteenth-century Germany reacting against French neoclassicism.

Subjectivism: Epistemological theories that limit knowledge to the states and elements of consciousness.

Theism: A doctrine that God, as creator and ruler of the universe, is in continuous contact with human beings.

Titanism: A marked tendency in expansiveness in expression, resulting in grandiosity and freedom from all restraints

Transcendental/Transcendentalism: Doctrines that propose to discover the nature of reality by analyzing the process of thought rather than sense perceptions.

Trifling Proposition (Locke): Same as Analytical Sentence (Kant)

Utraquism: The faith and organization of the Utraquist Church (*církev pod obojí*) in Czechia, originating from the Bohemian Reformation in 1415 and reabsorbed into the Roman Catholic Church during the Counter Reformation after the Battle of the White Mountain in 1620.

Bibliography

Archival Sources

Letters of Willa S. Cather to Tomáš G. Masaryk, Prague, Masarykův ústav - Archiv Akademie věd České republiky (MSÚ - A AV ČR), December 1, 1923, in Korespondence II, 41, 706; February 14, [1924], in Korespondence II, 41, 706; September 23, [1924], Korespondence II, 227, 738; February 2, 1925, Korespondence II, 57, 708; [2 letters during Masaryk's disability] February 14, 1935, and December 1, 1936, Korespondence II, 94, 717.

Letters of Tomáš G. Masaryk to Ernst Denis, Prague, Masarykův ústav - Archiv Akademie věd České republiky (MSÚ - A AV ČR), February 14, 1920, in Korespondence II, 11 (1920); December 18, 1920, Kor. II, 11 (1920); undated note of Prof. Jelínek concerning Denis, Kor II, 11 (1920).

Letters of Ernst Denis to Tomáš G. Masaryk, Prague, Masarykův ústav - Archiv Akademie věd České republiky (MSÚ - A AV ČR), March 1, 1895, in Korespondence I, 22-1; December 24, 1896, Kor. I, 23-4; December 20, 1905, Kor. I, 39-16; October 25, 1920, Kor. II, 11 (1920).

Letters of Tomáš G. Masaryk to Paul de Lagarde, Prague, Masarykův ústav - Archiv Akademie věd České republiky (MSÚ - A AV ČR), March 14, 1881, in Korespondence I, 7, 19; October 30, 1886, in Korespondence I, 7, 101 [?].

Letter of Virginia Woolf to Tomáš G. Masaryk, Prague, Masarykův ústav - Archiv Akademie věd České republiky (MSÚ - A AV ČR), April 7, 1930, in Korespondence II, 80, 713.

Personální spis Ludwiga Landgrebea, Archiv Univerzity Karlovy (AUK), fond Německá univerzita (NU), Filozofická fakulta, sign. NU P III 13.

Primary Sources

NOTE: For certain items, which are unusually rare, locations are given in LC (Library of Congress, Washington, D.C.) or NUK (National Library of the Czech Republic, Prague).

Bártová, Jana, and Jan Bílek. "Oldra Sedlmayerová ve vzpomínkách Pavly Mocové." *Tvar* 12 (1999): 14–15.

Bellows, Henry W. *Relation of Unitarian Faith to the Current Creeds of Christendom.* Albany: Weed, Parsons & Co., 1960.

Benda, Julien. *1867–1956, La trahison des clercs*. Introduction by André Lwoff. Paris: B. Grasset [1975]. English translation: *The betrayal of the intellectuals*. Translated by Richard Aldington. Introduction by Herbert Read. Boston: Beacon Press [1955].

Beneke, Friedrich. *Grundlegung zur Physik der Sitten, ein Gegenstück zu Kants Grundlegung zur Metaphysik der Sitten*. Berlin and Poznań: In commission bei E. S. Mittler, 1822.

———. *Lehrbuch der Psychologie als Naturwissenschaft*. 2nd ed. Berlin: E. S. Mittler, 1845; 1st ed. Berlin: E. S. Mittler, 1833.

———. *Ungedruckte Briefe*. Edited by Renato Pettoello and Nikola Barelmann. Aalen: Scientia, 1994.

Beneš, Edvard. "Nad rakví presidenta Osvoboditele." *Školská správa* 18 (1937): 114–120.

———. *Projevy, články, rozhovory, 1935–1938*. Prague: Masarykův ústav, 2006.

Bergmann, Ernst. *Die deutsche Nationalkirche*. Warsaw: F. Hirt, 1933.

Bergmann, Hugo S. *Das philosophische Werk Bernard Bolzanos*. Halle: Niemeyer, 1909. Reprint: Hildesheim: G. Olms, 1970.

Bergmann, Samuel H. "Bolzano und Brentano." *Archiv für Geschichte der Philosophie* 48 (1968): 306–311.

Bergson, Henri. *Matière et mémoire, essai sur la relation du corps a l'esprit*. 8th ed. Paris: F. Alcan, 1912.

———. *The Meaning of the War: Life and Matter in Conflict*. London: Unwin, 1915.

Bernard, Michel. *La mémoire de Prague: conscience nationale et intelligentsia dans l'histoire tchèque et slovaque*. Paris: Libr. académique Perrin, c1986.

Bittner, Konrad. *Herders Geschichtsphilosophie und die Slawen*. Reichenberg: Gebrüder Stiepel, 1929.

Bolzano, Bernard. *Der böhmische Vormärz in Briefen B. Bolzanos an F. Příhonský, 1824–1848: Beiträge zur deutsch-slawischen Wechselseitigkeit*. Edited by Eduard Winter. Deutsche Akademie der Wissenschaften zu Berlin. Institut für Slawistik. Veröffentlichungen, Nr. 11. Berlin: Akademie-Verlag, 1956.

———. *Gesamtausgabe*. Edited by Eduard Winter, Jan Berg, Friedrich Kambartel, Jaromír Loužil, and Bob van Rootselaar. 40 vols. in 57 parts. Series: Einleitug; I. Schriften; II. Nachlass; III. Briefwechsel; IV. Dokumente. Stuttgart-Bad Cannstatt: Frommann Holzboog, 1969– in progress.

———. *Über das Verhältniss der beiden Volksstämme in Böhmen. Drei Vortraege im Jahre 1816 an der Hochschule zu Prague gehalten*. Vienna: Wilhelm Braumüller, 1849. Reprint: Amsterdam: Rodopi, 1969.

Brentano, Franz C. *Aristotle and His World View*. Edited and translated by Rolf George and Roderick M. Chisholm. [Trans. of *Aristoteles und seine Weltanschauung*.] Berkeley: University of California Press, c1978.

———. *Aristoteles Lehre vom Ursprung des menschlichen Geistes*. 2nd ed.. Edited by Rolf George. Hamburg: Meiner, c1980.

———. *Aristoteles und seine Weltanschauung*. Leipzig, Quelle & Meyer, 1911.

———. *Briefe an Carl Stumpf, 1867–1917*. Edited by Gerhard Oberkofler with Peter Goller. Graz: Akademische Druck- u. Verlagsanstalt, 1989.

———. "Briefe Franz Brentanos an Hugo Bergmann," edited by Hugo Bergmann. In *Philosophy and Phenomenological Research* 7 (1946): 83–158.

———. "Epicurus and the War." In Brentano, *The Origin of Our Knowledge of Right and Wrong*. Edited by Oskar Kraus; English editor Roderick M. Chisholm; translated by Roderick M. Chisholm and Elizabeth H. Schneewind. London: Routledge & K. Paul; New York: Humanities Press, 1969.

———. *Geschichte der griechischen Philosophie*. Edited by Franziska MayerHillebrand. Bern: Francke, 1963.

———. *Geschichte der mittelalterlichen Philosophie im christlichen Abendland*. Edited by Klaus Hedwig. Hamburg: F. Meiner, c1980.

———. *Geschichte der Philosophie der Neuzeit*. Edited by Klaus Hedwig. Hamburg: F. Meiner, c1987.

———. *Grundlegung und Aufbau der Ethik: nach den Vorlesungen über 'Praktische Philosophie' aus dem Nachlass*. Edited by Francizska Mayer-Hillebrand. Bern: A. Francke, 1952.

———. *Kategorienlehre*. Edited by Alfred Kastil. Leipzig: F. Meiner, 1933.

———. *Die Lehre Jesu und ihre bleibende Bedeutung*, mit einem Anhang: Kurze Darstellung der christlichen Glauben. Edited by Alfred Kastil. Leipzig: Felix Meiner, 1922. [NUK: 31 H 270]

———. *Die Lehre vom richtigen Urteil*. Nach den Vorlesungen über Logik, mit Benützung anderer Manuskripte aus dem Gebiete der Erkenntnistheorie, aus dem Nachlass. Edited by Franziska Mayer-Hillebrand. Bern: Francke, 1956.

———. "Nietzsche als Nachahmer Jesu," in Brentano, *Die Lehre Jesu und ihre bleibende Bedeutung*, mit einem Anhange: Kurze Darstellung der christlichen Glaubenslehre. edited by Alfred Kastil. Leipzig: F. Meiner, 1922.

———. *Offener Brief an Herrn Professor Dr. Eduard Zeller*. Leipzig: Duncker and Humblot, 1883. [NUK: 12 F 791]

———. *Die Psychologie des Aristoteles, insbesondere seine lehre vom nous Poietikos*. Mainz: F. Kirchheim, 1867.

———. *Psychologie vom empirischen Standpunkt*. 2 vols. Leipzig: Duncker & Humblot, 1874; 2nd ed., 3 vols. Edited by Oskar Kraus. Leipzig: 1924–1928.

———. *Psychology from an Empirical Standpoint*. Edited by Oskar Kraus. English edition edited by Linda L. McAlister, translated by Antos C. Rancurello, D.B. Terrell, and Linda L. McAlister. London and New York: Routledge, 1995.

———. Über *Aristoteles: Nachgelassene Aufsätze*. Edited by Rolf George. Hamburg: Felix Meiner Verlag, 1986.

———. *Über die Zukunft der Philosophie; nebst den Vorträgen: Über die Gründe der Ermutigung auf philosophischem Gebiete, Über Schellings System, sowie den 25 Habilitationsthesen*. 2nd ed. Edited by Oskar Kraus, Paul Weingartner, Hamburg: F. Meiner, 1968.

———. *Untersuchungen zur Sinnespsychologie*. Leipzig, 1907.

———. *Versuch über die Erkenntnis*. Edited by Alfred Kastil. New edition revised by Francizka Mayer-Hillebrand. Hamburg: F. Meiner, 1970.

———. *Die vier Phasen der Philosophie und ihr augenblicklicher Stand*. Nebst Abhandlungen über Plotinus, Thomas von Aquin, Kant, Schopenhauer und Auguste Comte. Edited by Oskar Kraus, with a new introduction by Franziska Mayer-Hillebrand, 2nd ed. Hamburg: Meiner, 1968. [1st ed. Leipzig: 1926.]

———. *Vom Dasein Gottes*. Edited by Alfred Kastil. Leipzig: F. Meiner, 1929. [NUK: 12 H 395].

———. *Vom Ursprung sittlicher Erkenntnis.* 2nd ed. Leipzig: F. Meiner, 1921; 1st ed. Leipzig: Duncker and Humblot, 1889.

———. [Vom Ursprung sittlicher Erkenntnis.] *The origin of our knowledge of right and wrong.* Edited by Oskar Kraus, English edition edited by Roderick M. Chisholm, translated by Roderick M. Chisholm and Elizabeth H. Schneewind. London: Routledge & K. Paul; New York: Humanities Press, 1969.

———. *Von der Klassifikation der psychischen Phänomene.* Leipzig, 1911; 2nd ed. edited by Oskar Kraus. Leipzig, 1921.

Briand, Aristide. *La paix mondiale et l'Union européenne.* 2nd ed. rev. Edited by Achille Elisha. Louvain-la-Neuve: Academia-Bruylant, 2000.

Brooks, Jeffrey. "Vekhi and the Vekhi Dispute." *Survey* 19/1 (1973): 21–50.

Čapek, Karel. *Čtení o T. G. Masarykovi.* Edited by Miroslav Halík. Prague: Melantrich, 1969.

———. *Hovory s T. G. Masarykem,* Spisy 20. Prague: Československý spisovatel, 1990.

Cather, Willa. *The Selected Letters.* Edited by Andrew Jewell and Janis Stout. New York: Knopf, 2013.

Čechurová, Jana, and Jaroslav Čechura. *Edvrad Beneš: diplomat na cestách.* Prague: Karolinum, 2000.

Cibulka, Josef. "Jan Patočka a studenti pražské Filozofické fakulty v údobí 1945–1949." *Filozofia* (Bratislava) 52 (1997): 235 ff.

Comte, Auguste. *Auguste Comte and Positivism: The Essential Writings.* Edited by Gertrud Lenzer. New York: Harper Torchbooks, 1975.

Coudenhove-Kalergi, Richard N. *Aus meinem Leben.* Zurich: Atlantis-Verlag, 1949.

———. *Eine Idee erobert Europa; meine Lebenserinnerungen.* Munich: K. Desch [1958]; 2nd ed. with revised title *Ein Leben für Europa: meine Lebenserinnerungen.* Cologne: Kiepenheuer & Witsch, 1966.

———. *Pan-Europa.* Vienna: Paneuropäischer Verlag, 1923.

———. "Präsident Masaryk." In *Festschrift Th. G. Masaryk zum 80. Geburtstag.* Edited by Boris V. Jakovenko. Vol. 2. Bonn: F. Cohen, 1930.

———. *Crusade for Pan-Europe; Autobiography of a Man and a Movement.* New York: G. P. Putnam's Sons, c1943.

Doležal, Jaromír. "Jan Herben: T. G. Masaryk," *Masarykův sborník* 3 (1928–1929): 172–187.

———. "Masaryk na studiích ve Vídni," *Masarykův almanach.* Vienna: Akademický spolek, 1925.

———. *Masarykova cesta životem.* 2 vols. Brno, 1920–1921.

Drtina, František. "Vzpomínky," *Masarykův sborník,* 4. Prague: Čin, 1930.

Ehrenfels, Christian. *Metaphysik,* Philosophische Schriften. Edited by Reinhard Fabian. Vol. 4. Munich: Filosofia Verlag, 1990.

———. "Offener Brief an den Präsidenten der Tschechoslowakischen Republik T. G. Masaryk," in *Metaphysik,* Philosophische Schriften. Edited by Reinhard Fabian. Vol 4. Munich: Filosofia Verlag, 1990.

———. *System der Werttheorie.* 2 vols. Leipzig: O. R. Reisland, 1897–1898. *L'Europe nouvelle.* Edited by Louise Weiss. Paris, 1918–1940. [LC AP20.E88]

Evola, Julius. *Rivolta contro il mondo moderno.* Milan: Ulrico Hoepli, 1934.

Fechner, Gustav T. *Drei Motive und Gründe des Glaubens*. Leipzig: Breitkopf und Härtel, 1863.

———. *Elemente der Psychophysik*. 2 vols. Leipzig: Breitkopf und Härtel, 1860.

———. *In Sachen der Psychophysik*. Leipzig: Breitkopf und Härtel, 1877.

———. *Revision der Hauptpunkte der Psychophysik*. Leipzig: Breitkopf und Härtel, 1882.

Feder, Gottfried. *Der deutsche Staat auf nationaler und sozialer Grundlage*. 6th ed. Munich: F. Eher Nachf., 1932.

———. *Das programm der N.S.D.A.P. und seine weltanschaulichen Grundgedanken*. Munich: F. Eher Nachf., 1931.

Festschrift Th. G. Masaryk zum 80. Geburtstage. Edited by Boris V. Jakovenko. 2 vols. Bonn: F. Cohen, 1930.

Franta, Zdeněk. "Vzpomínky." *Masarykův sborník, 4*. Prague: Čin, 1930.

Funck-Brentano, Théophile. *La civilisation et ses lois. Morale sociale*. Paris: E. Plon et Cie, 1876.

Gašparíková-Horáková, Anna. *Masarykovcov. Spomienky osobnej archivárky T. G. Masaryka*. Bratislava: Academic Electronic Press, 1995.

Hálek, Ivan. *Vzpomínám na TGM*. Prague: Za svobodu, 1948.

Havel, Václav. "Český úděl?" In *Spisy 3*, 888–897. Prague: Torst, 1999–2007.

———. "The Legacy of Wilson and Masaryk Today," Part I. *Slovo* 12/2 (2011): 18.

———. *Spisy*. 8 vols. Prague: Torst, 1999–2007.

———. *Summer Meditations*. Translated by Paul Wilson. New York: Alfred A. Knopf, 1992; Czech original: Havel, Václav. *Letní přemítání*. Prague: Odeon, 1991.

Headlam, James Wyclif. *A Memoir of the Peace Conference 1919*. Edited by Agnes Headlam–Morley, Russell Bryant, and Anna Ciencila. London: Methuen, 1972.

Heidegger, Martin. *Die Selbstbehauptung der deutschen Universität*. Rektoratsrede, May 27, 1933. Breslau: Korn, 1933.

Herder, Johann G. *Sämmtliche Werke*. 33 vols. Edited by Bernhard Suphan. Berlin: Weidmann, 1877–1913.

Hoffmann, Roland J. *T. G. Masaryk und die tschechische Frage*. Munich: Oldenbourg, 1988.

House, Edward H. *The Intimate Papers*. 4 vols. Edited by Charles Seymour. Boston: Houghton Mifflin, 1926–28.

Houston, David F. *Eight Years with Wilson's Cabinet, 1913–1920*. 2 vols. Garden City, NY: Doubleday, 1926.

Husserl, Edmund. *Die Brentanoschule*. Part 1 of *Briefwechsel*. Edited by Elisabeth Schuhmann and Karl Schuhmann. 10 parts, which comprise vol. 3 of *Husserliana, Dokumente*. Dordrecht: Kluwer Academic Publishers, 1993.

———. *Briefe an Roman Ingarden. Mit Erläuterungen und Erinnerungen an Husserl*. Edited by Roman Ingarden. The Hague: Nijhoff, 1968.

———. *Logical Investigations*. 2 vols. Translated by John N. Findlay. London: Routledge, 2001.

Hýsek, Miloslav. "Masarykovy dopisy Leandru Čechovi." *Listy filologické*, 56 (1929): 136–149, 258–266.

Jahn, Friedrich L. *Deutsches Volkstum*. Berlin: Aufbau Verlag, 1991.

Jirásek, Josef, editor. "Z korespondence Franze Brentana a T. G. Masaryka." *Sborník prací filosofické fakulty brn nské university* 18 (1969), řada filosofická (B), no. 16: 94–103,

——. "Z korespondence T. G. Masaryka L. N. Tolstému." *Bratislava*, Časopis učené společnosti Šafaříkovy, 6 (1932): 610–612.

Kastil, Alfred. *Die Philosophie Franz Brentanos. Eine Einführung in seine Lehre.* Bern: A. Francke, 1951.

Kosík, Karel. "Váha slov." *Plamen*, 11/4 (1969): 16–17.

Král, Václav. *O Masarykově a Benešově kontrarevoluční protisovětské politice.* Prague: Státní nakl. politické literatury, 1953. Russian translation: *O kontrarevoliutsionnoi i antisovetskoi politike Masarika.* Translated by M. M. Khazanov. Moscow: Izdatel'stvo innostrannoi literatury, 1955.

Kraus, Oskar. "Biographical Sketch of Brentano." In *The Philosophy of Brentano*. Edited by Linda L. McAlister (Atlantic Highlands, NJ: Humanities Press, 1977).

——. *Franz Brentano: Zur Kenntnis seines Lebens und seiner Lehre.* Mit Beiträgen von Carl Stumpf und Edmund Husserl. Munich: Beck, 1919.

Krejčí, František. "Glosy k nynější filosofii u nás." *Česká mysl* 14 (1913): 225–242.

Krieck, Ernst. *Nationalpolitische Erziehung.* 14th ed. Leipzig: Armanen, 1933.

Kundera, Milan. "Český úděl." In Václav Havel. *Spisy.* 8 vols. Prague: Torst, 1999–2007, 3: 992–998; originally published in *Listy* 1 (1968), no. 7–8: 1, 5.

——. "Radikalismus a exhibicionismus," *Host do domu* 15 (1968–69):24–29.

Lagarde, Paul de. *Schriften für das deutsche Volk.* 2nd ed. 2 vols. Munich: J. F. Lehmanns Verlag, 1934. vol. 1: *Deutsche Schriften.* Edited by Karl August Fischer; vol. 2: *Ausgewählte Schriften.* Edited by Paul Fischer. [LC DD204.L35 1934]

——. *Deutsche Schriften*, Gesammtausgabe letzter Hand. 5th ed. Göttingen: Dieterich'sche Universitäts-Buchhandlung, 1920. [LC DD204.L27 1920]

——. *Deutsche Schriften*, Schriften für das deutsche Volk. Edited by Karl August Fischer. 4th ed. Vol 1. Munich: J. F. Lehmanns Verlag, 1940. [LC DD204.L35 1940 Bd.1]

——. *Deutscher Glaube.* Edited by Friedrich Daab. Jena: E. Diederichs, 1914.

Lange, Friedrich Albert. *Die Arbeiterfrage. Ihre Bedeudung für Gegenwart und Zukunft.* 5th ed. Winterthur: Geschwister Ziegler, 1894.

——. *Geschichte des Materialismus und Kritik seiner Bedeutung in der Gegenwart.* 2 vols. Edited by Alfred Schmidt. Frankfurt a. M.: Suhrkamp, 1974.

Laplace, Pierre Simon, *Essai philosophique sur les probabilités.* 3rd ed. Paris: Mme Ve Courcier, 1816.

Lenin, Vladimir Il'ich. *Filosofskie tedradi.* In V. I. Lenin, *Polnoe sobranie sochinenii.* 55 vols. 5th ed. Vol. 29. Moscow: Izdatel'stvo politicheskoi literatury, 1967–1970.

Lewes, George Henry. *Biographical History of Philosophy from Its Origin in Greece down to the Present Day.* 2 vols. New York: Appleton, 1857. [Also: London: Routledge, 1900, and also in German and Magyar transl.]

——. *Geschichte der Philosophie von Thales bis Comte.* 2 vols. Berlin: R. Oppenheim, 1871. Vol. 1: *Geschichte der alten Philosophie.* Vol. 2: *Geschichte der neueren Philosophie.*

——. *Fyziologie obyčejného života* [Physiology of Common Life] listed in Tomáš G. Masaryk, *Univerzitní přednášky I: Praktická filozofie*, Spisy 4. Prague: Masarykův ústav AV ČR, 2012, 26.

——. *The Physiology of Common Life.* 2 vols. Edinburgh and London: Blackwood, 1859.

Locke, John. *A Paraphrase and Notes on the Epistles of St. Paul to the Galatians, 1 and 2 Cor-*

inthians, Romans, Ephesians. 2 vols. Edited by Arthur W. Wainwright. Oxford: Clarendon Press, 1987.

Ludwig, Emil. *Defender of Democracy: Masaryk of Czechoslovakia.* New York: R. M. McBride, 1936; Czech version: *Duch a čin: Rozmluvy s Masarykem.* In Tomáš G. Masaryk. *Spisy* 38. Prague: Masarykův ústav, 2012.

MacCormac, John. "Masaryk, at Eighty, Toils on at His Task." *New York Times,* March 2, 1930, 3, 14.

Mann, Thomas, *Gesammelte Werke.* 13 vols. Frankfurt a. M.: S. Fischer, 1960–1974.

———. "In Memory of Masaryk." *The Nation* 145/15 (October 9, 1937): 373–374.

Mareš, František. *Otázky filozofické, národní a sociální v politice.* Plzeň: Česká národní demokracie, 1923.

Markov, E. "Kriticheskie besedy," *Russkaia rech* 6 (1879): 197.

Marty, Anton. "Franz Brentano. Eine biographische Skizze." In Marty, Anton. *Gesammelte Schriften.* 2 vols. Edited by Josef Eisenmeier, Alfred Kastil, and Oskar Kraus. Halle: Niemeyer, 1916–1920. I, pt. 1: 95–103.

———. *Ueber den Ursprung der Sprache.* Würzburg: A. Stuber, 1877.

Masaryk, Alice Garrigue. *Alice Garrigue Masaryk, 1879–1966: her life as recorded in her own words and by her friends.* Edited by Ruth C. Mitchell and Linda Vlasak. Pittsburgh: Center for International Studies, University of Pittsburgh, 1980.

Masaryk, Tomáš G: Books

Masaryk, Tomáš G. *Česká otázka. Naše nynější krize. Jan Hus.* Spisy 6. Prague: Masarykův ústav, 2000; earlier ed., *Česká otázka.* 6th ed. Prague: Čin, 1948.

———. *Cesta demokracie I.* Spisy 33. Prague: Masarykův ústav AV ČR, 2003.

———. *Cesta demokracie II.* Spisy 34. Prague: Masarykův ústav AV ČR, 2007.

———. *Cesta demokracie III.* Spisy 35. Prague: Masarykův ústav AV ČR, 1994.

———. *Cesta demokracie IV.* Spisy 36. Prague: Masarykův ústav AV ČR, 1997.

———. *Dopisy Oldře.* Edited by Dagmar Hájková. Prague: IN ŽIVOT, 2006.

———. *Ideály humanitní a studie z let 1901–1903.* Spisy 24. Prague: Ústav T. G. Masaryka, 2011. Earlier ed.: Masaryk.Tomáš G. *Ideály humanitní. Problém malého národa. Demokratism v politice.* Prague: Melantrich, 1968.

———. *Juvenalie: studie a stati, 1876–1881.* Spisy 16. Prague: Ústav T. G. Masaryka, 1993.

———. *Karel Havlíček: Snahy a tučby politického probuzení.* Spisy 7. Prague: Masarykův ústav AV ČR, 1996.

———. *Moderní člověk a náboženství.* Spisy 8. Prague: Masarykův ústav AV ČR, 2000.

———. *Národnostní filosofie doby novější.* 2nd ed. Prague: Melantrich, 1919.

———. *The New Europe.* London: Eyre and Spottiswoode, 1918.

———. *Nová Evropa; stanovisko slovanské.* Prague: Dubský, 1920.

———. *Otázka sociální. Základy marxismu filosofické a sociologické.* 2 vols. Spisy 9–10. Prague: Masarykův ústav AV ČR, 2000.

———. *Parlamentní projevy, 1891–1893.* Spisy 21. Prague: Masarykův ústav AV ČR, 2001.

———. *Parlamentní projevy, 1907–1914.* Spisy 29. Prague: Masarykův ústav AV ČR, 2002.

———. *Pokus o konkrétní logiku; třídění a soustava věd.* Spisy 3. Prague: Ústav T. G. Masaryka, 2001.

———. *Politika vědou a uměním, 1911–1914*. Spisy 28. Prague: Masarykův ústav AV ČR, 2011.

———. *Praktická filosofie na základě sociologie: Litografovaná příručka k přednáškám*. Prague, [1885]. [NUK: 54 D 7938]

———. *Přednášky a studie z let 1882–1884*. Spisy 17. Prague: Masarykův ústav AV ČR, 1998.

———. *Rusko a Evropa*. Spisy 11–13, 3 vols. Prague: Masarykův ústav AV ČR, 1996. English translation: Tomáš G. Masaryk. *The Spirit of Russia: Studies in History, Literature, and Philosophy*. 2nd ed. 3 vols. Translated by Eden and Cedar Paul, and W. R. and Z. Lee. London: Allen & Unwin, 1961–67.

———. *Sebevražda hromadným jevem společenským moderní osvěty*. Spisy 1. Prague: Masarykův ústav AV ČR, 2002.

———. *Les Slaves après la guerre*. Prague: Orbis, 1923. [Bibliographic note: a version originally published as "The Slavs after the War." *Slavonic Review* 1 (June 1922), 2–23; in Czech: T. G. Masaryk. *Slované po válce* (Prague: 1923)].

———. *Slovanské studie a texty z let 1889–1891*. Spisy 20. Prague: Masarykův ústav AV ČR, 2007.

———. *Světová revoluce za války a ve válce, 1914–1918*. Spisy 15. Prague: Masarykův ústav AV ČR, 2005. English trans. Tomáš G. Masaryk. *The Making of a State: Memories and Observations, 1914–1918*. Edited by Henry W. Steed. New York: George Allen and Unwin, 1927

———. *Univerzitní přednášky I: Praktická filozofie*. Spisy 4. Prague: Masarykův ústav AV ČR, 2012.

———. *V boji o náboženství*. 3rd ed. Prague: Čin, 1947.

———. *Válka a revoluce: Články, memoranda, přednášky, rozhovory, 1914–1916*. Spisy 30. Prague: Masarykův ústav AV ČR, 2005.

———. *Válka a revoluce II: Články, memoranda, přednášky, rozhovory, 1917*. Spisy 31. Prague: Masarykův ústav AV ČR, 2008.

———. *Z bojů o náboženství, 1904–1906*. Spisy 26. Prague: Masarykův ústav AV ČR, 2014.

———. *Z bojů o rukopisy, 1886–1888*. Spisy 19. Prague: Masarykův ústav AV ČR, 2004.

———. *Z počátků Athenea, 1883–1885*. Spisy 18. Prague: Masarykův ústav AV ČR, 2004.

———. *Základové konkretné logiky: třídění a soustava věd*. Spisy 2. Prague: Masarykův ústav AV ČR, 2001.

Masaryk, Tomáš G.: Articles

NOTE: Additional articles by Masaryk are included in his *Spisy* which are listed in the preceding **Books** section.

Masaryk, Tomáš G. "Alexander Bain: O vychování jako vědě." *Masarykův sborník* 3 (1928–1929): 330–344.

———. "Antwort des Herrn Präsidenten T. G. Masaryk auf den von Chr. Ehrenfels...an ihm gerichteten 'Offenen Brief'." In Christian Ehrenfels. *Metaphysik*. Vol. 4 of *Philosophische Schriften*. Edited by Reinhard Fabian, 294–295. Munich: Filosofia Verlag, 1990.

———. "Augustin Smetana a jeho filosofie sociální." *Masarykův sborník* 1 (1924–1925): 157–163.

———. "Časové směry a tužby." *Naše doba* 2 (1895): 16–37, 135–140, 193–212.

———. "Čisté němectví." *Naše doba* 4 (1895): 2–15

———. "Člověk a příroda." *Květy* 12 (1890), part 1: 95–106, 230–241, 353–365, 442–452, 588–598, 706–710; part 2: 69–77, 324–330, 490–496, 620–628, 734–738.

——. "Dopisy prof. T. G. Masaryka moravským theologům." *Masarykův sborník* 1 (1924–1925): 71–76.

——." Druhá universita." *Naše doba*, 1 (1893–1894): 672–676.

——. "Ernest Renan o národnosti." *Masarykův sborník* 1(1924–1925): 53–60.

——. "Ernest Renan o vědě a islamismu," *Masarykův sborník* 1(1924–1925): 69–70.

——. "Ernest Renan o židovství jako plemenu a náboženství." *Masarykův sborník* 1 (1924–1925): 61–68.

——. "Filosofie pacifismu." *Masarykův sborník* 3 (1928–1929): 146–152.

——. "Humanita a národnost." *Naše doba* 4 (1896–1897):193–205.

——. "K šestému červenci: Naše obrození a naše reformace." *Naše doba* 3 (1895–1896): 961–973, 1057–1071.

——. "Ke sporu o Kanta." *Naše doba* 10 (1902–1903): 108–111, 190–195.

——. "Ke sporu o smysl českých dějin." *Naše doba* 20 (1912–1913): 6–19.

——. "The Slavs after the War." *Slavonic Review* 1 (June 1922): 2–23.

——. "Moderní titanismus; A. De Musset: nemoc století." *Naše doba* 5 (1897–1898): 142–157.

——. "Můj poměr ke Goethovi." In *Goethův sborník*. Památce 100. výročí básníkovy smrti vydali čeští germanisté, 9–11. Prague: Státní nakladatelství, 1932.

——. "Několik myšlenek o literárním eklekticismu:'Twardowski' pana J. Vrchlického." *Naše doba* 2 (1894–1895): 314–337, 385–407.

——. [P., Č.] "O periodisaci českých dějin." *Česká mysl* 28 (1932), 131–142.

——. "O pověře rituelní." *Naše doba* 7 (1899–1900): 321–335, 481–491, 579–589.

——. "O povaze myšlenkové krise naší doby." *Čas* 1 (1886–1887): 51–55, 68–71.

——. "Potřeba pokrokové politiky." *Masarykův sborník* 1 (1924–1925): 168–179.

——. "Rozhled církevním životem v roce 1902." *Naše doba* 10 (1902–1903), 350–359, 440–446.

——. "Rukověť sociologie. Podstata a methoda sociologie." *Naše doba* 8 (1901): 1–12, 98–105, 173–181, 662–667, 735–741, 822–828, 906–910.

——. "Ruský absolutism v evropské publicistice." *Naše doba* 14 (1906–1907): 186–190, 255–259.

——. "Slovanské studie: Jana Kollára Slovanská vzájemnost." *Naše doba* 1 (1893–1894): 481–500, 588–598, 655–671, 720–760, 822–844, 891–920.

——. "Spisy F. M. Dostojevského." *Masarykův sborník* 2 (1926–1927): 21–33; originally: *Čas* 6 (1892).

——. "Studie o Lassalovi." *Naše doba* 12 (1904–1905): 513–517, 564–567.

——. "Svobodní zednáři." *Naše doba* 13 (1905–1906): 30–35.

——. "Thomas Garrigue Masaryk." In Alexius Meinong, *Philosophenbriefe: Aus der Wissenschaftlichen Korrespondenz*. Edited by Rudolf Kindinger, 1–17. Graz: Akademische Druck- und Verlagsanstalt, 1965.

——. "Vědecké náboženství ?" *Masarykův sborník* 1 (1924–1925): 167. Response to Gustav Tichý, "Vědecké náboženství?" ibid.: 164–166

——. "Vývoj evropské společnosti v devatenáctém století." *Masarykův sborník* 2 (1926–1927): 116–132.

——. "Z mravní pathologie společnosti české." *Čas* 1 (1886–1887): 21–25, 40–43, 129–132, 196–207, 307–415.

——. "Z nejnovější náboženské filosofie ruské." *Naše doba* 14 (1906–1907): 326–331, 425–429.

——. "Ze zápisníku čtenářova." *Naše doba* 10 (1902–1903): 312–319, 708–709. Pages 708–

709 also reprinted in ——. *Česká otázka. Naše nynější krize. Jan Hus*, Spisy 6, 430–432. Prague: Masarykův ústav AV ČR, 2000.

——. "Žena u Ježíše a u Pavla." *Masarykův sborník* 2 (1926–1927): 233–241.

——. "Život církevní a náboženský roku 1904." *Naše doba* 12 (1904–1905): 274–280, 353–358, 446–447, 518–524.

——. "Zolův naturalismus." *Naše doba* 3 (1895–1896): 423–437.

Masarykův almanach. Vienna: Akademický spolek, 1925 [NUK: D 63 107, 54 D 63325, 54 D 4844].

Masarykův sborník. Vol. 1–3. Prague: Čin, 1924–1925 to 1928–1929; vol. 4, subtitle: T. G. Masarykovi k šedesátým narozeninám, 2nd ed. Prague: Čin, 1930 [1st ed.: Prague: Grosman a Svoboda, 1910]; vol. 5–6, subtitle: Vůdce generací, pt. 1–2. Prague: Čin, 1930–1931; vol. 7, Prague: Academia, 1992; vols. 8–14, Prague: Masarykův ústav AV ČR, 1993–2009.

Maudsley, Henry. *Physiology and Pathology of the Mind.* New York: Appleton, [1876].

Meinong, Alexius. *Hume-Studien.* 2 vols. Vienna: K. Gerold's Sohn, 1877–1882.

——. *Philosophenbriefe: Aus der Wissenschaftlichen Korrespondenz.* Edited by Rudolf Kindinger. Graz: Akademische Druck– und Verlagsanstalt, 1965.

——. *Psychologisch-ethische Untersuchungen zur Werththeorie.* Graz: Leuschner & Lubensky,1894.

——. *Ueber philosophische Wissenschaft und ihre Propaedeutik.* Vienna: Hölder, 1885.

Miller, Herbert A. "Humanitarian Progress." In *Czechoslovakia.* Edited by Robert J. Kerner, 271–283. Berkeley, CA: University of California Press, 1945.

——. "The Slavs after the War." *Slavonic Review* 1 (June 1922): 2–23. "What Woodrow Wilson and America Meant to Czechoslovakia." In Czechoslovakia. Edited by Robert J. Kerner, 71–84. Berkeley, CA: University of California Press, 1945.

Münz, Sigmund. "Erinnerungen an Thomas G. Masaryk." *Masarykův almanach*, 48–55. Vienna: Akademický spolek, 1925.

Nečas, Jaromír. *Spojené státy Evropské.* Prague: Čin, 1926.

Nejedlý, Zdeněk. *T. G. Masaryk.* 4 vols. Prague: Melantrich, 1930–1937; 2d ed., vols. 1–2, Sebrané spisy, 31–32. Prague: Orbis, 1949–1950.

Nietzsche, Friedrich. *The Anti-Christ, Ecce Homo, Twilight of the Idols, and Other Writings.* Edited by Aaron Ridley and Judith Norman, translated by Judith Norman. Cambridge: Cambridge University Press, 2005.

Niklaus, Peter and Andreas Urs Sommer, editors. "Franz Overbecks Briefwechsel mit Paul de Lagarde." *Zeitschrift für neuere Theologiegeschichte* 3/1 (1996): 127–171.

Novák, Arne. "Světová revoluce," *Lumír* 53 (1926). In Arne Novák. *Nosiči pochodní; kniha české traduce*, 190–225. Prague: iterární odbor Umělecké besedy a Kruh českých spisovatel, 1928.

Palacký, František. *Úvahy a projevy.* Prague: Melantrich, 1977.

Papoušek, Jaroslav. "Masaryk und Slaventum," *Slavische Rundschau* 2, (1930): 169–189.

Patočka, Jan. "Bolzanovo filosofické působení." In Kateřina Trlifajová, editor. *Osamělý myslitel, Bernard Bolzano*, 203–213. Prague: Filosofia, 2006.

——. *Dvě studie o Masarykovi.* Toronto: Sixty-Eight Publishers, 1980.

——. "Husserl a Bolzano." In Kateřina Trlifajová, editor. *Osamělý myslitel, Bernard* Bolzano, 187–201. Prague: Filosofia, 2006.

———. "Interview. S Janem Patočkou o filosofii a filosofech," *Filosofický* časopis 55 (2007): 339–358.

———. "Pokus o českou národní filosofii a jeho nezdar (1946)," idem. Češi *I, Sebrané spisy* 12, 341–365. Prague: Filosofia/Oikoymenh, 2006.

———. *Sebrané spisy.* 22 vols. Prague: Oikoymenh, 1996–2011 (in progress).

Plachý, Jiří, and Ivo Pejčoch, *Masarykovy oprátky. Problematika trestu smrti v období první a druhé* Československé *republiky, 1918–1939.* Cheb: Svět křídel, 2012.

Plato. "Lysis," "Phaedrus," and "Symposium." In *The Dialogs of Plato.* Volume 2 of Great Books of the Western World, 14–25, 115–141, 149–173. Chicago: Encyclopedia Britannica, 1952.

Polák, Stanislav. *Charlotta Garrigue Masaryková.* Prague: Mladá fronta, 1992.

———. *Masarykovi rodiče a antisemitský mýtus.* Prague: Ústav T. G. Masaryka, 1995.

———. *T.G. Masaryk.* 6 vols. (Prague: Masarykův ústav AV ČR, 2000–2012).

Popper, Karl R. *The Open Society and Its Enemies.* 2nd ed. rev. 2 vols. London: Routledge & K. Paul, 1952.

Pražák, Albert. "T. G. Masaryk jako profesor." *Školská správa* 18 (1937): 126–132.

První světová válka moderní demokracie a T. G. Masaryk. Prague: Ústav T. G. Masaryka, 1995.

Rádl, Emanuel. "Locke." Česká *mysl* 28 (1932): 257–265.

———. *Válka* Čechů *s Němci.* Prague: Čin, 1928.

Rauschning, Hermann. *Gespräche mit Hitler.* Vienna: Evropaverlag, 1973.

Redlich, Josef. *Schicksalsjahre Österreichs, 1908–1919: Das politische Tagebuch.* 2 vols. Edited by Fritz Fellner. Graz: Böhlaus, 1953–1954.

Riezler, Kurt. *Die Erforderlichkeit des unmöglichen.* Munich: G. Müller, 1913.

Ritschl, Albrecht. *Die christliche Lehre von der Rechtfertigung und Versöhnung.* 3 vols. Bonn: A. Marcus, 1870–1874.

Ritschl, Albrecht. *Geschichte des Pietismus.* 3 vols. Bonn: Marcus, 1880–86. Reprint [?] Berlin: de Gruyter, 1966.

Robinson, Phyllis C. *Willa: the life of Willa Cather.* Garden City, NY: Doubleday, 1983.

Rolland, Romain. *Mémoires, et fragments du Journal.* Paris: A. Michel [1956].

Rosenberg, Alfred. *Blut und Ehre: Ein Kampf fuer deutsche Wiedergeburt: Reden und Aufsätze von 1919–1933.* 24th ed. Edited by Thilo Trotha. Munich: Zentralverlag der NSDAP, Franz Eher nachf., 1941.

———. *Letzte Aufzeichnungen: Ideale und Idole der nationalsozialistischen Revolution.* Goettingen: Plesse Verlag, 1955.

———. *Der Mythus des 20. Jahrhunderts. Eine Wertung der seelisch-geistigen Gestaltenkämpfe unserer Zeit.* 5th ed. Munich: Hoheneichen-Verlag, 1934. [Prefaces: February 1930, October 1931, May 1933].

———. "Paul de Lagarde," *Völkischer Beobachter,* September 10, 1927, in Rosenberg, *Blut und Ehre: Ein Kampf fuer deutsche Wiedergeburt: Reden und Aufsätze von 1919–1933,* 228–230.

Rychnovský, Ernst, editor. *Masaryk und das Judentum.* Prague: Marsvelagsgesellschaft, 1931; Czech version: Ernst Rychnovský, editor. *Masaryk a židovství.* Prague: Mars, 1931.

Sborník vzpomínek na T.G. Masaryka. Edited by Prokop Maxa and Lev Sychrava. Prague: Svaz národního osvobození, 1930.

Schenk, Antonín. *TGM: 'Proč se neřekne pravda?' Ze vzpomínek dr. Antonína Schenka.* Edited by Jindřiška Smetanová. Prague: 1996.

Schweinshaupt, Georg. "Nationalsozialismus und Lagarde." *Nationalsozialistische Monatshefte* 3 (November 1932).

Seton-Watson, Hugh, and Christopher Seton-Watson. *The Making of a New Europe: R.W. Seton-Watson and the Last Years of Austria-Hungary.* Seattle: University of Washington Press, 1981.

Seymour, Charles. *Geography, Justice and Politics at the Paris Peace Conference of 1919.* New York: American Geographical Society, 1951.

Shiriamov, M. "Whose Interests Did President Masaryk Defend?" *Current Digest of the Soviet Press* 20 (1968): n. 19, 8–9, citing from *Sovetskaia Rossiia*, May 14, 1968, p. 3.

Signposts: A Collection of Articles on Russian Intelligentsia. Edited and translated by Marshall S. Shats and Judith E. Zimmermann. Irvine, CA: C. Schlaks, 1986.

Silberstein, I. "L. N. Tolstoi und T. G. Masaryk," Neues aus den Archiven der Sowjetunion. *Slavische Rundschau* 7 (Berlin, 1935): 137–166.

Škrach, Vasil. "E. Radlow und Th. Masaryk." *Der russische Gedanke. Internationale Zeitschrift für russische Philosophie, Literaturwissenschaft und Kultur* 1 (1929–1930): 208–09.

——. "Edmund Husserl." *Česká mysl* 25 (1929): 189.

——. "K filosofickému obsahu *Světové revoluce.*" *Masarykův sborník* 2 (1926–27): 37–51.

——. "Masaryk," *Masarykův slovník naučný.* 7 vols. 4: 775–787. Prague: Československý kompas, 1925–1933,.

Smetáček, Zdeněk. "Filosofické základy Millova liberalismu." *Česká mysl* 28 (1932): 281–288, 353–358.

Šolle, Zdeněk and Jan Gielkens, editors. *Karel Kautsky a Československo.* Prague: Archiv Akademie Věd Č. R., 1995.

——. *Karl und Luise Kautsky Briefwechsel mit der Tschechoslowakei, 1879–1939.* Frankfurt: Campus Verlag, 1993.

Sommer, Andreas-Urs. "Zwischen Agitation, Religionsstiftung und 'Hoher Politik': Friedrich Nietzsche und Paul de Lagarde." In *Nietzscheforschung.* Edited by Volker Gerhardt, Jahrbuch Band 4, 169–194.

Soubigou, Alain. *Thomas Masaryk.* Paris: Librairie Arthème Fayard, 2002. Czech transl.: Alain Soubigou, *Tomáš Garrigue Masaryk.* Translated by Helena Beguivinová. Prague: Paseka, 2004.

Steding, Christoph. *Das Reich und die Krankheit der europäischen Kultur.* Hamburg: Hanseatische Verlagsanstalt, 1938. 3rd ed., Hamburg: Hanseatische Verlagsanstalt, 1942.

Steed, Henry W. *Through Thirty Years, 1892–1922: A Personal Narrative.* 2 vols. Garden City, NY: Doubleday, Page & Company, 1924.

Stumpf, Karl. "Erinnerungen an Franz Brentano." In *Franz Brentano: Zur Kenntnis seines Lebens und seiner Lehre.* Edited by Oskar Kraus, 87–149. Munich: Beck, 1919.

——. *Tonpsychologie.* 2 vols. Leipzig: S. Hirzel, 1883–1890.

Sychrava, Lev. *T. G. Masaryk: 1850–1930.* Prague: Orbis, 1930.

Treitschke, Heinrich. *Deutsche Geschichte in 19. Jahrhundert.* Introduction by Alfred Rosenberg. Berlin: Safari, 1933.

Trendelenburg, Friedrich A. *Logische Untersuchungen.* Berlin: G. Bethge, 1840.

Unger, Erich, editor. *Das Schriftum zum Aufbau des neuen Reiches, 1919–1. 1. 1934.* Berlin: Junker und Dünnhaupt, 1934. [9 books by Lagarde, 7 by Langbehn are listed.]

Vašák, Pavel. *Literární pouť Karla Hynka Máchy: Ohlas Máchova díla v letech 1836–1858.* Prague: Odeon, 1981.

Vondrák, Václav. "Docent Masaryk a naše první česká universita." *Masarykův almanach,* 40–43. Vienna: Akademický spolek, 1925.

Všetečka, Jakub. "Vzpomínky," *Masarykův sborník* 4, 323–336. Prague: Čin, 1930.

Weiss, Louise, editor. *L'Europe nouvelle.* Paris, 1918–1940. [LC AP20.E88]

Weiss, Louise. *Mémoire d'une Européenne.* 3 vols. Paris: Payot, 1968–1970.

Wilson, Woodrow. *The Papers of Woodrow Wilson.* Edited by Arthur S. Link et al. 69 vols. Princeton, NJ: Princeton University Press, 1966–1994.

———. *The State: Elements of Historical and Practical Politics.* Rev. ed. Boston: Heath, 1904; 1st ed. Boston: Heath, 1889.

Wirth, Wilhelm. "Eine Episode aus G. Th. Fechners Leben vor sechzig Jahren." In *Otto Glauning zum 60. Geburtstag.* 2 vols. Edited by Heinrich Schreiber, 2: 158–164. Leipzig: Hadl, 1936–1938.

Zimmermann, Robert. *Geschichte der Aesthetik.* 2 vols. Vienna: W. Braumüller, 1858.

———. *Philosophische Prepädeutik für Obergymnasien.* Vienna: W. Braumüller, 1853; 2nd ed. Vienna: W. Braumüller, 1860; 3rd ed. Vienna: W. Braumüller, 1867.

———. *Robert Zimmermanns Philosophische Propädeutik und die Vorlagen aus der Wissenschaftslehre Bernard Bolzanos.* Edited and introduction by Eduard Winter. Vienna: Verlag der Österreichischen Akademie der Wissenschaften, 1975.

Secondary Sources

Albright, Madeleine. "The Legacy of Masaryk and Wilson Today. Part II." *Slovo* 12/2 (2011): 19–21.

Baer, Josette. "Imagining Membership: The Conception of Europe in the Political Thought of T. G. Masaryk and Václav Havel." *Studies in East European Thought* 52 (2000): 203–226.

———. "Thomas Masaryk: Democracy as Czech Humanism," in Baer, *The Slavic Thinkers or the Creation of Polities: Intellectual History and Political Thought in Central Europe and the Balkans in the 19th Century.* Washington, D.C: New Academis, 2007, 15–42.

———. *Politik als praktizierte Sittlichkeit. Zum Demokratiebegriff bei Thomas G. Masaryk und Vaclav Havel.* Sinzheim: Pro Universitate Verlag, 1998.

Bartoš, František M. "T. G. Masaryk a studium české reformace," *Reformační sborník* 7 (1939): 3–9.

———. *Masarykova česká filosofie.* Prague: Kalich, 1919.

Batscha, Zwi. *Eine Philosophie der Demokratie: Thomas G. Masaryks Begründung einer neuzeitlichen Demokratie.* Frankfurt: Surkamp, 1994.

Bednář, Miloslav. "Česká a americká státní idea, souznění a přerušování tradic, dějiny a současnost." *Spory o dějiny.* Masarykův ústav AV ČR, 4 (2003): 99–106.

———. *České myšlení.* Prague: Philosophia, 1996.

Beld, Antonie van den. "Masaryk a postmoderní kritika: Potřebuje západní demokracie filosofické založení?" *Filosofický časopis* 51 (2003): 5–18.

———. *Humanity: The Political and Social Philosophy of Thomas G. Masaryk.* The Hague: Mouton, 1975.

Bradley, J. F. N. "The Allies and the Czech Revolt against the Bolsheviks in 1918." *Slavonic and East European Review* 23 (1965): 275–292.

———. "The Czechoslovak Revolt against the Bolsheviks." *Soviet Studies* 15 (1963): 124–151.

Brenner, Christiane. "*Zwischen Ost und West*." *Tschechische politische Diskurse 1945–1948*. Veröffentlichungen des Collegium Carolinum 118. Munich: Collegium Carolinum, 2009. Czech edition: *Mezi východem a západem: české politické diskurzy, 1945–1948*. Translated by Blanka Pscheidtová. Prague: Argo, 2015.

Brod, Toman. "Perspektivy Masarykovy republiky." In *Historik nad šachovnicí dějin*. Edited by Dagmar Hájková et al. 210–217, Prague: Masarykův ústav and Filozofická fakulta Univerzity Karlovy, 2011.

Broklová, Eva. *Prezident republiky Československé; Instituce a osobnosti*. Prague: Masarykův ústav AV ČR, 2001.

Bugge, Peter. "České obrazy Evropy za první republiky." *Evropa očima Čechů*, Sborník ze sympozia, Centrum Franze Kafky (October 1966), 22–23. Edited by Eva Hahnová. Prague: Nakladatelství Franze Kafky, 1997, 95–116.

———. Longing or Belonging? Czech Perceptions of Europe in the Inter-War Years and Today," *Yearbook of European Studies* 11:111–129.

Čapek, Jan B. *Záření ducha a slova*. Prague: Vilímek, 1948.

Čapek, Milíč. "Součastnost Masarykova myšlení." *Proměny* l7/4 (1980): 9–30.

Čapek, Milíč, and Karel Hrubý, editors. *T.G. Masaryk in perspective: comments and criticism*. Ann Arbor, MI: SVU, c1981.

Čapek, Norbert. "Masaryk po stránce náboženské." *Cesty a cíle* 2 (1924): 51–64.

Charlotta G. Masaryková, sborník příspěvků z konference ke 150. výročí jejího narození, konané 10. listopadu 2000. Edited by Marie L. Neudorflová. Prague: Masarykův ústav AV ČR, 2001.

Chisholm, Roderick M. "Opening Address." *Philosophie des Geistes, Philosophie der Psychologie*, Akten des 9. Internationalen Wittgenstein Symposiums, 19–26 August 1984, Kirchberg am Wechsel, Österreich.   [*Philosophy of Mind: Philosophy of Psychology*, Proceedings of the 9th International Wittgenstein Symposium, August 1984, Kirchberg/Wechsel, Austria]. Vienna: Holder-Pichler-Tempsky, 1985.

Chovančíková, Irena, editor. *Náboženská dimenze Masarykova myšlení*. Hodonín: Semináře Masarykova Muzea, Masarykovo Muzeum, 1995.

Crane, John O. and Sylvia Crane. *Czechoslovakia: Anvil of the Cold War*. New York: Praeger, 1991.

Croÿ, Jana. *Zámek Lány: 600 Years of History*. Prague: Správa Pražského hradu, 2007.

David, Zdeněk V. *Finding the Middle Way: The Utraquists' Liberal Challenge to Rome and Luther*. Washington, D.C.: Woodrow Wilson Center Press; Baltimore: Johns Hopkins University Press, 2003.

———. "Karel H. Mácha's Philosophical Challenge to the Catholic Enlightenment in Bohemia." *Sborník Národního muzea v Praze*, Řada C, Literární historie / Acta Musei nationalis Pragae, Series C, *Historia litterarum* 56, 1–2 (2011): 3–14.

———. *Realism, Tolerance, Liberalism in the Czech National Awakening: Legacies of the Bohemian Reformation*. Washington, D.C.: Wilson Center Press; and Baltimore: The Johns Hopkins University Press, 2010.

Demetz, Peter. "Nachwort des Herausgeber." In Thomas G. Masaryk. *Polemiken und Essays zur russischen und europäischen Literatur- und Geistesgeschichte: Dostojevskij, von Puškin zu Gorkij, Musset, Byron, Goethe, Lenau.* Edited by Peter Demetz, 384–394. Vienna: Böhlau, 1995.

Doubek, Vratislav, et al. *T. G. Masaryk a Slované.* Prague: Historický ústav, 2013.

Doubek, Vratislav. *T. G. Masaryk a česká a slovanská politika, 1882–1910.* Prague: Academia, 1999.

Dresler, Jaroslav. "Masaryk und die Kommunisten." *Osteuropa* 10 (1960): 663–68.

Dubin, Martin D. "Elihu Root and the Advocacy of a League of Nations, 1914–1917." *Western Political Quartely,* 19 (1966): 439–455.

Fajfr, František. *Masaryk a Comte.* Kdyně: Okresní sbor osvětový, 1925.

Fischer, J. L. "T. G. Masaryk: počátky a vlivy. Studie filosofická." *Česká mysl* 26 (1930): 132–160.

Frommelt, Reinhard. *Paneuropa oder Mittleuropa: Einigungsbestrebungen im Kalkül deutscher Wirtschaft und Politik.* Stuttgart: DVA, 1977.

Funda, Otakar A. *Thomas Garigue Masaryk: Sein phiosophisches, religiöses und politisches Denken.* Bern: P. Lang, 1978.

Gellner, Ernst, "The Price of Velvet: Thomas Masaryk and Václav Havel." *Czech Sociological Review* 3 (1995): 45–57.

Gillies, Alexander. "Herder and Masaryk: Some Points of Contact." *The Modern Language Review* 9 (1945): 121–128.

Glaise-Horstenau, Edmund von. *The Collapse of the Austro-Hungarian Empire.* Translated by Ian F. Morrow. New York: Dutton, 1930.

Hájková, Dagmar. "Constructing National Unity: Commemorations of Tomáš Masaryk's Death." *Střed* 1 (2012): 33–54.

———. "'Dokud člověk jí klobásy, tak neumře.' Oslavy narozenin T. G. Masaryka." In *Historik nad šachovnicí dějin.* Edited by Dagmar Hájková et al, 218–235. Prague: Masarykův ústav and Filozofická fakulta Univerzity Karlovy, 2011.

———. *'Naše česká věc': Češi v Americe za první světové války.* Prague: Lidové noviny, 2011.

———. "T. G. Masaryk, America, and the Creation of Czechoslovakia." *Slovo* 12/2 (2011): 12–14.

Hazdra, Zdeněk. *Šlechta ve službách Masarykovy republiky: Mezi demokracií a totalitními režimy.* Prague: Lidové noviny, 2015.

Headlam, James Wyclif. *A Memoir of the Peace Conference 1919.* Edited by Agnes Headlam-Morley, Russell Bryant, and Anna Ciencila. London: Methuen, 1972.

Heftrich, Urs. *Nietzsche v Čechách.* Prague: Hynek, 1999.

Heimann, Mary. *Czechoslovakia: The State That Failed.* New Haven: Yale University Press, 2009.

Herben, Jan. *T. G. Masaryk.* 3 vols. Prague: Mánes, 1927–1928.

———. *T. G. Masaryk: život a dílo presidenta Osvoboditele,* 5th ed. Prague: Sfinx, 1938.

Horák, Jiří,"Masaryk a Dostojevskij." In Jiří Horák. *Z dějin a literatur slovanských: stati a rozpravy,* 113–175. Prague: Jos. R. Vilímek, 1948.

Houška, Vítězslav. *Lidé kolem T.G.M.* Karviná: Paris, 2006.

———. *T. G. Masaryk: myslitel a státník.* Karviná: Paris, 2007.

Hromádka, Josef L. "Starý svět a tradice." *Naše Doba* 46 (1939): 261–267.

———. *Masaryk as European.* Vol. 2, no. 1 of the *International Philosophical Library.* Prague: International Philosophical Library, January 1936.

Hudečková, Viera. "Príspevok k vymedzeniu vzťahov T. G. Masaryka a F. Brentana." *Sborník prací filosofické fakulty brněnské university* 18 (1969), řada filosofická. B. no. 16: 86–93.

Hulička, Karel. "The Communist Anti-Masaryk Propaganda in Czechoslovakia." *American Slavic and East European Review* 16 (1957): 160–174.

Jarolímek, L. "Vzpomínejme, abychom nezapomněli!" *Školská správa* 18 (1937): 121–126.

Kalvoda, Josef. *The Genesis of Czechoslovakia.* New York: Columbia University Press, 1986.

Klimek, Antonín, et al, editors. *Vznik Československa, 1918.* Prague: Ústav mezinárodních vztahů, 1994.

Kohák, Erazim. "Ashes, Ashes … Central Europe after Forty Years." *Daedalus* 121/2 (1992): 197–215.

———. *Domov a dálava.* Prague: Filosofia, 2009.

———. "Úvod." In Jan Patočka. *Dvě studie o Masarykovi,* 9–33. Toronto: Sixty-Eight Publishers, 1980.

———. "Zdar a nezdar 'národní' filosofie: Patočka a Masaryk." *Filosofický časopis* 55 (2007): 441–456.

Kosatík, Pavel. "Češka z Ameriky: Charlotta Garrigue Masaryková." In *Osm žen z Hradu,* 10–70. Prague: Mladá fronta, 1993.

Košťálová, Michaela. *Rodokmen a soukromí T. G. Masaryka.* Prague: Petrklíč, 2013.

Kotyk, Jiří. "Tomáš Garrigue Masaryk a Jan Hus," *Teologické texty* 8 (1997): 133–134.

Kovtun, George J. *Masaryk and America: Testimony of a Relationship.* Washington, D.C.: Library of Congress, 1988.

———. *Masarykův triumf: případ konce velké války.* 2nd ed. Prague: Odeon, 1991.

———. *Republika v nebezpečném světě. Era prezidenta Masaryka, 1918–1935.* Prague: Torst, 2005.

———. *Tajuplná vražda případ Leopolda Hilsnera.* Prague: Sefer, 1994.

Kozák, Jan Blahoslav. *Masaryk filosof.* Prague: Svaz narodniho osvobozeni, 1925.

———. *Masaryk jako ethik a náboženský myslitel.* Prague: Slovanský ústav, 1931.

Král, Josef, *Masaryk, filosof humanity a demokracie.* Prague: Orbis, 1947.

———. "První období Masarykovy tvorby filosofické a prostředí vídeňské." In *Masarykův almanach,* 69–78. Vienna: Akademický spolek, 1925.

Kraus, Oskar. "Die Grundzüge der Welt- und Lebensanschauung T. G. Masaryks." *Slavische Rundschau* 2/3 (1930): 161–168. Also in *La pensée de T. G. Masaryk,* 105–113. Internationale Bibliothek für Philosophie 3/5 (1937).

Krejčí, F. V. *Češství a evropanství: úvahy o naší kulturní orientaci.* Prague: Orbis, 1931.

Kučerová, Stanislava, et al. *Bilance a výhledy středu Evropy na prahu 21. století: úvahy, svědectví a fakta. k 150 výročí narození T. G. Masaryka, 1850–2000.* Brno: Konvoj, 2000.

Lakosilová, Jarmila, ed. *Cesta a odkaz T.G. Masaryka: fakta, úvahy, souvislosti,* by Jiří Brabec and others. Prague: Nakl. Lidové noviny, 2002.

Leikert, Jozef, et al. *Politik s dušou filozofa; Miesto T. G. Masaryka v česko-slovenských dejinách.* Bratislava: Spoločnosť Pro Historia and Historický ústav SAV, 2007.

Machovec, Milan. *Tomáš G. Masaryk.* 3rd ed. Prague: Česká expedice, 2000; 1st ed. Prague: Melantrich, 1968.

MacMillan, Margaret. *Paris 1919: Six Months That Changed the World.* New York: Random House, 2002. British original edition: MacMillan. *Peacemakers: the Paris Conference of 1919 and Its Attempts to End War.* London: J. Murray, 2001.

Mamatey, Victor S. *The United States and East Central Europe, 1914–1918: A Study in Wilsonian Diplomacy and Propaganda.* Princeton, NJ: Princeton University Press, 1957.

Marzik, Thomas D. "Masaryk's National Background." In *The Czech Renaissance of the Nineteenth Century.* Edited by Peter Brock and H. Gordon Skilling, 239–253. Toronto: University of Toronto Press, 1970.

May, Arthur. "H. A. Miller and the Mid-European Union of 1918." *American Slavic and East European Review* 16 (1957): 473–488.

Meyer, Henry C. *Mitteleuropa in German Thought and Action, 1815–1945.* Hague: Najhoff, 1955.

Michel, Bernard. *La chute de l'Empire austro-hongrois, 1916–1918.* Paris: Laffont, 1991.

Nečas, Ctibor. "T. G. Masaryk v říšských volbách r. 1911." *Časopis Matice moravské* 114 (1995): 49–57.

Neudorflová, Marie L. *T.G. Masaryk: Politický myslitel.* Prague: ARSCI, 2011.

Novák, Josef, editor. *On Masaryk: Texts in English and German.* Vol. 13 in Studien zur österreichischen Philosophie. Amsterdam: Rodopi, 1988.

Novotný, Zdeněk. *Korektiv Masarykovy filosofie.* Prague: Filosofia, 2011.

Nový, Lubomír. *Filosof T. G. Masaryk, problémové skici.* Brno: Doplněk, 1994.

———. "Problémy s Masarykem-filosofem: Rekapitulační teze o filosofii T. G. Masaryka." In Irena Šnebergová, ed. *Po cestách naléhavosti myšlení: Věnováno Josefu Zumrovi k 65. Narozeninám,* 111–119. Prague: Filosofický ústav AV ČR, 1993.

Ogden, Charles Kay. *The System of Basic English.* New York: Harcourt, Brace, [c1934].

Opat, Jaroslav. *Filozof a politik: T. G. Masaryk, 1882–1893.* Prague: Melantrich, 1990.

———. "Glosy ke dvěma kritikám T. G. Masaryka." *Slovanský přehled* 76/3 (1990): 244–256.

———. *Masarykiana a jiné studie.* Prague: Masarykův ústav AV ČR, 1994.

———. *Masarykiana a jiné studie II.* Prague: Masarykův ústav AV ČR, 2006.

———. "Masarykovo pojetí češství." In Jaroslav Pánek et al., editors. *Idea českého státu v proměnách staletí,* 153–158. Prague: Lidové noviny, 2008.

———. *Průvodce životem a dílem T. G. Masaryka: Česká otázka včera a dnes.* Prague: Masarykův ústav AV ČR, 2003.

———. *TGM: Evropan světoobčan.* Prague: Masarykův ústav AV ČR, 1999.

Paukertová-Leharová, Libuše. *Vnuci prezidenta T.G. Masaryka: Herbert a Leonard Revilliodovi a jejich zvláštní osud.* Středokluky: Zdeněk Susa, 2009.

Pekař, Josef. "Masarykova česká filosofie." In Miloš Havelka, editor. *Spor o smysl českých dějin,* 295. Prague: Torst, 1995.

Pernes, Jiří. "O rozchodu dvou učených přátel aneb sto let České otázky." *Časopis Matice moravské* 114 (1995): 325–336.

Perman, D. *The Shaping of the Czechoslovak State: Diplomatic History of the Boundaries of Czechoslovakia, 1914–1920.* Leiden: Brill, 1962.

Peška, Vladimír, and Antoine Mareš, editors. *Thomas Garrigue Masaryk, européen et humaniste.* Paris: Etudes et documentation internationales: Institut d'études slaves, 1991.

Plachý, Jiří, and Ivo Pejčoch. *Masarykovy oprátky. Problematika trestu smrti v období první a druhé* Československé *republiky, 1918–1939.* Cheb: Svět křídel, 2012.

Pojar, Miloš, editor. *Hilsnerova aféra a česká společnost, 1899–1999.* Sborník předášek z konference na Univerzitě Karlově v Praze, 24. - 26. listopadu 1999. Prague: Židovské muzeum, 1999.

Pojar, Miloš. *T, G. Masaryk a židovství.* Prague: Academia, 2016.

Polišenský, Josef. "T. G. M. a angloamerický svět." In Josef Polišenský, editor. *Češi a svět; sborník k pětasedmdesátinám Ivana Pfaffa,* 147–150. Prague: Euroslavica, 2000.

První světová válka moderní demokracie a T. G. Masaryk. Prague: Ústav T. G. Masaryka, 1995.

Rádl, Emanuel. "Masaryk a Nietzsche." In *T. G. Masarykovi k šedesátinám.* Prague: Grosman and Svoboda, [1910]; also in Rádl. *Úvahy vědecké a filosofické.* Prague: Grosman and Svoboda, 1914.

——. "Filosofický realism." In Rádl. *Úvahy vědecké a filosofické,* 141–162. Prague: Grosman and Svoboda, 1914.

Rowell, Edward Z. *Masaryk's Realism and the Czech Nation: A Study of Philosophy and Its Significance in the life of a Nation.* Ph.D. Dissertation. Chicago, IL: University of Chicago, 1922. [LC:DB217.M3R68].

Šalda, F. X. "Těžká kniha." [*Rozhledy* 4.1894–1895.] In Šalda, *Kritické projevy.* Vol. 2, 267–301. Prague: Svoboda, 1950.

Schmidt-Hartmann, Eva. *Thomas G. Masaryk's Realism: Origins of a Czech Political Concept.* Veröffentlichungen des Collegium Carolinum, 52. Munich: Oldenbourg, 1984.

Schweiger, Hannes. "Bernard Shaw's Joyriding in Germany and Austria: A Politics of Cultural Internationalism." *Shaw: Annual of Bernard Shaw Studies* 28 (2008): 153–167.

Selver, Paul. *Masaryk: A Biography.* London: M. Joseph, 1940.

Shotwell, James T. "Czechoslovak Democracy: Was it Worth While?" In Robert J. Kerner, editor. *Czechoslovakia,* 441–447. Berkeley, CA: University of California Press, 1945.

Šimsa, Jaroslav. *V duchu T. G. M.* Prague: Laichter, 1946.

Skilling, H. Gordon. *T. G. Masaryk: Against the Current, 1882–1914.* University Park: Pennsylvania State University, 1994.

Slowiková, Katarzyna. "Patočkův projekt revize Husserlovy fenomenologie." *Filosofický časopis* 55 (2007): 511–536.

Šmíd, Marek. *Masaryk a Česká Katolická moderna.* Pontes pragenses, 47. Brno: L. Marek, 2007.

Sobotka, Richard. *Charlotta Garrigue Masaryková.* Prague: Dobra and Fortuna, 1999.

Srovnal, Jindřich. "Kolem Masarykovy 'Otázky sociální'." *Filosofický časopis* 50 (2002): 1005–1020.

Štěpán, Jan, editor. *Kazatel František Urbánek.* Prague: Oliva, 1999.

Strouhal, Evžen. "T. G. Masaryk a Vincenc Strouhal: přátelství ve světle dopisů." *Dějiny a součastnost* 3 (2000): 36–38.

Suppan, Arnold. "Zur Geschichtsphilosophie Tomáš Garrigue Masaryks." *Acta Universitatis Carolinae, Philosophica et Historica,* 2, *Studia Historica* 46 (1997): 75–81.

Švec, Luboš. "Herbert Adolphus Miller, psychóza útisku a středoevropská otázka." *Slovanský přehled* 93 (2007): 289–320.

——. "Masarykova koncepce střední Evropy a kontakty s polským exilem za první světové války: možnosti a limity česko-polské exilové spolupráce." Cracow, Polska akademia umiejętności, *Prace Komisji środkowoeuropejskiej PAU* 28 (2010): 91–108.

———. "The Mid-European Union: An attempt at Cooperation of Central and East European Representatives at the End of WW I." In E. Voráček, editor. *The Disintegration of Czechoslovakia in the End of 1930s. Policy in Central Europe*, 123–145. Prague: Institute of History, 2009.

Sweet, Paul. "Recent German Literature on Mitteleuropa." *Journal of Central European Affairs* 3 (1934–1944): 1–24.

Szporluk, Roman. *The Political Thought of Thomas Masaryk.* East European Monographs 85. New York: Columbia University Press, 1981.

T. G. Masaryk a česká státnos. Sborník příspěvků z mezinárodní vědecké konference pořádané Masarykovou   univerzitou ve dnech 4.-5. září 2007 v Brně. Edited by Helena Pavlincová and Jan Zouhar. Prague: Ústav T. G. Masaryka, 2008.

T. G. Masaryk a situace v Čechách a na Moravě od konce XIX. století do německé okupace Československa. Edited by Eva Broklová. Prague: Ústav T. G. Masaryka, 1998.

T. G. Masaryk a střední Evropa. Edited by Richard Pražák. Brno: Masarykova univerzita, Filozofická fakulta, 1994.

T. G. Masaryk: Bibliografie k životu a dílu. 2 vols. Prague: Filozofický ústav ČSAV; Národní knihovna, 1992–1994.

T. G. Masaryk, 1850–1937. 3 vols. Edited by Stanley Winters et al. London: Macmillan, 1989–1990.

T. G. Masaryk, idea demokracie a současné evropanství. Sborník mezinárodní vědecké konference, Praha, 2. - 4. března 2000. 2 vols. Edited by Emil Voráček. Prague: Filosofia, 2001.

T. G. Masaryk na přelomu tisíciletí. Sborník z VIII. ročníku semináře, November 15, 2000. Hodonín: Masarykovo muzeum, 2001.

T. G. Masarykovi k šedesátým narozeninám. Edited by E. Beneš et al. Prague: Grosman and Svoboda, [1910].

Tabor, Edward O. "Tři momentky z Masarykovy činnosti." In *Sborník vzpomínek na T. G. Masaryka*, 63–67. Prague, 1930,

Teeters, Negley K. "Herbert Adolphus Miller, 1875–1951." *American Sociological Review* 16 (1951): 563–564.

Tomáš Masaryk, filozof a pedagog. Sborník z 1. Semináře, November 19, 1992. Hodonín: Masarykovo muzeum, 1993.

Tomeš, Josef. *Viktor Dyk a T. G. Masaryk. Dvojí reflexe češství.* Prague: Lidové noviny, 2009.

Toth, Daniel. *Masarykova filozofie náboženství.* Hradec Králové: Gaudeamus, 2001.

———. *Studie o Masarykovi.* Hradec Králové: M & V, 2003.

Tothová, Martina, and Daniel Toth. "Masarykův vztah k náboženství a církvi." In Zdeněk Kučera and Jan B. Lášek, editors. *Modernismus: studie nebo výzva? Studie ke genezi* českého katolického modernismu. Pontes Pragenses 24: 174–197. Brno: L. Marek, 2002,

Tretera, Ivo. *Vzpomínky na Bohuslava Hrabala a na život vůbec.* Prague: Paseka, 2011.

Trotsky, Leon. "Professor Masaryk über Russland." *Kampf, sozialdemokratische Monatschrift* 7/ 11–12 (1914): 519–527.

Tucker, Aviezer. *The Philosophy and Politics of Czech Dissidence from Patočka to Havel.* Pittsburgh: University of Pittsburgh Press, 2000.

Uher, Jan. "Masaryk – demokrat." *Školská správa* 18 (1937): 132–136.

Unterberger, Betty M. "The Arrest of Alice Masaryk." *Slavic Review* 33 (1974): 91–106.

Valenta, Jaroslav, et al, editors. *Československo, 1918–1938: osudy demokracie ve střední Evropě*. Sborník mezinárodní vědecké konference, Praha, 5. - 8. října 1998. 2 vols. Prague: Historický ústav Akademie věd České republiky, 1999.

Veber, Václav. *Dějiny sjednocené Evropy: od antických počátků do současnosti,* 2nd ed. Prague: Lidové noviny, 2009.

Vorovka, Karel. "Česká mravní hegemonie a příští česká válka." *Ruch filosofický* 6 (1926): 99–111.

———. *Masarykova filosofie českých dějin*. Prague: Sfinx, 1928.

———. "Několik myšlenek o Masarykově filosofii a jeho *Světové revoluci*." *Ruch filosofický* 5 (1925): 257–283.

Vykoupil, Libor. "Zasloužil se o stát: Tomáš Garrrigue Masaryk." In *Osobnosti moravských dějin*. Edited by Libor Jan and Zdeněk Drahoš, 433–457. Brno: Matice moravská, 2006.

Vyšný, Paul. *Neo-Slavism and the Czechs, 1898–1914*. Cambridge: Cambridge University Press, 1977.

Warren, W. Preston. *Masaryk's Democracy: A Philosophy of Scientific and Moral Culture*. Chapel Hill: University of North Carolina Press, 1941.

———. "Translator's Preface." In Tomáš G. Masaryk. *Humanistic Ideals*. Translated by W. Preston Warren, 11–56. Lewisburg, PA: Bucknell University Press, 1971.

Wellek, Rene. "Philosophical Basis of Masaryk's Political Ideals," *Ethics*, 55 (1945), 298–304.

Werner, Arthur, *Th. G. Masaryk: Bild seines Lebens*. Prague: Roland, 1934.

Wirth, Wilhelm. "Eine Episode aus G. Th. Fechners Leben vor sechzig Jahren." In *Otto Glauning zum 60. Geburtstag: Festgabe aus Wissenschaft und Bibliothek*. 2 vols. 2: 158–164. Leipzig: Richard Hadl, 1936–1938.

Woolfolk, Alan. "Introduction." In Thomas G. Masaryk. *Constructive Sociological Theory*. Edited by Alan Woolfolk and Jonathan B. Iber, 1–37. New Brunswick, NJ: Transaction Publishers, 1994.

Žantovský, Michael. *Havel*. Prague: Argo, 2014.

Zeman, Zbyněk A. *The Masaryks: The making of Czechoslovakia*. London: I. B. Tauris, 1990.

Zmeškal, Vladimír. *T. G, Masaryk a Lužice: K osmidesátinám prvního presidenta Československé republiky*. Prague: Česko-lužický spolek Adolf Černý, 1930.

Znoj, Milan. "Masarykova kritika liberalismu a moderní doby." *Filosofický* časopis 51 (2003): 93–104.

Zouhar, Jan. "Jan Patočka a Masarykovo pojetí dějin," *Filosofický* časopis, 55 (2007), 457–472.

Zumr, Josef, "Patočka a Masaryk." *Filosofický* časopis 39 (1991): 448–455.

Zumr, Josef and Thomas Binder, editors. *T. G. Masaryk und die Brentano-Schule*. Prague: Filosofický ústav Československé akademie věd, 1992.

Index